The Vineyard Book of Devotions

Scattered thoughts from the camp's founder

L. DEAN BARLEY

WESTBOW
PRESS®
A DIVISION OF THOMAS NELSON
& ZONDERVAN

WestBow Press books may be ordered through booksellers or by contacting:

WestBow Press
A Division of Thomas Nelson & Zondervan
1663 Liberty Drive
Bloomington, IN 47403
www.westbowpress.com
844-714-3454

ISBN: 978-1-6642-1585-6 (sc)
ISBN: 978-1-6642-1586-3 (e)

Library of Congress Control Number: 2020924641

Print information available on the last page.

WestBow Press rev. date: 01/19/2020

3:00 a.m.

"No testing has overtaken you except what is common to mankind. And God is faithful; he will not let you be tested beyond what you can bear. But when you are tested, he will also provide a way out so that you can endure it." (1 Corinthians 10:13 NIV)

Several years ago I began to wake up around 3 a.m. with the weight of the world upon me. Like clockwork, I got anxious around that time *every morning* and ended up praying and praying for peace, comfort and sleep. One of the greatest lingering thoughts was that I would "soon be getting what I deserved," in terms of my lack of business acumen, poor planning, wishful thinking, or the lingering thought that I simply don't work hard enough. But the biggest fear I struggle with in the darkness is simply this: "What if I am wrong about everything I have trusted to God? What if it is all a mirage—it's just me against the world?"

And if God really is out there and hears me, what if I am wrong about His *willingness* to rescue me and take care of me? What if I am wrong about His leading and His *direction* in my life? What if I am *not* where I belong and I am *not* doing what He wants me to be doing in the first place? What if all my fears of missing His *true* calling in my life are right and what if *every failure I have made* is His message to me to give up? What if I am going to soon be very humiliated, revealed as a fraud, and paraded before all humanity as the one that was wrong about everything I boasted that I was sure about? Yes, what if every bad thing ever said about me—and all the *worst things that I think about myself*-—are all true and God has given up on me?

These are the things I fight with at the early mornings—*every morning*. And as a minister, a pastor, and a man that should know better, why am I so weak and vulnerable in the wee hours of the morning? I don't know the physiological reasons, but when day breaks I regain my vigor, focus and determination. Something about the rising of the sun every morning dispels those little demons that dance around my bed. Praise God for the morning.

…and I am reminded of these truths:

1. He *is* aware of my doubts and fears.
2. He *does* love me and has called me His own.
3. He is still the *sovereign*, Almighty God, and is 100% in control and able to change the circumstances that cause me concern.
4. He is *not* the source of my doubts, suffering, anxiety, or self-condemnation; Satan is the one who whispers to me at 3 a.m., not God.
5. *Nothing* is going to happen to me tomorrow that He cannot prevent, redeem, turn into a victory or use for His glory. I just have to let go and *let God be God.*

What about you?

What have done that you are ashamed of, worried about, losing sleep over? We're all in the same ark—this boat called the human struggle of reaching up for what we know we should be, while being ridiculed by demons laughing at how far we have missed the mark.

Is your God able to overcome all your sleeplessness, anxiety, desperation, and feelings of absolute helplessness? My God is. But I am *daily* dependent upon Him for peace and sleep. Until I am fully with Him in my new home in heaven I will always have tests and trials. I need Him every hour.

Fourteen Days in a Storm....

For over fourteen days Paul was aboard a doomed ship headed for Rome. Paul and some 276 people aboard endured over two weeks of hurricane force winds in the Adriatic Sea. They had given up all hope of surviving and yet they held on, waiting for the inevitable—the sinking of the boat and the drowning of all the passengers. There was no rescue in sight.

Of course God knew what was happening and had permitted all of this for a very good purpose. The ship and all its cargo were lost, but not "a single hair" on the head of any passenger was harmed, just as Paul prophesied. (See Acts 27:34, NIV)

God acts in odd and mysterious ways, it seems to me, and the way He handled this situation must have seemed strange to those sailors. Why waste the time, the boat, the grain, making these poor creatures suffer? Why did God not *immediately* stop it?

I need to be reminded of this fact from time to time. Sometimes, God allows what seems to be meaningless suffering, but later something incredible, wonderful and unexpected follows. Faith is trusting that God knows what He is doing and that He will not cause wasted suffering.

More than once over the past few years I wondered if God liked me. Yes, yes, I know that God loves me, but I frequently questioned if I was really one His favorites. I see many others in ministry that seem to never struggle, apparently living complacent, respected, and peace-filled lives. But Christ's redemption never included any assurances of protection from being broken-hearted, lonely, desperate, or feeling hopeless at times. It's all part of our pilgrimage.

I suppose that in the end, all of Paul's struggles and torments made him a man not easily frightened, not quick to surrender, and not subject to episodes of self-pity. Paul was not naturally the writer, missionary, zealot, saint, and martyr that he became. It took the humble submission of Saint Paul and the supernatural hand of God to allow all these things to work together for the good.

For God to give the world more Pauls, men and women will have to remain faithful to Him even when doom and destruction appear inevitable.

Joy in the Morning

God's way of getting things done and man's way are not always similar, are they? I look at how God answers my prayers, or how He speaks to me, or how He directs my paths and I see a different way: better, of course, but always different from how I would handle the matter.

I often find myself questioning why things happen like they do in my life, and the life of my church and the camp. I wonder why things can't be more perfect, why our reputations can't be more "sterling" and why things aren't a bit easier since I am a child of the Lord God Almighty! There are uncertainties, disappointments and a lot of scary things that happen in life (at least in *my* life) and I wonder, sometimes, if this is happening because I'm somehow missing the point He is trying to teach me; perhaps I'm not where I belong, or worse, I never was called by God to do what I am doing in the first place. These musings might not be the kind of thing that goes through your head, but I find myself a bit unsure if I am doing the right thing when times get tough and I feel too much pressure.

But last night I was reminded of the very life of Jesus Christ—the only man who lived and died *perfect*. Jesus *never* missed an opportunity to honor God, was *never* in the wrong place at the wrong time and *never* disappointed His heavenly Father. When Christ began His ministry, masses of people followed Him in delight! Thousands listened to Him speak for hours. He sent out not 12, but 72 disciples to share the good news. But later, as He taught more and more about His purpose, the desires of His Heavenly Father and His ultimate goal (to be the sacrifice for the sins of all mankind) people *stopped* following. His disciples shrank from 72+ to less than 12, and at the very end no one stood up to defend Him. He was tortured—alone; ridiculed—alone; mocked—alone; and finally crucified with only a couple of women and one disciple having the courage to watch.

Imagine what would have happened to the story and impact of Jesus in history if this were the *end* of the story! We would *not* have books written examining Him, see movies about Him, have churches all over the globe to celebrate Him—and 2.3 billion people would be worshipping a different kind of a god! But in the end God raised Jesus from the dead and the disciples were transformed from cowards into spiritual patriots! The world was shaken not because of the *life* of Jesus, but because of what God did with His humbled and surrendered life!

His death on a cross and God's power to resurrect Him from the dead is what changed the world.

It is the *surrendered life* of a man or woman to God that scares Satan—not the intellectually gifted or dedicated worker. A believer surrendered to God might have trouble, his friends might let him down, he might fail in business or relationships, be mocked or sneered at. But at the proper time—i.e. *God's time*—the surrendered life of a person in love can accomplish what no other life can come close to accomplishing. The journey will be lonely and seem desperate at time, but *that's the way God works with those that He loves the most.* The joy comes in the morning.

Look to the Son

"For my Father's will is that everyone who looks to the Son and believes in him shall have eternal life, and I will raise them up at the last day. " (John 6:40, NIV)

It struck me that it's clear that it is God's *will*, or His *desire*, that everyone—all people of all nations—will be in heaven, i.e. receive eternal life. But it's also clear that Heaven is *not* for everyone. Some will *not* look to the Son and believe, either because they *choose* not to look, or because they *have not heard* the good news. The latter, of course, is why we have missionaries and support missions. But note that there is <u>no</u> provision for those that simply don't hear or are never told where to look.

Contrary to a more liberal theology, Jesus taught that people *had* to look to Him, and Him alone, for salvation. There's simply no other means of receiving eternal life or hoping for a resurrection. It might sound severe, unfair or not kind, but it nonetheless does faithfully represent the gospel of Jesus Christ—He taught this stuff Himself.

We're careful in our nation to respect other folks' religion and beliefs, but I wonder, sometimes, if some use the idea of respect as an excuse for not sharing the good news to the lost. Throughout the Bible we're told that we *must* believe in Him—whatever that means. So it stands to reason that if I really believed that those that did *not* look to the Son and believe in him to receives eternal life are going to miss out, I should be more concerned for their eternal well-being.

And that of course is why we do what we do as "evangelical Christians": we define that "whatever that means" as teaching that Jesus *is* the only, incarnate, perfect and holy Son of God. That He came here, at God's directive, to teach us how to live and love, yes, but primarily to *die for us so that we could be with Him and His Father in Heaven.* We believe that those who look to Him will be able to admit and repent of their sin and commit their life anew, to become the new creature that God always intended. And we believe that *only* through this rebirth experience can a person have communion with God now and *forever.* And yes, we are mocked and more cruelly judged than folks of other religions and we get a lot of attention from those that disagree with our conviction. But it is because the Christian faith is *absolutely exclusive* in its call to belief and repentance that we are so disliked. We believe that there is *no other way* whereby a man can be saved except through Jesus Christ.

Only a fool sets out to be disliked, but if we have no enemies in this world, I suppose it's because we're not much of a threat to the enemy's attempt to keep others from looking to the Son and believing…

Stop Sinning or Things Could Get Worse

"Later Jesus found him at the temple and said to him, 'See, you are well again. Stop sinning or something worse may happen to you.'" (John 5:14, NIV)

So Jesus heals a crippled man at a well of Bethesda and then, later in the day, sees the man again and says, "See, you are well again. Stop sinning or something worse may happen to you." (John 5:14, NIV). If you read this in context, Jesus is clearly warning about what can happen if you are found to be sinning *after* God has blessed you. God hears our prayer, heals us, blesses us, answers our pleas, provides a miracle, but then, if we go back to the same old way of living, we are at risk. Christ suggests that God's discipline can be *worse* than our *previous* condition. America: Listen up!

We're praying up a storm right now for God to heal our nation, protect our way of life, restore our economic might, destroy this Covid 19—and I really believe that He will! But what does He require of us? To get our act together.

Jesus talked more than once about things like this and gave parables, such as the man *forgiven* of much (billions), who turned right around and strangled and threw into prison a man who owed him a few hundred dollars. In that parable the forgiven man was unforgiven and was himself thrown into prison *and tortured.*

These are the kinds of reminders that some of my friends don't like/agree with, because it sounds like a "works=righteousness" concept. But Jesus was not talking about salvation, but the consequences of being blessed and then *not* being a blessing to others and/or turning away from sin. The idea I get is one of "discipline"—i.e. God getting your attention and treating you as He would His own child.

Here's what I think this means: If He blesses us—i.e. heals us, answers our prayers, redeems us, restores us—we'd better be prepared to show a little gratitude. We'd better show a changed heart and acknowledge that we are in need of not only a Savior, but also a Lord.

The man at the well was healed *and was grateful.* But Christ also admonished Him to become devout. Will we, as individuals, communities and a nation return to Him *devout?* We risk a worse catastrophe if we don't wake up and turn away from sin.

"..stop sinning or something worse may happen to you." (John 5:14, NIV) These are words from the Son of God, and they make as much sense today as they did 2000 years ago.

Blame Circumstances or Upbringing?

I work with youth who have many reasons to feel disaffected. Many suffer from very poor self-esteem and no home life. These youth, like many of us, have had some disappointments, have been abandoned, and have seen the dark side of humanity.

One day, as I was wallowing in self-pity, I began to think of all the reasons Jesus too could have been excused for living a mediocre or futile life. Think about it: He was born in a barn. We might romanticize the nativity and imagine a quaint manger scene, but He was born in a place fit for animals, not a human baby. Dust, flies, manure, the stench of the animals—this was His first "baby picture." A child born in those conditions today would be removed from the parents' care and placed under the care of social services!

Later he lost His earthly father, Joseph, at an early age. This surely would have been another reason for some emotional scarring. Later when He began His ministry, His cousin, who knew that Jesus was God's anointed, sent his personal disciples to ask Jesus, "Are you really the 'One?'" (Matthew 11:3, NIV). It must have been disappointing to Jesus to know that His own cousin was unsure. Later, His brothers and sisters—His own flesh and blood—doubted His divinity.

His closest friends abandoned Him when things got tough, His best friend did not come to His defense, none of the thousands that saw Him perform miracle after miracle stood with Him to the end.

Jesus did great, selfless things and was routinely called bad names, insulted, threatened, and accused of misrepresenting God. Throughout His adulthood He owned no home and had only the clothes on His back to call His own. People used Him, attempted to trap Him, laughed at Him, ridiculed him, and hoped for his death. Did ever a man have reason to wonder if God was pleased with Him?

Yet He never returned insult for insult. He never blamed others for His underprivileged life or His choices. He never stopped trusting in God. He never became bitter towards humanity. He never doubted Himself. He was certain, confident, firmly planted, and absolutely aware that God would be glorified if He were obedient to His purpose and calling.

Ah, the piece and joy that envelops us when we know whom we believe and are 100% persuaded that He is in control. Jesus knew peace and joy. Oh, that I might fully enjoy the same and stop making excuses.

Before this Sentence is Finished

David once prayed, "Show me, Lord, my life's end and the number of my days; let me know how fleeting my life is. You have made my days a mere handbreadth; the span of my years is as nothing before you. Everyone is but a breath, even those who seem secure." (Psalm 39:4-5 NIV)

I am mortal, and whereas I have been redeemed to live forever, my time on this earth is limited. There are many things I would like to do that I will *never* do. That is sad. There are many things I hope to see and hear that will escape my "bucket list." I only have one life to live and there's only so much I can cram into it. Life is fleeting.

Therefore, it behooves me to figure out what is essential and what is a waste of time. And while not being "preachy," let me share what we have banned in our home—*television*. We don't have it, don't need it, and don't miss it. We also don't surf the Web (it is named the "Web" for a good reason), play video games, or use iPhones in our "free time." Yes, the oldest boy has an iPhone; he has more freedom to make his own choices, even if they are poor choices at times. His eyes will open.

But as I consider my "shelf-life," I am all the more compelled to seize the day, work to accomplish all that I can, and not regret that I did not make better use of my time. There are some 10,000 minutes in a week and what I do with those 2,000+ idle minutes represents "existing" versus living life abundantly.

Please do not think that I don't see the need of slowing down, smelling the flowers, walking in a stream, wrestling with the boys, and "goofing off" from time to time. But, I think that many of us live our lives as if we had a spare life to use later on! In particular, putting things off, waiting until the last minute, not planning/preparing, and not tabulating what it will require of me can turn a potentially abundant life into a befuddled and confused existence.

The question I sometimes ask myself is simply this: "What if today is my last day?" Would I live any differently? Jesus spoke about His return, the "parousia." And we know three things, for sure, about the second coming of Jesus.

- No one, not even Jesus, knows when that will be.
- He could return at any minute of any day.
- Therefore, we should always be ready!

Our time here could come to an end before I finish this sentence. Lord help us all to be ready and live each day completely.

Calling on God

In Second Chronicles we are told, "If my people, who are called by my name, will humble themselves and pray and seek my face and turn from their wicked ways, then I will hear from heaven, and I will forgive their sin and will heal their land." (II Chronicles, 7:14 NIV)

What a great promise to fall upon us, both as a society and individually. If I *humble* myself, if I *pray*, if I seek His face, if I *turn away* from those things that are not godly, then He will hear me from heaven! He will forgive my sin, and He will heal me.

Recently, I got a better understanding of the heart of God when the youngest boy in our home had an angry outburst, then became defiant, withdrew, and pouted. It's a common drama that I am becoming more and more accustomed to lately. But then something atypical happened. At the end of all the drama, the seven-year-old whispered something to me. I told him to come closer and then he whispered in my ear, "Daddy, I am sorry, will you please forgive me?" I was not prepared for that. It's not something any of the boys do very often, if ever, and it touched me. The fact that he whispered it to me illustrated humility and a desire not to grandstand in front of the other boys. He turned away by saying that he was sorry and I really could tell that he was sincere when he asked me to forgive him. How refreshing to have a son simply ask for forgiveness rather than point his finger at the other brothers, make an excuse for his behavior, or offer an "actor's apology." This was the real deal, and I could discern that he was not happy with himself over what he had done.

My friends, if I could take great joy and pride in what my youngest did, how much more does God take joy and pride in me (and my nation) when we offer the same to Him? Will He not hear me, forgive me, bless me, and heal me? And yet the question comes back to me, "Is this how I pray to my Father? Do I speak to Him as a child would, humbly, sincerely, privately, with no excuses or attempts to minimize my sin?"

I don't want to withhold forgiveness from my boys and it is all the more true of my heavenly Father! If I, imperfect and corrupted as I am, can treat my boys with grace and mercy when they approach me with sincere regrets and apologies, will not God, the perfect Father, do all the more for us? And will He not tax the most remote star to bless me if I humble myself, seek Him, turn away from evil, and pray?

Giving Up My Life in Love

As a follower of Jesus Christ I am *supposed* to be an imitator of Him. That is, I am expected to do things in His name—or *as He did*—with the same frame of mind, ultimate goal and heart. I have heard this so many times and sang about it so often that sometimes I fail to stop and evaluate my progress and have to ask myself to re-examine what imitating Jesus really means.

In short, to imitate Jesus, the Son of God, is to *love in the manner and extent* He did. *That* is a challenge. I am a *recipient* of His unimaginable love, but to copy or imitate that love is beyond my ability. And of course He knows this. I am *unable* to love as He loved, so I have to be the host for His Holy Spirit to love *through me and to teach me to love.*

And what kind of love is this that I am to imitate? A selfless love that thinks all the time of the other…. and not of myself. It's a love that *truly* considers the needs of the other (the beloved) more important than my needs. It involves the preparation to "do without" and suffer for the one(s) I love.

Ultimately, the love Christ has called me to exhibit is a love so devoted to the other that it would require me to give up my own life for the ones I love. Jesus Himself said that, "there is *no greater love in all the world* than this." (John 15:13, NIV)

So…do I love like Christ? Am I really prepared to die—or to *stop living for myself*—as an expression of love for the ones God brings into my life? Or are my needs, rights, desires for comfort and respect *primary?* Is my willingness to be abased, ignored and have my rights denied something I struggle with, or accept only as a distant secondary consideration?

I love many people but I am *not* where I ought to be in imitating Jesus Christ. I am not laying down my life each day as I could and I am poorer spiritually for it. But as I fall more in love with Him, I am learning. Praise God that He is patient with me.

Calling on Egypt for Help

God told the prophet Isaiah that He would pull His hand away from Israel (meaning stop blessing and protecting them) because they had sought help and deliverance from Egypt, and not God Almighty. (Isaiah 31:1, NIV) More than one of the prophets made the same point, and some of the prophets actually confronted the kings of Judah and Israel, at their own peril, to rebuke them for signing alliances with pagan kingdoms rather that seeking and trusting God.

It is easy to condemn the ancient kings and not look at "the log" in my own eye (Matthew 7:3, NIV. As I read these passages, I asked myself, "Have I looked to an 'Egypt' for deliverance and blessing and not to God?" Was there someone or something I was trusting for my protection and sustenance over the One who has loved me, redeemed me, and called me His own?

Regretfully, I must admit that this is true. I am not any better than the shortsighted kings of the Israelites. I have made alliances and signed treaties that I should never have agreed to. I have trusted in my own wits, imagination, energy, and intuition instead of the hand of God and the inspiration of the Holy Spirit!

Whom did I trust instead of God? The list could go on and on, but the greatest *king* I turned to, rather than God, was myself. At other times I have decided that if I work hard enough, long enough, and stubbornly enough, I would get what I wanted. I have also determined that when times are difficult and God does not move fast enough according to my plan, I turn people into my personal "Egypts," i.e. my secondary sources of protection.

In short, I have used people, as well as my own strengths and talents, to serve as a "Plan B" should God be unable to handle my needs and the desires of my heart in a "timely manner."

I am still accepting the need to re-learn total abandonment and child-like dependency upon Him, and unlearn adult thinking when things look difficult or even hopeless. It is when I am the weakest, the most vulnerable, and the surest to fall that He is the most present, visible, and persuasive in my life.….Lord, have your own way with me.

Do You Know the Same One?

The book of Hebrews tells us, "Jesus was made human in every way." (Hebrews 2:17, NIV) Why is that so important to know? Later on the author says, "Because he himself suffered when he was tempted, he is able to help those who are being tempted." (Hebrew 2:18, NIV)

That's the point. Recently, I was a little frustrated that my prayers were not being answered as expeditiously and precisely as I had hoped. I was feeling the pressures around me mounting and for the first time in my life I asked God if He really understood what a difficult situation He had allowed me to fall into. I thought to myself, "What's the point of all these weeks and months of prayer? God, you never worry or get anxious because you are God and have no reason to be apprehensive!"

But these verses in Hebrews remind me that such assumptions on my part are dead wrong. Jesus was made human in every way. That means He was vulnerable to attack, sickness, injury, sleep deprivation, dehydration, hunger, and so forth. But we're also told, most significantly, that He suffered when He was tempted. I really don't recall ever reading or studying that verse before. Jesus suffered through His temptations precisely because He did not surrender to those temptations!

I am guilty of doing bad, selfish, unkind, and reckless things, but Jesus, who was far more tempted than I ever will be, never committed these sins. He was tempted to do all the foolish things I surrendered to and more, yet He never got suckered into disobedience, though it caused great suffering in His life.

It is so much easier to give in to temptation and admit it was wrong, confess it, and ask for forgiveness! To resist temptation is hard and will lead to personal suffering.

The Bible tells us that terrible struggles, not immediate blessings, are on the way if we choose to do the right thing. Severe suffering follows all who choose obedience and it is amplified from what the enemy throws our way. Do we preach and teach this enough to new Christians? It's easy to be saved because it's all the work of God. But it's tough to follow Him some days because we live in a corrupted, upside-down world where the temptation to live a God-free life is seen as "cool" and glamorous, while resisting temptation and telling Satan to return to hell is considered passé and anachronistic.

Jesus understood pressure, lust, losing friendships, satisfaction of popularity, the passion of wanting to be properly understood, and so on. But He chose to please God. He never struggled with peace, joy, and love. He knew what mattered most and He knew who allowed, caused, or permitted all things for His good purposes. Do you know the same?

Why Not Just Say Thank You?

Recently I received a personal attack on my work and ministry. I went to bed and considered my response to the attack and what it did to me. It occurred to me that even though I waited quite a bit before responding, and even though I wrote, and then rewrote my response, and although I read my response to a brother to be sure it was not offensive or unchristian, I now wish I had not responded as I did at all…

Why not simply *thank* the person that chastened me and ask for their prayers? What would I have lost by doing that? It would have not only been a witness of how a Christian accepts insult and misunderstanding, but would probably have led to healing and an appreciation for my attempts to imitate Jesus Christ. As it is, I was "dead right" about what I said, but I did not need to prove my point and I compromised the cause of Christ.

I can see so clearly now that God *permitted* this insult and attack and that more is in store for the future for a good purpose. I had no need to defend myself or state my innocence. God "had my back" and always will, and I must simply humble myself and let go of my need to be vindicated.

Many years ago, it was rumored that Saint Francis of Assisi was confronted by a beggar while on his way to speak at chapel. Francis was near the end of his life and had to ride on a donkey; his feet were diseased and he could not walk. The beggar walked up to Francis as he sat on that donkey and reminded Francis of the need to be humble and preach the gospel properly. *An uneducated, dirty little beggar had the gall to speak to Saint Francis like this!* But the story goes that Francis got off the donkey, kissed the feet of the beggar, and thanked him for reminding him about humility… Oh Lord, I am not at that place yet! Give me the heart of Saint Francis.

Why not let the insult go unanswered, or better, *thank the one offering the insult* and ask for their prayers that we do not fall deeper into conceit, or arrogance, or whatever error we've been accused of representing? If I am *not* being insulted, slandered, and verbally abused in this world because of my stand for Jesus Christ, it's a sure indication that I am not *living for* Jesus Christ. So if I must learn to expect to be offended and keep my eyes focused upon God then when it happens so I will not be overcome or depressed. A person can hurt my body, steal my identity, and clean out my bank account, even destroy my ministry or reputation. But all of these things are temporal; they are of this earth. I have an inheritance waiting for me that no one can steal or defile. God Himself is watching over me.

Through a Translucent Glass...

It's amazing what *color* can do to your perspective. It seems so strange that the hue of something can cause me to be optimistic and positive, or bored and melancholy. Some days the sky can get very gray, signaling the oncoming of snow or sleet. And that gray cheerless sky gets me "down" before I am even aware of it. Then sometimes the sky is an incredible Egyptian blue and I am happy and look forward to the day. Can colors make me happy?

I was getting the last room in our new house painted, and one of my friends suggested "rose" for the small sitting room. As the painter finished the room I noted that it truly was a cheerful color, and then learned from a friend that prisons cells are often painted pink because the tint staves off depression! Again, why did He create us to be so motivated and vulnerable to external stimuli like the color of a room or the pigmentation of the sky?

We were wonderfully and marvelously designed to not only reflect His glory but also to embrace the very things that He embraces. God must love color, variety, and diversity! Look how He has established His glory, creativeness, and beauty on this planet alone. I truly believe that as we grow closer to Him, we naturally appreciate the colors, forms, and diversity He has created, and the moods they evoke within us.

In scripture, I have noticed His apparent "favorite" colors. Three must be scarlet, purple, and gold—colors He required to be used in His temple. White is a constant color referring to purity, holiness, and forgiveness; and darkness always refers to rebellion, the absence of God's peace and protection.

As I consider how God encourages, whispers, and touches me, it's clear that colors, landscapes, sunsets, snow falls, and even the twilight are His gifts, reminding me of where I came from and to where my eternal home is. "Eye has not seen, not has ear heard, nor has entered the mind of man the things that God has prepared for those that love Him." (I Corinthians 2:9 NIV)

Beauty is something He has given me to evoke a bit of homesickness. One day, sooner and sooner, the appetite He has given me for beauty, color, and perfect form will be thoroughly satisfied; for I will see Him in unimagined colors and forms. But for the present, I must, like Paul, settle for seeing some grays, fuzzy figures, and imperfect forms. And yet... He does offer glimpses of how life is supposed to be.

Am I Doing Enough?

"So when you give to the needy, do not announce it with trumpets, as the hypocrites do in the synagogues and on the streets, to be honored by others. Truly I tell you, they have received their reward in full. But when you give to the needy, do not let your left hand know what your right hand is doing, so that your giving may be in secret. Then your Father, who sees what is done in secret, will reward you." (Matthew 6:2-4 NIV)

It seems that Jesus is *assuming* that we *will* be giving to those in need—always. That's the first thing that grabs me when I read this and it leads to me to ask myself, "Do I give to those in need?" Frankly I could give more… and the giving that I do provide does not cause me to suffer or "do without."

It's been said that if your giving does not pinch you a bit, you're not giving enough. It causes me to think about how much I waste each day on things I *could* do without if I really wanted to.

But getting past the *responsibility of giving,* Jesus again is talking about the *motivation* for giving. When we help someone are we doing it for *recognition* or to show our *love for God*—secretly. A lot of the charity that goes on in the USA is driven by ego, personal recognition, the right to name a building or to honor the donor. Those folks *have* their reward, according to Jesus, and should expect *nothing* else from God.

But there *are* those who give because *He has already given to them abundantly.* I don't give so that God will give more to me (even though, in fact, He will); I give because He has given to me so much already that my charity is a mirror (dimly, but a reflection nonetheless) of His charity towards me.

I suppose that those that don't give—freely and with no expectations of tax benefits or congratulations—have never come to understand just how much He has already given them and how much *more* He is prepared to bless and give to them.

God, open our eyes to what we have already received and help us to share it! Forgive us for holding back our pennies when you have given us an immeasurable inheritance. Help us to be extravagant in our giving! Amen

Falling into Temptation

When Christ was about to be betrayed and face torture and execution, He took the disciples to an olive grove and asked them to pray for Him. Two times He warned them to pray that they not "fall into temptation." (Mark 14:32 NIV). I never noticed until today that He said this *twice*. Obviously Christ said things for a purpose—He did not waste words.

"Pray that you do not fall into temptation." (Matthew 6:41, NIV) All day I have wondered what He meant by that. I was reminded that He taught His disciples to pray,"...lead us not into temptation."(Matthew 6:13, NIV). In the prayer of Jabez, Jabez requests that God "protect him from evil." (1 Chronicles 4:9-10 NIV)

It seems clear that, as believers, there is an obvious and omnipresent danger to *fall* or *stumble*. Regardless of how close we are to Christ—and no men have ever been closer than the eleven Jesus was speaking to—there is a danger—perhaps even *more profound the closer we are to Him*—to FALL into temptation. This does not mean that we pray to never be tempted; that would mean we would not be alive. But to fall into temptation seems to suggest that we are *not looking where we are going*.

Jesus was warning us to k*eep our eyes open*. We stumble because we are not paying attention to where we are, where we are going, the purpose of our journey and whom we travel with. "Falling" implies a lack of focus, getting too comfortable with our surroundings. I've been told that the ones that are most likely to get hurt with a tractor or a chainsaw are not the novices, but the professionals. The pros get too used to it, don't pay attention and end up injured or dead.

The danger for those of us that know Him is that we begin to think too highly of our own holiness and forget how easily—how *very easily*—we can fall flat on our faces! When God redeems us He doesn't place us on a shelf as a trophy to be looked at. He uses us for His work in a world that is full of challenges, temptations and "pitfalls." I need to pray daily that I not fall into temptation by losing my focus. It provides a sober reminder of what I am without Him.

Discipline = Knowledge

We have seen some extraordinary media events here in the USA in recent times. Very famous and powerful men have been accused, frankly, of being quite dull-witted. They said, touched, suggested, and requested sexual things from women to whom they are not married and they got caught.

What surprises me about these men and the many others that have fallen, is that they would normally be the first people to accuse, denounce, and condemn anyone else of the very same things that they did. Surely, they knew that what they did was wrong (at least they're saying that they realize it now), and certainly they had the ability to say "no" to their impulses and not indulge in inappropriate actions. But it appears that they lacked discipline, the very discipline that would have demonstrated an understanding of how important it is to be wise about how they should treat people.

Prior to these scandals, Vice President Mike Pence said he never eats alone with a woman other than his wife and that he won't attend events featuring alcohol without her by his side. The media ridiculed Pence for saying this, but this is the same standard the late Billy Graham lived-by for over 90 years. Pence, in my view, is living wisely and with discipline. The same might be said about Barack Obama or Jimmy Carter or any other politician that was careful around the opposite sex. I am not arguing one political party over another. I am thinking about the need for men in power to use their brains and show some character! Proverbs 12:1 (NIV) says, "Whoever loves discipline loves knowledge, but whoever hates correction is not wise." No one likes to be disciplined, rebuked, or chastened. But, a wise man (or woman) welcomes it as a gift from God because it's a barrier and hedge to keep them from falling into disgrace.

Yet, there's always a temptation to feel good when the driver in the fancy sports car gets pulled over for speeding, and we may feel the same "satisfaction" when these powerful men get fired and humbled. But of course it's very wrong and dangerous to crow or gloat over someone else's failures. The question should be, "Am I behaving the same way?" Perhaps I'm not behaving in the same *circumstances*, but am I one that loves discipline? Do I appreciate wisdom for what it is preparing me for and protecting me from? Do I understand that God disciplines me because I am His child and He loves me? Do I reflect upon the absolute need for discipline regardless of my age? Discipline from God is training that makes me more willing to obey and more able to control myself.

God trains me by allowing things to happen (or not happen) in my life in such a way that I look up to Him, cry out and say, "Speak, Lord!" And like Mike Pence, I can choose discipline and not allow myself to be placed in the wrong place, at the wrong time, with the wrong people.

May God have mercy on us all and teach us with His gentle hand to accept His discipline and rebuke. Speak to us, Lord Jesus!

Being of Use to God or Trying to Use God?

Most of you reading this devotion would join me in agreeing that we *believe* in God and trust that He uses His hand in history to work "all things together towards good." (Romans 8:28, KJV) We *say* this, but do we *believe* this when bad things are happening to us? Do we still hold that lofty notion that He is sovereign when torment comes to *our* emotional life (consider the prophet Jeremiah), or do we whine, worry, fret, or (worse) go on the attack by suggesting that *someone else* is responsible for bad things coming our way? It's funny how we can clearly see God working to open the eyes of someone who we think needs to be shaken up a bit, while seeing things quite differently when it happens to us.

In talking to other Christian leaders of late, I am surprised that many of the methods they propose for handling hardship, giving good leadership, addressing problems or even preparing for evangelism focus more upon "what works" to get the desired result in a worldly sense, than in doing the *right thing* as taught in scripture, and going about it openly and transparently.

Is it right to try to manipulate God—and His servants—to accomplish *our* agenda and dreams—even if these goals are noble? Is it right to "do whatever it takes" to stop suffering or torment within our own souls, or have we forgotten abandonment and trust in God?

I was moved to write this after talking to many folks in the past few years about "marketing" our ministry to families (we're a summer camp) along with fund raising, capital drives and so forth. But the *consistent* counsel I get back from the Christian "pros" is the same kind of reasoning and advice I would expect from a publicist for a movie star! And I am not trying to be unkind, but somehow Madison Avenue and Wall Street seem often to have replaced the spiritual, "other-worldly" direction for doing God's work. I have *not yet* heard or seen a plan that focuses solely on God and His people—it's all about strategies, "development of resources," having succession plans, properly packaging the message, yada, yada.

I struggle in my work and spiritual walk as all men trying to follow God do, but I hope never to be found to be struggling *with God* about my work and walk. He is aware of all my challenges and dreams and hopes. It's good to act wisely and circumspectly in business, family life and ministry. But living for "results" rather than living an abandoned life *for* Him leads to frustration and depression. *He* is the goal and the desired end result—nothing else. If I order and plan my life accordingly, I will found to be a good and faithful servant and a blessing to those I know.

To Whom Much Is Given

For as long as I have been a student of the Bible, one of the most soul searching verses for me has been Amos 3:2 (NIV), "You only have I chosen of all the families of the earth; therefore I will punish you for all your sins."

Amos was preaching to the divided kingdoms of Israel and Judah when he uttered these words. These two kingdoms were *special!* God called them into existence for a purpose, and they had woefully failed to produce the results He intended. To whom much is given, much is required. I wonder: Do we talk about this enough?

One reason that verse has haunted me is that many of us—myself included—are like Israel. We're blessed, protected, and (when compared to the other citizens of this world) quite affluent. God has blessed most of us with good health, a prosperous culture and a very secure land in which to live. It is as if He chose to bless us especially—and yet we have not considered the responsibilities that go with great blessings.

I can never match, in my good deeds or donations, what God has given to me. Like the ancient Hebrews, I do feel that God's hand and His blessings have been upon me and my brethren more than others. But I do believe that God *expects* more from those of us who have been *given* more. I am convinced that He holds the ones He blesses with, for example, greater intellect (I am not one of these) or profound gifts and talents, to higher expectations! And why shouldn't He?

So in light of His goodness, mercy, grace and gifts, why would I ever expect God to not expect a more robust response of obedience and gratitude from me than from one who was not so blessed? Why do I choose to compare my <u>goodness</u> with the worst possible example rather than with the highest example?

Now I don't think that God is up in heaven looking down and waiting for a chance to upset my apple cart, and I am certain that Christ has already taken the *full* punishment for my sins, yet there is also a lingering realization that I am obliged to be a better man because He has chosen not only to redeem and rescue me from what I deserve, but has provided a home, a family, a community that is far *better* than I deserve.

I do not serve the King of Kings or give my tithe to the church to receive God's blessing. I serve Him and give my gifts to Him because I *have already been blessed indeed.*

Nonetheless, Pressing On

What do you do when you've done everything you possibly could have done to stave off defeat and yet see destruction coming? Or when you have done your level best to be obedient and faithful to God and *still* find that things are not working out like all the songs and motivational speakers insist they will? And what happens when night after night you go to bed dreading the morning and all the frustrations and certain troubles you know you will have to face based upon what happened that shouldn't have, or did not happen that should have, the day before?

I know that I am not the only one that suffers from these torments described above, and yet as I go through this I often feel that way. I was wired, conditioned, trained, and educated to *succeed* and complete the tasks that I take on. My parents taught me to do a job well or don't start it. No one who knows me would call me a "quitter." Something within me *hates* the idea of losing, failing, giving up, admitting defeat, or throwing in the towel. But my ultimate question is simply this: Am I pleasing Him, right now, where I am, doing what I am doing, being what I am…? Or have I somehow missed the mark and mistaken His call for something else?

My need, daily, is to be reminded and reassured that He *is* pleased with me and that *His hand is upon me*, regardless of the present circumstance or outward appearances of my life. Honestly, on days like these, I think that if people knew the pressure that was upon me and the innumerable issues that I must address, they might suggest that I simply "curse God and die."(Job 2:9, NIV).

I hope I don't appear to be bragging about how difficult my life is! In fact, I am blessed far more than most. But sometimes I feel like "butter being spread a bit too thin over toast." At the end of the day, all that I am trying to do could fall and I might well be called the biggest failure in Christian summer camping; or all things might come together perfectly and I could be celebrated as man of vision, tenacity, and prayer! Of course, *both* of these things might also happen. I might fail miserably (from the world's perspective, as did Amos in the Old Testament) and yet be found by God to have been faithful and loyal.

Right now I must endure the "quiet" of God, the nerve-wracking "wait" and the attacks of the enemy who continues to call me a failure and fool for thinking I could fulfill the vision and burden God placed upon me 40 years ago.

Friends, be sure of what He has called you or led you to do, and then burn your bridges and follow that vision. If there's a way to retreat you'll never reach the goal He has set before you. I am not totally there yet, and I have been beaten down more often, but I know in Whom I have believe and I do not believe that He has wasted any of my sleepless nights for nothing. Good things must surely be in store.

Angels in France?

One of the things that grabs my attention immediately when I visit France are all the handicapped, crippled, blind and slightly demented people I see on the streets of the cities. I am not saying that France has more than we do in the USA—perhaps they have fewer. But they are *seen* in France, and I just don't see these kinds of people that often in North Carolina. Perhaps it's because we are such a rather rural state (North Carolina); in our state people hardly ever walk *anywhere.* We use a car and rarely walk down the streets. That might be why I never see folks that are handicapped very often, but I also wonder if we are more inclined to "put them away" in my country. Maybe we prefer to put people that are blind into blind colleges, blind communities and working at places just for the blind. Perhaps the same is true for those a bit demented. Maybe we put them into special homes where no one else has to see them. Maybe we justify that by telling ourselves that it's for their own protection and treatment.

We might have good reasons for putting away all the folks who have physical or mental shortcomings, but one thing was clear to me today: I had compassion on those that I could see and touch in a way that isn't possible just by reading about them or seeing a TV special regarding their plights. Walking right up to them made them individual beings in a way a poster or special campaign to assist does not.

I also noted that *my* troubles and challenges quickly receded to the back of my mind as I thought about all that these folks are up against. I whine and whimper about how hard my work is and how unappreciated and misunderstood I am—and then I am literally face to face with a man with no legs—begging for food… or an old lady bent and twisted so much that she has to strain to see what is in front of her… or a man muttering and arguing with someone that is not there as he crosses the street. What on earth do I have to complain about? Thank God for letting me see how difficult life is for some—and yet they never seem to complain.

The Bible speaks about angels and how God sends them to protect the "little ones." (Matthew 18:10, NIV). The author of Hebrews admonishes us to be kind to strangers because it *might* just *be* an angel. (See Hebrew 13:2, NIV).I wonder sometimes: *Was* that a bent up old lady… or an angel? Was that man really insane… or was he a messenger of God?

One of our staff and I were in Puebla walking through a bazaar several years ago, and a young man walked past us begging for food. We both recalled that he did not appear to fit in, and as we both turned to look at him again *he was gone—vanished.* It was as if we were being tested to see how we would respond to cries for help. We failed the test.

What if I treated every strange man, woman and child as if he or she were really an angel? What if I treated them if they were really *Jesus Christ?* Isn't that *precisely* what Jesus told me I was supposed to do?

Puppies, Pets and Little Boys

The eldest son approached me last night about the possibility of getting another puppy. I thought it was some sort of sick "Covid-19" joke. We have our hands full with four dogs, an Arctic wolf and the seven people that now live here with big appetites. We're living through a pandemic, for crying out loud, the last thing I need is another animal.

But he was serious. After getting a Pit-bull mix less than two years ago, now he wants another one, albeit a puppy, for the purpose of one day breeding the two and selling the puppies. It seems madness to me, but he rarely asks for things for himself, so we're "talking" about it. But I *know* it's not a good idea.

Simultaneously, and truly coincidentally, the other three boys have all been dreaming of their own puppies as well. To make all four boys in my home happy by acquiring four new puppies in the house, I would be ready to *seek* quarantine. So I must carefully navigate what all four young men are wanting versus what is really needed. But I have noticed, over many years that people who are kind to animals are most often kind to people, and people who are cruel to animals are almost always also cruel to people. Watching my sons hug, pet, spoil and give little treats to the dogs we have reminds me that there is purpose and meaning for all God's creations and creatures. Truly, He reveals His nature and His glory in His created order—even dogs and puppies (I am not so sure about cats and kittens).

Puppies are adorable and we want to pick them up and love them. Why is that? My sons are instinctively drawn to the innocence, gentleness and frailty of a small puppy. Something within them wants to protect them, provide for them, speak to them gently and cuddle them. I have seen children who are unable to accept a touch or give a hug to an adult but find it quite easy to stroke and hug a pet.

The ancient Hebrews as well as the folks of Jesus' time despised dogs, so I don't want to draw too many analogies here, but there is "divine revelation" (e.g. the holy scripture, the prophetic word, miracles, and of course Jesus Christ) and there is "natural revelation" (rainbows, sunsets, the majesty of nature—and puppies). Frankly, I get more headway in explaining God and His love for man with puppies than I do trying to explain the synoptic gospels or systematic theology with the boys in my home. I thank God for puppies and the natural things He provides to help hapless dads like me.

It looks like we'll be getting another puppy this weekend………..

Friends Can Disagree

"Some time later Paul said to Barnabas, "Let us go back and visit the believers in all the towns where we preached the word of the Lord and see how they are doing." Barnabas wanted to take John, also called Mark, with them, but Paul did not think it wise to take him, because he had deserted them in Pamphylia and had not continued with them in the work. They had such a sharp disagreement that they parted company. Barnabas took Mark and sailed for Cyprus, but Paul chose Silas and left..." (Acts 15:36 NIV)

Disagreements are inevitable even among spiritual giants like Paul and Barnabas. And sometimes it's not a matter of right or wrong, but simply a difference of opinion. These Christian missionaries simply did not agree about the character of John Mark, and rather than demand that the other see his point as the more valid, they simply parted ways—-that is, the literally took different paths. And it appears that, as they departed as friends, they got more accomplished.

Anyone who has studied the Word of God would quickly come to the conclusion that there *are valid* points of dogmatic disagreement in the Bible regarding matters that are not essential for salvation, but that have nonetheless led to a lot of angry debates and name calling. I have never met a Christian man or woman with whom I agree in all matters—*not once.*

I was personally raised in a large, conservative, Protestant church. But while at my university I was a youth pastor at a church that was borderline "fundamental." Later in graduate school, I served in a *far* more liberal church. But in each church I found this to be true: the most tolerant, open-minded, even-handed, gracious and "ready to learn" were the mature Christians; men and women quite secure in what they believed and therefore not easily angered by someone with whom they disagreed.

There is plenty of room at His table for various opinions about the Holy Eucharist (the "Lord's Supper"), the inerrancy of scripture, what we should eat, wear or drink, etc. But I don't believe that our host (the Son of God) appreciates bickering and arguing at the table. I say this because I find it amazing that some very educated people seem far more dedicated to their opinion, or to a denomination, or a creed, or a particular version of the Bible than for the One whom all this passion is about.

I have served in Baptist, Methodist, Presbyterian and non-denominational churches; my best friends are both Catholic, Orthodox and Protestant; the men that influenced me the most came from Rome, Nashville, Scotland, England and Germany—and the common thread with each of those influences was their modesty and humility—I find that compelling and irresistible in a friend.

If I am certain in whom I believe and I know where I came from. Therefore I am able to listen and learn from the least and best.

Against Thee Only I Have Sinned. (Pslams 51:4, NIV)

A day ago, one of my boys rushed to tell me that one of my other boys had broken one of our "nice" drinking glasses in his bedroom. I asked him if he knew who broke it, and he said that he "knew for sure" that it was the other brother. After our typical ten-minute investigation, it became clear that it was not the other brother who had broken the glass, but rather the very boy that snitched in the first place. I thought to myself, "Well, surprise, surprise…."

I asked him why he would falsely accuse someone else and why he did not come to me with the truth. He retorted that he knew I would be angry and he did not want to be the subject of my anger. As disappointing as my discovery was, it points to a fact that has been true of mankind since the creation. We humans have always wanted to shift the blame to someone else. Adam blamed Eve, Eve blamed the serpent, but no one "fessed up" and accepted the consequences with contrition or repentance.

It is within mankind's twisted DNA to always try to blame someone or something else for our poor choices, selfishness, or weakness. It's become culturally acceptable to blame our parents, our genetic make-up, our chemical imbalance, or a lack of proper recognition as a child. It is claimed that these deficiencies give us a "right" to be different, which causes us to sin, or "miss the mark," and commit an act that is morally unacceptable.

Sin is the root issue between the ideal man that I want to be and the actual man that I am. And despite my 1001 excuses, the sins I commit do severe damage to my association with others, my own self-image, and my relationship with God. Making excuses, blaming others, whining about how I am misunderstood, and complaining about not being properly pitied, does nothing to deal with the root of the problem – *sin in my life.*

I've read many times that real maturity begins when a man or woman can look at the bad things (sins) he or she has done and say to God, "against you (God) only have I sinned." (Psalm 51:4, NIV). I did not fully understand this as a young man. How could my offenses against another man be "only" against God? But now I understand that each time I lie, exaggerate, shift the blame, boast, show unkindness, or fail to keep a promise, it is God that I am offending. This is because as a redeemed man of God, one born again by the blood of Jesus, my life is supposed to express something new, something different from the old way I used to live! The reality of the cross of Jesus is most easily proven in the way I live a new and transformed life. Each time I fail God by failing to live the way He intended, my reputation as a servant of Jesus Christ suffers, and indeed I have sinned only against God. Even though my salvation is not at stake, I have let Him down and have called into question the efficacy of the cross!

My life cannot undo the work of Jesus Christ, but it can cause those outside the Christian community to hesitate or have pause, and it can cause those within the Christian community to slow down in their desire to follow Him. In the end, it is God Himself that I am wounding.

But once I see my sins as *my sins*, and that it is God Himself that I am wounding, I can abandon all excuses and embrace the power of the Holy Spirit. Only then can I overcome those things that cause me, and others, to stumble.

A Legacy of Kindness

Unkindness is something I can easily identify in others, but can others see it in my life? To be unkind is to act in an unnecessarily dismissive or hurtful way to another soul. I see this behavior as I raise four young men in my home. They instantly and correctly point out the rudeness and unkindness of the others throughout the day. But when *they* are being unkind, they are quick to explain and justify the reasons why.

I need to be careful when discussing politically improper things, I suppose, but just today my blood boiled when I heard about how our summer camp's foreign staff are treated at U.S. Embassies around the world, particularly in Kenya. I am venting right now, so forgive me, but I am shocked at how unkind and dismissive officials are to Kenyans seeking work visas. They wait weeks, prepare for months, and dream for years of coming to the USA on a work or tourist visa, then are summarily dismissed for no apparent reason. Their hearts are broken, tears are shed (as I heard today), and no compassion is shown or expressed. But it's not just Kenya; I experience the same lack of courtesy at tollbooths in New Jersey and cafes in NYC.

However, over the past few years I have noticed how some workers and managers, like the folks at Starbucks and Chick-fil-A, are consistently kind and how those companies have continually experienced growth. It appears that most folks would rather be treated gently and courteously, and are prepared to patronize companies and organizations that treat them with respect.

Of course this causes me to be somewhat introspective about my church, and the thousands of other churches that claim an association with Jesus. Although the church I attend has it challenges and problems, I am quite certain that it is because of the kindness of its members and leaders that my family and I have chosen to join it. Consistently, they have showered us with encouragement, kind words, and smiles. They give us the impression that they are glad we are there and that they authentically care about us.

What about my ministry (a summer camp) for children? Do I and the members of our board and our staff exhibit such compassion? Is it obvious that we are glad to see the arrival of every new camper or staff? Do we welcome them? Do they feel cherished, important, appreciated, and special? Do we flood them with kindness in such a way that there is never any question of how much we approve of them?

Finally, I think of my own home. I often brag about the fact that most of the time I am right when I tell my boys not to do something. I am on target almost always about how they could do more, behave better, and be more Christ-like. But am I kind?

My boys, and the campers and staff, will soon forget my lectures, my tirades, and the times I have been disappointed in them. But what they will most likely remember is how they were treated and if it was kind. When I have the opportunity to shine as someone who has abandoned all for Christ, I am able to bear the fruit of kindness during the most stressful moments. This sets an example and legacy that these sons of mine, and my camp staff, may never forget. It is my *hope* to set this example in a practical way every day of my life and every summer at our camp.

Being Hungry

"Blessed are those who hunger and thirst for righteousness, for they shall be filled." (Matthew 5:6, NIV)

This is:

- A plea for satisfaction…
- A description of folks that have a *passion* for what is right…
- Encouragement for those who want justice, fairness, and equality.

Those of us who *hunger and thirst* for what is right, will get angry over injustice to others, unkindness to the small or weak, and attacks on those who are incapable of defending themselves.

To make this more appropriate for a summer camp like ours, you might say that, *blessed* are those that stand up to the bully in the cabin, or stop the staff that gets a second cookie when some campers haven't gotten their first, or is impatient about cheating in a game even if his team is the one cheating—and winning.

It's easy to dismiss the teachings of Jesus as being more appropriate for those dreaming of an ideal that is totally impractical. But Jesus was not simply blowing smoke. He meant what He said. *Hurray* for those who are passionate and determined to do all they can to make the world a better place by standing up to the bully, rebuking those that are deliberately offensive, and calling things *wrong* that are clearly *wrong*!

If you thirst and hunger for these things, be encouraged. You're going to be satisfied—partially in this life and *totally* in the next! My ability to yearn for what is right is a sure sign that I am growing closer to Him; my complicity in what is patently wrong is a sure sign that I do not know Him well at all.

If You Declare with Your Mouth, "Jesus is Lord" (Romans 10:9 NIV)

"If you declare with your mouth, 'Jesus is Lord,' and believe in your heart that God raised him from the dead, you will be saved." (Romans 10:9 NIV)

In sharing the gospel, these are the two absolutely central and essential truths about Jesus: (1) *He is Lord*, (2) *God raised Him from the dead.* These two inseparable truths sum up what I *must* believe and confess if I want to inherit eternal life.

Is He Lord? That is, do I believe that He is God in the flesh and have I abdicated my throne to Him? There was never a call from Jesus to come to Him to simply escape hell, but rather a call to *turn away from blindness and deafness and be born again* into the original kind of creature God intended.

And do I *believe* that God really did raise Him from the dead? In my understanding of the Bible, this is what changes a man's life in regard to God. *If* God really raised Jesus from the dead, then all that Jesus said and did is authenticated and validated—He *is* the Son of God and the Christian faith is all that the New Testament says it is! If I am unsure of the resurrection I will always be crippled spiritually, no matter how hard I try to believe. But I have come to the conclusion that God *did* raise Jesus from the dead and that He *is* Lord—and that's made all the difference in my life.

But I am also *required* to "confess" or "admit" these truths. The criminal on the cross did this, and so did the tax collectors and prostitutes—I am no better. I was redeemed not to brag about my own merits, *but in spite of them* to proclaim that He loves me and has saved me. *He* did all the work—my job is to tell the truth: He is Lord, He paid my debt on the cross and He rose from the dead.

There are other things Christians *should* do, and some Christian fellowships put more emphasis on those things: communion, baptism, giving, being a member of a church, etc. But the thief on the cross did not receive communion, baptism, never tithed, was not a church membership—he simply *believed* and *confessed*.

It's really quit simple, but only God and I know what's really going on in my heart when I talk about believing in Him, and my confession either rings true or hollow when it is compared to the way I live and the good deeds that naturally spring from my soul.

"For God so loved the world that He gave His only Son, so that *whoever believes in Him* might not perish but have eternal life". (John 3:16, NIV) It's the greatest news of the New Year.

Humble Yourself in the Sight the Lord (James 4:10, NIV)

Jesus went into a Pharisee's home and a prostitute followed him in, washed His feet with her tears, wiped His toes with her hair and then poured perfume on His feet. Most of us have read this story many times, but what He said to her **at the end** of the story surprised me:

"Your faith has saved you; go in peace." (Luke 7:50, NIV)

He did not just say, "Your sins are forgiven," but *"your faith has saved you"*. (Luke 7:50, NIV) So, if I read this correctly, a lady that lived her whole adult life doing something *very bad in God's eyes,* simply has to cry and pour some oil on Jesus' feet and everything is fine?

Evidently so! And this is where I see Jesus turning all religious thinking *upside-down*. It's not the "right living" souls that Jesus came to save, but the sinners. And sinners like this prostitute recognized that her life was so messed up that it was "hopeless" short of Jesus' compassion. That's where she "placed all her eggs", so to speak, spiritually. She positioned all hope in His love and believed in her heart that if she *truly humbled* herself (she sat at his feet and wiped His feet with her hair), acknowledged her sins (she never stopped weeping and used the tears to clean His feet!) and recognized Him as the Messiah (she anointed His feet with an expensive perfume) she might be redeemed and saved. And her faith proved right.

What an incredible sense of lightness must come when someone hears Him say, *"Your faith has saved you!"* (Luke 7:50, NIV) Friends, that means that "All is well—you are now a redeemed, restored, justified member of the family of God". It's the sick that seek a physician—the poor that seek a philanthropist. Conversely, those that are well or <u>well off</u> never have need of such intervention. The sad truth is that there *are* folks in our world that *think* they are wealthy, clean, pure, healthy—and therefore in no need of a savior. And so Jesus correctly said: *"Blessed are the poor"* (Luke 6:20, KJV). It means, **blessed** are those that know just how poor they are!

This woman was far wiser and more in touch with God than the Pharisees. She knew how dirty and in need of cleansing she was. And *that* is what we are to preach to a world that is so confused about wealth, health, and purity. When any man or woman stands next to Him, then, and perhaps only then, can he/she really begin to grasp how wretched and crooked he/she is.

My goal at this camp is to help young people and maturing young adults *seek Him, find Him, kneel before Him and experience the restoration to fullness and holy living that only He can give.*

Am I Satisfied with Him?

In reading the Old Testament I am often dumbfounded at how the people of God could be so thickheaded and quick to forget the lessons of history. How could Josiah be such a good king and his son and grandson so rotten? Were they not watching how God blessed Josiah's obedience? How could Solomon be such a wise king and yet Rehoboam (his son and heir) be so unwise? Did he not see the ineptitude of acting rashly and without thoughtful consideration?

How could the church be so on-fire for Jesus Christ and expand so rapidly in the first few centuries and then fall into such troubles during the next 1000 years? Were they not aware that the persecution kept the church pure, God-dependent and narrowly focused upon His Kingdom? Did they not consider that being too secure and safe, or too prosperous and self-sufficient, would certainly lead them away from the security, purpose and place of the cross? Paul said this: "For you know the grace of our Lord Jesus Christ, that though he was rich, yet for your sake he became poor, so that you by his poverty might become rich" (2 Cor. 8:9, NIV). Jesus's words were, "One's life does not consist in the abundance of his possessions" (Luke 12:15, NIV).

So what is it within *us and our children* that makes us look for greener pastures and an easier life when we know, from the Biblical record, history and personal experience, that the grass is *not* greener and life is *not* easier when we try to "cut corners"? Why do we crave to do things our way when we know, good and well, that eventually our sins will find us out?

Arrogance somehow causes us to think we could run our life better if we were our *own* god. We worship our own instincts, ideas and notions as if they were "divine". Though we would never announce it publicly, we think we're better than others—and perhaps even God.

Of course Jesus Christ was the *antithesis* of these vices—-so why don't we follow Him rather than enemy? Because we're not content. We never seem ready to accept the good things that He sends to us or the proper instructions He has provided. And so, ultimately, we are not content with Him.

Paul said, "Not that I am speaking of being in need, for I have learned in whatever situation I am to be content. I know how to be brought low, and I know how to abound. In any and every circumstance, I have learned the secret of facing plenty and hunger, abundance and need." (Phil. 4:11-12, NIV). Paul was clear that possessions and the good life are not signs of God's blessing—_contentment_ is. And the secret to holding on to contentment is to get into the habit of praising Him in all circumstances. Paul said we should "rejoice in the Lord always." (Philippians 4:4, KJV). That's a sign that we are content—and that we have received the full measure of His blessing.

Am I thanking Him, rejoicing in all things, praising Him throughout the day? Have I learned about the inner peace that comes from being content with what He has given me?

Delighting in Rules

When the Psalmist says that he, "delights in God's law" (Psalm 1:1-2, NIV), I used to wonder how in the world anyone would get happiness from rules and regulations. As a younger man, I felt the need to challenge the rules from time to time, and question the wisdom of those older than me.

But it was *God's* law, not man's law that David was talking about when he spoke of "laws." In addition, I have come to understand the delight that comes in knowing God's law and the benefit that obeying it brings to my own life. I am learning that reciting, remembering, and reflecting on God's law does not only lead me to see how rotten and derelict I am, but also to see His law as an operator's manual for a precision made piece of equipment. This fine piece of equipment, of course, is mankind, or more specifically, me. God tells me in His Holy Word how this finely tuned machine works best and most efficiently, as well as what will foul up the engine and cause it to sputter and fail.

As I read and re-read His word, I realize more and more that it is true. His directions for caring for this machine, my soul and body, are absolutely correct. All the shortcuts I have attempted have caused my life to be less effective, more uncontrolled, poorly maintained, and improperly operated. God's Word is meant to bring me to a place of "delight" because I can begin to live and thrive as the creature (or machine) that He intended.

I suppose this is why I crave His Word more each morning. It's the "gasoline" that my engine requires. It provides the checks, maintenance, and occasional "overhauls" that my soul desperately needs. As I begin to see His Word as His manual for living the abundant life, I increasingly desire to remember it, abide by it, and live it.

The pity, of course, is to see so many human "machines" that have been ruined because they lacked a qualified mechanic, i.e. Jesus Christ, to open their hearts and minds to the truth contained within the owner's manual. Please pray that our summer camp leads more souls to the Master Mechanic and His manual.

Fatherhood 101

I think that a crisis can reveal what we are really made of, but a nine year old boy and his six year old brother living in your home can be even *more* revealing of what you're made of.

I agreed to accept into my home two brothers whom the local DSS thought I might be able to help. Whereas I might have served as a father figure to youth over the past four decades, this is the first time that I have had two children living with me like this. *It is exhausting!* I am amazed at the energy they have as well as their inability to exercise self-control. It's non-stop questions, talks, warnings, explanations, confrontations—with two very excited boys. Truly I had no idea that being a parent required so much dialogue, explaining, reasoning, reminding, reinforcing, *threats*, and at times having my *own* meltdowns.

Of course these boys have also brought into our home laughter and tenderness, revealing an open-minded desire to know how things work and an incredible longing for belonging. I am reminded again and again that after being in various foster homes, they do *not* want to be relocated again. And that's where my heart breaks for them—regardless of their temper tantrums, lack of good manners, selfishness, silly behavior, et al. They want a home, stability, the assurance that no matter what they do, *someone* will always be there for them and *never* give up on them.

But that's what being a father is all about—and I am both experiencing this first hand *and* being reminded of how my heavenly Father loves me, forgives me, tolerates me, and *never lets go of my hand.* These two boys want, more than anything else, to know that my love for them is unconditional and transcends their common mistakes, errors, and poor choices. I can offer that to them, not because it comes naturally from me—it most assuredly does not!—but because *I am a recipient of such incredible love because of the sacrifice of my Father's only begotten Son.*

In loving these boys I am no more than a flawed reflection of His love for me. But with God's help, that love (from me to them) will become a bit less fractured and a bit more in keeping with how He first loved me.

I am learning that anyone can have a child, but it takes *all you have* to be a daddy.

The Sickness of Complacency

The book of Hebrews talks about believers who were once persecuted (by the Romans) and yet persevered, but some of the very ones that held strong during the suffering were "slipping" after conditions improved. The author of Hebrews warns against the wrath of God for those who "*deliberately keep on sinning*" (Hebrews 10:26-27, NIV) particularly after they have maintained their faith in the tough times.

I think that this is still true today. Some of us hold up with great courage when we are suffering or under attack for doing the proper thing, but then we fail morally and behave quite unlike the saints we were redeemed to be when God blesses us! I observe that persecution and personal suffering quite naturally can draw us closer to Him, so why are we so shortsighted when things go well? In the "good times" I tend to drift away from my intimacy from the *very one that brought me to the good times.* I call this, in my own life, "SAD" i.e. Spiritual Attention Disorder.

King David, Samson, Solomon, priests, pastors, popes and incredible men and women of God throughout history have experienced the same spiritual malaise. They were men and women of spiritual *iron* when their very lives were at risk or they were suffering incredibly, but when they were blessed with peace, prosperity, or "success" they suddenly became spiritual midgets and simpletons.

I have witnessed the same in my life; I recognize that happiness and popularity are not the things those following Jesus should admire or desire. And if I *do* find myself respected and free from conflict, I think that the only prudent thing to do is willfully draw *closer to Him and ask Him to protect me from the spiritual disease that afflicts many Christians who succeed.*

I am aware, naturally, that there are many good folks that are not apparently suffering and are not under attack, and yet are quite well respected and honored in their communities. These same folks have not surrendered to pandering habits or vanity. *But I would argue that they are rare.* Humility *and* popularity rarely are seen in the same person, even in the body of Christ. Success and a maintained focus on the Kingdom of God is not common, even among the most educated warriors for God.

May God grant me all the good things that make a man satisfied, but may He *always* remind me of just how quickly success, people, and life can change. The *essential* thing is my relationship with God; all good things and all blessings can potentially eat away at that priority.

Crises

When Jesus was told that His good friend Lazarus was ill, Jesus was fully aware that it was a severe illness. Yet He took two full days to leave before beginning the long two-day walk back to Lazarus' home. By the time He got there, Lazarus had died and had been in the grave for three days. (Read the entire narrative in John 11:1-44, NIV)

What strikes me, most humbly, is how Jesus responded to a crisis compared to how I respond to a crisis. I have a long way to go in my walk with Jesus.

First, Jesus did not get frantic, upset, or lose His self-control. He never did and He never does. He also simply never let Himself get caught up in a frantic attempt to solve the problem or "take control of the situation." He took His time, finished His tasks, and later addressed Lazarus' sickness (by that time, Lazarus was dead). Excited, hurried, fearful actions never seem to be in the narrative of men and women properly connected to God. The inner peace and reliance upon God's sovereignty dispels any need for rushing or losing their heads!

Second, it was not about the calamity of Lazarus being at death's door that was of primary concern to Jesus, but rather it was God being glorified in the midst of the calamity. The crisis was necessary for God to be glorified, for Jesus' power over death to be manifested, and for billions of future men and women to have a concrete example of how God can take an absolutely heartbreaking event and turn it upside down! What if the crisis you or I are going through will one day inspire millions or even billions of people by the manner in which we calmly trust Him?

But what if Jesus had done what Martha and Mary begged for and had rushed back and cured Lazarus of his disease? This narrative would have been lost to history and we probably would never have heard much about Lazarus!

Can you imagine the testimony of Lazarus? He suffered, died, was buried and then was brought back to life! This was a precursor to the same thing that would soon happen to His Savior. It would be a profoundly difficult thing to deny the reality of Jesus if you lived in Lazarus' neighborhood. Here's living, breathing, walking evidence of the Son of God's power over death!

Crises in our lives are God's gift, not only enriching our capacity to exercise trust, but far more importantly, providing His opportunity to bring others to Him. Others witness His miraculous intervention in our lives and how He preserves us. Friends, _are_ we walking testimonies to what God can do? Is my church or your church an epistle of God's miracle?

The Gospel

When I first entered Christian ministry, my purpose was to introduce young people to Jesus Christ and help them become true disciples of Jesus. In a few words, my goal was to lead youth to a "rebirth" experience. But as I grew up in my ministry, I often focused on other things that are *associated* with the Christian faith—from good works to being involved with "religious" programs and running a summer camp.

But as my sons have talked to me about their struggles lately, I realize that my first call has sometimes been ignored. I say this because for the past week, as the boys have continued to make the same poor choices (lying, disobeying, talking back, breaking promises) I have asked them, *"Why do you keep doing this?"* But of late, I have seen them "come clean" and tell me, meekly and quite bluntly, "I don't know why and I can't help it." And that is what lies at the heart of the matter in ministry. Those outside the body of Jesus Christ don't know why they do the things that they *do not want to do,* but are powerless to stop.

I am not suggesting that we are *not responsible* for what we do, but we often do the wrong thing and wonder, "Why in the world did I do that?" Sadly, like an addict, we are infected with these wrong things (sin) and are unable to stop!

My boys *know* when they do the wrong thing, but since they find themselves unable to change, they have grown somewhat comfortable with their foibles. On the other hand, they are *quite* unaccommodating to the weaknesses of the other brothers and are less than charitable when one tells the other that, "He can't help it."

That of course points to our need for "rebirth." My boys (and I) readily admit there are some things we simply cannot change or stop doing on our own—we need outside help. Jesus Christ came for this very purpose and *that* is what I was called to preach and teach. There is no means whereby I can live the life I was called, created and destined to live, short of Jesus being *reborn within me.* That's the good news (gospel) of the New Testament. My boys will continue to wonder why they do they things they do and why they cannot stop doing the things that they know disappoint and sadden me, until they receive *supernatural* intervention. That intervention is Jesus Christ, the Son of God, the One who died in my place and provides a new mind—one set upon God—for those that surrender their lives to Him.

It seems so simple, and yet I somehow forget the main point sometimes. Thank goodness that God is merciful to me and that He preaches to me through my children.

Am I Hurting Jesus?

"A man with leprosy came to him and begged him on his knees, "If you are willing, you can make me clean." Jesus was indignant. He reached out his hand and touched the man. "I am willing," he said. "Be clean!" Immediately the leprosy left him and he was cleansed. Jesus sent him away at once with a strong warning: "See that you don't tell this to anyone. But go, show yourself to the priest and offer the sacrifices that Moses commanded for your cleansing, as a testimony to them." Instead he went out and began to talk freely, spreading the news. As a result, Jesus could no longer enter a town openly but stayed outside in lonely places…" (Mark 1:40-45 NIV)

The man did not obey—-he had a better idea. He thought he knew more than Jesus.

As a result, Jesus *suffered* because now He could not walk and commune openly and freely with people. Also, countless others were denied intimacy with Jesus because of this man. Who knows how many others *were not healed* because of Jesus' inability to walk freely among the crowds?

How has my disobedience to Him hurt Jesus? Have I caused His work to be diminished or compromised because of my *selfish obstinate habit to do things my way?* How many people have not been able to hear Him, see Him or touch Him because I have ignored and disobeyed Him?

This young man with leprosy did not *willfully* hurt Jesus; he did not intend for Jesus to be forced to spend the next three years on the outskirts of towns in lonely and desolate places; it was never his plan to keep others away from being healing of leprosy or blindness or being crippled—but these bad things happened because he was not willing to humble himself and obey.

God asks for our obedience…not our opinion.

Moved by the Holy Spirit

Many years ago I traveled to Kampala, Uganda, to speak at some schools about our camp and to interview some potential summer staff. While there I had a day or two free, and after speaking to some folks at the church that was sponsoring our visit, I was encouraged to visit a small village in the bush—about an hour drive from Kampala.

I traveled to the village and met two young boys who had just lost their father to sleeping sickness and their mother to AIDS. Tragically, the older of the two little boys had found his father, in the brush, a few days after he succumbed to the disease. The boys were sad, worried, hungry and unsure about their future. They were orphans in a nation with many, many orphans.

I asked the leader of the village for permission to take these children back to Kampala with me for a couple of days to give them some hope. I was the first white man they had met, and they were hesitant, but the leaders talked the boys into coming with me. Honestly, I did not know then why I made this offer.

To make a long story short, I reserved the boys a room at the Sheraton Hotel, where I was staying, bought them some clothes, let them go swimming in the pool at the hotel, feed them a few meals, and then said good-bye to them and headed back to Kenya the following day.

Their time with me represented their first time in an elevator, the first time in a hotel, the first time in any body of water (the pool) and the first time to be around a "muzungu" (a white person). I never heard from these little boys again, and some folks chided me, over the years, about what I did, in that it was actually a bit self-serving and heartless. The boys would probably never go into a pool again; they now knew just how poor they were, and now they realized how hopeless their situation was. Of course, that was not my intention—I merely wanted to extend kindness, some relief from the dust, heat and dry air, and give them some reprieve from the sad home they came from. I was hoping to offer them some joy and tell them, in effect, "You have value—you matter."

Anyway, 23 years later the eldest child called me today—23 years later! He is now living in Houston, Texas, with his wife and two sons. They were able to apply for and receive a green card and moved here. But what broke my heart was to hear that it was my visit to him, 23 years ago, that served as the single event that gave him and his brother hope; they received a vision from God of their worth and purpose—and it changed their lives. Two little boys were esteemed by an eccentric white man in Uganda as having purpose, worth and a future.

I cannot save the world—-but I am able to make a difference if I ignore the naysayers that say that planting seeds is "unkind", etc. These little boys mattered to me, 23 years ago, and were ignored by many others. No, I am not the hero here and don't claim or want to be the hero. The hero is the Holy Spirit. He spoke, and on that occasion, I listened.

His Pleasure and Delight

David wrote that: "His pleasure is not in the strength of the horse, nor is his delight in the legs of the warrior; the Lord delights in those who fear him, who put their hope in his unfailing love." (Psalm 147:10 NIV)

Those things that impress us probably don't "move" God too much. The massiveness of our aircraft carriers, the destructive power of our hydrogen bombs, our incredible infrastructure and industry—these are absolutely *awesome* when you consider what they represent in terms of our construction, protection, etc. But God's delight is *not* in our building enterprises and "development" but rather in our humble determination to place Him foremost in our lives and recognize Him as *Almighty God.*

Two things David comments upon which I must remind myself: He is *delighted with me* when I recognize and worship Him as the One He is, God… and, that I trust in Him, His promises *and His unfailing love.* What a promise! What an assurance! If I choose Him as my Savior and humbly acknowledge that *He is Lord*, He is pleased with me and will not let me down! "Some trust in chariots and some in horses, but we trust in the name of the LORD our God" (Psalm 20:7, NIV). It's a choice that I make, and my life is forever blessed and I am sealed with His unfailing love i.e., a love that is not fickle, or fading, or temporal.

How then should I live if I *truly* fear Him, put my hope in Him, and trust in His unfailing love?

- I would choose to be obedient; He is God and has stated succinctly what is right, what is wrong, and what is pleasing to Him. If I have a proper fear/respect for God I will be an obeying son.
- I would decide to not worry or be anxious about tomorrow. "Hope" is more than wishful thinking. It's believing that He will see me through the tough times and worrisome events in life.
- I would see myself as special: *He loves me.* That sets the standard for human self-esteem. If God is for me and loves me and cares for me, what does it matter what anyone/everyone else thinks?

But sadly, I am not all three of these things all the time. I am, at times, disobedient; I do get anxious about my work, friends, and family members some days; I wonder if He *likes* me at certain seasons in my life! He becomes so quiet, so removed and I ponder if He is fed up with me some days. But these things do not represent my new life, but the residue of the old life that's not yet been consumed by His total presence in my life.

I am not where I want to be yet, but neither is any man or woman with the body of Christ. We all struggle from crawling, wobbling, walking, jogging…. to running.

Disciplined for our Good

The author of Hebrews wrote about discipline and how it always seems unpleasant at the time, but "produces a harvest of righteousness." (Hebrews 12:11 NIV) It's a fact that God disciplines the believer because He loves him or her and the discipline is always for our good.

Clearly, the recipients of this letter were undergoing some discipline. God was preparing them for something by allowing hardships or sending unusual challenges into their lives for the purpose of righteousness. I don't always understand why God does things like this, but He does.

My *right living* will not come about by being pampered and spoiled and elevated like a trophy on a shelf. Instead, righteousness is the result of being strained, bruised, and poured out. If this is how God gets us to a higher level of living, and if this is the manner in which man is brought from being common to being holy, then why is discipline in our society so frowned upon?

It seems that my "right" to do whatever I want, whenever I want, to whomever I choose, is to be more desired and protected than my call to be holy and set apart for Him. The Christian was not redeemed to exercise his rights, but rather to surrender those rights and lay down his ambitions submitting to the leadership of Jesus Christ—and that always involves discipline (i.e., being required to do, endure, or accept things that we would rather avoid).

How is He disciplining me now? It is with constant changes to my schedule, spontaneous requirements for me to break with my routine, and seemingly wasted time doing menial tasks! But right now that's how He is preparing me, somehow, to be of greater use to Him later. He knows what He is doing even if I am bewildered at times.

How is He disciplining you?

Some Trust in Chariots, (Psalm 20:7 NIV)

Each time I "give up" or "surrender" something to God, strange things seem to happen. Not that strange as I look back on them now, but quite strange at the moment. Over the past thirty-four years I have seen many, many things turn out quite differently and very often *contrary* to what I had hoped and prayed for. Some months (and years) later, I recognize that His familiar hand was upon what transpired—and I thank Him for blessing me even when I could not see it and when I was totally unaware of how incredibly He *was* blessing me.

"Surrender" means laying down my arms, admitting defeat or acknowledging that a superior force is now in charge. My surrenders to God must be unconditional and complete; I cannot hold on to anything in my present struggle that I feel I *must* maintain when I surrender something to God—it's either all or none in these matters.

But I am ever learning that even though the cliff seems quite high and the danger of falling is all too real and eminent, He never lets me down—*never*. That's not to say that I really might be the biggest loser on this planet in the minds of some people, but by choosing to capitulate to His will I am not only redeemed from deserved annihilation, I am set apart, set above, and set upon a rock that cannot be shaken.

"Some trust in chariots and some in horses, but we trust in the name of the LORD our God." (Psalm 20:7 NIV) And so, what was true when David wrote this in the 20th Psalm 3500 years ago is true in our lives. *He is aware of my battles, fears, personal attacks and humiliation and He is more than able to move heaven and earth to keep me from stumbling.*

I have let others down and I have been let down… but He is incapable of breaking His promises to me, letting go of my hand or losing me. I am safe and secure matter what storms may come my way.

Today Was One We Will Celebrate

I noticed a change within me recently: I sleep better, I am in a more positive state of mind, and I am less anxious and tense. Again, there are ample reasons for me to *not* sleep well and many, many reasons I could site that should give me cause to worry. But two things have changed:

In the first place I have made a decision to both *be* positive and *associate* with people that are positive. The people that choose to be close to me truly do have an affect on my mood, my outlook and my sleep. By making a move towards those that are kind, positive, full of faith and mirth, l have found that I am not only a happier person, but that I am *a greater source* of joy to others.

Secondly, and far more importantly, He (God) has brought me into a more intimate relationship with Him and I fear for the worse less and look for the good surprises more. I am believing, more and more this year, that He is able take care of me and the dreams and desires of my heart if I let go and allow Him to bring about the solutions to my challenges *in His time and in the manner of His choosing*. My prayers are less about what He *has to do to keep me safe*, and more about surrendering to whatever He chooses to allow to happen for His glory. I see myself more and more shielded under His wings and in the safety of His mighty hand, and less and less as vulnerable to the world and its changing affections.

I am reminded of those "perfect" days at camp where the breeze is cool, the sky is blue, the campers and staff are happy, the events transpire flawlessly and spiritual insight is shared. One day, in a few years perhaps, many campers and staff might look at those days, at our camp, as one of the "golden days" of their youth. I am glad that He allowed me to be a part it. But I had to be in a proper relationship with Him and my fellow laborers to see this day.

A Shoulder to Lean Upon

While on a trip in Uganda, my brother told me of a memorable encounter in the countryside. While he and some other missionaries were traveling in a van, they offered a ride to a lady and her son on the side of the road. The young boy immediately wanted to sit beside my brother. Then, the boy wanted to lean against him. It surprised my brother a bit, but the lady with the boy encouraged my brother to permit this.

Later, after the boy had departed from the van, the lady explained to my brother that the boy had recently been hunting with his father when they stumbled upon some honeybees. The father unintentionally ate some of the honey containing a live bee. Tragically, the bee stung him in the throat and he suffocated right in front of his son. Her son had been grieving horribly ever since. My brother became, as it were, a surrogate father to this young man for a few hours.

This boy yearned for someone to sit beside, lean upon, allowing him to remember the warmth, touch, love, and security of being with his dad. In regard to showing compassion to those who are hurting or in need, Jesus said, "Truly I tell you, whatever you did for one of the least of these brothers and sisters of mine, you did for me." (Matthew 25:40, NIV) I wonder sometimes if God sends His angels to appear as "the least of these," to test us and open our hearts to the brokenness of this world.

As a very imperfect adoptive parent, I understand a little about this testing. It takes so little of my resources to offer the hope, love, and touch that a scared, homeless child needs. But there are many selfish reasons to deny them that attention and time. (This represents my confession, not my attempt to shame someone would never consider adoption or foster care. If you're feeling guilty, talk to the Holy Spirit about it, or call your county DSS office.)

From a human, fleshly perspective, I truly do not have the time to care for these boys in my home. Frankly, the demands of my ministry are far beyond my skill-set, experience, and stamina. And yet, I am learning (or remembering?) that each time I put down my laptop computer to hear about my son's new pet toad, or other son's imaginary battle as a Power Ranger, or my third son's excitement about being in his new home (ours), I am reminded that nothing is as important to them than my willingness to lay aside my work, and other adult pre-occupations, and allow them to lean against me.

In my brother's story, I do not believe that the tragedy this boy experienced caught God by surprise, nor was this something God caused to happen. And I don't believe that He is incapable of stopping such heartbreaking events in life. No, these things are echoes of our rebellion against God, the collateral damage of our determination to live without God and outside His plan. But the beauty of all these things is how God can change a tragedy into victory (e.g., the horror of Jesus' torturous execution transformed into the resurrection and redemption of all mankind).

My brother, and anyone who shares in his kind of hands-on evangelism, is blessed by being of service to the King of Kings. In this case, all the more, because he was able to offer a shoulder for a little boy in Uganda to lean upon.

Conformed to His Character

Around the fourth week of camp I tend to look a bit more introspectively in regards to not only which people (staff) cause me to be at peace the most, but also which ones remind me that I am far away from where I want to be in my walk with Christ.

The things I value most in the staff, volunteers, and even the campers are probably the same things you value in your fellow workers, students or friends. But as I pray for my mind and attitude to be *conformed* to *His* mind and attitude, I am beginning to appreciate more and more what *He* longs for as well. With that said, I realize that I find great peace in being around adults, staff and campers that are:

- Humble
- Servants
- Full of smiles and laughter
- Ever saying good things about someone else
- Ready to help me or someone else any way they can
- Never attempting to manipulate me or others
- Genuinely interested in what I have to say
- Uninterested in unkind talk about *anyone* else
- Full of wonder and excitement!

I am drawn to people like this because that's the kind of a person *I want to be.*

Isn't it noteworthy that *none of us* wants to be around people that are the opposite, i.e. the arrogant, self-serving, haughty, unkind, lazy, rude, dull and gossipy? But am I striving to be the kind of person that we see as the ideal?

I understand better why people hated Jesus so much. He lived what He talked about and proved that it was possible to be the very man we all crave to be, but seem to be unable to become. And that's the part of the gospel that we often fail to proclaim. The *only* way to realize the ideal life, the one for which we were created, is to put to death the old habits and life and allow a new life to be created within us. It is *not* a matter of God merely trimming my branches, but pulling up the entire tree and planting a new one!

It's not bit-by-bit that I can be reborn. But in the very moment I admit I am not the man I want to be and am not likely *ever* to achieve the traits and graces I admire in others, I begin that process of being sanctified. *Then and only then,* can I begin to be one that draws others to Him—-not on my merits, but rather on my acknowledgment of what a wretched man I was without Him.

Fear of Men = A Snare

"Fear of man will prove to be a snare, but whoever trusts in the Lord is kept safe." (Proverbs 29:25 NIV)

Sometimes I realize that what I have been reading for years does not seem to make sense because when I first read it, I lacked the *experience* required to totally comprehend the truth. What a pity that I did not begin earlier in my life to *trust* God's word and allow Him take more authority in my life and provide more light.

But *now* I get what Solomon was saying here, *precisely* because I have wrestled with the "fear of man" (Proverbs 29:25 NIV)—which includes being consumed and overwhelmed with the anxiety of what other men and women—or the institutions of men and women—can do to me. Banks, creditors, vendors, payroll companies, the IRS, the Department of State, embassies all over the world—these are all man-made institutions, but they wield power and are capable of making *anyone's* life miserable. And even more so a disgruntled co-worker, parent, or neighbor! They can make your life a nightmare if you're not wise and careful in how you handle them. It's just a matter of fact.

Yet Solomon realized that it's not man or his bureaucratic institutions that represent "reality," but rather God Himself. We get all lathered up about the "what if's" of business, money, security, reputation, et al, and we fret that if we make one mistake or if someone decides to go after us, we're doomed! But in fact it is the Creator that needs to be the focus of our security, future, and protection. If God is for us, who can be against us? Who is it, in reality, who is finally in control of everything that happens? Is it not God? And are not men and his institutions a mere mist, something here today and gone tomorrow?

Do I trust in Social Security, the Federal Government, the U.N… or God? Do I fear what men can do *to* me or have I not witnessed time and time again what God is prepared to do *for* me?

Napoleon Bonaparte, the emperor of France in the 1800s, was a man who was driven by his insane determination to rule the world. On the morning before the Battle of Waterloo, Napoleon mapped out his strategy to defeat Wellington and the English army. He told his officers, "By the end of this day, England will sit at the feet of France and Wellington will be the prisoner of Napoleon!" One of Napoleon's generals said in response, "But we must not forget, sir—man proposes—but God disposes." Napoleon flew into one his common rages and said, "Napoleon proposes and Napoleon disposes!" Of course, later Napoleon lost that war. Victor Hugo wrote these words: "From that moment, the Battle of Waterloo was lost. God sent a storm of wind, rain and hail—and Napoleon's troops were immobilized. By nightfall, Napoleon was the prisoner of Wellington—and France sat at the feet of England."

Do I fear man or do I trust in God? Put another way, do I trust in my own skills, instincts, and efforts of self-preservation and aggrandizing, or do I surrender all to Him and humbly seek shelter beneath His wings? Am I a Napoleon or a Moses—a man of arrogance or a man of humility? Do I seek Him and Him alone for direction, strength, courage, and resolve… or am I looking for it somewhere else?

Whoever *trusts* in the Lord is kept safe. He wants to be our source of Joy, but we must look to Him as our "All in All."

The Right to Work…

I have fought and fought with one of my adopted boys about "work." Each of us has chores to perform in the home, and one thing I have discovered with the foster care program is that either foster parents *don't* encourage the kids to work, or it allows them to whine their way out of work, or it requires very little effort on the chores meted out to the foster kids. No foster child that has visited my home, or that I later adopted, is accustomed to any sort of responsibility when it comes to chores or work. They look at me like I am from a distant planet when I discuss the value, personal reward and satisfaction that come from doing a job well. To them work is punishment—plain and simple.

The fight got heated today with one of the boys; he simply does not like to work and sees no "joy" in doing his tasks thoroughly—let alone excellently. So rather than go through another hour of lectures and debates about the virtues of "hard work" I told him that he no longer had to do any more work in the house and that the other boys would pick up his work, but he would forfeit all TV, movies and anything "high in carbs" (which is most of what he prefers to consume) until he earned the "right" to work again. He is ecstatic.

Try as I might to instill a work ethic in some of the children—and staff—that attend our camp or live with us, work seems to have become the new "four letter word" for many. But I *know* that this is true: *Work is good.* How do I know this? Because *Jesus* worked with His hands, and He continued to teach that God works *still.* "Now because Jesus was doing these things on the Sabbath, the Jews began to persecute Him. But Jesus answered them, "To this very day My Father is at His work, and I too am working." (John 5:16-17, NIV)

My boys are not yet enjoying the pleasure of doing a job well—*not yet*—but God willing, they will one day! Satisfaction from work is joy from God—it's *good* to look at the work we've done and be satisfied, and it's a crime and pity *not* to be able to work.

With many people now at home *legally not permitted to work,* I am reminded that even retirement has its pitfalls and is certainly *not* a Christian notion. It's been said by someone that, "a retired husband is often a wife's full-time job." And having three boys at home, with one of them disinclined to work, my task of watching them and keeping them positively occupied is similarly a full time job.

Lord lift this virus soon…

He Understands!

Today I missed my Bible reading and the time I set aside for prayer for the first time in many, many months. There was a time when I thought that if I failed to read my Bible and spend the early morning in prayer that God would be disappointed in me—I even feared that something bad might happen to me or that I would miss His blessings by omitting this ritual from my life each and every day.

But today I missed my "morning watch" because I was *slightly* sick (a cold) and very tired (four boys to care for). Rarely do I allow myself to "sleep in," but last night and this morning I was totally spent—I could not rise early and even ended up getting the boys to school late.

I have opined before about how frail our bodies really are and how easily we can be sapped of strength in a split second. But raising four young men has caused me to micro-manage my life, time, strength, and resources as never before. And what I have found is that I *still* have enough time to do the essential and required things in life, but I don't have much time to "chew the fat." I now rarely watch movies, TV or surf the Internet. There are more important things in my life now.

I'll get back into my routine tomorrow, I believe, and I will be happier doing it. But I don't believe that God loves me less or is disinclined to bless me because I failed to have a quiet time this morning—He's a much "bigger" God than that... and He *understands*.

And that's my big word today—He *understands*. It gives me courage and confidence to go out into the world and make some choices that could be quite bad for my business and ministry if I choose wrongly. But God understands my limited abilities and experience. And if I humbly admit, "I am tired," "I don't know what to do," "I am not sure I can trust him/her Lord," "I am afraid about this situation," *He understands and directs my path.*

I don't have to stammer and stutter as I explain why I slept in late today—*praise God, He understands and is on my side in this matter.* But the same is true, of course, when I attempt to deceive others or myself in regard to the true intentions of my heart. Although He loves me grandly, He also holds me to a higher standard than those that do not know Him.

Talking and Listening

Strange how I find myself just "talking" to the staff that are now stranded at the camp with my family and me. At night we can't go out for a coffee or to a movie or even shopping. So we stay here each night and end up just *talking*. These conversations have no purpose and end up with no final benedictions and summations. We're just yakking and listening to each other.

It's refreshing, new (for a lot of us) and needed—just to converse. Talking with no agenda can be a challenge for those of us so conditioned to getting a lot accomplished in a very restricted time, and to those who see "chit-chat" as a waste of time and really not natural at all! But maybe we were wrong. Maybe staying home with the TV turned off, along with all other means of entertainment or technology, is okay. Maybe it's better to listen to some nice music, enjoy gentle conversations, small talk, spontaneous laughter. Maybe reminiscing and dreaming are actually good things that need to be resurrected.

Jesus spoke to crowds for hours and they always left wanting more. But evidently that talking was combined with questions and requests for clarification. It's good to be able to ask questions, make clear what we really mean, illustrate our point, and, most emphatically, *to listen*. Jesus did all of this. And that's what I have been forced to discipline myself to do the most, of late—-*to listen* to a nine-year-old, eleven-year-old, and twelve-year-old and three young people in their twenties as they share their fears, dreams hopes and fantasies. We're talking about puppies (all three boys for some reason have determined that they each need a new puppy to add to menagerie of five) as well as creating a time machine (to bring back Tony Stark, and also, secondarily, so that if I die they can quickly go back in time and rescue me). The older ones talk about finishing their studies, starting their careers and getting back to "normal"—whatever that means.

But my younger boys are *constantly* referencing the Covid 19 and they sense an inevitable reckoning on the horizon with our economy, etc. As I listen to them I wonder if they know something I don't! They also are quick to ask "why" China allowed this to happen and what's going to happen. Again, they put two and two together better than the most folks that work in popular media.

They worry about going to the fourth, sixth and seventh grade and if they can play sports in the fall. Small matters for most of us, but for a boy, the world revolves around sports.

And finally, they talk about "What if this doesn't stop?" Their questions might seem puerile, but the boys are honest—perhaps more so than the folks whom we pay to listen to.

What my sons are teaching me, again and again, is that I need to *listen to them*. We've never been through a crisis like this before, but children look to the parents for the *experience* and knowledge that they lack. In this situation, no parent has any experience or knowledge about what is happening and how it will end—-and yet we can still provide the courage, confidence and steadfast faith that God will provide what they still lack.

Let's listen to our children! And let's honestly answer them about what we know **and** what we don't know—-and of what we can be *sure: I know that my Redeemer lives, that God loves me (and them) and that He does not want anyone to be lost.*

"Feed my lamb. Take care of my sheep. Feed my sheep."(John 21:15-17, NIV)

"When they had finished eating, Jesus said to Simon Peter, "Simon son of John, do you love me more than these?" "Yes, Lord," he said, "you know that I love you."

Jesus said, "Feed my lambs." Again Jesus said, "Simon son of John, do you love me?"

He answered, "Yes, Lord, you know that I love you."Jesus said, "Take care of my sheep."

The third time he said to him, "Simon son of John, do you love me?"Peter was hurt because Jesus asked him the third time, "Do you love me?" He said, "Lord, you know all things; you know that I love you." Jesus said, "Feed my sheep." (John 21:15-17, NIV)

These were Christ's *final* words to Peter. I am struck that He did not give Peter any demands upon how to establish the hierarchy of the church, or how to administer the Eucharist, or how long to preach or even how to teach. He told Peter to *feed* the lamb (the young?) and *feed* the sheep (the more mature?) and "take care of the sheep"(John 21:15-17, NIV)

—i.e. sheep can be ignorant and do the dumbest things, so look out for them (that's my take on this, but I could be wrong).

Peter was the first "pope", the head of the church, the rock… but is what Jesus requested of Peter any different from what He requests of me or any other Christian worker? I was not called to create a ministry, or establish an international camp or write these little devotions. I was called to feed sheep and lamb and care for His flock. Imagine a church or community or nation that lived with *that* as their "constitution."

Dale Carnegie famously taught that, "You can make more friends in two months by being interested in other people than in two years trying to get people interested in you." Even truer in ministry, I can envision that the cause of the Kingdom could be furthered *far* more easily if we *cared and fed* those in our flocks (that is, provided those things essential for spiritual growth and development) than by any amount of time or resources invested in "feel good" worship services, air-conditioned auditoriums or eloquent/entertaining speakers. (Please forgive my soapbox.)

Feeding the lamb and sheep is not something that brings us fame or fortune and it's not likely to be something that brings quick gratification. Those who care for others are often the most over-looked and less celebrated members of a church or Christian organization, but according to Jesus, Peter, *the head of the church,* was supposed to about the "menial" task of looking after the needs of others. Perhaps we have our priorities in ministry backwards.

What speaks to me is that the most important thing I can do in ministry is to be sure that those in my care are being properly "fed" the good things that God would have them consume (spiritually speaking) and to keep an eye on them for whatever things are needed for their well being. *Imagine a community that really lived like that—where everyone was looking after the well being of the other!*

May this camp become such a place—a place where everyone that is hungry or thirsty is fed—and where no one is carelessly tended.

Not a Very Popular Dad Today...

My two youngest boys came home from school excited, as always, and we talked about their day, what they learned, and the upcoming weekend. Then the trouble started. One of the boys had broken a promise and we discussed the consequences. He was very, very unhappy about me keeping my promise (no iPod music for five days) and begged and begged for another chance. Of course this is the consequence he agreed to and in light of what he did, it was fair; but when it came to accepting the discipline he simply was not pleased with me.

For two hours he whined, complained, pleaded, screamed, begged, told me what a horrible parent I was; he demanded his way, threatened to make me quite "unhappy" if I did not give him another chance and so on—for two hours! Moments later, when I walked back into the house, the *other* boys were fighting and one was crying. Good grief!

But strangely enough, an hour later we were able to have our meal, say our apologies, tour the now completed new house and then come back to our home ready for bed. In fact, the time *after* the "meltdown" today was one of the best evenings we've ever had. My challenge is how to positively parent these boys whose behavior my parents would simply *never* have tolerated! (But then, I must remind myself, my parents raised ten of us from infants, whereas these boys came to me at 7, 9 and 10 years old.)

What I have learned is that establishing expectations, talking about consequences, and encouraging them with rewards is easy; but following through and keeping *my* promise is far more difficult than I ever imagined. It would be infinitely more pleasant, and our home would be far quieter, if I just showed mercy and gave "second chances" to the boys. But that's not what a father is. My task is *not* to be loved or liked, but to train them in true love and kindness, though frankly, my sons are not fans of this "tough love" notion of child rearing.

Unlike most of my Protestant friends, I have a crucifix in both my home and office. Both were gifts and I cherish them. And while some argue about that the "cross of Jesus is empty" and that we should not place such emphasis on the death but rather the resurrection of Jesus, I beg to differ; the man on that cross suffered for my broken promises, bad behavior, and dishonesty. That man received the punishment I deserved. That bruised and bloodied man, Jesus, and only He, has a right to look down upon others—and yet He chooses to instead lift them up.

God did not give me a "second chance" or simply forgive me each time I messed up; He held me and all men before and after me accountable, just like I hold my boys accountable. But unlike me, God provided someone else to receive the just consequences for all mankind's poor choices and outright rebellion. God forgives me not because He is a mild-mannered Father and a good guy, but because of the cross and Jesus Christ. He is the righteous God that rightly requires His children to be righteous.

One day I hope that my boys will appreciate the connection between "choices and consequences" as well as the connection between God's expectations, our failures, and Christ's vicarious suffering for us. Until then, I pray that I can remain steadfast, firm and fair with these boys, even when they choose to not like me because of it. This job is not for the man that wants to be popular.

How Could God Let Bad Things Happen

I often wake up in the morning around 4:00 am and pray about things that are burdening me. I have prayed about some things for years and years, but sometimes it seems that God is just not listening. *That* is the time, of course, that the enemy suggests that God does not care, is uninterested, has better things to do, and is not concerned about human suffering.

While all this is going on I wonder about things like, "Why did God allow the Communists control half the world for the past 100 years and murder 100,000,000 people?" "Why did God allow a man like Hitler to start WWII and kill another 60,000,000 people?" While the Nazis and Communists were exterminating entire villages, millions of Christians were praying for God to intervene and bring an end to the insanity. But the killing went on for decades and even now it is continuing, albeit on a smaller scale.

I don't have an answer as to why God did not stop Hitler, Lenin, Stalin, or Mao. But I do know that it was not God's doing… it was the fault of the morally failed leadership in Russia, China, Europe, and elsewhere that allowed these monsters to come to power. In a real sense, the 160,000,000 souls that were lost represent what happens when the leaders in power *have no fear of God—all these men were avowed atheists or non-believers.*

So how can I expect God to hear my prayers and effectively intervene in problems like mine that are *minuscule matters* in comparison to the world's issues? I believe that this is precisely how the enemy would like me to question and reason. This is his method for causing me to give up praying, believing, hoping, and trusting. The enemy would have me forget that while bad things *do happen*, good things *also* happen… all the time. And while bad choices, godless living and arrogant leaders can lead to the suffering and destruction of an entire nation, it's not a 20th century phenomenon; it's recorded in the Bible by the inspiration of the Holy Spirit as something that's been going on since recorded history! Nations (and their citizens—young and old) are held accountable for the sins of the their kings, dictators, despots, emperors. When catastrophes happened to Israel, Judah, Rome, or Babylon, the people did not question, "How could God allow this?" but rather, "How could we have been so brainless?"

I pray for my nation and the nations of the world that I have come to know and love. But, when I turn my prayers to my personal needs *it is with a different understanding.* I pray for the nations by *interceding* for their leaders and citizens. True, I cannot effect change in their hearts, and God will not *make* them bend their ears to Him. But when I pray for my own hurts, dreams, hopes, and needs, I am able to responsively *listen to what He tells me to do and choose to be obedient.* There is an absolute, positive correlation between the effectiveness of my prayers and my choice to obey.

I cannot make a nation obedient. I can only pray for God's mercy to fall upon it and for those in power to open their ears and eyes.

Is He Pleased With Me?

It seems to me that the two most annoying kinds of people to be around are those who do not care what others think about them and those who are consumed by what others think. On the one hand, it's important to not walk over other people's feelings or opinions, and one should never deliberately offend or hurt another person. But at the other extreme are those that are so focused on being liked that they are never able to enunciate the truth or take action when action is required.

I find myself at both extremes, at times, but I have come to see that I am so concerned with the risk of "letting someone down" that I frequently can't sleep or eat. Pleasing others can become such a distraction that I can't live and enjoy the good life He has given me. And, whereas it's truly unchristian to deliberately disappoint a friend, no man of God should be a person-pleaser or sycophant.

Yes, if I choose to follow Him, grow ever closer in intimate relationship with Him, others will at times be offended and I will inevitably disappoint people. But what *should* burden me is the question: "Have I let *Him* down? Have I *offended* Him? Is *He* disappointed with me?"

As a pastor I am embarrassed to confess that just recently I lost sleep because I thought I had failed someone (a friend); but for the life of me I cannot recall the last time I lost sleep because I let God down. That's a pitiful thing to say from a man who should know better, but it's true.

The question I must ask myself is this: "Are my conflicts, losses, embarrassments, and disappointments pushing me farther from Him or drawing me ever closer to Him?" The spiritual truth about pleasing God or man is this: If I choose to please God, I shall be pleased with myself, and others, though not all, will also be pleased with me. But if I try to please others, neither God, others, nor myself will be pleased.

Daily Bread

"And give us this day our daily bread". (Matthew 16:11 NIV)

1. GOD is the provider: not us, not our government, or our friends or family. He wants us to *depend* upon Him and is clearly against human "self-sufficiency." After all, will He not *give* if we ask for basic things for life? Is He not able?
2. Give us what we need for *today*—not for a week or a year.
    a. With too much we hoard like the Israelites in the desert.
    b. With too much we stop looking to Him—we forget very quickly where the bread came from.
    c. With too much we get fat and spiritually lazy.
    d. With too much we become independent in our minds—just like Lucifer.

Final notions:

*   God *might* give you too much if you keep asking Him—but you will regret it and learn a hard lesson, like the Israelites that whined about wanting more than just manna and getting so much quail they gorged themselves to death. Be careful of asking for what you ought not to ask for. (See Numbers 11:33, NIV)
*   *Nowhere* is it suggested or demanded that we do nothing and simply let God shower us with blessings! We are commanded to "work with our own hands." (I Thessalonians 4:11, KJV) We are told that, "by the sweat of our brow" (Genesis 3:19, NIV) we will bring forth a harvest. Yes, we *must work*. But unless we dedicate our work to Him and recognize that *He* orchestrates the harvest, we're no different from those who perished in the desert *because they did not trust God.*

Blameless, Righteous, and Honest

"Lord, who may dwell in your sacred tent?
  Who may live on your holy mountain?
The one whose walk is blameless,
  who does what is righteous,
  who speaks the truth from their heart" - (Psalm 15:1-2 NIV)

The Kingdom of God, is... *God's Kingdom.* It is *not* a place I am entitled to, or that is my reward for being better than most people, or a place that I can "earn" by my actions when I die. David is clear about the matter here: God's house—or "tent" and His "holy mountain" are reserved for people who are:

- Blameless
- Righteous
- Speak truth from their hearts

These are not merely "requirements" but refer to the *character* and *composition* of those who will live with God eternally—as well as those who can enjoy friendship with Him right now. Am I blameless? And I righteous? Do I speak the truth *from my heart?* These things can only happen by (1) a decision on my part to allow Jesus to be re-born within me, and (2) a sober acknowledgement that *only* God can bring me up to this standard.

But I can also be certain that if I am deliberately living a life that is deceitful, reckless, unkind and self serving; if I am ignoring what I know is right and proper; if I am a fraud, an "actor" and charlatan, then I *most certainly* will have no place in God's Kingdom to come.

It's not a matter of me changing and being good enough—that's never going to happen— but rather of me admitting just how *bad I am* and asking Him to *make me holy, pure, righteous and blameless.* It comes from outside and enters into me when I am ready to admit I cannot generate it myself.

And those of us who have received "it" are well aware that our new lives have nothing to do with our own "goodness" or hard work, but His perfection, love and mercy.

America's Preacher's Greatest Sermon

Billy Graham died the day I wrote this devotion in 2018. He was 99-years-old. I had the privilege to briefly meet him on three occasions. Two times I simply shook his hand after he preached. The third time that I met him, I was a cabin counselor at a camp near his home. I was walking around the camp lake and saw a man fishing in the lake. I knew that he was not a part of our camp staff, so I politely walked up to him, tapped him on his shoulder, and told him that the lake was private and that he should not be fishing there. The man turned around and told me that he had permission from the owner. The man was Billy Graham and I was speechless. Within a few minutes the campers and other staff recognized him and swarmed him for autographs. He quietly put up his fishing gear and headed home. I felt sorry for him and wish I had not interrupted his private time of angling.

I studied a little about Dr. Graham while I was in seminary, and I recall that his sermons were basically all from John 3:16. He was an evangelist – period. He also authored 30 books, counseled U.S. presidents, and traveled the world. But he saw himself as an evangelist first, called to preach salvation to anyone that would listen.

Tonight, the news channels and editors will speak about Dr. Graham in great detail. But for me personally, the greatest thing about Billy Graham is that I know that he really believed what he preached. I never sensed any doubt in his faith in Jesus Christ, nor his certainty as to the veracity of God's Word. As a young Christian, my faith often wavered, but Billy Graham was a hero of the faith. He believed it, and many, many times I found courage and confidence knowing that this good man could not be wrong about that which he believed. Atheists, agnostics, and non-believers must have hated him. He proved by his very life the efficacy of the gospel. The earth might be poorer now, but heaven is immensely richer tonight because he is there.

I often have compared my life to Billy Graham's and wondered, "Would he have ever said or done some of the outlandish things I've done and said?" And as I measured my life against his, I am ashamed that I have not come even close to his level of dedication and purity. I am keenly aware that eyes watch me, no less than my eyes watched Dr. Graham. But as they watch me, are children, youth, and adults being drawn to Him? Is their faith increasing? Are they more certain now than they were before because of my life and witness?

Dear God, raise up another man of God like Billy Graham for the next generation! A man after your own heart. I pray that I might remember that the greatest sermon is the one preached without words.

In Action or In Word Only?

When the followers of Jesus were first called "Christians" it was not meant kindly; it was an insult. They were being ridiculed as being "little Christs." Tertullian remarked that Roman soldiers said, "See how they love each other," when describing the Christians; again, this was not a compliment but was intended to deride their "weakness."

What attracts the non-believer to the follower of Jesus *should* be love, that is, how we love one another, and how we love those outside the family of Christ. But do I love in *such a compelling manner that it is clear I am one of His?*

Saint John wrote in his first letter: "This is how we know what love is: Jesus Christ laid down his life for us. And we ought to lay down our lives for our brothers and sisters. If anyone has material possessions and sees a brother or sister in need but has no pity on them, how can the love of God be in that person? Dear children, let us not love with words or speech but with actions and in truth." (I John 3:16-20, NIV)

Laying down my life seems to mean much more than just dying. It means *living,* but *not* living ambitiously for my own purpose and pleasure, but instead for His purposes and for the joy of others. It is, of course, an absurd way to live, and that's why most of us who call ourselves "Christians" don't live that way. But there *are* those that did live lives of love and self-denial like this, *and we admire and adore them for it!* People like Saint Francis, Mother Theresa, George Mueller, Dietrich Bonhoeffer (to name a few) had the idea that Jesus (and the writers of the New Testament) *meant what He said* about denying ourselves and following Him; putting the needs of others first; loving without partiality.

What *I* love about men like Saint Francis is that they *did* what others only talked about doing! "Let us not love with words or speech but *with actions and in truth."* I John 3:20, NIV). I do not think it's outrageous to proclaim that if even a significant minority of the Catholics and Protestants that claim to know Jesus Christ *proved it with their actions, the world would by and large be converted.* It is not that we do not know *about* Him (Jesus) but rather that we do not *know* Him. Bonhoeffer, Saint John, Saint Francis, Mother Theresa, Saint Paul, all knew Him intimately and they all loved others because of it. It is impossible to *know* Him and not love others deeply.

Do I Listen?

A question to consider today: Do I listen? Most people do not and usually I am just like them. It takes time and energy to listen. It's hard work! Most of us can talk and expect to be listened to, but when my mouth is open, I am not listening or learning anything.

But listening is important, particularly in the body of Christ, and especially now. I realize some people will take advantage of my willingness to listen and never stop, but it's worth the frustration. Those who come as campers or staff to my camp, and those that come to our churches, are worth listening to. After all, we're taught that if we were kind, or listened to the smallest child, we were listening to Jesus. So, are we listening or just hearing?

I have to remind myself that listening is a form of loving. It costs me nothing to listen and it shows not only respect, but sets up the opportunity for me to be heard later. The greatest among us is also the greatest listener.

Listening to the smallest (i.e., children) is essential in ministry and the life of a camp and any church. Hearing is a passive occurrence that requires no effort. Listening, on the other hand, is a conscious choice that demands my attention and concentration. Camp directors, pastors, and Christian leaders need not only to hear, but also listen.

Aren't you glad that you have people in your life who listen to you? And more than all else, how blessed we are that God hears our voices. God not only has spoken, but He also listens! He stops, patiently waits, and wants to hear from me. He stands ready to hear my voice. We have an audience whenever we want—it's called prayer.

The world would be a better place if people listened more to each other. Communication would be real, everyone would be able to say what they wanted, conflicts would lessen, and people would find new strength to follow their hearts.

Listening is an art, a path to other people's hearts, and an effort that requires patience. At times I must fight the urge to talk and just listen. The only way we learn is by listening, reading, or observing, never by talking or controlling a conversation.

Many years ago in San Francisco, a young man, lonely and depressed, jumped off the Golden Gate Bridge. When the police went to his apartment afterward, they found a simple note he'd written and left on his dresser. It said, "I'm going to walk to the bridge. But if one person smiles at me on the way, I will not jump."

No one smiled at him, talked to him, or listened to him about the hurt he felt inside. The next time you have a chance to listen to someone, try to stop thinking, discard the smart and witty things you can't wait to say, and just listen. Listen with all your heart, mind, and soul. You might be saving a life and giving hope to a person at the end of his or her rope.

I need to listen more. Those of us who lead in camps or churches must listen more to our campers, church members, community, and especially to the lonesome.

Faithful or Successful?

In the book of Acts, the first martyr to the Christian faith, Stephen, is introduced explaining the good news of Jesus to a very hostile crowd. At first they listened to him. Indeed, it's reported that he had the "face of an angel" (Acts 6:15, NIV) and they stood still and paid attention. His appearance and speech were attractive and captivating.

Stephen *could* have won the crowd over had he told them what they wanted to hear or simply "diluted" the story about Jesus' life, death, resurrection and divinity. But he did not speak cautiously or in fear of the power of those listening or the danger of the mob at hand. He spoke boldly, fearlessly, and honestly about what he *knew* was true. He *could not bring himself to deny His Savior.* And, as you know, the mob went wild; they "gnashed their teeth, threw dirt in the air, covered their ears and ran to him demanding that he be pelted with stones until he was dead." (Acts 7:57, NIV). Stephen was murdered for speaking of God's love.

Stephen knew the dangers of speaking for Jesus Christ, but he humbly accepted it rather than deny the Savior of his soul. Speaking the truth is often dangerous and even today, in many parts of the world, could result in a man or woman being killed.

I wonder how many of us who stand behind a pulpit, or lead a Christian camp, or claim to be a follower of Christ, demur from speaking the truth if we think it will cause someone we respect to think less of us. I am not talking about politics or cultural issues, I am referring to discussing Christ's death on the cross and His call to discipleship. Some of the preaching and teaching I have witnessed from mega-churches to small chapels seem to be more of the "feel-good" Christianity than the religious tone that Paul, Peter, John and Stephen expounded. These men *suffered* for the truth. I won't be executed for speaking the truth in the USA—nor would any other pastor. But I *might* be ignored or fail to attract a large crowd on Sundays—or at my camp—if I continuously spoke of Jesus Christ.

Stephen was an utter failure as a deacon and preacher in the eyes of the world. His first message was his *last*. But he was *faithful to the call.*

God has *not* ordained us to be successful, but like Stephen, *faithful.*

Does My Life Cause Others to Wonder?

I recall reading in the gospel of John of events that occurred right after Jesus raised Lazarus from the dead and just before the Passover was celebrated in Jerusalem. Christ was at a home visiting some friends and crowds of people were pressing in trying to see Jesus *and Lazarus,* whom Christ raised from the dead. The following verses tell us that the Pharisees wanted to kill Jesus *and Lazarus,* because many were now following Jesus because of Lazarus' resurrection. (John 11:38-53, NIV)

Lazarus had *nothing to do* with what Jesus did for him—that is, brought him back from the dead *four days after he was buried.* But because Jesus had performed a miracle in Lazarus' life, Lazarus was as much of a problem to these Pharisees as Jesus! Every time people saw Lazarus it was a reminder that Jesus *was* the Messiah—the Son of God who had power over the grave.

Am I a threat to those who want to stamp out Christianity as well? Has the resurrected life in me caused others to put their faith in Jesus? Do people see how I have suffered and then how He has rescued and restored me, and do they then determine that they want a Savior like that also? Or am I so concerned about my personal comfort, reputation, standing in the community and personal gain that my display of the living Christ is muted, faded, and of no concern to those who deny Christ?

When the Holy Spirit filled Paul, Peter, James, and John they became *threats* to the forces of evil and the kingdom of Satan. When Lazarus was raised from the dead he became a marked man. He was the embodiment of what Jesus can do. *May the same be said of me one day!* May my *reborn and reformed* life reflect something different, miraculous, outstanding, extraordinary, not of this world and may the people who oppose Christ *hate me because of it.*

In a real way I suppose I need to wonder why I am not *more* opposed and why I am not under *more attack.* It would seem that an easy existence is a sure sign that my life does not represent the resurrected Christ very convincingly.

Fill Me!

I woke up very, very early a few nights ago, and began to consider the chores and jobs I had to perform once I got out of bed—my calendar, the meetings, the deadlines. The mundane drudgery of life can oftentimes push me down, but I know that little eyes in my home are watching me so I am supposed to appear cheery and optimistic at all times.

So that night I stopped my fretting and simply prayed, "Lord please *fill me up, right now*, with your Holy Spirit, and let me be over-flowing with the new life that I want my sons and others that I meet to see today." It was *not* some sort of pious, elaborate or pontificating prayer—I really, sincerely, humbly meant it. "God, fill me up with you so that there is *no more room for me!*"

At that very moment, inexplicably, my bedroom door flew open and I heard the sound of rushing wind! My bedroom is on the second floor of the house and the outside doors were closed tight and all the windows were sealed. I realize that some folks hearing this might be rolling their eyes at such a story, but I know what I heard and what I saw that night—no one can tell me that what happened did not happen, and it's not the first time I have seen His hand move in a totally unexpected, marvelous and breath-taking way.

Pnuema (πνεύμα) is the Greek word used for "Spirit", "breath" or "wind". In scripture, breath or wind is often associated with the coming of the Holy Spirit, so this "coincidence" got my attention and gave me great peace—it was an epiphany from God. He heard my plea—as He hears *all* our pleas. We just have to be listening and believe that He will answer us in unconventional and unexpected ways. "*Fill me Lord*" is a plea that He does not ignore or delay. He is ready to fill me—but am I ready to make room for Him and receive Him fully? And do I ask for it enough?

Fill me!! Why ask Him to fill me? So that there's not room for anything else and so that there is *less of me*…I have that discovered that what it is in my soul and heart that brings me depression, unhappiness, a loss of focus, and discouragement is *I!* But I have been filled with the Holy Spirit sent from Jesus, and I *know*, first-hand, the consummate joy that comes when I do not have to be preoccupied with thinking about myself or my short comings *at all*. There's nothing I want more than to be filled with Him so that I can be led and motivated, focus and concentrated, upon the things that He has set apart for me to do.

God speaks to us in two ways—natural revelation (sunsets, the wind, physical catastrophes, and more) and divine revelation (the Bible, miracles and Him breaking into our bedrooms). Am I looking for the ways He does speak to me each day—in ways I never expected? He is there, nonetheless, regardless of whether I am paying attention.

Dark Water....

"Then Jesus was led up by the Spirit into the wilderness to be tempted by the devil." (Matthew 4:1 NIV)

"While they were ministering to the Lord and fasting, the Holy Spirit said, 'Set apart for Me Barnabas and Saul for the work to which I have called them.'" (Acts 13:2, NIV)

"And now, behold, bound by the Spirit, I am on my way to Jerusalem, not knowing what will happen to me there." (Acts 20:22, NIV)

The water out there is dark and inky...and yet when Jesus was taken out into the deep, dark waters of life (temptation), He never thought twice about it. And it never entered the mind of Saul and Barnabas *not* to follow the Holy Spirit as He led them to dangerous places and unimaginable challenges.

Friend, it's safer near the shore. The water is shallow, rescue is nearby, the surf is never too choppy nor are the waves going to destroy you. Even the fish that might nibble at your toes are smaller when you are near the shore. It's safe on the beach or near the shoreline—away from the unknown deep waters of the ocean.

But God calls those who will listen away from assumed safety of the beach, and onward to utter abandonment and a total dependency upon Him. In this world there's simply no other way for us to come to know, for sure, that He is there or that He is able to be our Savior than for us to give it all up and head out into the dark, inky blue waters of life. It's a brave decision to make, but one you won't regret.

Are you on the shore, or maybe in the shallow water, or have you ventured *out* of the harbor into the ocean. Yes, it can be scary, and if you look down the water can be downright dreadful. There's something about black water that brings out fear and dread for all of us.

And yet it is only away from the safety of the harbor and the shoreline that we can really enjoy and experience the vastness of the ocean and the incredible sensation of the wind in our sails! And so it is with trusting God and leaving the safety of our homes, or our familiar acquaintances, or the certainty of a staid and secure job. Letting go and venturing into the vastness of God's purposes and plans is not for everyone—only for those who would really and sincerely know the depth of His love, provisions, power and ability to preserve.

What does it mean for *you and me* to venture out into the blue?

1. To be in mortal danger and to face the reality of "failure."
2. To be alone at times.
3. To have no other source of security than God—who is our "ark."
4. To at times be lost and not know where the waves and winds are pushing us.

But the *joy* of the deep blue is:

1. The incredible adventure of it all!
2. The certainty that *He* knows the depths and secrets of the deep—nothing surprises or startles Him.
3. The exhilaration of allowing His Spirit to blow and lead us where it will.
4. The beauty of the incredible expanse of His universe and creation.

Let's get into the boat and start the adventure!

Whose Side Am I On?

I was recently reading a book about the Reformation that a close friend gave me. I am blessed to have as many friends that are Catholic as Protestant, and I am quite certain that both my Catholic and Protestant friends worship the same God and follow the same Son, etc.

What caused me pain and concern last night was not what I read about the conflict with Catholics and Protestants, but what I read about the persecution of the Anabaptists of Switzerland. The Anabaptists believed that the true sign of being a follower of Christ (i.e. a Christian) was baptism *after* one was old enough to make a decision of accepting (or rejecting) Jesus. Since all people in Europe at this time were already baptized as infants, the Anabaptists believed in a *second* baptism.

These people were opposed to capital punishment, war, torture, bearing arms, and fighting. They refused to defend themselves if attacked and were known for their kindness, modesty, love and humility. Yet the Protestants of Zurich, the Lutherans of Germany and the Catholics in general rounded them up *by the thousands and drowned them*. By some estimates, fellow Christians (Catholics and Protestants) martyred more Anabaptists than the Roman Empire martyred Christians for three hundred years! And all of this was being done in the name of God.

I don't see how an entire *community* of believers (let alone a *nation*) could be so cruel and heartless to such gentle and kind people, but I wonder what the church will say of *me* and my generation in 500 or 1000 years? What am *I missing* that Luther, Calvin, Zwingli and the leaders of the Catholic Church missed 500 and 1000 years ago? Where am I living in prejudice and totally *outside the love of God today*?

Just because the majority says that something is right (or wrong) does not make it so. Frequently the majority is *wrong*. I want to be not merely on the "right" side of the argument, but on **God's side.**

I am confident of this: My Savior would never say, write, blog, suggest or take part in many things that are happening right now in some Christian communities and churches.

I pray for **His** discernment, **His** courage and **His** determination to stand for what He stood for... and still stands for today; not what is politically, ecclesiastically or socially expedient.

Essential Matters of Life

The "Spanish Flu" of 1918 was the most severe pandemic in recent history. It is estimated that 500 million people, one-third of the world's population, became infected with this virus. The number of deaths was estimated to be 50-100 million worldwide with about 675,000 occurring in the United States!

Far worse was the plague of the 14th century. An estimated 75-200 million people, including a third of the Europe's entire population perished. The *"black death"* lingered on for centuries, particularly in cities. Outbreaks included the Great Plague of London (1665-66), in which at least 70,000 died.

As bad as the current Covid-19 virus is, things *have* been worse and *could* get worse. Can you imagine where we would be today if *this* virus had happened only 50 years ago? With no social media, a lack of coordinated clinics all over the world and limited technology, the present pandemic could have been more catastrophic than the black plague. Evil as life can be, we will survive this sad chapter in human history and we will be stronger, wiser and, prayerfully, more humble about our limitations.

While some of our politicians are presently telling us that attending church and prayer meetings, tending to our lawns or visiting the hardware store for supplies for our homes, is not "essential" during this crisis, the leaders maintain that the sale of marijuana, alcohol and lottery tickets *is* essential for life (this really happened just a few days ago in Michigan!).

Sane people are no longer talking about climate change, the legalization of pot, or the urgency of immigration reform. Important as these issues might be, suddenly the *survival of the species* and the continuation of our "flawed" democracy, a return to our "selfish capitalist economy" replete with its inequalities, and the ability to congregate in worship seems a *lot* better than the repressed life we're now forced to endure.

We're being required to decide what is *essential* and what is *non-essential*—and that's a good thing. And for the record, the Governor has it wrong about liquor, pot and gambling—they are not essential for living. She's got it backwards and is pandering to her constituents' worst instincts. What *is* essential in life our lives—and the life of our nation—is to humble ourselves before our Creator and enter into the sober confession: we have chased insignificant and erroneous things that *do not* add value to life; we have celebrated the *wrong people* that are doing *the worst* things; we have chosen to believe that *banal* things are necessary for a full life and that *destructive things* are indispensable. How insane and indefensible. Sometimes it takes a plowshare of suffering and tragedy to wake-up a soul …or a nation…

Enemy Territory

It occurs to me that the challenges I face in my family and in my ministry are not the *external* obstacles of government, laws, marketing or finances, but the *internal* challenges of maintaining peace, harmony, and a shared sense of purpose among our leaders here. When I think about the opportunities this camp has, this year, for the cause of Christ *worldwide* I become soberly aware that we are invading the enemy's territory. Certainly we can expect attack.

That might sound fanciful, but just as Christ believed in demons and the devil, and just as Paul believed that our fight was *not* against flesh and blood but "spiritual principalities", (Ephesians 6:12, NIV), so I too believe that it is the *darkness* we must not only fight but also protect ourselves against.

If the men and women that lead this camp are truly together in one mind this summer, young lives *will* be re-directed, challenged, reborn, and restored—but that is *not* what the enemy wants. It seems that the most effective means of stopping the work of God in the lives of our leaders here is to create discord, distrust, jealousy, and lukewarm enthusiasm for the gifts, talents, and opportunities that He has given each us. The enemy (Satan) wants us to argue and fight amongst ourselves.

We must pray that the leaders of our nation, our ministries and our own families might not be seduced into believing the devil's lies, and that we might confront our own errors and shortcomings before pointing out the flaws in others. We should all pray that we might esteem each other as being superior, in some regards, to our selves. I trust God to give me the grace to *put up* with the other and thus stop the enemy's taunts and attempts to hamstring our work.

There are no perfect families, congregations, parishes, or Christian camps. But there might be a small camp in the foothills of North Carolina that becomes a real burden and worry for the devil. I hope that our men and women can choose to cast off petty complaints about each other and focus on the prize and purpose of this camp: Jesus Christ, and Him exalted.

To Love As He Loves

Talking about love, but not living, acting, planning and giving in love makes love a meaningless or hollow part of our vocabulary. If love costs us nothing, I wonder what kind of love it is? It's certainly not the love of God, His Son or His saints.

If my love is always calculating, always measured and reserved in the same response to how much I have received in love, it's not love... it's 'accounting. Love must sometimes be careless and extravagant in terms of how it is expressed. It must be exposed not in mere words, but in unrestrained actions and demonstrations! Not as *proof* of our love, but as uncontrollable eruptions *because* we love. We *cannot help but go overboard at times for the one we love.* That is the kind of love He has given to me.

To me, nothing, *nothing....* is so hurtful to the cause of Christ as members of the faith who talk about love and use the word constantly, but fail to *live* in love. Truly, we are *annoying and become an aggravating noise* when we talk about God's love and our love for another, but fail to live a life that is not spent, emptied and poured out for those we profess to love.

Love requires more than mere sentiment or verbal expression—it naturally finds expression in sacrifice, living without some of the things we like to have but are forced to give up (happily!) for the one(s) we love. At other times, love is shown in stunning and surprising things we do or get for the beloved in our lives. *That* is true love—and it was first expressed by God.

The idea of love as taught by Jesus is pretty simple, really.

1. The originator, creator, and first One to love was God—He knows more about it than any other being. *Learn from Him*—i.e. love purely.

2. God loved us—in the pure sense of love—before we knew Him or loved Him. *Practice what He did*—i.e. love others *before* they love you.

3. If you really love someone else you will go to great extents to love them—-even to the point of giving up your life. *Consider the needs of the one you love more essential than your needs and you will be loving as the original Lover loves.*

Stigmata

When I was five years old my mother accidentally shut the door on my right hand. It created a moon shape scar on my middle finger that's it's still there today. I will have it till the day I die. It reminds me of that old maroon Chevrolet station wagon and my mom trying to handle four or five kids at one time.

Do you have a scar? From an accident…or surgery…or something really foolish you did as a kid? If we live long enough we *will* have scars and they all tell a story.

At the end of the letter to the Galatians, Paul said this: "From now on let no one cause me trouble, for I bear on my body the marks of Jesus." (Gal. 6:17, ESV)

Paul had some painful marks, or scars, on his body. In reading this passage in context, it sounds like Paul was sick and tired of people challenging his authenticity and his authority to preach the gospel. He tells the Galatians, in effect—look at my body and what I have endured because of my love for Jesus Christ. *These* are my credentials.

"The marks," translated in Greek is "stigmata. It does not necessarily refer to the same scars Jesus had, though some would argue that they were. In the ancient Greek, stigma could also refer to a *brand*, as when a master branded a slave. Or it could even be a *tattoo*. But Paul was not talking about a tattoo or some branding he received. I mean, could you imagine the disciples walking around with tattoos to show their dedication to Jesus?

The term stigmata also could mean the *scars* resulting from deep wounds. Think about it: In Lester, Paul was stoned and presumed dead because of all the wounds and blood. At Philippi he was beaten with "many stripes" with rods (II Corinthians, 11:25, NIV). And by "many" he acknowledged that he had received "stripes beyond count". (II Corinthians, 11:25, NIV)

He received five beatings by the Jews. Each of these produced thirty-nine wounds that would leave the body disfigured. Think about that. Wouldn't the average man have quit and picked up a different vocation? What propelled this man to tolerate such suffering and hate?

Three other times he was whipped with rods. His body would have been grotesque by the time he wrote the letter to Galatia. Those rods would have broken bones, remembering that the Romans tasked with beating a prisoner were quite proficient in their vocation.

Now a modern pastor or missionary would probably be ashamed of just how ugly and scary those scars were. Others might have found them hideous. But to Paul they authenticated his dedication to Jesus Christ.

And yet, Paul does not spend chapters and chapters bragging about how much he has suffered—the suffering was not the point! They were inevitable events in life that follows if you are serving the King of Kings in a fallen and perverted world. In fact, Paul only spent *six verses* to reference the appalling abuse he experienced. He was *not* trying to call attention to himself.

Paul was reminding the Galatians that his message wasn't just one that he had heard about and trusted. He had *lived it* and he *suffered for it*. If you want to see the handwriting of Jesus, look upon Paul's body.

What handwriting is upon my body—or yours? Or, what suffering have we shielded ourselves from that Paul would have readily endured? Where have I shirked because of the certainty of insult or pain or humiliation? Where and when have I failed to receive His marks?

There's something wrong in our individual pilgrimage or a congregational confession when we avoid doing or saying the right thing because we don't want to risk getting our feelings hurt or being branded as a "zealot" or "fanatic". Lord: bring the stigmata onto our churches and into our lives that we might be accounted as sold out for Jesus Christ. Forgive our whimpering and whining.

God Is My Refuge

Sometimes the Psalmist seems to be speaking the very words I am thinking but have a hard time expressing.

In Psalm 46, David wrote that, "God is our refuge and strength, an ever-present help in trouble. Therefore we will not fear, though the earth give way and the mountains fall into the heart of the sea, though its waters roar and foam and the mountains quake with their surging." (Psalm 46:1-3, NIV)

David knew what he was talking about, of course. He lived a daring life full of love, tragedy, surprises, victories, setbacks, restorations, treachery. Was there a man in the Bible with such a full life? What that man learned is invaluable to me precisely because he was so "human." He messed things up, blundered and stumbled and stammered—and yet the man loved God and never forsook that first love.

And so when I read Psalm 46 I see *great truth and hope* for my life as well. God *is my refuge—and God alone.* The biggest discernible difference in my life this year, over every other year in my life, is the abiding conviction that God *is in control and has my back protected.* Now David wrote about this far more eloquently in Psalm 46, but that's what he was saying: '*God has my back.*'

My life is certainly not as glamorous, fabled, and storied as David's, but just like David I have struggled, worried, wondered about my future, felt abandoned and even experienced the heartbreak of an Absalom or two. But God has been an ever-present help in (my) troubles. It is that knowledge that allows me to brush away the fears of the early morning, and the dread of facing one Goliath after another during the day.

David did not go out and court evil, but evil came his way and into his life by his own bad choices, lack of good judgment, absence of courage, or simply because evil is present all around us. The same holds true for me and all of us in Christian ministry. None of us is free from of our ineptitude and poor choices, but anyone that is never attacked, or struggling, or wondering about "what is going on?" is not very effectively engaged in Christian ministry.

I am no match for earthquakes, roaring waves, or the incredible forces of nature, and neither was David. But he *remained* "a man after God's own heart" (I Samuel 13:14, KJV) regardless of what nature, other men, the enemy or life threw at him; and so, God help me, I will be too.

Following the Cloud

I was reading in the book of Numbers recently about the Israelites in the wilderness with Moses. God moved the Israelites around from where they were, to a new location—for no apparent reason. But the Israelites packed up and moved *each* time the cloud moved. Sometimes they stayed in the same place one day, and at other times it might have been for weeks: but they were ready to move *as God moved*.

We often focus on how stubborn and rebellious the Israelites were, but they were commonly *obedient*. How many of *us* are willing to pull up our "tent stakes" or familiar connections, leave our comfortable and known environment, and enter into the "who knows what" when God's cloud leads over the horizon?

Imagine living a life where *every morning* when you got up you would not know what to plan for? Imagine *not* being in the driver's seat in regard to your destiny, where you would live, who would be your neighbors, what path you would have to take to the next destination. And now imagine this: *That's how God wants us to live.*

Am I following the cloud by day and the column of fire by night? *Would I follow Him* if I could see those symbols of His presence each morning and evening??

Is His church—not the building, but the body of believers—*following Him,* or putting tent stakes into concrete? What if following the cloud meant changing our focus or doing something brand new or taking an unknown path?

Do I plant roots too deep? It's so common to our nature to want to put down roots and stay put, but children of God—those redeemed by blood—have been purchased and rescued for the purpose of being of *use* to God is His work. He might allow us to stay where we are for a long time—perhaps our entire lives—but there's always a need to be ready to go—just like Abraham was when God told him to pack up and move. "The Lord had said to Abram, "Leave your country and your people. Leave your father's family. Go to the land I will show you. "I will make you into a great nation. I will bless you. I will make your name great. You will be a blessing to others. I will bless those who bless you. I will put a curse on anyone who calls down a curse on you. All nations on earth will be blessed because of you." So Abram left, just as the Lord had told him. (Genesis 12:1-4, NIV)

Does what He tells us to do have to "make sense" if we are going to obey? Or are we prepared to blindly and boldly follow him—even if it appears totally nuts? He did not "make sense" to the Israelites or Abraham or the early church apostles—but they obeyed.

And do we have to see the "end game" if we respond to His directives? It's a bit disappointing to have to say it, but quite often a faithful follower *never* sees the benefits that the obedience lends to the Kingdom for what has been done. The Billy Grahams are the exception—they saw, first hand, how their faithfulness blessed God. And yet, how blessed to be trusted by God to be called to be faithful to Him when all the while we *fully accept* that we will probably *not* see the spiritual fruit of our labors.

Don't Go on a Diet in France

This is now my sixth day on the road. I am in Versailles, France, and have already had several presentations in the homes of former campers. It's been a very good trip, but being alone can cause me to get a bit down. In truth, I've never enjoyed travel, but it's something I must do for our camp each year.

On this trip, I decided to lose some weight by eating less and focusing on no or low carbs. It began well at the airport and on the plane, and my first day in France I did pretty well. But France is the worst country in the world to start a low-carb diet!

This country, like none other, is known for its food. If you think of France, what immediately comes to mind is cheese, baguettes, pastries, champagne – the best food in the world! No, this is definitely not a place to start a diet; it's a place to experience your first heart attack!

So I tried for three days to avoid the desserts, bread, and pastries, but I finally crumbled and ate a croissant. I simply surrendered to the bakery (they seem to be on every corner of every village) and enjoyed my one-day limit of carbs on a single croissant.

There are some spiritual similarities. Again, one should not begin (or even attempt to maintain) a diet in France – or while touring the Ben and Jerry's Ice Cream factory in Vermont! But there are places I should not frequent, websites I should not surf, and companions I should not entertain if I want to maintain my intimacy with Jesus Christ. It's foolish to deliberately tempt my "fleshly impulses" by being in the wrong place or placing myself in a situation where I know I might falter and succumb to temptation.

There's nothing wrong, I suppose, with breaking a diet from time to time, but you can't use that justification for deliberately setting yourself up to fail spiritually. To my shame, I have done that in the past and was always quick to justify my surrender to temptation. But Jesus was tempted and did not surrender. Being one who is born again, I can choose not to surrender to the enemy's temptations when they confront me. And as a wiser man, I should choose to stay away from those places where the temptations may occur.

All those things by which I am tempted represent a desire that God placed in my heart that has became corrupted and perverted after the fall. Sin turned good things upside down and now we must make choices about what's right and wrong. Oh, to be in a place where the corrupted way of seeing things is gone and the fight is over! But until I get to heaven, I have to maintain a physical diet and spiritual focus. And when that focus moves from Him to my cravings, self-pity, or self-centeredness, I am right where the enemy wants me to be—where he can really compromise my witness.

He Denied Jesus Three Times

Peter was a zealot for Jesus Christ. He endangered his own life when he drew his sword and cut off the ear of one the guard's of the Chief Priest the night Jesus was betrayed. He *honestly* told Jesus that he would die with Him; he had already turned his back on his career and family to follow Jesus; he was the foundation, or *rock* upon which Jesus would build the church…and yet he *did* deny Jesus three times.

You know the story: "Then seizing him, they led him away and took him into the house of the high priest. Peter followed at a distance. And when some there had kindled a fire in the middle of the courtyard and had sat down together, Peter sat down with them. A servant girl saw him seated there in the firelight. She looked closely at him and said, "This man was with him." But he denied it. "Woman, I don't know him," he said. A little later someone else saw him and said, "You also are one of them." "Man, I am not!" Peter replied. About an hour later another asserted, "Certainly this fellow was with him, for he is a Galilean." Peter replied, "Man, I don't know what you're talking about!" Just as he was speaking, the rooster crowed. The Lord turned and looked straight at Peter. Then Peter remembered the word the Lord had spoken to him: "Before the rooster crows today, you will disown me three times." And he went outside and wept bitterly." (Luke 22:54-62, NIV)

I realize that there are scholars far more learned than I who they can explain why Peter did what he did. But I often see *myself* (and other preachers) in Peter at times, and I can understand why he did what he did. Peter was full of bluster, bravado and loud-spoken confidence when the others were there to hear him (or when Jesus was there to bridle him in). He was also passionate, tough, strong, and a rock when it came to dependability and believing in the cause.

But Peter was *alone* when Jesus was being humiliated and slapped around this particular night. He was surrounded by folks in that courtyard that were *not* fond of, or impressed with, Jesus. Peter was in enemy territory and he was watching what he said. There was *no* audience there to cheer him on or to offer approval for his tenacity and convictions. No, it was just Peter by himself—the solitary little fisherman with hostile objectors menacing him—and he was afraid, outnumbered and in risk of dying *alone*. We can be brave, or at least hold onto some dream of a "grand finale," when others are watching…but what about when we are absolutely alone or, worse, surrounded by others that do not share our passion, love, conviction, values or basic beliefs?

And that's when Peter decided to lie, hide and show his true colors. Tragedies, pandemics and catastrophes don't "make us" (nor do they make a Speaker of the House, a President or a Governor); instead, they reveal who we really are. And Peter was a lot smaller than he realized when the rooster finally crowed.

The rooster is crowing in America and around the world right now. We're seeing the mettle and mind of our national leaders, our pastors, spiritual super-stars and heroes. And what about us? What about you and me? What are we doing? Are we denying Him or courageously acknowledging Him?

Peter changed after he realized what a coward he had been—and he became a lion. His pitiful denial was replaced by an undeniable transformation *after* he met the risen Christ and received the Holy Spirit. He would never again be ashamed of His Lord. Once you meet the risen Messiah and receive His Holy Spirit you cannot be the same creature.

Counting Them Today

Some of the old hymns I sang as a child seemed quite boring and almost un-sing-able in the octaves in which they were created. But now, as I think upon my life (and many of my errors), I realize how incredibly helpful those same old hymns are.

One that has helped me as of late is "Count Your Blessings." It was written by Johnson Oatman, Jr. in 1897—but how profoundly insightful those words have been for me today! And without throwing "cold water" on modern praise and worship music, the old hymns are biblical and focused on theology. They approach the challenges of life in a different way than contemporary praise songs.

To "count my blessings" is to ask how many things went right today that could have gone wrong. I should, like others, keep a daily journal of all the answered prayers and small, kind things that happened. People, total strangers, were kind to me at the Paris train station today. An attendant at the hotel was sweet and helpful and encouraged me to come back next year at a discount. I have enjoyed incredible meals over the past few days with our hosts in France.

And by counting my blessings, I can see my attitude change become infectious. Why do I allow things to drag me down? It brings everyone, especially those I love the most, down with me. I let the "what ifs" hamstring me and turn me into a worried, anxious man. How much time was wasted today counting the troubles and not celebrating His blessings?

Consider these words from Mr. Oatman (he says it far more eloquently than I ever could):

> Count your blessings, name them one by one,
> Count your blessings, see what God has done!
> Count your blessings, name them one by one
> Count your many blessings, see what God has done.
> And it will surprise you what the Lord has done.

We need to sing more of the old hymns in our churches.

Dogs, Cats, and a Pig

We have had many pets at the camp: a potbelly pig, ferrets, ducks, cats (many kittens), dogs (right now two dachshunds named Jude and Biscuit, and a mixed breed named Maggie), and wolves (Kalah is the most recent). Some folks are cat lovers and others love dogs. But the pets that are dearest to me are my dogs and my wolf. Why?

- They are faithful. If I fail to feed the cats, they will find someone else. My dogs and the wolf prefer my words of praise for them to food. I doubt that anything could cause them to abandon me for another master.
- They forgive me. I might be gone for a night or a month, but when I come home the dogs and Kalah are all about celebrating the return of Dean. If I could only be the man that my dogs and wolf think that I am)!
- They seem to know when I need some attention, when I am "down," and when I need a friend. The black dachshund (Biscuit) and the wolf (Kalah) truly seem to enjoy being with me and appear to catch my mood and disposition.

This reminds me of how God reveals Himself to us in two ways: supernaturally, as in the divine incarnation of His Son, Jesus Christ; and naturally, as in nature, human interactions, and particularly with animals. The Bible is full of Christ's parables of foxes, doves, goats, lambs, and so forth. To me each of my pets is a message from God; I just have to take the time to allow God to speak to me through their behavior.

Part of seeking God's Kingdom is to be ever on the lookout for things in the natural order and supernatural order that reveal a poignant truth about God. God is faithful, He is forgiving, and He knows when I need to be encouraged. God speaks to me through all things bright and beautiful. But in order to hear Him, I have to be listening.

The Danger of Success

If you listen to the political discourse going on right now (and how can you ignore it?), you will hear a lot of arguments on the merits of socialism. It's amazing to me to even hear the suggestion that socialism would work, based upon the historical failure of it over the past 100 years. It's been said that capitalism does represent equality—-and that's true. But socialism and communism reward inefficiency, laziness and a disregard for ambition. Regardless of what some pine for, our present society is geared towards capitalism. And I whereas we could all argue that capitalism has many faults, and it does to a large extent reward greed and fierce competition, socialism makes the erroneous assumption that all people really want to work and the that government needs to re-distribute wealth so that we are all equal. Sadly, this does not work—anywhere.

So our culture and my generation are wired for "success" and the rewards associated with competing in a capitalistic economy. And why should we not seek success and financial security? Who wants to live in a society wired for failure, mediocrity or dependency on a government? In socio-economic terms, capitalism *rewards* success, and conversely socialism rewards "adequacy" and encourages everyone to finish the race at the same time.

Obviously, based upon the other alternatives, I am a capitalist, but I must remind myself (and all my capitalist comrades) to be careful of living for and seeking *success*—because we might have the misfortune of succeeding, and then find that success is quite hollow and that we nothing else to live for. What *is* success anyway? Is it reaching all my goals?…. collecting the most toys?… being the most respected/envied/idolized in society? Do **I** really love those that succeed more than those that slip or fail? Am I secretly envious of those that do really well? Do I admire those that are successful or do I secretly hope for them to be brought down?

There is a danger of thinking that God's purpose in my life is to make me successful, or that the intensity of His pleasure with me is best be measured by how auspicious and accomplished I am. God's favor has *nothing* to do with what I have accomplished, but rather for what Christ has *reconciled and completed.*

The opposite of failure is success, in the world's understanding of life's challenges, but in Christianity, the opposite of failure is *faithfulness*—worldly success has *nothing to do* with following Jesus or of being assured of His approval and love. As a matter of fact, success can cloud the vision and dilute our devotion to Him.

Success, even in ecclesiastical enterprises, can lead to pride, arrogance, self-absorption, and a sense of entitlement. There's *no pride* like spiritual pride and nothing hinders the work of God more than a pastor, church leader or Christian camp director that takes himself too seriously. "If I had only one sermon to preach it would be a sermon against pride."– G.K. Chesterton

Milk-toast Prayers versus Mighty Prayers

I don't believe that I have ever asked God to do too much, nor do I think that my longest and most earnest prayers have had the least drain, *whatsoever*, on God's capacity to hear me and at the same time tend to all the matters of the universe. Quite the opposite, I believe that I have asked for (and anticipated) too little and then complained about getting just what I prayed for.

There is a real danger of praying and expecting too little and thereby limiting what God is *prepared to do.* Men like Elijah prayed for *incredible things* and were spectacularly answered! Paul and the other apostles not only healed and cast out demons, but also, by prayer and faith, on at least one occasion caused a man to become blind for a few days in order to get his attention. They prayed for some mighty things.

Today it hit me that I have *continuously* asked God for a "sardine" when what I needed was sea bass. I have asked for "just enough" because I have assumed God *could not give more.* How bafflingly foolish of me. My Father loves me *infinitely more* than I love the four boys I am raising, and yet I would *never* deny them what they needed—and more—if they asked me.

Why this revelation today? I have been praying and fasting for God to give me "just enough" to get by until a legal matter we filed is settled, and I have been praying for God to help us meet our modest goals in our business. But I have withheld, for some reason, from asking God to *bless me abundantly and indeed*, for some silly fear that it might tax His resources.

Today His Spirit reminded that me that it *pleases Him to bless His children.* No, He's not going to spoil me or give me so much that I lose sight of heaven, but He is quite willing, I now believe, to take away my fears and anxious thoughts and replace them with those things I need to minister and survive.

I doubt that anyone reading this devotion has ever asked God for the full measure of what He is prepared to give. I want to be bolder in going to His altar and humbling asking for His help, His hand and His blessing.

Extravagant Love

There's a story of a woman (Mary), that poured an "alabaster jar of pure nard" on the head of Jesus—a very holy and outrageous act of love (Mark 14:3, NIV). Nard, an aromatic ointment, was very expensive and the woman was roughly criticized for the waste. After all, it was pointed out, that nard could have been sold and the money used to help the poor. Jesus rebuked her tormentors and told them that she had done a very good thing and that what she did would not be forgotten. (Mark 14:4-6, NIV)

I love these kinds of stories because they show Jesus turning common assumptions and accepted mores on their heads. Yes, yes, the money used for the nard could have been sold to help poor people. But Jesus probably knew that none of those condemning the woman would have used the nard for the poor *or* to anoint His head—they would have kept the money! "Fine, why don't you go out and sell something valuable that *you* have, such as this woman possessed, and give the money to the poor?", is what someone should have said! They were frauds and Jesus knew it.

But more importantly, this woman was honoring the King of Kings and Lord of Lords with the best she had. She gave God's Son her ultimate possession—not what was left over. That's how it's *supposed to be* in life. We give Him our best… and He takes care of the rest. I give Him the best time of the day (the morning) to seek Him, I give Him the best (first payment) of my paycheck, I offer Him my highest devotion, attention and commitment—and He looks after me (Matthew 6:33, NIV). *That's the plan.*

I recently heard a young Christian speaker comment that, "The two primary commands of "Loving God with all your heart, mind soul and strength" and "Loving your neighbor as your love yourself" (Mark 12:30-31, NIV) are inseparable parts of the front and back of a coin. Both are essential. You can't do one without the other. But this is contrary to scripture and displays a lack of an understanding of God. If I love God *totally, radically, extravagantly and with all my being, I **will** love my neighbor as I love myself.* It will happen naturally and uncontrollably. But the reverse is not the case. If I love others totally, radically, there is *no* assurance that I will *find*, let alone *fall in love with*, God. I might become a wonderful humanitarian, or a philanthropist, but I will never develop the deepest possible love for my fellow humans unless I am first exposed to and immersed in the love of God.

This woman did an excessive, abandoned, and over-the-top thing for our Lord. *Praise God that she did and that there are still people that do the same.* May God provide witness of utter abandonment to God at our summer camp and may we all be incurably infected.

Oh to Be Able to Move the Mountains!

Jesus said more than one time, "Ask for anything, believing, it will be done for you." (Mark 11:24, NIV)

How many times have you prayed, *believing this to be true,* and your prayer was not answered? Truthfully, I have prayed, *believing* (or at least thinking that I was believing) and my prayer did not seem to be answered. It strikes at my faith.

Have you ever felt like He was not listening to your prayer, or that Christ meant that prayers would be answered *only* for these twelve men, or, that, although you don't want to admit it to fellow Christians, this idea that you can ask for anything is all a bunch of foolishness?

- My dad had a stroke many years ago and I prayed and prayed, earnestly and tearfully for his recovery. But he still died.
- At my first camp a staff was hit by lightning. For twelve days I prayed for her and begged God *to take my life* and *please* restore life to that sixteen year old junior staff. But she also passed away.
- Early this morning, in my time of prayer, I asked God to send me a word or encouragement, but the first two emails I opened after my prayers were anything but encouraging. What happened?

As I read *the entire Bible* and not just a verse here and a verse there, I note that sometimes Jesus prayed and things *happened just like He said—immediately.* But other times He prayed, and things did not happen as He initially intended—for example, "let this cup pass from me" (Matthew 26:39, KJV), or in Nazareth where He "*could not* perform many miracles because of *their* lack of faith." (Matthew 15:38, NIV)

Similarly there are some personal prayers God seems to answer *immediately,* such as, "God please keep me humble", or "Lord please send something in my life to test my patience." Pray those prayers and watch how swiftly He answers!

So why does it not happen *at all* sometimes? Because He answers "no", "yes" and "not now" when His beloved pray—and if we are praying *in His will, as Jesus did,* we can pray with total faith, *knowing* that He does answer, but not in the manner we think is best.

I think that if you look at what Jesus said about praying it's rather obvious: A follower of Jesus has the super-natural ability to petition God Almighty to intervene in ways that defy our understanding of science, physics, natural law and so forth. But again, Jesus was talking to men and women that truly *believed that He was the Son of God and were living lives obedient to Him.* What kind of obedience? Not a morbid life of doing *nothing* so that they would not offend God, but deliberately choosing what they *knew* was right and eschewing what they *knew* was wrong! The disciples were not flawless human beings, but they lived and died *knowing Jesus in an intimate and personal way.*

We ought to pray more, be bold, and not be afraid to ask! When you decide you want to play basketball or tennis or to swim, you don't wait till you have perfected the skills, strokes or techniques before you try to play! You have to pick up the basketball, tennis racket or jump in and learn *as you play—and get a coach or master athlete to teach you.* Jesus understands our immaturity, our foolish prayers and our tendency to ask wrongly. But Jesus *is* our "prayer coach" … the "prayer master"… and

He's is happy to help us earn a black belt in prayer—if we're ready to let Him teach us and put them it to use. It is Satan's lie that God will not hear you until you learn to pray a perfect prayer! The Devil *does not* want you to get closer to God—and prayer is the quickest path to the heart of God.

You'll never learn to pray *in power* and you'll never see the miracle of prayer if you don't *do it.*

You'll never to swim if you don't jump in the water. Pray—and pray without ceasing (I Thessalonians, 5:17, KJV)—those are the words from Paul to fellow believers. Pray and don't give up…pray and believe that He hears…pray and trust that He is good, able and prepared to give us the desires (true desires) of our hearts

Church People

Recently, I had the opportunity to talk to a few folks that are uninvolved with any church or any religion, for that matter. Without giving too much information about them, they all had the same reasons for not being involved in an organized religion or church. It was not doubts about God, or questions about the Bible, or issues with a particular pastor or priest. In each case it was about a member of their family that had turned them off to the Christian faith and church attendance.

All of them spoke about being "talked down to" by a parent, sibling, or partner about how much they needed to go to church. But for each of them, something was annoying about the manner in which they were being lectured or even cajoled into going to church. In some ways, the good intentions of the family members had the opposite effect.

Making a person feel that they are wrong or somehow inferior for not attending church will never cause our churches to grow. Neither will any appearance of aloofness, spiritual pride, or pious pity upon the un-churched. What will make a difference is genuine interest in the other person. It's "pre-evangelism" if you will. But until I can be sincerely kind and caring for the person regardless of their willingness to come to church or become a convert, I will never be much of a fisher of men.

I say all of this because the folks I talked to this past week are good people. In fact, they display more humility and character than some of us within the church! Perhaps that's part of the problem. They look at the lives and dealings of those that never miss a Sunday mass or worship service and conclude, "I am as good as they are and I never go to church!" And perhaps they are right, but you should have met the same church members *before* they came to Christ and joined the church.

Nevertheless, to some, I am the only proof that the Christian faith is real. Some look at me and are inspired to increase their faith, but how many more think twice about being a disciple of Christ because of my inconsistent life, poor choices, sins, and selfishness. Eyes are always upon those of us who bear the name "Christian." I am not able to maintain an act for long. Either He dwells within me and bears fruit or I am an artificial tree. May I, and those at this camp, be well rooted in Him and draw others to Him.

Temptation

"And lead us not into temptation, but deliver us from the evil one." (Matthew 6:13, NIV)

Towards the end of the most famous prayer in human existence, Jesus reminds us that we are in a fight with evil. It is not the temptation, of course, that represents sin—-Jesus Himself was tempted on more than one occasion. But temptation *leads* to spiritual failure. Eventually, if you *place yourself* in tempting situations, you *will eventually give in and be defeated.*

I don't know how many times the serpent tempted Eve to eat the forbidden fruit, but *eventually,* it worked. It would have been better to keep *away from that part of the garden* in the first place!

The best way to avoid evil? Keep away from temptation. That might include certain people, certain websites, certain stores in the mall and certain types of daydreaming!

Pray that God shields you from being tempted in the first place! Jesus understood that we are *frail creatures that are easily persuaded to do the dumbest things! That's why he referred to us as lamb and sheep!* No one that raises sheep could hate a lamb—but they're not the brightest barn animals! And that's what I am when I get close to something that is tempting me—I get dim-witted!

What helps me are these three things:

1. I pray that God directs my paths *away* from temptation!
2. I try to be so full of that which is good and holy and pleasing to God that there is simply no room for the garbage of the enemy.
3. I try to have people in my life that can be wise when I am thinking about doing something witless.

If I Could Go Back and Do It Again

As I consider our devotions for our summer camp, as well as giving some advice/counsel to my sons, I often think about the mistakes I have made in my youth that I wish I could have avoided. There are some things I would have given up altogether and others I wish I had never abandoned.

The wisest among us are those who listen, weigh the counsel being offered and have a sober understanding of just how inexperienced and uninformed they are.

That being, said, if I could go back to my childhood and my days at the university and graduate school, I would have:

- Taken more classes in English, literature and creative writing! I would have benefited in nearly all aspects of my work and ministry were I better educated in these skills.
- Signed up for more business classes in college. There's no doubt all things I have touched financially would be better off if I had done this.
- Studied theology far more diligently in graduate school. *Nothing* would have prepared me better for the work I am doing with youth from all over the world than a better grasp and appreciation of theology.
- Never stopped playing tennis! I loved this as a teenager but stopped playing years ago. What a pity to have your parents pay for years of tennis lessons (as mine did) and then, when I have four courts in back yard, stop playing. I loved the game and the friendships it provided, but I let my hobbies go by the wayside the busier I got.
- Never gone into debt! Borrowing and debt become monsters, and whereas I do not know how I would have sustained this ministry without having a mortgage, there's got to be a better way to live and grow.
- Never lent to anyone what I could not afford to *give* away. If I had back all that I have lost in loans to others I would be far better off—*and so would they.*

Finally, I wish I could have invested the money I wasted on "8-track tapes" in Apple stock; I wish I had read a lot more and watched TV a lot less; I wish I had locked up all my childhood toys when I left home and kept them away from my mom's car-port sales; I wish I had spent more time hanging around all my aunts and uncles.

We can't do it all over again though, can we? Oh, that my boys would listen to me and trust me better than I listened to and trusted those that gave me similar advice as a young man.

Oh, to be able to move the mountains!

When God Says, "Don't Ask Again" (Duet. 3:26, Paraphrased).

Moses begged God for the chance just to *see* the promised land. As I read it I thought to myself, After forty years in the desert and all the rebellion and bellyaching Moses put up with, why not let him go in and at least spend a few days there before he died. But God said, "No more of this." (Duet. 3:26, NIV).

This is one of passages I don't totally "get," because when you first read it, God seems too rigid. Why couldn't He give the same grace to Moses that Moses begged God to give to the Hebrews when they rebelled against God? God was merciful and patient with them but seems unwilling to give Moses a second chance.

I never have fully grasped what Moses and Aaron did that God so upset when they struck the rock and water came out, but what they did it wrong, somehow, and they *knew* it. But I have to remember that *God* is the perfect Father—I am far from it. So when Moses is recorded to be *begging for what he wanted* (after God already told him "no") it is not the posture of a humble man, but rather of a stubborn man. Moses was a great man of faith but he did not always do the right thing. As we look at the great heroes of the Bible and Christian history, we should *never* put our total confidence in a man or woman—only One is truly "good" and totally worthy of trust.

With God, "no" means "no." A good parent does not waver in regard to his/her standards or what's best for the child and family. They place their love of their child above begging and temper tantrums. Why do my kids beg and beg when I say "no"? Because sometimes because I don't love them enough, I think. I am weak—and they know it. Do I want my children to trust me? Teaching them to accept "no" and to trust me is preparing them to one day trust Him and to accept His no's as well.

There's a point when God tells us, "That's enough"; (Duet. 3:26, Paraphrased). there *is* a point to stop asking for what He is clearly saying "no" to. And my observation is that I do *not* know what is best for me; I don't know what is going to happen tomorrow that might *totally* upend all my detailed life plans; my heart does not always "pine" for the best things; I sometimes change my mind!

I thank God that is a better Father than I am.....

Mercy, Grace, and Forgiveness

Often while praying I think about how *much* I want and need God's mercy. "Mercy" refers to God's compassionate or kindly forbearance shown toward a person like me—one who deserves punishment. It has to do with God, the One power, having compassion, pity, or benevolence towards folks, again like me, who have done the wrong things. If I am held accountable for all the bad things I have *thought*, or all my *hidden* purposes, or all the sins of my youth or all stumbling as an adult, I am in deep trouble.

I also think about how much I want and need God's grace, which is the unmerited, undeserved favor of God to those who should be condemned. I need His blessings, His help, His hand to protect and direct me; and more than anything else, to know that I am being held as the apple of His eye.

Finally, I considered how much I want and need God's forgiveness. Although I *really* try to keep myself holy and set apart for Him, I am forever slipping and failing to be the real man I know that I *could* be and that He has called me to become. God please forgive me for my ineptitude and bad choices!

With these three thoughts in mind, how do I treat *others*? How do I respond to staff that disappoint me? How do I treat the waiter at the restaurant that forgets about me and keeps me waiting for thirty minutes? What do I say (or think) about the lazy, surly hotel desk clerk who speaks unprofessionally as I attempt to check in?

These are not theoretical questions, but real life examples of my being able to declare, "He lives, He lives, Christ Jesus lives… within my heart." Or I must admit that once again, I messed up the opportunity to prove that Jesus lives and Dean has died to self?

I want mercy *all the time*… but do I give it all the time? I want grace *abundantly*, but do I give it extravagantly to others during the day? I plead for His forgiveness for once again messing things up… but am I willing to forgive 70x7 the brother that complicates things up for me?

I hope that God never says, "Ok, that's enough. I have had it. I am done with you. Get out of my face and out of my life." In fact, I *know* He *never* will give up on me. He expects no less from me when I get exasperated with others.

Dependency On Him

If you have read these "daily devotions" of mine for very long you know that I am writing primarily of things that happen to me during the day that catch my attention or my imagination. As I re-read them I am instantly reminded at how rudimentary they are spiritually speaking. But it is the basic things that I need to be reminded of in my life. Most of my adult life I am *remembering* things I learned earlier but have forgotten!

When our little camp opens every summer, there is *no turning back* for three months. Whatever is not finished before we open *won't* be finished; whatever is lacking will be lacking all summer! One year in particular was exceptionally challenging for many reasons. I was building a new home, welcoming and training new directors and operating with full-time staff that were almost *all* new to the camp. I would often wake up in the middle of the night and remind God of how much was on my plate, how much I had to complete, how limited I was, how I needed more of His help and *more* of His blessings. I began to *carefully* complain to Him that I did not feel His presence and His help intensely enough, and I complained to Him that I needed more evidence of His approval, more certainty that He would be there for me all summer.

It occurred to me while I prayed that night, that in all my complaining I never took time to *thank Him* for being as involved and present in my life *as He is*. I began to imagine how life would be if God were *removed* from my life. Friends, I could not go on. I would have no compass, no inspiration, no joy, and no confidence. Such is my dependency and need for Him.

I pray my dependency upon Him might grow more and more *desperate* and that I might lead others to the same dependency. He is the wind I soar on and the air I breathe. I hope that those who come here this summer might experience the same sense of flight, exhilaration, and total dependency.

Bitter Tears

At the time Christ was being interrogated and falsely accused, Peter was nearby watching, but not revealing who he was and denying any association with Jesus. He was *watching* to see what would happen to his friend and hero, Jesus of Nazareth. Christ had warned Peter to pray that he would not fall into temptation and had bluntly prophesied that Peter would *deny* he knew Jesus *three* times before the rooster crowed. (See Luke 22:54-62, ESV)

Sure enough, as Christ was going through that humiliating time of taunts and jeers with the Roman soldiers, Peter was repeatedly asked if he knew Jesus and he steadfastly denied it. But the third time when he was asked if he was a companion of Jesus he swore down *oaths* that he did not know Jesus. And then two horrible things happened: the rooster crowed and Jesus looked straight at Peter. Peter *knew* he had failed. He was *immediately overcome with remorse, left the square and wept bitterly.* He had let Jesus down, he denied his best friend, he showed himself to be a coward!

It's so easy to condemn the failures of Peter, Solomon, David, Samson, and so many other characters in the Bible. But I know that I am *no better* than them. There's a reason these "flawed" men are recorded in the Bible—they are our spiritual ancestors. We do the same dumb things they did—and worse. Each time I refuse to forgive, or love the unlovely, or allow my temper to get the best of me, or refuse to respond gently when rebuked, or fail to live in integrity...*I deny Jesus Christ.* I suggest, by my lack of resolve to allow the *new* man to be made in me, that Christ does not dwell within me and is a fraud.

What if I am *truly* the only "Jesus" people can see? What if another man's salvation were to be determined by the manner in which I *profess,* by the way I live, that Jesus is the Christ? The truth of the matter is that people are asking us, each day, "You are one of His disciples, aren't you?" And either we admit that we are by the character on display and the "Christ within me" life we are leading, or we deny it by our indifference to the souls that are thirsty to *see* a true disciple of Christ.

If we deny Him, pray that we are confronted by the gift of tears—tears of repentance.

Afraid of Bears

I go to our outdoor weight room almost every day and my youngest son always wants to be with me. As I lifted weights in our gym he told me that he was afraid and wanted to stay close to me. I asked him what it was that frightened him and he told me, "Bears." Then I remembered that we had just seen a bear on the camp property a few days ago and I had warned him about how powerful they are.

I reminded him that I would protect him and that bears were not going to bother us in the first place, but this did not satisfy him. Then I asked him if he believed in God, and if he did, did he also believe that God would protect him? He told me that he was not sure about God, and that if God really did exist, he would like for God to "swoosh down from the sky and protect him." I explained that this is precisely what God had already done through His son Jesus.

As we talked more, I asked him if he would like to pray to God and ask God to look after him. He quickly agreed, and without any instructions from me, he prayed to God silently and at the end said, "I am afraid, God. Please protect me from the bears." Then he looked up to me with excitement and said that he had "heard God." I asked him what he meant and he said he heard the sound of a "sigh" or a "breeze" after he prayed. At that point, I thought of the Holy Spirit, God's Comforter, and recalled that the Greek word for spirit is "pneuma," meaning "wind," "sigh," or "breath." Had my son actually heard God speak the first time he prayed?

I then asked him how he felt? He told me that he was no longer afraid. He never again spoke of being scared, and he never has since. Something instantly dispelled that anxiety and fear. As we left the gym he asked me one last question: "Does God ever sleep?" I told him that God never sleeps and always hears our prayers, all day and all night long. This was the reassurance that he was looking for, that God can be trusted to always be there, and that he doesn't ever have to be afraid of bears again.

My son preached to me that night. I too am afraid of things and often fail to pray to God first, sincerely, and simply by saying: "God I am afraid, please protect me." It is such a simple thing to do and such powerful thing at that. I am reminded that, "unless you become as a little child, you will never enter into the Kingdom of God." (Matthew 18:3, NIV) And, unless you pray like a little child you'll always be afraid of something.

His Word Cannot Fail

"The angel answered, 'The Holy Spirit will come on you, and the power of the Most High will overshadow you. So the holy one to be born will be called the Son of God. Even Elizabeth your relative is going to have a child in her old age, and she who was said to be unable to conceive is in her sixth month. For no word from God will ever fail." (Luke 1:35-37 NIV)

Has God given you "a word"—i.e. a promise...a word of comfort...a guarantee...an epiphany? Make no mistake, His word cannot fail—He is *incapable of lying, deceiving or leading us astray.* I need to remind myself of this, because sometimes I forget His promises to me. *This* is the reason I need to have *daily times* of devotion—times set apart to be only with Him. *This* is the reason I must meet together each week with others to remind myself and encourage myself to not let go of what I am *so sure* was whispered to me when I first came to know the love of God through Jesus Christ.

God has wired us to need each other for the very purpose of keeping each other on fire, as it were, and to hold each other accountable for what we clearly know we ought, or ought not, to be doing. When we are together we are reminded of the very things we thought we would never forget or wonder about. We find ourselves spurring each other on when our minds might be tempting us to panic or give up.

But as we are each faced with time alone, or time limited to only our families, let us recall that God cannot fail us and that He is not limited! One of my sons recently remarked that He does not pray to God about little things because He knows that God has better things to do. *The devil's lie!* God delights in hearing our smallest and most "insignificant" prayers and is the *author and regulator of time! He has time for me (and you) right now and is neither taxed, tired nor challenged by the smallest petitions with which we come to Him.* In fact, He is disappointed that we are unwilling to trust Him with the small stuff of life.

Has He spoken to you in the past? Remember His promise—He cannot and will not break it. Have you not heard Him lately? Perhaps you need to listen...

He Deserves Our Best—Not What's Left Over

One of the last books of the Bible is Haggai. He was a prophet of God sent to the Israelites after they returned from exile. He explained to the Jews that they had made a mistake when they stopped working on the temple (which had been utterly destroyed) and were instead working on rebuilding their own homes. This small book addresses why the people were not being blessed and how they needed to get their priorities re-directed.

Haggai's point was simple: Build the temple first, then trust God to bless you with the rest—i.e. homes, farms, security. When I was quite young I recall being taught that the Pilgrims came to the new land and *first* established a place of worship and *then* spent time on their homes. Our founders had it right.

But something has gone terribly wrong, in my opinion, in Europe, North America and other lands that were once faithful, Christian nations. Something has slipped into our way of thinking that has shifted our priorities and causes us to look a lot more like the folks that Haggai was talking to than the ones that celebrated in Solomon's time.

I understand that many pastors today talk about the need to make churches more attractive to non-believers or new converts. Many churches allow casual dress from-flip flops and shorts to camouflage and t-shirts. The bigger churches even create Starbucks cafes within the entrance to the sanctuaries. It's a "come as you are" mentality with "Christianity lite" being preached from the pulpit.

Why? Because the reasoning goes that "the church needs people and we've got to change our approach to get them in." To which I humbly reply: *Pure rubbish*. The bride of Jesus is not desperate for people—people are in desperate need of becoming members of His body. *All* people are in *a great need of God—but God does not "need" us…He loves us.* God will be no less God if churches cease to have *anyone inside or if the entire Christian community ceases to exist.* And the church might very well disappear if we continue to water down the gospel and continue to anthropomorphize God.

*As a nation we've lost our compass—somewhere, somehow…*and it will not be found in suggesting that God wants us to come and worship Him *anyway He can get us.* And to be clear, I dress casually for worship and I would *never* refuse attendance to anyone that desired to worship Him or hear the gospel *regardless of his or her dress, hygiene, political leanings, etc. But God deserves our best in worship, our sincerest forms or praise and the honest preaching of the Word irrespective of how those observing respond.* The audience is God—not the congregation.

Active Hope

We have been taught to have faith, believe in God, and hope for the best. That's what Christians are supposed to do, right? But sometimes it is unspeakably *hard*. Not only do things frequently *not* work out like I had hoped and planned, but things seem to get *worse* the harder I pray and try to make them right. It does not diminish my faith in God—I do know Him and I do not doubt His love for me. But the truth is that I often find myself *impatient* with how long it takes Him to get things done.

Why do some folks seem to do so well and prosper so quickly in their endeavors, and I seem to be growing at the pace of a lichen! I realize that patience is not my strongest suit, but truly I dream of using my limited gifts and energy for His Kingdom—if He would merely remove all the obstacles that haunt me each day.

But as I whine about such things, I am reminded that I am not the first man to wonder why God takes so long to fulfill His promise and answer my prayers. He told Jeremiah: "For I know the plans I have for you," declares the LORD, "plans to prosper you and not to harm you, plans to give you hope and a future." (Jeremiah 29:11, NIV)

He has plans for *me!* Now that is exciting. His goal and plan is not to harm me, hinder me, suppress my energy or life, but to give me *hope*…and a future. I have been learning to live for hope more and more over the past few years. Not just the idea of getting "lucky" or the slim possibility that something good "might" happen. But rather the whisper of His Holy Spirit that I do not need to worry, be anxious, lose sleep or feel like the world is passing me by. *He has my back and is allowing all of this to cause me to prosper and have a marvelous future!*

If my hope rests in Him—and I truly *trust* Him, I can proclaim as David did:

"Many are saying of me, 'God will not deliver him.' But you, LORD, are a shield around me, my glory, the One who lifts my head high. I call out to the LORD, and he answers me from his holy mountain. I lie down and sleep; I wake again, because the LORD sustains me. I will not fear though tens of thousands assail me on every side." - (Psalm 3:2-6, NIV)

Amen and Maranatha.

How Much Does He Love Me?

I got a little sick recently on a trip, having not been able to sleep well for two nights in a row, and trying to finish too many things in too short a time. Perfect conditions for being irritable. These are days I just want to "check out" and head home. But I have responsibilities, four young men to raise, and I was redeemed and purchased by the blood of Jesus Christ to serve Him—not to simply talk long strolls in the park. In short, I am here for a reason and whether I like my present circumstances or those placed upon me in a year or ten years hence, I am not my own and in these matters I am expected to reason like an adult, not a spoiled child.

But today, as I was praying and reminding God of how frail, inept and inadequate I am, my youngest son interrupted me, crawled into my lap, kissed me several times on the cheek and told me over and over that he loved me. He just wanted to be near me and fall back asleep. What an epiphany and humble wake up call *for me*. This little boy loves me, dysfunctional father though I am, and I love him and would do *anything* under the sun to help him, protect him and provide for him.

Then it hit me: God, *my* heavenly Father, whom I know and love, *loves me far more than I could ever love my nine-year-old.* But if I can be counted upon to love, protect and care for my sons (as any good father does), have I forgotten that He will do the same—*and more than I can imagine?* He is not going to provide a stone when I ask for a piece of bread or hemlock when I ask for a drink. He will withhold no good thing from *me* and has purposed and promised to give me the desires of my heart. "I can do *all* things through Christ!" (Philippians 4:13, NIV)

For reasons I cannot explain, I sometimes fail to remember spiritual truths like this. God *loves* me and cares about me even when I get too busy and too squeezed. I begin to slip when I start pondering that it's "all up to me" and that "God expects me to figure this thing out and wrestle it to the ground," when, in fact, what He really wants is for me to tell Him that I love Him (i.e. praise Him) and meekly admit my needs, haunting thoughts, dreams and hopes.

He's a very good Father and I can rest assured that each time I come to Him, even before I ask, He knows my needs and His arms are open wide to pick me up, wipe every tear from my eye and remind me that He will *ever* love me and be there for me.

But I would bear in mind that just because my boys can manipulate me, try to tease or trick me into getting them things they don't need or allowing them to go to places the should not, my Father is wise and able to give me the best, not simply the things I pine for now and then regret tomorrow. Yes, He may on rare occasion give in to my constant pleading, but I cannot wear Him down or exasperate Him; He loves me too much to give me the wrong things at the wrong time. And of course, if I am a good father, I will follow that example with my own sons.

L. DEAN BARLEY

Blind No More

The New Testament tells of a young man who was *born blind* and was healed by Jesus. This miracle had never occurred in the history of Israel until then. *There is no recording of a blind person's sight being healed until Jesus came.* There were cases of leprosy being healed in the Old Testament and even the dead being restored to life, but the blind being able to see had never happened. (See John 9:1-2, NIV)

The religious leaders were simply unwilling to believe the obvious. They denied what was *clearly* an incredible miracle because to acknowledge that this *really happened* would have caused them to admit that Jesus was obviously (at the very least) a "prophet." And to do that would have upset the entire apple cart of their religious organization. So they made fools of themselves in front of the crowds of on-lookers by arguing over "who" really did the healing and if the man was *truly* blind in the first place (and of course everyone in the crowd knew he was!)

These were the *spiritual leaders* of the Jews: So why were *they* so blind? Would you not expect these scholars and clerics to be far more enlightened and in touch with God after reading and reading the books of the prophets and the Torah? Christ explained that the problem was that these men had become "religious" externally, but were full of pride and conceit internally. Being *religious* does not mean that you are in love with God or that you follow His Son. Memorizing Bible verses might make me appear very devout, but the Scribes, Pharisees and Sadducees memorized the *entire Old Testament* and were, according to Jesus, more fit for hell than those that knew nothing of the Old Testament! "Knowledge puffs up…Love builds up." (I Corinthians 8:1, NIV)

What God wants from me is not "religious devotion" to an idea or a creed, but my absolute devotion to the Son of God. These folks were committed to the Torah and the books of prophecy, but not to the One that inspired the same books! Am I a loyal fanatic to the Bible, or to the One of whom it speaks? Am I dedicated to a church/denomination, or the Groom of the true church? Am I in love with my idea of who I want Jesus Christ to be, or who He *really* is?

Jesus has a habit of upsetting tables in our temples and seeing through the external into the heart of the matter.

Change my heart, God, to see you as you are and to become as you intended me to become. Remove my denial to truth and give me the courage to see the miraculous! —Amen

Intimidating or Inspiring?

The anticipation of all that must be done before opening the camp for the summer is sometimes makes me a bit "prickly." By that I mean that I can be cantankerous and not as talkative and friendly as I should be. I have no excuse for exhibiting this kind of temperament, but I do recognize a disconnect between what I *want* to be and what I *am* at this time of year.

Today, a camp staff delivered to me the worst insult any man could level at me. He told me, quite carefully and haltingly, that I "intimidated" him. I suppose that some men and women would not be too bothered by that complaint, and indeed many of the people we look up to as heroes did in fact scare the daylights out of their adversaries! But I am not one of those men; I am a follower of Christ and my goal is to imitate Christ. Christ had the capacity and power to *cause* anyone to tremble when He spoke. But He did use that power or His relationship with His father to make others cower or shake with fear. Quite the opposite, He was the most humble man to ever walk upon the face of the earth! Little children would climb into His lap, older children wanted Him to place His hands upon their heads, prostitutes would wipe His feet with their tears and dry them with their hair, *the worst of the worst* would be unafraid to talk to Him, invite Him to their homes and ask Him questions.

If anyone should have caused others to be impressed and have reason for intimidation in His presence, it was Jesus…but He was not like that. I never want to cause others to be afraid or intimidated because of me—it's simply unbecoming of a disciple of Christ. I was ashamed—truly ashamed—that my brother in Christ was intimidated of me. And yet it's not the first time I have been told that I intimidate some people. *God have mercy on me!* Who am I that *anyone* should be afraid of me, let alone be menaced because of me?

I hope never again to have anyone tell me that they are scared to talk to me. If anything, people should feel more at ease in my presence and more able to become close to me if I truly becoming more like Him…but it appears I have a long way to go yet.

Have I Hid His Word In My Heart?

Psalm 128 speaks to my soul. In fact, it *nourishes* my soul on days when I need it the most. The Psalmist was speaking to others who believe in, worship, and "fear" the one Holy God. (Psalm 128:1, NIV) But as I read these passages I have come to grasp a bit clearer the meaning of "fearing" God and of being an obedient child.

"Blessed are those who fear God and walk in obedience" (Psalm 128:1, NIV) is something akin to saying, *"Congratulations to people who use seatbelts and don't drive intoxicated."* It's not a matter of being afraid of God, though we have reason to if we are outside the body of Christ. But think about it: we consider congratulatory remarks about wearing seatbelts and not driving drunk to be self-evident and proven truths…people that obey these two laws are the kind that live longer lives and don't ruin the lives of others; it's a statistical fact they are "blessed." Why, then, question the wisdom of respecting God's commands and laws and wonder if they will *really* make us happier, more content, and at peace?

Funny that we trust the education, training, and the instincts of those that run statistics on seatbelt use and drunk driving, but not the cumulative wisdom *of the entire universe (i.e. God)* when He promises blessings and prosperity *if we obey Him*. The Psalmist goes on to explain specifically how God does bless those who choose to obey Him.

I am *not* advocating a Pharisaical observation of every letter of the law. But something is wrong when we assume that we can live *any way we want* and yet still expect God's peace and blessing. I have been born again and redeemed, but if I expect His blessing, I had better be *paying attention to what He prescribes for me to live and focusing on what pleases Him!* And arguing that I have a different opinion of God's law really does not matter… *His opinion is the only one that matters.*

The Ten Commandments are the foundation, of course, of God's commands, but I am also required as a citizen of the Kingdom of God, to learn to *love* what God loves and *hate* what He hates. I know that He hates a lying tongue, hands that shed innocent blood, failure to keep one's word, and above all, all displays of pride and arrogance. Do I have the same hatred for these traits in myself? And do I tolerate those behaviors in my family, my church, or with those that I elect to represent me in my country?

If I would enjoy all the abundance in this life that He wants to offer me, why would I not *read and study His Word, hide His words in my heart, meditate upon them and embrace them as a way to live my life?* He knows more about me, my nature, the dangers that await me tomorrow and what lies around the corner *than I could ever imagine*. Why would I presume to make up my own rules or assume I know how to operate in this world? This is my first and last time to pass through life. There are no second chances. But if I humbly admit my shortcomings… if I continually attempt to determine His will for my life… if I read His word and determine to follow His commands… I *will* be blessed; nothing under heaven can stop it.

> "Blessed are all who fear the Lord, who walk in obedience to him.
> You will eat the fruit of your labor; blessings and prosperity will be yours.
> Your wife will be like a fruitful vine within your house; your children will be like olive shoots around your table.
> Yes, this will be the blessing for the man who fears the Lord.
> May the Lord bless you from Zion; may you see the prosperity of Jerusalem all the days of your life.
> May you live to see your children's children—peace be on Israel." (Psalm 128:1-6 NIV)

What Does "I Love You" Really Mean?

How many times during the day do you say, or hear someone else say, "I love you"? Beautiful words that can change your mood and add light and encouragement for the whole day. But saying, "I love you" means more than just, "you're okay," or "I like working with you." Sometimes I have to remind myself that saying "I love you" has more to do with a decision of how I will treat the one I love more than sentimental affection or acknowledgement of their existence.

Saint Paul is clear about real love:

- Love is patient.
- Love is kind.
- It does not envy.
- It does not boast.
- It is not proud.
- It does not dishonor others.
- It is not self-seeking.
- It is not easily angered.
- It keeps no record of wrongs.
- Love does not delight in evil but rejoices with the truth.
- It always protects, always trusts, always hopes, always perseveres. (I Corinthians 13:1-13, Paraphrased)

So when I tell someone in my family or inner circle of friends that I really love them, I am saying *all* of this. I am making a statement of my determination to be patient and kind with them, as well as how I will conduct myself around them—i.e. to be humble, to not be quick to get upset, and to not bring up past offenses. As a Christian, if I tell you that "I *love* you," it should generate quite a sensation of protection, peace and assurance. It means that I am there for you: to be your shield, to believe/trust in you, to hope for the best for you and never give up on you. Wow! Don't you want to be loved like that by a *lot* of people? What a wonderful world this would be if we all loved like this. But if I aspire to such love in my life, it must also flow out of me to those around me. The people who are loved the most are those that also make the decision to love.

We all want to be loved—it's quite natural. But are we also prepared to love others in demonstrable ways? It's not just a feeling—it's a personal discipline and courageous determination. I *will* love that person… I *will* trust, protect, hope for the best and *never* give up on that person. That is love.

From Boys to Men

When Christ was betrayed on the Mount of Olives and lead away to be tortured, the disciples scattered and ran away. No one came to His rescue or defended Him. Peter denied Him, later Thomas doubted Him, the rest kept as far away from Him as possible. Only John was loyal enough to watch Him die on the cross.

Prior to The Passion these young men fought among themselves about who was the most important; they complained amongst themselves; and they had a hard time taking in all that Jesus was trying to teach them about humility, suffering, and desiring God with all their hearts.

But in a very short time *after* the resurrection and the ascension these young men became very different apostles. After they received the Holy Spirit they were *not* the same men. In the book of Acts, for example, Luke explained how the Jewish leaders had Peter and the other apostles flogged for preaching the good news about Jesus. After the flogging (which was a painful and humiliating punishment) *they left praising God that they were considered worthy for suffering and being humiliated for "The Name."* (Acts 5:41, NIV) These were not the same boys. Something happened to them.

Friends, these men didn't simply *believe* in the resurrection of Jesus, they *met the resurrected Jesus and ate a meal with Him!* These men were not merely converted from their previous way of thinking; *they were baptized with the Holy Spirit and became new men!* This is what I pray for every summer! This is the goal of any man or woman that has been appointed to share the good news of Jesus Christ's redemptive work for His Father. I don't want just to tell kids about God and show staff how to be godly. I hope and pray that they might be *transformed into new creatures.* That is the goal.

And it *happens* when someone meets the true, living Jesus Christ in a personal and private way and receives, through His Holy Spirit, a new mind and is truly *born again.* Please, please pray that our words and actions might bring young people into a passionate desire to meet Jesus at our camp.

An Ideal Community

I read the last chapter of Hebrews recently and realized for the first time what a perfect recipe it offered for an ideal Christian community, whether it be a summer camp, church, Christian fellowship, or village.

Hebrews thirteen suggests nothing surprising or unique in the Bible, but remember, this book was written for a mature Christian community that needed to be reminded of the basics of Christian living. It was not meant as sustenance for non-believers, but rather as food for followers of Christ who were still struggling in the dark world of the Roman Empire.

Here is the counsel with which Hebrews closes regarding how we are to treat each other:
- "Keep on loving one another as brothers and sisters". (Hebrews 13:1, NIV) Regardless of what anyone has done, don't stop loving each other! Why did he say this? Because Christian communities are always at risk of becoming indifferent to the others in the community. That's why we make ourselves unite with other believers each week to be *reminded* of the truth.
- "Do not forget to show hospitality to strangers." (Hebrews 13:2, NIV) Don't get too smug with those in your fellowship and always reach out to those who are not yet "in." God does not want us getting too comfortable within our church membership or those at our camp! We should expand our borders—increase our fellowship. This must be our hope; we need to be willing to feel a bit uncomfortable with new folks in our fellowships.
- "Continue to remember those in prison as if you were together with them in prison (Hebrew 13:3, NIV)—-or the hospital, bedridden, or even out of fellowship because of quarrels and disagreements. "Remembering" (Hebrew 13:3, NIV) refers to missing them and wishing they were back! You will treat them different if you miss them.

Here's the counsel with which Hebrews closes regarding how we are to live:
- "Marriage should be honored by all, and the marriage bed kept pure." (Hebrews 13:4, NIV). We're supposed to shine as the ideal in terms of how we conduct our own families and how we reject society's ideas of what is morally right or wrong.
- "Keep your lives free from the love of money and be content with what you have", (Hebrews 13:5, NIV). Don't fall in love with "things"; instead be content with what you have! This is a call to stop whining and complaining.

In regrade to how we should handle the matters of our churches, camps, and Christian communities, it's clear that we should: (See Hebrews 13:7-19, NIV)
- Respect those who lead and serve. Leading is harder than following because the spotlight is always on leaders—and should be. But if they get it right, give them some respect. They deserve it.
- Don't believe everything you hear—check it out to be sure it is right! Just because a camp director, deacon, president, priest, or pastor says it is true does not make it so.
- Pray for those who pastor you, those who teach you, those who serve you, and those who are dedicated to you.

Praying an authentic, heartfelt, earnest, sincere prayer is key, and it will move mountains. Did you pray today for those who lead your church, city, state, and nation?

Free Indeed

"Jesus replied, 'Very truly I tell you, everyone who sins is a slave to sin. Now a slave has no permanent place in the family, but a son belongs to it forever. So if the Son sets you free, you will be free indeed.'" (John 9:34-36 KJV)

If you are a slave, you do *whatever* your master demands—you are not your own. Your master has *absolute* control over your life and your destiny and you have no real "place" or "seat" at the family table, so to speak. It's bad to be a slave—but good to have a place in the family.

I have never owned or even met a slave, but did you know that *40,000,000 people* still live in slavery? China, Democratic Republic of the Congo, India, Indonesia, Iran, Nigeria, North Korea, Pakistan, the Philippines and Russia still practice some sort of slavery. But in the ancient world 30%-40% of the world was in slavery! It was an economic means of life.

No sane person talks about the virtues of slavery—it was and is a bad thing. And in the context where Jesus uses it, "sin" is the slave-master of those who those who live apart from God. "Sin" (or Satan) does not want the best for me but instead pushes for my destruction. Sin's purpose is to keep me from the table of God (the Father) and from becoming formally and legally part of *the* family.

If you think that "slavery to sin" does not exist in our society, consider those that are "mastered" by alcohol, drugs, sex (porn, prostitution, etc.), gluttony, or their own egos—just to name a few. Once a habit or a hankering like this enslaves you, it *owns* you. It's funny, but most things that end up becoming an addiction or sin were, as God originally intend, *gifts* from the Father. But sin tempts us to have it all, right now, and with no restraint or respect for the same standards we expect from others. Sin causes us to "understand," or even wink at, our own addictions or excesses, but show disgust and reproach at the failures of others.

So who is the master of my life? (a) Sin (a self-centered existence that must have it now, with no limits) or (b) God (a trusting relationship where I know that my Father will always have a place for me at the table)?

And note the promise: Once we turn to Jesus, we become freed from the slavery of sin and become a *true* a son or daughter—forever! We never need to be a slave again—we're free to live the overflowing life He talked about and promised. Why would anyone want to be a slave (to sin) when he or she can be a child of the King of Kings?

Maybe Jesus Knew What He Was Talking About

"'Enter through the narrow gate. For wide is the gate and broad is the road that leads to destruction, and many enter through it. But small is the gate and narrow the road that leads to life, and only a few find it.'" (Matthew 7:13-14, NIV)

Wide and broad—the way most people live—including families. (Matthew 7:13, NIV)

Most folks live like this "because everybody else does." Small and narrow is the road that leads to life—"eternal life"—*and "only a few find it".* (Matthew 7:14, NIV)

This is a bit disconcerting. Only a few will find heaven? Is God only interested in a few?

This is one of the statements of Jesus we don't like to consider. It goes contrary to what we have decided that heaven must be (i.e. where *most* people end up). This suggests that most people are *not* going to heaven, and it is not commonly discussed. But either it is true or Jesus was not aware of the true heart of men and women. Maybe He was mistaken and perhaps people have progressively gotten better and better since He was on earth. Or maybe now, because of better education and a keener comprehension of how the human mind works, we know that God will accept most people into heaven, because we *know* that most people are not *really* responsible for the way they live; they can't help it; people have chemical imbalances, emotional disorders and trauma from their past that explain why they are as they are. It's not fair to limit heaven to only the emotionally healthy and un-traumatized.

Or maybe Jesus *is* the Son of God and He saw beyond the conclusions of Freud and Skinner, et al. Maybe Jesus does not care what polls tell us or what we have decided on as "fair." Maybe, just maybe, He sees what we do, today, this very day, as being no different in terms of sin and separation from what God intended for us, than what He saw 2000 years ago.

And if the latter is the case, *maybe* He's right. Maybe most folks *do* follow the crowd and maybe only a few really look for God and what is pleasing to God. Perhaps, one day, we will find that heaven's citizens are *only* those that wanted to be with Him for eternity (a minority of all humanity) and hell is full of those that *did not* want to spend eternity with Him—and maybe hell really will be full of the vast majority.

My New Home!

I have had dreams for years about an incredible house I was building that was not yet complete, but nearly. In most of the dreams I am living in another home, but for some reason I suddenly "remember" that I have second home that is grander than the one I am living in and that I must go and complete the construction.

The new house is basically the same in all these dreams. It's under construction, it's two stories tall and has an enormous attic and basement. In each dream I am so *proud* of that house and ask myself why I have not finished that home and moved into it.

I believe that this "second house" is the one that He has prepared for me in heaven, and at night He gives me glimpses of the glory to come. Always in my dreams, I don't want to leave that special built home. It was created especially for me and I know it. I am homesick for the place He has prepared for me.

I had a similar "homesickness" for heaven for some reason today. At certain times, for no apparent reason, I just get weary of the way things work here on this earth. The vanity, the greed, the dishonesty, the selfishness, the pride, the hurry and the worries of tomorrow (and these are just *my* sins!) cause me to want to leave. I know that this world, like the house I live in now, is not what He ultimately wants for me, and all others who call Him Lord, to enjoy. In a real sense, my "home-sickness" for God's perfect kingdom is a good sign that I *am* seeking it and that I am reminding myself that, "This world is not my home, I'm just a'passing through…"

It makes me think that if this is really the case, why in the world am I ever greedy, selfish, worried or in a hurry? This world is a mere stage of what is really coming—we're seeing through a cloudy glass what heaven will really be… and *that* thought pumps me up. The One who created you and me knows how we crave beauty, order, purity, perfection—and He will one day satisfy our cravings and the deep desires of our hearts.

On Having His Mind...and Him on My Mind

I have never fully understood what "having the mind of Christ" (I Corinthians 2:16, NIV) means, and I am still trying to completely receive it. But I know that it has something to do with also *having Him* on my mind—all the time—as well as seeing things as He sees them.

His ministry and the ministry of the disciples are totally out of step with most ministries today. Jesus' laser-beam focus on God's Kingdom, and the disciples' dedication to sharing the gospel and establishing churches, is a far cry from the heartbeat of many of us in ministry. Most of us are bent on *self-promotion* rather than *promoting Jesus Christ and Him crucified.*

I heard an inspirational speaker once remark that if you wanted to "make it" in business, you had to follow the "2 Ps" of business: *patience and persistence.* Sometimes folks in business are nearer to Christian principles than pastors! These folks have it right. I was called to not *give* up and to not be *anxious* about God's timing for getting it done. After all, what will really matter when it's all over is not my little private enterprises, but those things I faithfully executed for *His Kingdom.*

Of course I need to eat, sleep, pay my bills and raise my children. And I yearn to be a blessing in my community and neighborhood—not a burden or a curse! But these hopes and needs are *not* primary. He has reminded me time and again, that *if* I put Him first (*that* is primary)...*if* I will trust Him and *not* worry...*if* I choose to live for Him and not those appetites the world says I should be perspiring for... He *will* take care of me and give me more than I ever hoped for—-pressed down and overwhelming.

So how do I maintain this state of mind? How can I continue to have Him on my mind and avoid the pitfalls of self-pity, worry and getting my priorities backward?

Well, it's always good for me to look back and recall how He rescued me in the past and how much better my life is because of the things He did, or the things He allowed to happen in the past—painful as they might have been.

He *cannot lie or deceive us.* That encourages me when I am tempted to wonder or doubt. But I must also consider the lilies...they simply "are."

He Anoints My Head

"You prepare a table before me in the presence of mine enemies: you anoint my head with oil; my cup overflows." (Psalm 23:5 NIV)

How inspiring to know that *if* He is my Shepherd (i.e. I yield to Him and follow Him in my heart) *He will honor me in spite of what others may think or imagine about me.* Isn't that something that everyone wants? Some *respect*? His promise to me is that He is going to cause others to one day look upon me with admiration, and regret the unkind things they said about me or the unfair things that they did to me. He will stand up for me and defend me: *if* I am humbly following Him. I don't have to worry about defending my endeavors or arguing about my integrity—He will do it for me. What a blessed riddance! **He** will defend me!

Here's what I am learning and re-learning every day: If I will praise, adore, trust and follow Him—He will *lift me up.*

It's *not* the others in my church, camp, family or even my own home that are the source of my "ok-ness." It is God Almighty—He is the One that will bless me and make me feel whole; He will remind me that I am "*somebody.*"

And at the end of the day, I will find that He does not just take care of me, but that He is *extravagant* in the way He shows His pleasure with me and approval for me. *He anoints my head with oil. I will not be able to take it all in because He overwhelms me.*

Such is the life of the ones who follow the Good Shepherd and obey His voice. Is there any reason to follow anyone or anything else?

The Log in My Eye

More than one time I have begun to write these "thoughts" and erased everything and began again. This time, I began to share something, but a more important theme stirred me and caused me to open my heart. More often than not, that "theme" is not something necessarily noble or enlightening. It's quite frequently "confessional": some remorse for how far I still am from my Master's intention and purpose for my life.

I have seen that I struggled with my own temper, anger, and frustrations as my days grow longer. There might be 1001 things that would give any normal person a reason to explode or throw a tantrum, I suppose, if he/she ran a summer camp such as I have. But much of what annoys me is self-inflicted, and regardless, I am *not supposed to act and react like a normal person.* And that's what causes me such shame at the end of a day like this.

I was born again, redeemed, chosen and adopted by God for a single purpose: to be holy. I am not *supposed* to be "normal." One way or another, God intends to have His way in my life through that process called "sanctification." And only one person on the face of the earth can thwart or delay God's ultimate goal for me: *me.*

And for me, more than anything else, it's my temper that reminds me I have a long way to go yet. It is the knowledge that I am still a man who is not totally "self-controlled" that allows me to have more patience with other brothers and sisters in Christ who are immature in other areas of their walk. I know all too well that I often "lose it" over some of the most ridiculous occurrences at my home or the camp, and then find I have a hard time "winding down" from my explosion.

I don't want anyone who reads this to think *good* about their anger and fits of rage since I have them too! No, but I do want to say that growing closer to Him does help me dwell on my *own* shortcomings a bit more soberly, and *less* on the shortcomings of others. I still have a *log* or two in my own eye to remove and at my age it's time to get those logs removed!

I think I *do* get angry over the *right* things, but that anger rarely, *if ever,* is so effective as walking away from the situation, praying about it, and then walking back into the situation. I have never flown into a rage and had a graceful landing.

May God give me more discretion, self-control and understanding.

A Boyhood Treasure Almost Lost

Today, I had to take the two younger boys to their pediatrician. They had to leave school early and were elated! We drove to the doctor's office, and after the appointment, we went next door to an Ingles grocery store. We spent twenty minutes shopping, but on this occasion, I let them each have a cart to "help" me shop. Of course they picked up a lot of junk food, stuffed animals, and things we did not need. But they had a great time even though I made them put most of it back.

Then we drove to an old country store where I allowed them to purchase one snack each. Again, this is not something I normally do. They spent ten minutes finding the perfect snack. For one it was an ice cream sandwich, for the other it was a bag of potato chips. As we left the store and drove to pick up the third boy from track practice, I realized how happy the boys were that we shared an "adventure"—at least that's how they described it. It was really nothing more than going to the grocer, to an old country store, and taking a drive while listening to their favorite music.

I suppose the music is what really set the backdrop for our adventure because each boy got to choose his own song. We listened to Christian praise for a while, then "Puff the Magic Dragon", "A Lover's Concerto", and "YMCA." And as we drove through the mountains to our last destination, it hit me that this day would probably be one that the boys looked back on as one of those "perfect days of boyhood." It was a golden, happy adventure. An afternoon of their childhood, that as adults, they surely will long for. And it could easily have all been lost if I had not thought of them and their needs, more than my needs and the requirements of my little business.

How many times during the week have I allowed opportunities of a golden moment, or worse, a "God moment" to be lost because I was too busy or too preoccupied with a more "pressing" considerations. Today alone, I had more than four contacts or conversations with some very special people who were suffering, and truly needed someone to listen to their concerns. In reflection, I realize that when those phone calls and meetings began, I was looking at my watch and wanting to find an excuse to cut the meeting short and do anything to get back on my schedule. But each time, something (and I believe it was the Holy Spirit) told me to shut my mouth, turn off my phone, and trust Him. If I would allow Him to work through me on His bigger matters, He would handle my little concerns. As he showed me, the big things are investing time in the lives of those that Jesus died to redeem.

Today, three of us had a marvelous adventure because one of us remembered to not be a self-absorbed adult. God, please forgive me for majoring on the minors and looking through the microscope and not the telescope!

Living a Life Worthy of the Name

"As a prisoner for the Lord, then, I urge you to live a life worthy of the calling you have received. Be completely humble and gentle; be patient, bearing with one another in love. Make every effort to keep the unity of the Spirit through the bond of peace. There is one body and one Spirit, just as you were called to one hope when you were called; one Lord, one faith, one baptism; one God and Father of all, who is over all and through all and in all." (Galatian 4:1-6, NIV)

We often talk about the need to be more like the "New Testament church" as if *that* church had its act together all the time. Read the Pauline epistles or the letters that Peter and John wrote and you'll get a different impression. Those Christians had a lot of the same flaws we have and some of their behavior was scandalous!

But there is one thing they *had* and one thing that they *did* that we lack: They *had* men like Paul, Peter, John, Barnabas, Stephen and other apostles and leaders that had the passion for Christ **and** the backbone to courageously, and graciously, remind the good folks in the Church what they were foolishly forgetting.

And they *did* one thing differently when it came to reprimands or "putting someone in their place." They directed discipline to those *they loved* within the churches regardless of who it was. Nothing is more cruel than a passivity which abandons others to their sins. Jesus' most direct and bluntest words were saved for Peter and the disciples—not those outside. It seems to me that we are quick to point out the errors of those outside the Christian faith and yet remain silent about the things within our churches that *ought* to be confronted. If Paul, another apostle or Jesus Himself were standing here today, what would they say to leading church folks—the bona fide Christians in our communities and at our camps?

They would tell us:

- Show true brotherly love to each other. They would confront those within the church that are not "nice." There's just no place for unkindness. There's no record of Jesus ever screaming or yelling at anyone—or of the apostles doing so.
- Don't forget that you are also a *servant* of Jesus Christ. Jesus is not <u>our</u> servant or a genie in a bottle. He is not the one we call on to do the work for us *that we ought to be doing* or the one we turn to make our lives easy and full of pleasure—we've got it backwards. *We are His to be used as He chooses in the work of Kingdom of God.*
- Keep yourself humble—or don't be surprised if He intervenes and does the humbling for us. There's no place in God's Kingdom for arrogance and boasting
- Be gentle!! If we must rebuke or reprimand or offer correction or even advice, be gentle. Yes, being gentle is a fruit of the Spirit, but Paul tells us that if we're not being gentle, something is wrong with our spiritual connection in general. Being gentle is not being weak. Jesus was not weak, God is not weak—but they are gentle. To be gentle I must at times restrain my temper, learn to empathize and have compassion. I have to put myself in their shoes, so to speak, and recall how I want God to treat me.
- Be patient and put up with each other. In a few words, do to others what you hope God will do to you. He certainly is patient and forbearing with me and certainly does put up with me—and

He demands that I express the same virtues and spiritual attitudes to the other. This is why God gives us children—to test us in this matter.

In closing this passage, Paul reminds us that, *"There is only one god, one body, one faith on baptism."* (Ephesians 4:5, NIV). If we know Him and have declared that He is Lord, and believe that God raised Him from the dead, one day, soon perhaps, we will be in a place with many folks from various denominations, political parties, races, colors. We might be with some that we thought would *never* get into heaven, and some there might have thought that *we* would never get into heaven. But I believe this: Heaven is a place for those who love God and His Son and desire to be there. God is going to bring His children into that place of rest and peace. Therefore, let's get used to spending time with each other and play nicely together.

Moses' Anger...and Mine

"He (Moses) said to Aaron, "What did these people do to you, that you led them into such great sin?" "Do not be angry, my lord," Aaron answered. "You know how prone these people are to evil. They said to me, 'Make us gods who will go before us. As for this fellow Moses who brought us up out of Egypt, we don't know what has happened to him.' So I told them, 'Whoever has any gold jewelry, take it off.' Then they gave me the gold, and I threw it into the fire, and out came this calf!" (Exodus 32:21-25, NIV).

So Moses came off the mountain and found that the Israelites had made a golden calf. He asked Aaron, "What in the world is wrong with you? How could you have allowed this?" Aaron lamely responds, "We just threw the gold into the fire and out pops this golden calf." (Exodus 32:21-25, Paraphrased).

Moses *exploded!* He broke the stone tablets to pieces, berated the Israelites, ground the calf to powder, made the Israelites drink this "golden cool-aid" and then, on top of all this, ordered the Levites to take a sword and kill thousands of those that took part in the idolatry.

Point: God chose Moses and loved Moses partly because of his *incredible passion for God.* The man got mad about the right things!

Do I?

Moses saw the immense danger of what they had done and made a *big deal about it. Do we do that at my summer camp or our churches or in our nation?* Have you ever noticed the things that are "big" to God, are usually not such a big deal to us? (Just ask a politician.)

It was the *idol* that got under Moses' skin—i.e. anything that would cause the people to worship or place their trust in *anything* other than God Almighty. How *silly* to worship a golden calf, or a fish (like some people in the promised land did) or a totem pole or anything other than living God! Of course, we *also* have things that often get our focus off of God, and in my opinion, the gravest danger to worshipping God, the greatest "idol", is church or mission "work". Sometimes we equate activity and physical presence with *passion and yearning* for Him. We must be careful in Christian camps and church life to not assume that "work" for God becomes the "good" thing that keeps us away from the "best" thing.

Moses saw the difference between *good* and *best*. He understood the danger of looking to the wrong things for protection and deliverance and purpose. He properly *got really mad* when those he loved did something that dishonored or offended God.

Later, after Moses calmed down, he asked God to please be patient with the Israelites and to continue to lead and protect them. And the Lord said to Moses, "I will do the very thing you have asked, *because I am pleased with you and I know you by name.*" (Exodus 33:17, NIV)

Wow! That passage from rocked me. *I will do everything you ask because I am pleased with you and I know you by name!* The Israelites were saved because of *one man's holy petition to God.* Think about that the next time you intercede in prayer for someone—it might be the prayer that changes the course of history.

I want Him to be pleased with me—and it's a decision I must make each day. But because of Jesus interceding for me, I can be sure that He hears me, and because I have received the broken body and spilled blood of Jesus to cover my sins and I have confessed and turned away from sin, He knows my name! Praise be to God—He knows my name! And if you have received Jesus as your Lord and Savior —He knows your name as well!

Is He pleased with you and does He know your name? If so, pray boldly and know that He will hear your petitions and give you the desires of your heart...

Are You Praying for Another?

In my life I have seen God answer my prayers in wonderful and unexpected ways. He has amazed me and at times perplexed me. Sometimes He has told me "no," sometimes, "not now." But lately I have come to understand the need to depend upon *others* for prayer.

This does not come easily for me. I would rather handle my personal matters and concerns of my ministry with the strength of *my* relationship with God and not lean or depend upon others. But it appears that's not what God intends for me—and for any one of us that are a part of the "family."

More and more I am discovering not only the *strength,* but also the efficacy of *corporate prayer.* At times I have been burdened by some needs at the camp, and whereas some folks tell me that they are "praying for me" there are few that I *trust* to *pray for me.* I have asked those trusted few to pray about some important matters because my prayers seemed to be going nowhere. I have been humbled in seeing *immediate* answers to my prayers when people of faith intercede on my behalf.

I have also noted the reciprocal effect. People come to *me* with personal needs and I stop what I am doing and concentrate on their need, intercede on their behalf *and things happen—much faster than when I pray for my own needs.*

Obviously God wants me to depend upon Him—but also reach out to others when it comes to my personal struggles, my challenges in ministry and concerning unanswered prayers in general.

Perhaps *you* are also perplexed about why your prayers are not being answered. I challenge you to ask someone you know *who has an intimate relationship to Christ* to personally and emphatically intercede for you. Miracles will follow.

Produce Fruit in Keeping

John said to the crowds coming out to be baptized by him, "You brood of vipers! Who warned you to flee from the coming wrath? Produce fruit in keeping with repentance. And do not begin to say to yourselves, 'We have Abraham as our father.' For I tell you that out of these stones God can raise up children for Abraham. The ax is already at the root of the trees, and every tree that does not produce good fruit will be cut down and thrown into the fire." "What should we do then?" the crowd asked. John answered, "Anyone who has two shirts should share with the one who has none, and anyone who has food should do the same." Even tax collectors came to be baptized. "Teacher," they asked, "what should we do?" "Don't collect any more than you are required to," he told them. Then some soldiers asked him, "And what should we do?" He replied, "Don't extort money and don't accuse people falsely—be content with your pay." (Luke 3: 7-14, NIV)

It seems to me that the Bible often records things that were said that we tend to ignore or de-emphasize. Can you imagine a priest or pastor today preaching *this* (see passage above) to the folks in a church? What would the elders, deacons, presbyters or bishops say if our clergy preached like John preached! *Imagine* the idea of telling people that they had better offer *proof* that they were serious about God and His Kingdom. To hear John preach you would think that John *did not* believe that God, or His Kingdom, were desperate to bring in all the people He could! John's preaching would turn some folks off, offend others and anger others because he spoke of God as if God were some sort of "perfect" being that expected us to choose to do just as He commanded and just what He expected. The God John the Baptist preached about offered forgiveness, but on His terms alone. You could accept them or you could go out and look somewhere else for purpose, fulfillment and an eternal life of glory without Him.

I believe that this is what we should be preaching and teaching—not a saccharine-laden message of "come as you are and leave as your are." What we *should* be preaching is the good news that Jesus Christ has come to save us from certain death and destruction and that salvation is based upon God's dictates, not man's choices. If we choose to accept salvation and escape God's judgment, John would say that we *must repent* and *give proof of it*. This would suggest that it is not merely a matter of admitting sin, but acknowledging (i.e. confessing) that what we did was wrong, make amends (if possible) and *stop doing it!* I don't recall hearing that very much in today's preaching. Jesus told the adulteress, "Neither do I condemn you, (but) *go and sin no more.*" (John 8:11, NIV)

God have mercy on me if I fail to preach the gospel—which includes what we are *yearning* to hear and what we don't like to hear as well. As a follower of Jesus I have been redeemed to shine and walk in the light—not the shadows or darkness. The message I must present requires that I honestly explain the need not only for remorse, but also repentance and a determination to give up those things that stand in contradiction to holy living.

John the Baptist eventually lost his head for speaking truth. Some people don't like to hear the truth and want to silence the messenger. But may God send us more men like John...

Putting Away Childishness

"When I was a child, I talked like a child, I thought like a child, I reasoned like a child. When I became a man, I put the ways of childhood behind me." (1 Corinthians 13:11 NIV)

In terms of *love* Paul reminds me that I am to be an *adult*. In terms of faith—a child.

As a child I *loved* those that protected and provided for me—my parents, aunts and uncles. Later I loved my teachers, coaches and professors for the same reasons. But as I grew, I learned about *my responsibility* and wonderful *opportunity* to love those that offered *nothing* back to me.

Christ called Peter, James, and John away from their fishing boats and offered to teach them how to catch men. And the first step in "catching" others for the Savior was the determination to love them, and put away the childish personal yearning to be protected, provided for and shielded by others. Adults, in Christ, are required to *become* the protectors, providers and shields—not the other way around.

Maturely loving means that I am becoming more like the Master and less like an adolescent. I am moving away from the demand to be understood, appreciated, applauded, recognized and complimented. I put away childish love and instead embrace the "adult-love", if you will—one that understands, appreciates, applauds, recognizes and compliments the one I love! And as an adult, I am able to come to the *greater* joy of *loving with no expectation of being loved back,* all the while knowing that He loves me and is proud of me for the manner in which I have learned mature love.

Salt and Fire

"For everyone will be salted with fire." (Mark 9:49, NIV)

I have spent a day thinking about this verse. It's one of those enigmatic verses in the Bible that we don't talk about very much, though we shouldn't shy away from these kinds of passages. Jesus was talking about *everyone*. We will be "salted", (Mark 9:49, NIV) that is, brought to a place of being made pure—that's what salt means when it is represented in His teachings every time. Salt was a source of purifying a sacrifice or making something "preserved"—holy. And fire represented that which removes the "dross" or the impurity that is found with something "dirty." So fire was used to make gold or silver or iron or copper *pure*. The impurity was burned away and what was left behind was the essential, whole element.

I have come to understand in my ministry and my walk with God is that He *does* intend to permit suffering. We go to great lengths to avoid suffering, *but even God Himself suffers,* so we should not think of suffering as an unholy or inappropriate thing. Jesus *suffered* at Calvary and prior to the crucifixion. God was *grieved* (i.e. He suffered in heart) when He saw how evil men had become and was forced to destroy His creation with the flood.

So if I can get into my head that suffering is *not* a bad thing and that it does *not* represent God's punishment or displeasure with me, I am able to experience peace and joy—even in suffering. Pain gets our attention to "get our attention", from time to time, to spiritual concerns; it is essential if we would become the creatures He had imagined us to be.

If I truly aspire to become a part of His body, I must be able to accept and bear suffering. To become like Jesus I have to remind myself that He was "a man of sorrows, and acquainted with grief" (Isaiah 53:3, NIV). To be conformed to Jesus requires that I accept suffering.

I think of Job and His suffering and wonder: What an honor to have been considered *worthy* to suffer for His glory. Job himself asked, "What is man, that you make so much of him, and that you set your heart on him?" (Job 7:17, NIV). Job's suffering *surely* brought him closer to God in a manner that physical blessings never could. Oh, that I could be one that God could point out to the accuser and say, "Have you considered my servant Dean?"

No sane person should ever go out and look for persecution, trouble, or suffering. But what a witness to a non-believing world we can become when we accept the "salt and fire" (Mark 9:49, NIV) and shine for Him. What unspeakable satisfaction is ours when we find that we have been made pure and holy by "holding up" as His process of sanctification and perfection is brought into our lives.

Shine Jesus

I had one last night *to be still,* and enjoy the sites of France on one of my business trips. I had a dinner meeting at 8:30 pm near Notre Dame, but I arrived in the city early simply to sit at a cafe and reflect a bit, pause and appreciate this wonderful city and country.

I was alone, of course, but many years ago I came to learn to appreciate the peace of being alone from time to time. I learned to tolerate "me" — and it has helped me to learn to tolerate others as well. The people of France have never been anything other than generous, kind and helpful to me. And although every single Uber driver is France seems to be Muslim, I must *salute* each of them as well as being consistently kind, alert and respectful.

Even as I was writing this devotion, a family called me from the North of France asking me to please join them at their church tomorrow morning and then for lunch. Some may query how there could there be a God with all the evil in the world, but how could there not be a God with all the charity and selfless love that *is* in the world?

The fight seems to be with a world created by a God who *is love;* this "image" or "pattern" of love is embossed in sunsets, smiles, a light snowfall and "senseless acts of kindness"; and yet the world is also marred and scarred by an "enemy" that attempts to draw all attention to the perverse and the self-serving alternatives of love.

God help us, because if the news we hear each night is any indication of "progress" towards "heaven on earth," we're in trouble, for it appears that the enemy has won more hearts than God Almighty. Of course that's nothing new or surprising, I suppose, and Jesus talked about the wide path that leads to destruction and the narrow one that leads to eternal life. In Matthew 22:14 (NIV)He said, in a rather foreboding manner that, "many are called but few are chosen." Yikes!

And yet I have been blessed to be with men and women whom He has surely chosen. How do I know? Clearly from the fruit they bear in their lives and their love of Him that causes them to act uncommonly and "alien" when compared to the way those in the "enemy's camp" live. And it has helped me in my work and ministry to remember that this world is really "enemy territory." Just because I *do* see good and hope and love all about me these past two weeks in France, this is not the way most men live—and there are surely many who masquerade as "creatures of light" who are absolutely not living for God; they are actors, or better described as hypocrites."

So what am I to do? I have to applaud and celebrate those things that are good and represent what is godly, but I have to admit that things will *never* be the way they should be until God rescues His redeemed and creates the new heaven and earth. I am *not* anxious that this happens tomorrow—many would be lost. But if I can see those who are in the enemy's camp as *lost* and not *my enemies,* perhaps God's light, reflected (poorly) through me might bring them over to His camp. That is my task and the first task of everyone in the body of Jesus Christ, i.e. to remain connected to Him (my *first priority*) that I might bear fruit that glorifies God and draws other from darkness—or shadows—into the light.

Shine, Jesus, shine. Fill this land with the Father's glory. Blaze, Spirit, blaze. Set our hearts on fire. Flow, river, flow. Flood the nations…(Crystal Lewis)

The Messenger or the Message

I have become more aware, the longer I look in the mirror, that I treat what I *hear* differently, depending on who says it. I might be told the same thing by a person I respect and I person I don't particularly care for, and I will thank the person I respect and ignore the opinion of the one I hold in lower regard. This is blatantly "unchristian" of course, but I know that I do it all the time.

It seems that lately God has been using people that have offended me or with whom I differ greatly in most matters, to be His instruments of sanctification in my life. I have experienced (at least three times recently) a messenger that gave me counsel that I did *not* appreciate. I found their tone and method of delivery haughty, self-righteous, arrogant. When they pronounced their opinion on my errors I quickly dismissed their remarks as being judgmental, unkind and unneeded. But later (not at first, but *later in the day*), I began to reconsider what they had said and had to admit that they were *right*. Not only were they right, but also I would not have discovered my errors if they had not pointed them out to me—I was simply blind or too stubborn to recognize it on my own. I am grateful for their words of caution.

Today I came to realize that it was not the *message* that annoyed me, but the *messenger.* If the same thing had been said to me *lovingly* by one of my best friends, it would not have been hard to accept. But when a person (or persons) that I know have no room to talk began to lecture me, my pride rises up and I am unable to *listen.*

But this time I did listen—and I think I am better because of it. I won't name the three folks that told me truth, but I will say that I believe they were agents of God for a good purpose. I need to listen to rebukes, insults, questions of my actions, etc. and *thank God for those that remind me to be circumspect and humble in my work.*

I am not looking for criticisms or rebukes, but I am in no place to complain to God about the messengers He sends. Lord have mercy on me.

You're Getting Older—No Matter Who You Are..

The honesty of children: It's something that keeps those of us in summer camps "young at heart," I think. I was asked today by my seven year old, "Daddy, why do you look so old?" I quipped back, "Because I am old!" But his honesty reminded me that I can't hide who I am, what I am, or how I look from my four sons—particularly the younger ones—they simply have no filter. What they think comes out of their mouths instantly.

This can be a good thing, perhaps, or a very embarrassing and awkward thing. I appreciate their honest evaluations of me, at times ("Why are you always mad at me?" "Why is your face like that?" "Why is your hair turning gray?") but at other times, they spurt out the same pronouncements on total strangers—e.g. "Why are you so fat?" "Is he/she going to die soon?" ...and so on. They have not learned how to speak and respond tactfully and politely to things they see and the opinions that they form.

It's funny, though, how they are comfortable asking about aging and death, but in general, the church and our society seems to shun the same conversations. We know that we're all getting older and we know that we will all eventually die, but we don't like to talk about it much—even though it is an inevitable and certain part of our existence.

As I get older I find myself yearning, more and more, for that ultimate place for which I was created and redeemed; I do think more about the joy that must be associated with freedom that comes from finally, one day, being totally emancipated from the worries, trials, frustrations, uncertainties, aches, pains and disappointments that life on this earth places upon every human being. I think that all men/women, both Christians and non-believers, have the same hankering for such a place of peace—a surrounding where things are "as they should be"—and we all know, innately, that things are *not* the right way on this earth right now.

So why do we hate to talk about death, dying and aging? I think it must be the fear that we are not "sure" that we will continue. There's that hesitation of not being 100% positive that all this talk about God, heaven, eternal glory, et al is real. But the more I know Him, the more I see His hand working in my life and the lives of those I love, the more certain I am not only of heaven and my place in it, but also of His desire to calm my soul for the time I have remaining here.

One day we will look back at our struggles, or aging, or aches and pains and we'll probably smile and say, "Can you believe we ever doubted Him? Look at what He had prepared for us all along...

We Need a Revival

A friend recently shared with me a short story about a Welsh revivalist named Evan Roberts who preached around 1904. He was *the man* God used to bring over 100,000 souls to Jesus Christ. But his message was *so* simple and the delivery *so* very short.

His message was as follows:

- Confess all your sins
- Remove anything doubtful from your life
- Give yourself completely to the Spirit—and then speak and do all He requires of you
- Publicly confess Jesus Christ

He could preach for hours, it's said, but he could also, if led by the Spirit, speak for only a few minutes. It was this *short, brief message that sparked a revival. Oh that preachers today would listen to the Holy Spirit and speak no more, (or less), than prompted.* Where did this idea come from, that a preacher *must speak* thirty minutes, forty-five minutes or an hour?

Evan Roberts merely preached the good new about Jesus Christ, and the Spirit moved. But as I think about *my* nation and Christendom as a whole, I wonder if we rely *way too much* upon persuasive arguments or an impressive presentation of Christian dogma, rather than the *need* for everyone of us to: *confess sin* (and quit referring to it by any other name); turn away from those things that we doubt are pleasing to Him; obey God as He speaks to us and stop making excuses for ignoring Him; forget what is politically correct and instead, with courage and passion, confess that Jesus Christ is Lord of all.

Speak, Lord Jesus. Open my eyes to the things that I have done that have offended you or compromised my walk for you. Show me all things, hidden or in plain view, that are not needed or inappropriate for a man to possess or display that *he is in love with God.* And give me the opportunity to profess that Jesus Christ is Lord to all whom you place in my path.

The Urge to Worry

"Therefore I tell you, do not worry about your life, what you will eat or drink; or about your body, what you will wear. Is not life more than food, and the body more than clothes? Look at the birds of the air; they do not sow or reap or store away in barns, and yet your heavenly Father feeds them. Are you not much more valuable than they? Can any one of you by worrying add a single hour to your life?

"And why do you worry about clothes? See how the flowers of the field grow. They do not labor or spin. Yet I tell you that not even Solomon in all his splendor was dressed like one of these. If that is how God clothes the grass of the field, which is here today and tomorrow is thrown into the fire, will he not much more clothe you—you of little faith? So do not worry, saying, 'What shall we eat?' or 'What shall we drink?' or 'What shall we wear?' For the pagans run after all these things, and your heavenly Father knows that you need them. But seek first his kingdom and his righteousness, and all these things will be given to you as well. Therefore do not worry about tomorrow, for tomorrow will worry about itself. Each day has enough trouble of its own." (Matthew 6:25-34, NIV)

Read What does Jesus tell us about worry? One word: *Don't*. And I would confess that I have disobeyed Him in this command on more occasions, perhaps, than any other command...to my shame. There's *nothing* positive, helpful, Christ-like, purposeful or meaningful about worry. It accomplishes *nothing*.

Perhaps *that* is why the enemy tempts and lures me into worrying late at night. What do I worry about? This ministry's effectiveness, the safety of the campers, our finances and debts, those who live with me, my pets, etc. So you see, I worry about *good* things. The enemy never tempts me to worry about things that are not noble or praiseworthy. He's sly. He tries to convince me that maybe bad things will happen or not go my way because:

- I am not good enough
- I have not worked hard enough
- I am not worthy of God's blessing and protection
- There are people out there that are able and ready to hurt and destroy me

...And he is right about all of this. *All* of this is true! I have good reason to worry! ...or so it seems from Satan's perspective. After all, *he* has good reason to be sleepless at night.

But hear this! When Jesus told his disciples not to worry *He meant it. This was a command, not a suggestion or recommendation. His point was pure and simple: obey me in this matter.*

After I exhaust myself, from time to time, anxious and worrying about one thing or another, I am reminded, "Wasn't that a ridiculous waste of time once again?" "I am *not* good enough—but He has called you as His own—I am now a joint heir of His inheritance—all that His Father has set aside for me is also mine!" "I have *not* worked hard enough, but He has done more than enough and I have been faithful—He will take care of the rest." "At one point I was *not* worthy, but because of my acknowledgement of my failures and my need of Him, I am now worthy to be called a son of God." "There are people out there that want to see me fail and fall—but He is *not going to let it happen because I have loved Him and chosen to humble myself before Him.*"

So when I worry I am demonstrating one thing: *I do not trust God.* How foolish! Either He does love me and is able to answer my prayers, rescue me and send 10,000 angels to my defense or I am in this battle alone.

God wants to bless me, not hurt me. God wants to protect me, not humiliate me. God wants to give me peace, joy and abundant love, not the paralysis of fear, doubt and worry. But I must let go and let God be God in my life.

A Character of Love

"Love must be sincere. Hate what is evil; cling to what is good. Be devoted to one another in love. Honor one another above yourselves. Never be lacking in zeal, but keep your spiritual fervor, serving the Lord. Be joyful in hope, patient in affliction, faithful in prayer. Share with the Lord's people who are in need. Practice hospitality. Bless those who persecute you; bless and do not curse. Rejoice with those who rejoice; mourn with those who mourn. Live in harmony with one another. Do not be proud, but be willing to associate with people of low position. Do not be conceited.

Do not repay anyone evil for evil. Be careful to do what is right in the eyes of everyone. If it is possible, as far as it depends on you, live at peace with everyone. Do not take revenge, my dear friends, but leave room for God's wrath, for it is written:

> 'It is mine to avenge; I will repay,' says the Lord. On the contrary:
> If your enemy is hungry, feed him; if he is thirsty, give him something to drink.
> In doing this, you will heap burning coals on his head.
> Do not be overcome by evil, but overcome evil with good." (Romans 12:9-21, NIV)

What a perfect picture Paul paints of a *concrete* expression of love. We talk about Christian love, but here. Paul makes it inexplicably clear what I should be *doing*—in real time, right now—if I am sincerely practicing my Christian faith and living a love of love.

This is a wake up call for me when I think I am progressing in my walk with Christ. It's really a very, very simple quiz for me to take every month or so to determine if the Christian faith is really taking a hold of me. Am I literally living and walking a life of love?

So here's the personal quiz:

1. Can I read every verse listed above and state that I have *met* that standard?
2. Do I really treat my enemies kindly? (That's the real test.) It's not how I love those who love me, or those who are lovable that defines my walk with Christ, but how I treat those that do not like me, want to harm me or are unlovable.
3. Am I allowing evil done unto me to compromise my witness, or am I allowing personal attacks and setbacks to serve as a springboard to allow the risen Christ to be manifested in my life?

I Don't Know Why I Did That!

As the staff and campers began to descend on the camp last summer I found that the boys in my home were torn between wanting to be at the camp, *all the time,* to experience all the new things and meet all the new people, and at the same time maintain normalcy and a set agenda they've had for the past school year.

But with all the changes, new faces, new schedules and routines, the boys have also had a hard time adjusting and knowing *how* to act. The resulting behavior has been, quite honestly, the *worst ever,* and we've sat through the most dramatic meltdowns we've ever had since I first adopted the boys. They've been horrible—and my response has been *worse.*

Yesterday I got one of the boys alone and asked him why he had committed a litany of foolish things over the past week, and quite exasperated, he blurted out, "I don't know why I do those things!" And it's true—he does not. I don't believe for a second that these boys plot to make their OCD dad angry. In truth, I don't think that they are *thinking* about *anything* when they do the dumb, dangerous, outrageous things that they do. They do it and then really don't know why.

Paul said that same thing, in effect, in the book of Romans: "I do not understand what I do. For what I want to do I do not do, but what I hate I do." (Romans, 7:14, NIV). Paul was pretty mature and advanced in his walk with Christ when he wrote those words, so perhaps I need to be a bit more charitable when my boys do what they do—and perhaps all of us dealing with children need to remember the same.

But why did Paul, the boys and I do the things we did *not* want to do last week, last year or 2050 years ago? It is because of the struggle still going on within us all. Even though we've been born again, the struggle to do the *right thing* fights against the urge and temptation to do the wrong thing. Regeneration provides me with the *option* of living a life totally dedicated to Him—I have the tools, the manual the blueprint! But it's not automatic; it does take dedication of my mind, heart, body and strength.

Yes, at my age I am aware of the areas where I am weak and the need to build a hedge to protect my heart and mind from the things that will produce garbage in my soul—but these boys have not learned that yet. I have come to understand that I am not as pure and holy as I would like folks to believe that I am. I know that I am twice as guilty as the worst criminal if I were held accountable for what I *think* sometimes! I *know* that at times I am powerless as I allow my temper, my frustration, the pressures of running a business and ministry—rather than my Savior—to rule my life! Yes, I know this and I am *disgusted* at my own weakness and inadequacy!

But the point is that I *do* know this—-but young boys and girls and those immature in their faith *do not.* And that's why I have to be careful about judging them or casting them down for the perverse, unkind, selfish and rude things that they do. *Truly, they don't know why they do these things.*

But getting back to me—and to those of us that do dumb things—i.e. sin—why don't we choose to stop? The power of the Holy Spirit within us *does* give us the ability to give up sin. We *can* stop being violent, we *can* give up bad language and screaming at our kids, we *can* turn away from dishonesty, unfaithfulness, etc. *Yes, it is possible!* But can only happen when two things occur:

1. We stop blaming our past, our parents, our society, etc. for our sins.
2. We stop thinking that our sins are somehow more understandable and acceptable than the sins of others. Instead, we determine to *hate* the things *we* do that dishonor Jesus Christ.

Being a Sheep

"Surely goodness and mercy shall follow me all the days of my life; and I will dwell in the house of the Lord for ever." (Psalm 23:6 NIV)

Those that follow the Good Shepherd are optimists—*plain and simple.* These are the kind of folks you want on committees, projects and capital campaigns!

When I am following Him and I *know that He is leading me,* I am certain of my destiny even though I am unfamiliar with the terrain and the path. I *know* that my Shepherd is leading me to green pastures and clear, still waters, so even if I come across some thorns and mud in the journey, I am well aware that something better, cleaner, brighter and indescribably incredible is over the horizon. *This* keeps me going and pushes me to higher ground. And so I can rest, knowing that although I will make mistakes from time to time (as all sheep do) *He will show me mercy* and will remember that I am but a sheep—i.e. it's my first time on this earth and I am quite fallible and dull at times. He knows this; it's been factored into the path on which He is leading me and He's prepared to give me time to catch up and get disentangled from the briars and thorns I sometimes fall into.

And finally, *one day,* the journey will be over and I will never again struggle with decisions of right or wrong, left or right, up or down—I will be in His House… and I will rest and be at peace. But between that transformation that will take place in the "twinkling of an eye" (I Corinthians 15:52, NIV) and today, I can be sure that although I might stumble, I will not fall so long as I follow Him.

It is good to be a sheep when I have such a good Shepherd.

A Lamp and a Light

Often, while lying down, I and think about all the things I must do when my feet hit the floor, along with all of life's demands. There are many days I would prefer to just stay in bed. There's something about being on my back, lying down flat, that causes my mind to wander, wonder, and worry about all the things that I should not be concerned about in the first place.

But each time when I get out of the bed and off my back, I see things differently and I become energized. There's a connection between getting on my feet and out of bed that changes my way of thinking about life and what I must get done. I was not meant to lie down but "rise and shine."

In the book of Proverbs, King Solomon wrote a lot about lazy people, e.g."As a door turns on its hinges, so a sluggard turns on his bed." (Proverbs 26:14, NIV). I don't believe that God calls us to be paupers for the sake of the Kingdom of God, though we are all spiritual paupers—and many paupers *are* incredible witnesses for Jesus Christ. I was brought up to believe that working diligently, rising early, eschewing excuses for missing work or school, and taking care of my body (i.e. what I eat, what I do in my free time, what I read) would lead to an abundant and successful life.

To this very day I am uncomfortable with adults who get up late, do less than their very best at a given task, or use "sickness" as a constant excuse. I must be careful, I know, because some people have congenital issues or diseases that sap their strength. But I also know how easy it must be to slide down that slippery slope of just "getting by" and doing only what is essential in order to live.

It is said that the biggest problem with the average worker in the USA is that they either don't do what is asked of them, or they *only* do what is required. I hope that I am raising four young men in my home, and equipping 100+ staff each summer, to think differently. Without sounding too "fundamental," let me attest that no book I have ever read explains how to live a productive, praiseworthy, satisfied, and "successful" life better than the Bible. No book in the Bible covers everything on those topics as succinctly as does the book of Proverbs, written by Solomon, the wisest man to ever live. God especially and personally endowed him with that wisdom. As I re-read Proverbs each year I nod and tell myself, "Yes, he's right. I can see now that this is spot-on once again."

I don't like to preach in these devotions, but I am amazed at the number of my friends, both Protestant and Catholic, that have never read the Bible. God's word is both a lamp and a light in our lives. In particular ways it may go counter to the common culture, but it has stood the test of time by remaining relevant for 4000 years!

If you are not one that reads scripture, I would challenge you to try it. Begin reading it early in your day, not at night in order to put you to sleep. Before each reading, pray that His Holy Spirit might illuminate the Word in a purposeful way in your life. I believe that you will walk out of your door each morning more prepared for an abundant day. By spending only minutes in the Bible, you may find the answer to what's been troubling your soul for years.

A Time to Shudder?

With three young boys in my home there's always some competition when it comes to *everything*. If I do one favor for one, the others are quick to request a compensating favor. If I read to one, I must read to all. And when it comes to sports or games, typically there ends up being a fight to see who comes out "on top." I recall playing "king of the mountain" as a child, and that's the best way I can describe how these boys interact with each other. One is always trying to exceed the others.

In their young minds, the short-term goal is to have more toys than anyone else in the house—and then hoard those gifts. We have *footlockers* full of toys they never play with and yet they are determined to have more and more. Sadly, they're living lives that are really quite common and *natural*—at least "natural" in terms of normal human behavior.

But as I scold them for being selfish or for bragging or hoarding, I know what I am swimming upstream when I take into consideration *all* that they see in magazines, television, advertisements and movies. We really don't know what to do with folks that act *contrary* to "normal" human interacting, so we ignore them, ostracize them, even crucify them.

The *joy* I am attempting to impress upon my sons is the joy that comes from *giving,* from letting others get to the top *ahead of you* and from *denying your own rights and defending the rights of others.* But when I say these things they look at me as if I have two heads. It's as if they are muttering to themselves, "Daddy is out of his mind?" So whom do I point to as *examples* of living a selfless life? Who can direct them to what would instill within them the hidden but incredible satisfaction and union with God that comes about when we truly live a life like Jesus? Can you think of a national leader, national athlete or even a clergyman that could be pointed to?

Obviously *Jesus* is the hero to look at, but He is not still walking the earth—only His disciples are, people like you and me. We are here to mirror the kind of life a young person *should* live. And this is why I am somewhat critical of folks, like me, who minister in the "name" of Jesus but forget that little eyes are ever upon us. Are we exhibiting, daily, the humility, selflessness, love and devotion to God that we *should* be showing? Are we industrious, hard working, *honest*, trustworthy… and do we love as He loved? As I take time to examine my own life and bear in mind that for the time being I am the closest example of Jesus these boys have, I should shudder a bit. "Woe to him who causes one of these *little ones* to stumble…." (Matthew 18:6, NIV)

The Greatest of These

One night I offered a devotion to the campers about love as described by Paul in his first letter to the Corinthians. The last verse concluded, "These three remain: faith, hope and love; but the greatest of these is love." (I Corinthians 13:13, NIV)

Love, of course, is what our faith is all about. But I am reminded that *talking* about love versus exercising love is the same as looking at a fitness magazine versus working out. The first might stimulate you, but the latter makes the difference.

What I am learning is the need to love not like I see people love, or how it is written about in novels or portrayed in movies. *My role model for love is Jesus Christ.* And as I read and meditate upon His level of love I understand that I have not yet "arrived."

You see, Jesus really *meant* that I should *pray* for my enemies and *bless* those that attempted to misuse me for their own purposes. For the longest time this teaching didn't really made sense to me, but I now see that the real purpose of my praying, forgiving and blessing those that are mean and unkind to me is not because they *need* my prayers, forgiveness or blessing, but rather because in doing these things *I am taking on the very nature of Jesus Christ!* I need these people in my life more than they need me in their lives! (See Matthew 5:44, NIV)

I am *becoming like* Him in my response to attacks upon me and the mean-spirited things done to me when I *refuse* to respond in kind, and instead allow Him to shine through me. God permits me to be the recipient of callous attacks, derisive talk and vulgar insults for one reason: to permit Him the space and place to reveal the Son of God living in me.

Faces of Angels

The book of Acts states that one of the first martyrs, Stephen, had "the face of an angel" (Acts 6:15, NIV), as he was being accused of sedition and blasphemy. That's always struck me as something quite unique in the Bible. I can't think of anyone else ever referred to in this manner.

Since Donatello first produced "cherubs" in his paintings, we've had this whimsical idea that angels are chubby, naked little winged babies, flying around church steeples. But that idea is nowhere found in scripture. Are the angels dazzling, handsome? *Yes,* that's biblical—not the renaissance notion of a pretty, soft, androgynous being. The "face of an angel" that I think Luke was referring to in the book of Acts was a countenance that was holy, pure, resolved, brave, unflinching. And if I may be so bold, that's the face that a true follower of Jesus (such as Stephen) should portray. Ahhh, but do I? Does my face show grace and tenderness, but also determination and courage to be about God's work—even if my co-workers, family and friends abandon the call?

People killed Stephen anyway, so his angelic face did not sway them any more than Jesus' face did—and Jesus displayed the very face of God! In fact, Jesus was murdered even though he had the most pure heart, the greatest humility, and was filled with total truth, perfect knowledge and had command of language that swayed thousands. But in the end an angry crowd wanted Him dead—just like they wanted Stephen dead. Dead for just for speaking the truth?

I am reminded that my face, my convictions, my determination, my faith and my love for Jesus do not provide a force field of protection from those that are offended by God's truth. In fact, it appears that the very things that we think should draw men to God oftentimes bring out hatred and violence. There are a few great men and women of God who ended their lives peacefully enjoying their grandchildren, I suppose, but I can't think of many of them—even in our modern day.

And yet, at the last, when Stephen was being pelted with stones and near death, he looked up and saw Jesus standing at the right hand of God! *Jesus was <u>standing</u>! Waiting for this hero—Stephen—to come home.* Oh, that it might be so in my life! Oh, that He will tell me, "Well done, man of faith and courage." But am I being a man, like John the Baptist, who fearlessly confronted Herod about breaking God's law"? Am I speaking the good news of Jesus even though those near me might sneer, or worse, ignore me? Am I standing for Him, living for Him, being spilled out and broken for Him each day? Or I am denying Him in the way I confront my assailants and look out for "number one"? (See Acts 7:54-59, ESV)

God Almighty—give me and the men and women that work with alongside me in this ministry the faces of angels.

Making Our Father Proud

The prophet Hosea was asked to *marry a prostitute* to make a point to the Kingdom of Israel. (" When the Lord began to speak through Hosea, the Lord said to him, "Go, marry a promiscuous woman and have children with her, for like an adulterous wife this land is guilty of unfaithfulness to the Lord." Hosea 1:2, NIV). The nation was unfaithful to God and He wanted to make a bold statement about how bad things were. So He told *a righteous man*, Hosea, to do something quite unthinkable—have marital relations with a woman whose entire vocation has been dedicated to adultery! It was a sin for Hosea to even associate with her, and here's God telling him to *marry her and treat her like a good wife should be treated.*

I do not doubt that God loved Hosea, but God calls His servants to do some *unusual* things at times. Yet Hosea did not demur or protest; he allowed God to use Him for a greater purpose. Something *within* Hosea saw what God did with his life as bigger than his own "religious spotlessness"; he surrendered his "need" to keep himself unsullied by the sins of others. He was prepared to do *whatever he was called to do to please God.* He is referred to as a "minor prophet" because of the length of his book in the Old Testament, but any man that would live the life he did and choose to be used by God in such an unheard of way is a "master/major" prophet in my opinion. Most men would simply ignore the call, but men like Hosea, Amos, Moses, Joshua, Abraham and other giants of the Bible paid attention and faithfully executed the assigned tasks.

Why did they obey? The youngest one in my home taught me why these heroes and martyrs obeyed Him. They wanted *Him* to be proud. It sounds almost childish, but as I have listened to the youngest respond to me when I am disappointed with him, or when it takes two times to get his attention, he looks at me and whispers, "I just want you to be proud of me." And he *does*. Nothing dissuades him or causes him to stop dead in his track so much as the suggestion (from me) that if he does this or that, I would not be proud of him.

A seven-year-old *wants me to be proud of him more than anything else. It is his greatest goal and his coveted reward that His dad is proud of him.* Can there be a better reason for obeying God—my *heavenly* Father? Can there be *any greater* satisfaction than to hear Him say, *"I am so proud of you!"*

And so a child has helped me understand the devotion of the great men of old where professors and theologians could not. "I want my father to be proud of me." What a powerful rule to live by.

Maintaining the Focus

Sometimes I wonder if He is paying any attention to my prayers and endeavors. I pray, plead, fast, enlist legions of "prayer warriors" to intercede for me and this ministry; and yet it seems that either God is simply not interested in my petitions at this time, or something is very wrong in my "prayer formulas."

Please forgive me if I sound sarcastic or negative: I am *certain* that He hears my prayers and that He is *completely* capable of taking care of my concerns and headaches. And yet God is never in a "hurry" to answer my prayers… and He is *never early!* I wonder out loud why He allows me to be so humiliated and defeated so often while I attempt to do good things in His name.

Yes, I run the risk of falling into self-pity if I continue down this line of reasoning—I know that. Yet it seems incredible that God would waste so much of my energy and time raising money, re-financing debts, begging creditors for another week, when He could quite easily eliminate all my debt, establish an incredible trust fund and keep my bank accounts well in the black each month! It would be a very, very simple task for God and it would *make my life so much easier!* With my extra time I could focus more on evangelism, bible study, helping in my local community, and more. So why doesn't God cause my PayPal account to "overflow"?

Maybe God *wants* to keep my life a bit difficult… God-dependent …absolutely in need of His miracles. Perhaps He has chosen the best means of keeping me humble and "busy" so that I do not become conceited or a "busy-body." It is possible that though He owns 1,000 cattle on a 1,000 hills (Psalms 50:10, KJV), I am not yet able to handle more than *daily manna*.

Friends, I wish that I never had to raise another dollar to keep this ministry functioning. But He thinks it is good for me to keep living totally dependent upon Him. "Though he slay me, yet will I trust in him: but I will maintain mine own ways before him." (Job 13:15, KJV)

Fruit From the Vineyard

Isaiah encouraged his listeners to "sing about a fruitful vineyard." (Isaiah 27:2 NIV) Amen! May God cause *this Vineyard* (our summer camp for children) to bear good fruit for His Kingdom. And may He use me to tend to the Vineyard by whatever means suits Him best.

Jesus told His disciples clearly and unmistakably that the *greatest* in God's Kingdom (or His Vineyard) is the one that serves the other. I thought about that today, and wondered about the character, habits, and customs of a true servant. Saint James told us to not "grumble, or you will be judged." (James 5:9 NIV). That's one of the first things a true servant would not do—complain and whine. We're called to do our Master's work, not whine about how unfair the work is, how little we get recognized, or how little the other servants work. We were called simply to *serve.*

But in the same chapter of James, he says, *above all,* don't swear (James 5:12, NIV). "Above all"? (James 5:12, NIV). Is not swearing, i.e. "promising," that important? Evidently it was to Jesus as well—He commanded His disciples to simply say yes or no, and that any other means to convince people we were telling the truth was from the devil. The point is that *our word* should mean something and not require swearing, taking an oath or signing in blood!

Bearing fruit comes not by my efforts, but by my decision and discipline to *remain in Him,* regardless of my circumstances. But it appears that bearing fruit also requires that I determine to take on the character of a true *servant* of Jesus Christ—and that necessarily means I do the work, the chores, the tasks He gives me and give up my penchant to complain about things, and most importantly, that it befits my reputation to simply say yes or no and *never have the need to "give my word", "swear" or "promise."*

Abiding in Him will naturally leave no space for serving myself or looking out for #1. But I *will* bear fruit and I will draw others unto Him if I am an obedient servant.

I Don't Have to Understand

"Unless you change and become like little children you will never enter the Kingdom of God…"(Matthew 5:35-36, NIV)

One day during prayer I was so overwhelmed with the tasks at hand and my personal challenges that I cried out to God: "I don't understand why this is happening! I don't see how this is going to help me or the work of your Kingdom! I am not able to handle all this pressure—why are you letting this happen to me?"

And as I listened to myself talk to God, I realized that I was not speaking as a child to his father, but as an employee to his employer, or as a private to his sergeant. I was placing myself into a relationship with God that He never intended and that was *totally* inappropriate! Christ reminds us that we *must* come to God as a "child to a father" if we would have our prayers answered and be a part of His Kingdom. The same holds true if I would *enjoy* the blessings, peace, purpose and joy that is *mine to claim*. I must understand that there are *no* adults (or teenagers) in heaven. Only children.

A child does not *have* to understand things, because he knows that his dad does. A child does not have to worry about shelter or food or clothing, because he knows that his father takes care of those things. A child does not fret about how things are going to work out, because his father always is looking after him to be sure that things *do* work out. In fact, childhood, if in a proper relationship to good parents, is the most secure and peaceful time of life. There are no worries, no pressure, no need to be afraid or uneasy. *This* is what Jesus was talking about.

Oh, the joy of knowing that He loves me and is proud of me! What peace I have in relaxing and trusting Him to figure things out. Yes, I do not understand many, many things in life—but He understands *everything… and I belong to Him.* This is my source of "self-esteem" and personal confidence: *I am His and He approves of me.*

My quiet times are not so much revelations of new spiritual truths but reminders of things I have known all along. After He reminded me to simply be a child, I spent the next many minutes simply *praising Him*. It might sound strange to someone that's never done that, but something is "released" within me when I merely praise Him and ask Him for nothing. I was created and born again to praise Him, not whine about how difficult I have made things!

Change does not come easy for any of us. But a condition for an abundant life is to change and become (and remain) like a child.

On Mowing and Painting

Since I was a child one of the things I *enjoyed* doing the most was mowing the grass. In truth, I have not mowed grass for over thirty years now, but as a young teenager I truly liked mowing grass. Later, I found pleasure in painting a room, a closet or hallway. I found the same pleasure in painting that I once enjoyed in mowing; for the past many years I have found the same satisfaction in cooking. No, I am not a chef or very accomplished in the kitchen, but I do nonetheless enjoy it. In fact, I have guests over to eat with the boys and me once a week or more often.

I discovered years ago *why* I enjoyed these exercises… mowing, painting and cooking: it is because I can start and *finish* the endeavor. There is something inside me that takes pleasure out of *finishing something*. In ministry and leading a camp there's never really a finished product. Even as one camp season concludes, we're already building another. Camp work—and Christian ministry in general—is never a finished job; there's always more to do.

God started the process of creation and finished in six days. Then He rested i.e. He sat back and appreciated His labors. That's what I felt, I think, when I finished mowing a yard. It was *done* and I was proud of my good work. When I painted a room I did a *good thing* in turning a dingy room into a brighter, cleaner room because of my efforts. I started and finished the task… *done*!

This is the challenge of ministry; *never being able to take pride in the finished product.* It's always a matter of faith that perhaps someone *else* will finish or harvest the work I began or continued. It's an honor to minister, but a burden to almost never see the end result of your efforts.

My point is that when I get to paint a room or start a project I will see completed, I am excited about being able to *begin* and *finish* a good task. That's how God has "wired" me; I get great satisfaction in doing things well. That's part of the challenge to all believers: "Whatever your hand finds to do, do it as unto the Lord" (Ecclesiastes 9:10, KJV)… do it well and *finish the task.* Except, in appears, when it comes to spiritual endeavors. We must be willing to allow *Him* to get the satisfaction of seeing the task completed as one of us plants, one of us waters and tends to the work and one of us *harvests* the work. Not a single one of us are able to complete the task of discipleship—but we can all do *what He has designed for us to do* and then, in faith, leave the completion to Him.

It Doesn't Take Much

I recall one summer an older camper got pneumonia and had to be kept away from activities and other campers. He was a very good camper but was bored to death in the infirmary. I had an extra room in my home so I offered him a private room and bath, along with TV and internet access so that he could have some peace and rest, but also a little time to entertain himself and not have to watch all the campers having all the fun at the camp.

My action was not calculated, it was rather impulsive. I felt compassion for this young man and helped him for a couple of weeks by letting him live in a vacant room. In truth I spent little time with him except for the meals I would bring him and the few minutes I spent with him the day he left. But the gratitude his family has shown me since I helped him has been humbling. Again, what I did cost me very little time and energy—it seemed to simply be the proper thing to do. But the kindness his family displayed to me at dinner in their home reminds me that small acts of kindness can leave long lasting feelings of approval and deep affection. I thought in my own life about the times people have done small things for me that I have *never* forgotten; they represent "embossed" memories to me and I am a better person because of some of the unheralded little acts of kindness shown to me.

Having recently accepted the task of raising three boys, I am keenly aware of the other side of the coin in terms of the "little things" we do for others. If it's true that a little kindness can make your day, then a little meanness can ruin your week! I have come to see, first-hand, how unkind words, thoughtless remarks, disapproving glances, and scowling faces can enter a little boy's mind with such destructive power that it will take *substantially* more kind words, reassuring remarks, loving glances, and spontaneous acts of approval to undo the damage. The bad things we say to people seem to be far more potent and far-reaching than the good things.

Saint James talks about the tongue and the challenge of controlling it. I am *still* learning that I do *not* have to always say what I think at the moment (unless it is positive). Just because it is *true* does not mean it is helpful or an act of Christian compassion and love to say it. I wish that some of those that I love very much could have been saved sooner from hearing the things that still haunt them. "For by your words you will be justified, and by your words you will be condemned."(Matthew 12:37, NIV)

It does not take much to bring about appreciation and gratitude—just a little spontaneous time and some words of kindness. But it takes *less* to damage children and leave them afraid and unsure for years or the rest of their lives by speaking carelessly and cruelly.

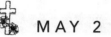

If My People Who Are Called By Name

With all the politicians jockeying for political positions in our government, I am reminded that the proper position for our leaders, and the one position that none seem to be taking, is on their knees. How many of those folks running for office today do you think are *truly* on their knees, humbly seeking Him and His will? Where would our nation and our communities be if we elected men and women of prayer and conviction, and then held them *accountable* for telling the truth, keeping their promises and living as *examples of what a politician of character* (now *there's* an oxymoron) *really should be?*

The sweet humility of Jesus: There's really no fitting place for it in our world today, but was there ever a place for it? And if it is to be witnessed...if it does "fit"...should it not first be identified in our pulpits, seminaries, Christian organizations, Christian authors and (yes) Christian camp directors?

The practice of humble prayer produces the power of spiritual stamina and inner conviction that can withstand insult and what might appear to be imminent defeat. But the arrogance of trusting in our own wits and instincts lies at the heart of human failure and has produced oceans of tears throughout human history.

The more I read the headlines about our politicians, I wonder why *no one* is counseling them of the *benefit* of complimenting and praising the *other* guy; of *not* taking credit for things you merely helped bring about. What about this Christian concept of *being forgotten* and letting someone else receive the celebration and adoration? We love to see these effacing qualities in others, so why do we not demand it from our national leaders, professional athletes, our clergy—and our very selves?

As I read, listen, and watch all of that is going on in my state and country, the *less and less I feel like I fit in*—and perhaps that's a good thing. That's not to say that I am walking with the spiritual giants yet. But it does mean that after I have tasted the spiritual food that God offers, it's hard to appreciate what the world throws at me and call it "haute cuisine."

Lord, please raise up gentlemen and ladies to lead us and inspire us—we're starving for it.

Truly Committed to Him Alone

King David once said, "Truly my soul finds rest in God; my salvation comes from him. Truly he is my rock and my salvation; he is my fortress, I will never be shaken." (Psalm 62:1, NIV)

I do not think that I was able to grasp the truth and satisfaction of these words as a youth or a young man. I was focused on the right things, I believe, but my focus was more of an "action figure" plan than leaning upon God. Like the Iron Man, my attack plan was: Attack. There was a time when I believed that by hard work and determination a man could do almost anything—including creating a community that was exactly as it should be. My motives were actually very good, but my goal was not right. I was not so much seeking Him as I was seeking the things that are *associated* with Him—such as peace, rest, stability, purpose.

David has it right. *Rest* does not come from seeking to be holy, righteous or blameless. A *sure foundation* for a ministry or church does not come from being well endowed with lots of a positive cash flow and a well-organized office. Stability in my personal life is not the result of carefully raising my sons, or watching my diet, workouts and personal habits. No, enjoying *rest*, having a *rock for my foundation* and being *immovably stable*, are the *by-products* of my intimacy with, and preference for, God in all of life. Jesus was clear: If you don't hate your mom or father in relation to how you "love" the Son of God, (See Luke 14:26, NIV) you are not going to experience the oneness with Him that David described.

And that is something that a young person (at least something *this* one-time young person) never grasped—or was never properly taught. He (God) is not the means to the goal, and He is not the One that will lead me to the goal, nor is He the gateway to the goal—*He IS the goal and He alone!* That's what produces this rest and salvation! This is what becomes an immovable rock of confidence and sense of purpose in my life! *He* is the reason. *He* is the source. *He* is my all-in-all.

The true heroes of the church, those that were truly *in love* with Him, were frequently not very celebrated in their lives. They caused others to be a bit uncomfortable because of their unwavering devotion to Him—their lives made others feel a bit embarrassed about their own lives!

I don't think I make folks very uncomfortable yet. Pity. May it change soon.

A Legacy

King Jehoshaphat was a good king, but Jehoshaphat's son, Jehoram, was not. He only reigned for eight years and did some pretty dumb things. When he became king he had his eight brothers executed for *no reason.* Then he followed the *bad* example of the evil king of Israel and refused to repent or listen to God's prophets.

When he died, at a mere forty years of age, the Bible says, "He passed away to no one's regret and was buried in the city of David, but not in the tombs of the kings." (II Chronicles 21:20, NIV) What a pity, a waste, and a horrible legacy. Who wants on his gravestone: "No one is sorry you are gone"?

But what about *my* legacy? It's so easy to cast stones at a dead man like Jehoram, but surely the man did not wake up one day and say, "Hey, I think I will be a total fool, turn away from God, and have my whole kingdom hate me." I think these things happen over time—not in an instant. Jehoram slipped, I imagine, a little at a time and finally was deaf and blind to how evil and senseless his life had become.

My hope in avoiding such a life lies in an honest evaluation of where I have *been*, where I am *going* and what *adjustments* must be made. I am in need of not only the *maintenance* of my spiritual connections (private devotion time, Christian fellowship, etc.) but also an occasional overhaul of my priorities, focus, and journey. I don't think that it is possible to simply *coast* or *relax* as a follower of Jesus; there's always higher ground to climb, more of my selfish nature to be exposed and more of "me" to be refashioned into *His* image. There's no holiday when it comes to living a life that will leave behind a lasting legacy for Jesus Christ. I hope that our lives here at camp will inspire others to walk taller and climb higher.

Watch Yourself!

"So watch yourselves. If your brother or sister sins against you, rebuke them; and if they repent, forgive them. Even if they sin against you seven times in a day and seven times come back to you saying 'I repent,' you must forgive them." (Luke 17:3-4 NIV)

How often do I absorb something that has been done wrong to me, allow the matter to infect my soul, and then lose a relationship. Why don't I rebuke those I love when they are clearly offending me or doing something obviously wrong?

Most of us prefer to talk to *others* about the friend that let us down, disappointed, wounded or offended us. But can you imagine Jesus or the apostles acting like that? Of course not. They were all transparent and direct—life is too short to let things go on like that!

Jesus rebuked Peter to his face and told Thomas to stop doubting. He called the religious leaders frauds and snakes! Paul minced no words in setting things straight when friend or foe stood in the way of the gospel—no matter who it was and what the setting!

I realize that during the present pandemic, our political leaders are *not* at a loss for words of rebuke and correction for their opponents, but that's not the same thing here. The words from our leaders are angry and vicious—they are an embarrassment, not an example, of human compassion.

But when I consider my own life, I refrain from confronting and rebuking a brother or sister for one of three reasons:

A lack of love. I simply don't care enough about their well being to give them a hard word. It's easier to be indifferent to the offender than to engage with the person who's hurt me.

A lack of courage. There are times that I *have* done the right thing and rebuked one that I love— and I have done it in great affection—but I have been blown away by their response. Quite often if you follow Jesus' commands, people *do not* respond in kindness and appreciation, but with venom and vengeance. I won't mention names and places, but I have, on occasions, told one I loved very much *the truth*, and have been cut out of their lives. Things have never returned to where they were before; I became an enemy. So I retreated, determined that it was more important that *they love me* than that I show them true love—and this was cowardly on my part.

I am doing worse things! This is the most disgusting and pitiful excuse. Even though I know that those *I love* are doing things that are bad for them and inappropriate, I refrain from rebuking them because of the log in my eye! And it's a shameful way to live to have to always walk around with a log in your eye! I need to get the log(s) out of my own eye *so that I can help (rebuke) my brothers and sisters who are walking around blinded!*

God is showing me these logs, and perhaps He is presently showing the nations the logs in our national agendas. Let us *live in love* and be unafraid to rebuke those we love, from the heart; let us *love each other sincerely* enough to invest the time required to talk to them and point out the offense that has harmed us; let us *listen to the loving rebukes* of those who love us and are trying to help us remove logs from our own eyes.

…And pray that our politicians might have similar goals.

Is Something Amiss?

For a moment, think of how *differently* would we would live, worship and plan our lives if we *really* believed that Jesus meant what He said? I personally ponder the words of Jesus each morning and I must ask myself if I am *truly* living by the recorded narrative of Jesus.

Consider these promises from Jesus: "With what you give it will be given to you."(Luke 6:38, NIV) Am I stingy, careful with what I own, conservative with my possessions, always looking out of myself? Or worse, am I hiding behind my family and saying I can't "give" because of my children's needs? Or am I known for my generosity, for my tendency to go over the top, to donate beyond my means? Am I one that has to pinch my budget because of how much I freely contribute?

"Forgive and you will be forgiven… if you do not forgive, from the heart, neither will my Father forgive you." (Matthew 6:14-15, NIV). *Do* I forgive—or do I store the offense away for future revenge? Am I quick to forgive—even *anxious* to let go of the offense—or do I wait for the offender to come crawling to me after he/she has suffered long enough from the guilt?

"What you did (or did not do) to the least of these you did (or did not do) to me."(Matthew 25:40, NIV)

The *least*? Does that include wacko Democrats, Republicans, Socialists… the wacko supremacists… the gay, lesbian, transgender…or others whose lifestyles/beliefs I don't appreciate?

Listen to these words from Luke 6: "'But to you who are listening I say: Love your enemies, do good to those who hate you, bless those who curse you, pray for those who mistreat you. If someone slaps you on one cheek, turn to them the other also. If someone takes your coat, do not withhold your shirt from them. Give to everyone who asks you, and if anyone takes what belongs to you, do not demand it back. Do to others as you would have them do to you. 'If you love those who love you, what credit is that to you? Even sinners love those who love them. And if you do good to those who are good to you, what credit is that to you? Even sinners do that. And if you lend to those from whom you expect repayment, what credit is that to you? Even sinners lend to sinners, expecting to be repaid in full. But love your enemies, do good to them, and lend to them without expecting to get anything back. Then your reward will be great, and you will be children of the Most High, because he is kind to the ungrateful and wicked. Be merciful, just as your Father is merciful. 'Do not judge, and you will not be judged. Do not condemn, and you will not be condemned. Forgive, and you will be forgiven. Give, and it will be given to you. A good measure, pressed down, shaken together and running over, will be poured into your lap. For with the measure you use, it will be measured to you.'"(Luke 6:27-36, NIV)

Here's the point of biblical exegesis: What did Luke *mean* to tell us here? And the answer, I think is this: *Exactly what Jesus said.* Luke may have left the interpretation up to the readers, but this is not tough to figure out. What did Jesus say that those that *expect and hope* for eternal life must practice, embrace and exhibit?

- the ability to love your enemy
- the habit of doing good to those that treat you badly
- not returning slaps, insults or unkindness

- not being attached to material possessions
- being able to give others *literally* the shirt off your back
- treating others *exactly* like you want to be treated
- lend to those in need and don't expect the money back
- don't judge other people's actions—*don't do it!*
- forgive—*from the heart*
- give to others
- be merciful

Jesus went on to say that if we *believe* that by doing these things God will be pleased with us, *He will* bless us! I need to get it into my head that *He is the source of all good things*—not Mr. Trump, not my employer, not my bank account.

A Christian is one who has not only been saved from hell but has determined to allow God's Holy Spirit to be the transforming process of sanctification whereby *I take on the character of God* by doing all these things—the very things that *He has already done for us and has shown us!*

But here are some grave warnings as well:

- If I don't forgive-I *won't* be forgiven!
- If I don't have compassion—He *won't* have compassion!
- If I judge others—I *will* also be judged!
- If I am unmerciful—He *will* be unmerciful!

It appears to me that part of the reason we find ourselves entertaining children and adults when we should be focused on worship, is that we have translated a holy God into a jolly Grandfather. Friends, I was redeemed by the precious blood of Jesus *not* to succeed, *not* to be constantly beg God for superlative blessings, not to be shielded from pain, disappointment, heartbreak and suffering—*No!* I was redeemed to bear testimony of what Jesus has done for me, and to share this primarily in the manner I exhibit the graces He has extended to me! And if I am not—something is wrong and I might be surprised when He says, "Depart, I never knew you." (Matthew 7:23, NIV)

I don't believe that I am redeemed because I forgive people or because I am charitable, or because I am kind and merciful, or because I don't judge people. I am saved solely on all that Jesus did on the cross. But if I have come to the cross and humbly received the broken body and spilled blood of Jesus—*transformation follows!* If not, something is amiss.

Poor Soil = Best Wine

I travel to many places that produce exceptional wine—especially France, Italy, Spain and parts of South America. Wine production in the USA is growing and especially in our state of North Carolina. The name of our ministry and camp is "The Vineyard"— we've grown grapes here from the beginning.

But as I have learned more about vines and grapes, the common remark I keep hearing by oenophiles is that the best wine comes from the poorest soil. In fact, some of the best wine in the world is produced from some of the poorest quality soil imaginable.

It's been explained to me that if you plant vines next to a river in very healthy soil, the vines develop what it is called 'lazy grape syndrome." They soak up all the water to grow their leaves and shoots, and although the grapes look plump, juicy and delicious, the real truth is they're just oversaturated with water. The grapes are okay for eating, but not the best for making jellies, jams, preserves or wine.

So why does poor soil create some of the best wine? Instead of putting their focus into vibrant leaves and shoots, they push their roots deep into the ground in search for more nutrients and water. The rest of their energy goes straight into the grapes. When planted in poor quality soil, a vine is forced to dig its roots deeper into the soil looking for what it needs to produce grapes.

Point: We don't need to be spoiled by God and we should not live for His blessings. Instead we need to be pushing our spiritual roots deeper into seeking what God, and God alone, can give us. Don't think that because you are not of a super IQ, or born into wealth, or from the right ethnicity, nation or gender, that God can't use you! Are you poor? You're blessed, according to Jesus! Yours is the "kingdom of God" (Luke 6:20, NIV)—i.e. everything is yours!

Why are those of us poor blessed? Because we realize our poverty and look to God to fill us up! We can't afford to be lazy—we have to work for all that we have and we have to sink our roots deep into Him! He is our strength, our hope and our vision. I pity those who have everything; those born into great riches and those of stellar intelligence or physical prowess—things come easy for them just like the grapevine planted in rich soil by a mighty stream! Jesus spoke about the great difficulty those of wealth would have in entering into heaven.

But those of us who have been required to struggle, dig down deep, and endure drought, poor soil and tough seasons are able to produce fruit that is of the highest quality to Him.

Suffering and "doing without" brings this about—not His abundant blessings, being born with a silver spoon in your mouth or being of the "right" race (whatever that might mean to you), or the preferred gender, high intelligence or of a "superior" nationality. Those of us born in poor soil need to stop whining about our circumstances and start producing unrivaled wine!

God has called us to be a part of His vine and produce good fruit. We're not expected to complain about the soil, location or irrigation, but rather to dig deep into the soil and seek Him.

Water From a Rock

Reading His Word is essential for me. He seems to speak *directly to my challenges* as I meditate upon what the Psalmist, Isaiah, or James wrote thousands of years ago.

The Psalmist recalled how God made a *spring* flow out of an old, dusty, arid rock in the desert. Isaiah reminded those in exile that, "steadfast trust in God leads to perfect peace, (Isaiah 26:3, NIV)" and James exhorted his flock to, "not pray for pleasures, but humble yourself and He will answer your prayers." (James 4:10, NIV)

Those might appear to be jumbled, unconnected points, but they *all* connected with me when I read them at 6:30 am this morning. It was what I needed—the fire in my belly— the wind in my sails—the very voice of God that I heard this morning. That's what I get from *enthusiastically* reading His inspired word each morning. It's as if He wrote the next chapter in Psalms, Isaiah, and James the night before I read them.

If God can pour a *spring of water* out of a huge, solid rock, can He not provide for me the things I need today? (See Exodus 17:6, NIV). *Since* His peace is the very thing I need more than anything else in order to maintain my focus each day, should I decide, then, to keep my eyes *trusted on Him? And if my prayers are not being answered*, is anyone to blame but me? Are my prayers pure—or am I seeking personal pleasure? Am I truly humble throughout my day and am I asking Him *to point out an area of pride and replace it with the sweet humility of Jesus?*

I don't assume the right to tell anyone reading this devotion what he/she should or should not do. But I would urge anyone who is struggling, afraid, unsure, uncertain, or lacking peace to read the Word each morning—and ask Him to open your eyes and ears.

Mean People

If I asked you to think of a "mean" person, does anyone come to mind? Would anyone ever conjure up *my* name, or *your* name, if we asked that question? When was the last time you did something really mean? Meanness...I've seen it a lot this year; I have seen it myself lately and I wonder why it's still within me.

Jesus was angry...disappointed...frustrated. God shows anger and is recorded as having some "regrets" about creating mankind; more than once said that He was fed up with men's disobedience. (See Genesis 6:6-7, NIV). But neither of these instances would be described as "mean." Meanness is a human trait—not a godly one. You might think that hell is a pretty mean thing, but it is not something God created for His entertainment, but rather the ultimate "means" of discouraging the self-destructive of mankind.

But I *am* mean, at times. Are you? People who have been regenerated and are in fellowship with Jesus become, quite naturally, like Jesus—that is, kind and gentle. As we take on *His nature*, we are going to become less mean, less eager to see others suffer, less anxious for others to get what they deserve. And if my *occasional* mean outbursts don't cause me personal embarrassment and remorse, something is wrong with my walk with Jesus. People who reject God will eventually lose touch with God, and the result is that their hearts, without His Holy Spirit to keep them tender, become hard. Hitler, Stalin, Mao, the pharaohs, dictators, the Roman Emperors all became men that delighted in meanness and denying their captives and enemies any mercy or kindness. They devised weapons and machines with the single purpose of carrying out their meanness. Their hearts were hardened.

But Paul reminds us to "do nothing from rivalry or conceit, but in humility count others more significant than yourselves." (Philippians 2:3, NIV) What would happen in our church and my camp if we did that? If we treated *every* new camper and staff, or every visitor in our churches, as if they were more important than we are? To our shame, we often do *not* do this. We display meanness. And in my life as a pastor and camp director, I can tell you what I think two things cause us to be mean: *Jealousy* and *insecurity*.

And what's the cure?

1. Basking in the love of the Father and the certainty of His continued approval of me.
2. Obedience to the single command of Jesus: <u>that I love the other as He loves me</u>. (See John 15:12 NIV)

There's no place for bigotry, prejudice or meanness in the love of Jesus. It is impossible to look down on others when are at the foot of the cross.

He Cannot Break His Promises

Have you ever considered the shock and devastation the disciples must have experienced when their hero, Savior and Messiah was brutally tortured and executed on Easter Friday? They had seen Him perform never-before-seen miracles; they knew that no one could stand up to His responses to the questions His enemies presented to entrap Him; they had seen Him walk *on water*, and untouched, through mobs of angry people bent on killing Him. He was the real thing and they *knew it*.

And yet, *not a single one of them* understood why He suffered and died until *after the shock and disappointment*. But with Easter Sunday something happened within their hearts and minds that transformed them and their understanding of the Messiah and His Kingdom. They became *lions* for Jesus Christ.

In the final years of the Judah, Hezekiah, a very good king, became ill and was at the point of death. "The prophet Isaiah son of Amoz went to him and said, 'This is what the Lord says: Put your house in order, because you are going to die; you *will not recover*.' Hezekiah turned his face to the wall and prayed to the Lord, 'Remember, Lord, how I have walked before you faithfully and with wholehearted devotion and have done what is good in your eyes.' And Hezekiah wept bitterly. Before Isaiah had left the middle court, the word of the Lord came to him: 'Go back and tell Hezekiah, the ruler of my people, 'This is what the Lord, the God of your father David, says: I have heard your prayer and seen your tears; I will heal you. On the third day from now you will go up to the temple of the Lord.'" (Kings 20:1-4, NIV)

Hezekiah was supposed to *die*, but cried bitterly to God and God relented and added 15 years to his life—and then made the sun go back ten hours to prove it! Is this the same God you and I pray to? Is He able to turn our anguish, broken-heartedness and despair into indescribable joy? He certainly did this for Hezekiah and more so for the disciples. Those eleven young men were never the same brawling, whining, scared young men they were again after the resurrection.

We're not supposed to live our lives based upon *how we feel at the moment* but rather based upon our trust that He will do what He promises. David said, "Trust in the Lord and do good; dwell in the land and enjoy safe pasture. Take delight in the Lord, and he will give you the desires of your heart. Commit your way to the Lord; trust in him and he will do this: He will make your righteous reward shine like the dawn, your vindication like the noonday sun. Be still before the Lord and wait patiently for him." (Psalm 37: 3-7, NIV)

So is it true or false? It can't be both ways. Can these words from David, the record about Hezekiah and the narrative about the disciples be trusted?

David learned that if he did his best *and* honored God, that God could be trusted to hover over him. But David *still* had sorrows, setbacks and disappointments even after this Psalm was recorded. People betrayed him and his own kids were rotten at times. David is talking about life in perspective—not under a microscope.

Funny how I often think that God is required to answer at beck and call as if I alone understand the severity and timeliness of my troubles. How often do I allow small things—truly *tiny matters*—to steal the peace of God from my heart? The disciples suffered for three days—but Jesus kept His promise—He always does. That gives me peace and keeps trouble from my heart.

The Battle is His

"Listen, King Jehoshaphat and all who live in Judah and Jerusalem! This is what the Lord says to you: 'Do not be afraid or discouraged because of this vast army. For the battle is not yours, but God's.'" (2 Chronicles 20:15 NIV)

The King was facing an unbeatable army that surrounded the city. There was no hope of rescue, but God told him to not be afraid or discouraged—"the battle is not yours but God's." (2 Chronicles 20:15 NIV). Is it any less true today than it was 4,000 years ago? Are the things we fear and the battles we face really *our* battles or *God's opportunity to reveal His power and sovereignty?* Is there anything my God cannot do? There are certainly things that surround me that could be cause for alarm, but the battle is *not* mine, it is God's fight—*that* is reassuring.

In sports and military actions the best defense might be a good offense, but in the spiritual domain the best defense is *deference,* i.e. humbly submitting to His sovereignty in all matters and meekly trusting Him to accomplish the things that I cannot. It's so easy to fall into the trap of worry, doubt and discouragement—and so uncommon to trust in God. But Jehoshaphat did trust—and Jerusalem was saved. It was God's hand that saved them, but it required Jehoshaphat to let go of his fear and trust in God.

The hero and heroines of the Bible were never the stuff of Hollywood—i.e. supermen that obliterated the bad guys or were in destructible when attacked. No, the Bible's heroes were shepherds, tenders of sycamore trees, simple fishermen or carpenters. They were often beat up, locked up, or chased around the countryside by angry mobs. But people *did* listen to them, follow them and revere them—but not because of who they were, but because of *Who* they represented. The real heroes, then and now, don't speak about their own gifts or greatness—but the greatness of God—the One that has gone before them to win the battle.

When clouds begin to gather I have to remind myself—this is *His* holy place, I am *His* servant and ambassador, and He has already made the battle plans to see me through whatever storm is upon me presently, this summer or in summers to come. But I must *choose* to not be afraid or discouraged, regardless of how enormous the challenge and difficult the odds.

Being Still

During the camp season, Wednesday night has become my favorite night of the week. This is the evening when the older teens go to town for movies or a cafe and the younger campers have a cabin camp out with their counselors. It is the night that I am not needed for the evening message or for any kind of administrative tasks, not even to unclog a toilet or fix a broken rail. It's the evening when I can truly *rest.*

Many times during the summer I am reminded that I am blessed to work at such a marvelous place as The Vineyard. The sunsets across the meadow are incredible. Sunrises at the lake are inspiring. The smell of the jasmine at night or the sound of the whippoorwill at dusk; the solemnity of the mountains on the horizon and the loud laughter of children and teens causes me to stop and thank God for the gift and *honor* of laboring here. I am indeed blessed.

But the need for rest, an evening alone to relax, a space to reflect and simply be still is *essential* if I am to continue my labors here. Those who know me are aware that I don't watch TV, play video games, or even put on a DVD at night. What I crave is the ability to be still, quiet and alone for a time. I need to both hear Him and put all those things that compete with my senses at a distance so that I might regain the vision and dream that came to me thirty-five years ago. In a word, I need time to reflect—and I cannot do that if I am being distracted by entertainment.

I am a big fan of most that has come about because of the Internet, iPhones, and other incredible technology. But the need to be alone, solitary, solemn and un-entertained is absolutely essential for me to be able to articulate to others the gospel of Jesus Christ and the new things I am learning of Him every day! I need time to get re-fueled spiritually. Wednesday night is my time.

Many times during the camp's nightly Bible studies, I have asked campers to describe Paradise. *More than one* has said it was a place with two or three TVs and free movie-on-demand! I pray that I am able to persuade campers to seek a time each day *free* from entertainment and replace it with space to dream, reflect, and experience something that will fill their souls and change their lives for eternity.

Love Deeply, From the Heart (I Peter 1:22, NIV)

This is what Peter told the early Christians in his first letter. It's a common theme from the time Jesus first began His ministry. But the apostles *reminded* the same folks who knew Jesus first-hand… who had received the gift of the Holy Spirit… who were fairly mature in their faith, to *do* the Christian thing and *love from the heart.*

Here's what Peter was trying to make clear:

1. There *are* loves that are *not* rooted in the heart. Those loves have more to do with affection for someone or perhaps a sentimental appreciation for someone. But Peter here is talking about a *deeper* love that we must have for one another as new men and women in Jesus Christ—one that is bolder, more sincere, and everlasting.

2. There's a need to be reminded to act in love. Why? *Because Christians are always forgetting the important things.* That's one reason we should be a part of a church. Not to be re-saved or re-redeemed each week, but to be reminded and challenged of *essential* Christian living.

3. It's not possible to follow through with this kind of love, i.e. to all people, on your own strength, unless you've got the power from somewhere outside and greater than yourself. There are some people I am naturally at odds with and it is not easy for me to love them—that's the sad truth. Sometimes, I simply don't feel like loving the ones He's placed in my path to love. They're annoying, immature, ungrateful, unsophisticated, bad mannered, politically lost in space, irrational, and so forth. They're *not* lovable in their present condition, and so I am not inclined to have a very deep affection for them—*and I know it.* But that's the *very* time, the most *important moment* to call upon the Holy Spirit to help me love him or her through Him! We are vessels for His love, and that love is to be communicated to the lovely *and* the unlovely. We're not supposed to discriminate.

But why do we hold back this love for each other—even to those we find no fault with? C.S. Lewis said that, "To love *at all* is to be vulnerable. Love *anything* and your heart will be wrong and possibly broken. If you want to make sure of keeping it intact you must give it to no one, not even an animal. Wrap it carefully around with hobbies and little luxuries; avoid all entanglements. Lock it up safe in the casket or coffin of your selfishness. But in that casket, safe, dark, motionless, airless, it will change. It will not be broken; it will become unbreakable, impenetrable, irredeemable. To love is to be vulnerable." (The Four Loves by CS Lewis © copyright CS Lewis Pte Ltd 1960. Reprinted with permission.)

He went on to say that, "Friendship (love) is unnecessary, like philosophy, like art…. It has no survival value; rather it is one of those things which give value to survival." (The Four Loves by CS Lewis © copyright CS Lewis Pte Ltd 1960. Reprinted with permission.)

For our churches and Christian camps to survive, thrive, and be the proper bride of Jesus Christ, we must *love* one another—from the heart—especially those that are hard to love…He will fill our cup to overflowing. Amen

My Life, A Mist

Speak to me *today,* Lord Jesus. Examine what I am thinking, writing, planning, hoping and the very goals I have set before you. *Remove* any relationship, text, email, imagination or dream within me that would disappoint you! Hold my feet to a holy fire.

Help me to see things *and people* from your point of view. Teach me to treat them better than they treat me and to serve them as if I were serving you. Forgive me for allowing the words and actions of others to steal my attention from you and your kingdom. Keep whispering to me that my ultimate goal is to glorify *You,* and not merely to vainly "succeed." More than anything, have mercy on me for every poor choice or thoughtless action that brings shame on the name of Your Son.

Protect me from the very ones that I love—because they are the ones that harm me the most. Shield me from the ones that *don't* love me and the one that desires to destroy me. I am far too dependent upon the approval of those that I care deeply about and I let the blows and assaults from those that are indifferent to me wound me far too easily and deeply.

Father, help me to have more compassion on those that are lukewarm to You or challenge my devotion to You. I listen too much to the taunts and half-truths of the enemy and find that my energy and zeal is drained because of it. Help me to be deaf to him! But most of all, have mercy on me when I take my own self and my own needs *too seriously* and consider my reputation and standing among my own brothers and sisters to carefully, leading to *reckless abandonment of You!*

I know many of my own frailties and vanities. I wish to be *vindicated* when slandered or when thought of poorly. When I have been wronged I wish to have the matter "righted" and for all those whose opinion I covet to know that I was wrongly accused. Lord, deliver me from this urge to be absolved and appreciated by others.

My life is a mist—please hear my pleas and come quickly. Maranatha.

Indifference

"There was a rich man who was dressed in purple and fine linen and lived in luxury every day. At his gate was laid a beggar named Lazarus, covered with sores and longing to eat what fell from the rich man's table. Even the dogs came and licked his sores.

"The time came when the beggar died and the angels carried him to Abraham's side. The rich man also died and was buried. In Hades, where he was in torment, he looked up and saw Abraham far away, with Lazarus by his side. So he called to him, 'Father Abraham, have pity on me and send Lazarus to dip the tip of his finger in water and cool my tongue, because I am in agony in this fire.'

"But Abraham replied, 'Son, remember that in your lifetime you received your good things, while Lazarus received bad things, but now he is comforted here and you are in agony. And besides all this, between us and you a great chasm has been set in place, so that those who want to go from here to you cannot, nor can anyone cross over from there to us.'

"He answered, 'Then I beg you, father, send Lazarus to my family, for I have five brothers. Let him warn them, so that they will not also come to this place of torment.'

"Abraham replied, 'They have Moses and the Prophets; let them listen to them.' "'No, father Abraham,' he said, 'but if someone from the dead goes to them, they will repent.' "He said to him, 'If they do not listen to Moses and the Prophets, they will not be convinced even if someone rises from the dead.'" (Luke 6:19-26, NIV)

Recently the Prime Minister of Great Britain, a staunch conservative, was placed in intensive care in a hospital in London because of the Covid 19. He might not survive, but in a blog one British citizen wrote, "Good, he deserves it."

Why would any human being say this of another human being? I suppose because he disapproves of the Prime Minister's belief about Brexit, the virus, economics, immigration, etc. But to suggest that he was "glad" about a man's suffering and probable death is sad. It means that the man does not know God, let alone the love of God. *I* am willing to make that judgment based upon the Word of God.

In Christ's parable, the rich man went to *eternal* place of suffering with no way out, but able to *remember* how good he once had it. He had a chance to show love and compassion and failed the test. The poor man, obviously loved by God, went to a place of eternal peace and rest.

There *is* a place of suffering and a place of rest and peace. People don't like to talk about this, but Jesus sure did. And from what He said, *nobody* in hell wants to stay there. There are no "zealots" of hell—only folks that wish they could get out.

This rich man was not mean to Lazarus, any more than the British citizen was directly mean to PM Johnson—but they were indifferent to the suffering. The rich man probably did not even know that Lazarus existed.

But Jesus *noticed* the folks like Lazarus—the crippled, the bent over, the blind, the lepers—and he did not avoid them. He helped them—and so must any of us that claim Christ as our Lord. Quite bluntly, helping *someone poor* is what a person on his way to heaven does. Ignoring *someone poor* is what a person on his way to hell does.

We're not saved by works, but our heart towards the poor and towards sinners is a compass to tell us where we are headed. When we are born again we begin to take on the "mind of Christ." (I

Corinthians 2:16, KJV). If your mind is *no different* now than it was prior to your salvation experience, *something did not happen—something is wrong.*

Those that knew Jesus intimately would call us liars if we *claimed* to know God (i.e. we were born from above) and yet failed to love others. Christ said that He would disown us when we attempted to enter into heaven if we failed to show love and compassion for the poor, the sick, the imprisoned and the lowly. (See Matthew 7:21-27, NIV). Which way are we headed in this nation? Which way are *you* headed?

Have Mercy on Us, Lord

David wrote: "Have mercy upon us, O Lord, have mercy upon us, for we are exceedingly filled with contempt." (Psalms 123:3 KJV)

David was crying out to God: "Help us!...but *not* because we deserve it." (Psalms 123:3 Paraphrased)

This is the language of earnest pleading; repeating it represents the emphasis of the prayer. David knew that help could come *only* from God; he was looking only to Him, and he looked to God like a small child looks up to a parent. "Dad—please help me!"

Perhaps you are one that needs help, or you feel maybe for the first time that you are under great pressure that you cannot overcome, or you do not know Him, or you have strayed far away from him. Perhaps this is your prayer today. *"God please have mercy on me and help me."*

To David, he cried out to God that he and his people had been stuffed with hatred, loaded down, heavily burdened with the disapproval of others…"for we are *exceedingly filled with contempt*." (Psalms 123:3 KJV). The Hebrew word used means to be saturated, i.e. entirely full, and the idea here is that so much contempt had been thrown upon them that they could not possibly experience any more. Contempt had been shown to them in every possible way. They were thoroughly despised. Do you feel that way sometimes?

If you do the right thing, sometimes people *do* hate you. David knew this first hand. People can be incredibly mean and oftentimes the same ones call themselves "Christians" or worse, are part of special Christian "society" determined to be above sinning or to even associate with people who sin ("New Pharisee Societies").

How can you avoid being treated unkindly and never be served with contempt? Well, you can be sure that it is far safer to take *no* stand for Christ than to stand up and be counted a follower of Jesus Christ. On account of your faith, many will make fun of you; you might be called in irritant in your school or local government.

For these and other reasons, David knew about contempt—it was plentifully poured upon him. Why? Because he was a man after God's own heart and the world *hates that*. May the world hate me as well…

This prayer from might be appropriate today:

"God sustain us, bless us and protect us from those that are opposed to the good news of your Son and your everlasting love. Protect us from our own foolish choices and decisions—give us a new, clean, pure, and wise heart! God, also give us the fortitude and courage that we might continue to be held in contempt by those who do not love God and have those who disavow His Son."

You can't live for God on your own. You need two things: An intimate relationship with Jesus Christ and fellowship among others who hold your same love.

Eyes Opened to His Amazing Love

Jesus asked Peter three times if he loved Him and three times Peter said "yes." It was embarrassing for Peter to be asked three times, but it represented a chance for Peter to redeem himself after *denying* Jesus three times.

As most folks know, the New Testament was written in Greek and many of the nuances of the Greek language are lost in translation. Seminarians and Bible students are aware that when Jesus asked Peter if he loved Him, He used the word *agape*—i.e. the highest, purest expression of love. *Three times* Jesus used that word, but each time Peter responded, "Yes, I love you," but he used another Greek word for love: *Phileo,* which refers to an "affectionate" or "brotherly" love. (See John 21:17, NIV)

So what's the point? Does it really matter? It means a bit more to me now than it did a couple of years ago, because I have a better understanding of this *agape* love. The oldest love in the universe is *not* the love of man for a wife (romantic love) or the love of a friend (*phileo*), but the love of a Father for His Son…and the Son for His Father. This love, agape love, is not the common love we find in most songs and it is not applauded at the Grammys, nor is this the love that we celebrate on Valentine's Day. Agape love, as I understand it, is the *only* love that God exhibits; all other loves, regardless of how noble or celebrated, are inferior to His agape love. Agape love is a love that loves *by nature* and loves *regardless if the one being loved returns the love.* Agape love does not love one day (as in romantic love) and then stop loving a few weeks later after a lovelier prospect comes around. Agape love knows no end and no limits. It is unconditional and always looks for the best means of expression.

In raising my boys I have been brought to a *better* understanding of this kind of love. There are times these boys *do not appear* to love me back. In fact, I wonder at times if one of them hates me! But agape love is not threatened, or defeated, or diluted by the negativity of the one being loved; it is not connected to "getting something back." Agape love is a profound yearning for the beloved to be well, safe, happy, secure, protected, educated, well fed and properly clothed. And all the while, the one offering true agape love is unfazed when the one being loved is ungrateful, sullen, selfish, lazy, unresponsive and indifferent. I have *finally* come to a better understanding of just how much God loves *me.*

It is His Holy Spirit that enables me to love and understand love, and it is the same Spirit that opened Peter's eyes at Pentecost. I pray that my eyes might be opened to the incredible love of God— and the fruit of abiding in God, which is agape love.

If the Lord Wills

I've always had a hard time identifying with folks that always seem to know exactly what they are going to do and precisely where they are going. It appears to me that God wants all good things in our life *except* this. My personal experience has been that sometimes there's no real map for life's adventure; you just have to keep on walking—blind at times. If you are waiting for God to give you a clear vision of where you will spend the rest of your life you'll never get anywhere.

At other times, even though I know that God has put work before me and the work *has* to be done, I wonder if it makes a difference. I am not attempting to sound like what I do does not matter, but if I live my life expecting immediate gratification for what I am doing, I will soon lose heart and stop working. Sometimes we do the work just because it *has* to be done and we're *able* to do it.

Although it's often been illustrated otherwise, working for a church or Christian ministry is mainly perspiration and very little inspiration. Yes, those serendipities do come—there are epiphanies on rare occasions and they make all the difference in the world. But you can't live for those rare occurrences of revelation and God-sent surprises…you have to *force yourself, at times, to not give up* even though you have no vision and you feel that you are losing your passion.

I don't ever recall hearing about this in the university or graduate school. I wrongly assumed that everything would make sense and I would be constantly reminded by God of how pleased He was with me if I went into a full-time Christian vocation. In fact, however, a lot of what I do is based upon waiting—and waiting and waiting—for God to act and intervene, and being patient (and trusting) that though He is quiet and does not seem to be moving fast enough, He still is bringing all things together at the proper time.

Responding to what God brings to (or allows to enter into) my life is simply not something that I can prepare for, organize or plan. He blows away all my ideas of where I will be and what I will be doing in five years, or even next week, with the wave of His hand! So do I plan and prepare to execute tasks each day, month, year? Absolutely. But I do so knowing that God will be God and intervene and upset the apple cart whenever it suits Him. It's best to say, as Saint James admonished us, "…you ought to say, 'If it is the Lord's will, we will live and do this or that.' (James 4:15, NIV). *That's* safe ground—*if it is the Lord's will.'* Therefore I have no map for my life, my family or my ministry that is specific at all, except to say, "Whatever He wants of me… wherever He places me… in His own time" .

God Will Bless My Work, Not My Excuses

"Bless me indeed…" (I Chronicles 4:10 NIV)

A man of *honor*, Jabez boldly asked God to not only *bless* him but "bless me indeed," (I Chronicles 4:10, Paraphrased) i.e., *a lot.*

Is it wrong to ask God to help me—a lot? Or to beg Him to shower me with all the good things He has for those that He loves? Or to fill me up to *overflowing?* Obviously, if you read the Word, it's okay and quite acceptable to God.

However, it's one thing to ask God to make our lives pleasant and another to ask for an easy, luxurious, carefree life. But Jabez was not asking for this—and neither should we. He was asking that God *bless his efforts, prayers, work, attempts and sweat.* God did not bless Noah with an ark—He blessed Noah's work to *build* that ark.

Neither did God cause the temple of Solomon to rise out of nothing; but He blessed the artisans and craftsmen to create a temple that we *cannot imagine* today. God did not bring people of other nations to believe in Jesus Christ just because godly folks prayed in Jerusalem; but He did bless the toil, suffering, and determination of Paul to allow the gospel to overtake the Roman Empire and shake the gates of hell.

No, God is not going to bless my laziness or my dreams as I lie upon my bed, but God **will** bless me as I put my hand to the plow and get about His work. It's incredible what we can accomplish, for His glory and His Kingdom, when we shrug off our lazy excuses, believe in Him and decide that He *is able* to do far more than we can imagine if we dedicate our efforts to Him and trust that He will bless us.

But we have to get out of our cots and put our hands to the plow. God does not bless inaction or lazy excuses. (See the Prayer of Jabez in I Chronicles 4:9-10, NIV)

Loving All His Children

What was the *one command* that Jesus gave His disciples? *That they love one another.* (John 13:34, NIV) And yet 2000+ years later, we are still challenged to be obedient to that solitary command. I tend to love those that love *me,* that are *like* me, that *treat me nice,* that *share my point of view,* and that are… well… "lovable".

But the command was not to love the lovely, or those that were helpful or of the same opinion, but to love the "other" or "one another." Jesus loved the very ones that denied Him, abandoned Him, even the one that betrayed Him. He expects the same of me. But do I really love those kinds of people?

What kind of love is He talking about? The kind of love that would lay down his/her *life* for the other. Jesus used the word the Greek word *agape* to describe this love, the highest love possible. A love that loves regardless if the beloved loves in return. It is a selfless love that wants what is best for the other whether or not the one being loved has any feeling at all for the one that is extending the love. It is the same love that God has for me. I am, in effect, *commanded* to be become a creature of the love that is reflected in God's love.

Of course as I attempt to keep His command, I am at times confronted by the sobering fact that some folks are hard to love (even though I sincerely try). But that is where His Comforter comes to the rescue. If I admit that I am having a hard time loving this or that person, and I humbly admit my need for the Holy Spirit to intercede, I find that I am able to see that soul *differently* than I did before; I begin to see him/her as *God sees that person.* And with that new perception of who they *are,* as well as who they are destined to *become,* I am able to love them as the sister or brother they are.

Oh God! Have mercy on me for only loving those easy to love! Bring the ones that *you have called "beloved"* into my life; those that others have rejected: help me to love them *through you* with the intensity that you have loved me. Give me the grace to see men and women, boys and girls, not as who they are, but more so as you do, *as the objects of love you for which you sacrificed your Son.*

Holy, Holy, Holy

I am struck by how many people immediately fell to their knees when they came to Jesus. These were people who were demon-possessed, pleading for their sick children, aware of their own sin, in need of a savior. But they were not, in my opinion, any less intelligent than modern man. And whereas they were less *educated* in terms of technology and the sciences (perhaps), they were no less astute when it came to the existential matters of life and death. They realized that all men are born and all men will die. What happens *after* death has been debated for thousands of years.

But these people saw Jesus for what He was—a one-of-a-kind, "not of this world," unique man. They might not have been ready to call Him "God in the flesh" but they saw Him do things that *no human being had ever done before.* Even those who were unaware of His miracles were awed by what He *said* ("No man ever spoke like that man" (John 7:46, NIV)… "Surely he was the Son of God" (Mark 15:39, NIV).

And, so when they came to Him they *humbled themselves before Him and pled for His help.* And this, friends, is one thing that I don't see so often in Christian worship today. I am *all for* contemporary music and worship; I love the entertainment found in Christian skits and dramas, and I am fond of Christian comedians. *Anything* whereby the gospel can be communicated to youth that have turned a deaf ear to the traditional means of preaching and worship.

But I fear that we have misplaced or forgotten our proper appreciation, at times, for the Savior and the Father. I am referring to the flippancy with which He is worshipped and spoken of at youth rallies, on Christian radio, by the mega-church pastors and even in traditional church services. *He is holy*—and "wholly other"—and I am neither worthy nor can I make myself worthy—and worship is supposed to be all about *Him.* And I suppose that what burdens me at times with contemporary worship is this question: *Is it* all about Him and are we humbly (figuratively if not literally) falling to our knees when we come to Him?

Personally, I never feel as close and approved by Him as when *I am on my knees praising Him and asking for His mercy.* Do we teach this to our youth, our own children, those who would be leaders in our worship? Or has God's Kingdom become so desperate for workers that nothing is holy and sacrosanct?

His Kingdom is in need of *no one and nothing*, but I am in desperate need of the Son and His kingdom.

Grace

I read some remarks from Dietrich Bonheoffer about "cheap grace" and "costly grace." Any seminarian or pastor is familiar with Bonheoffer and his use of these terms, but the idea of God's grace, which is the love and mercy given to us by God because God desires that we have it, not because of anything we have done to earn it, is something that many of us *do* take for granted. Cheap grace is the preaching of forgiveness without requiring repentance; it's baptism without church discipline; it is grace without discipleship; grace without the cross; grace without Jesus Christ. Costly grace is that grace delivered by Jesus on the cross when He paid for our sins in full. Saint Paul said that, "You were *bought* at a *price*; do not become slaves of human beings." (I Corinthians 7:23, NIV)

As a Christian, my *faith* in God's grace and mercy brought about my salvation, *but my obedience to Him* is the *evidence* of my salvation. If I have truly come to God by faith, my obedience to Him proves it, but if I am disobedient to Him, it is a sure sign that something is terribly missing—i.e. that I have claimed "cheap grace." That's not to say, of course, that no man who follows Jesus would *always obey* Him—none of us are there yet, and neither were Paul or Peter. But it *does* mean that the Holy Spirit is grieved within me when I act in disobedience… and He convicts me of how unbefitting it is. I can be sure of my salvation not because of how "good" I feel, but because of how "bad" I feel when I know I have discounted His work on the cross. Another indication that I have experienced "costly grace" is my acknowledgement that *no one* makes me disobey Him once I have been redeemed; that's a conscious choice I am making and I have no one to blame but myself.

And so, although I have my faults and although I do not always represent Jesus Christ as perfectly as I could and should, I am nonetheless aware that I know Him and I *am* a part of the redeemed. What grieves me are the people that claim faith in Him, but have a total disregard for *obeying Him*, and if pressed on the matter will inevitably blame others for their disobedience or dismiss their disobedience as being of no consequence relative to the sins and disobedience of the *really* bad guys.

Of course that line of thinking is not what a true child of God would exhibit. If I have come to Him by faith, I realize that God's grace *cost Him* the life of His only son and that my acceptance of that grace requires my confession *and* repentance. It is obvious that I have become a new creature when my only human reference, in terms of relative comparison, is Jesus Himself—not some half-hearted churchgoer.

Am I living obedient to what I *know* is right? Are we, as church members and a part of His body, giving evidence that we have received and are living testimonies of God's grace to us? Or have we become slaves to our passions, our habits, and our desires to lift ourselves up?

Four Letters and Five Letters

When I adopted my boys, I was not aware of the new language they would bring into my home. As a boy, I recall the stories of how my older cousin, Dougie, got his mouth washed out with soap by my mother for using a bad word. That story, passed around among my cousins and siblings for aeons, more than anything else caused me to *not* use a bad word. Profanity has never been a part of my vocabulary. But more and more it's not uncommon to hear *a child* use what my folks would have called "dirty" words.

Growing up we called them the "four-letter words." I won't list them, but if you are an adult, or you watch TV, you can probably recite all those four-letter words. As a father, I consider the use of those words to be a crude display of a lack of education, taste, and upbringing. But as I thought about the four-letter words that I won't let my boys use, I thought about something that causes me more consternation than all the four-letter words boys speak: it's the *five*-letter words that can ruin a life. As I lay in bed thinking about those words last week, I was surprised at how many of life's vices are *five letters.* Consider these words and the devastation they bring to life:

- *Money (the worship of it)*
- *Pride*
- *Anger*
- *Greed*
- *Power*
- *Worry*

I have not been able to altogether avoid these vices in my life, and neither will the four young men that live in my home. Our society and our culture *celebrates money, pride, power and greed.* And *worry* and *anger* are common (and mostly accepted) to all men in all societies. There are only two ways to put to death these five-letter words:

1. Dedicate your life to such an ascetic existence that you live apart from society in a cloistered environment that eschews all these desires and expressions; or…
2. Be filed with something that surpasses the desires of money, pride, greed, power and leaves no room for anger or worry.

It is the latter, of course, that represents the abundant life in Christ that is ours… if we choose it. Christ offers this new life to us as we maintain our intimate relationship with Him. You see, it's one thing for me to *make* myself not use profanity, but it's another to live a life where four-letter words serve *no purpose.* Likewise, it's one thing to hide from the five-letter words that *represent the world*, and quite another to be born again and live a life that *represents the new world* (His Kingdom) to come.

My task is to encourage my young men to be different and experience the new life—not merely act different and avoid the old.

Doing the Boring Things

I have noticed that when I travel each year I have less time to roam around the towns and sightsee. I tend to have far more business dinners and meetings to attend. That suits me fine, of course, and I am glad to have a full agenda when I come visit these familiar countries.

However, some days I do desire to pull away from the promises I made to myself (in terms of emails and calls to return) and simply rest on what has been accomplished. But one thing I learned in college was that if I was not first true to myself, I could never expect the same from others. So I began to stop making long lists of things I could not or would not complete, and instead stuck to goals and agendas that I could honor.

I don't consider myself a successful businessman, but I have come to trust myself when I say I am going to do something. This might sound a bit schizophrenic, but what I mean is that I make myself complete things I do not want to do once I put them on my agenda. It's made me happier, regardless of how happy or unhappy it might have made others.

My point is that on some days I may not want to send out the twenty emails on my to-do list, but I have promised myself I would not give up or let up. It seems that I am blessed when I make myself do the things I don't want to do, and the results are sometimes outstanding.

On those outstanding days, I relearn that I like myself more as I do the tough things I promise to do, and refuse to hide behind excuses. Also, I am reminded that while work can be fun, a lot of the time it's just not. That's why we call "work," work.

It has caught my attention that spiritual endeavors are no different from common labor in this regard. If I do what is good and proper for my soul and as a means of honoring God (going to worship on Sundays, praying, reading my Bible, sharing my faith with someone seeking light, even writing one of these devotions) but have an expectation that I must "feel good" about doing it or experience some sort of ecstasy, I will soon be missing church and back-sliding in my relationship with God. There is no immediate gratification for doing "good works" any more than there is immediate gratification for going to the gym to work out.

One reason I give my sons for their daily chores is to instill in them the satisfaction that comes from doing the chore properly. In addition, I hope it gives them discipline, good habits, and then becomes second nature to do what has to be done without whining or whimpering.

Anyone that thinks being a pastor, priest, or Christian camp director is principally about spiritual mountaintops has not lived with one of us very long. The work is often boring and tedious, as all good things are at times, but sticking to it produces a harvest.

How to identify a Christian

"When Paul had finished speaking, he knelt down with all of them and prayed. They all wept as they embraced him and kissed him. What grieved them most was his statement that they would never see his face again. Then they accompanied him to the ship." (Acts 20:36-38, NIV)

It's been said that in the early church, members of the body of Christ could easily be identified by how they loved each other. Throughout the history of the church there are other examples of how this means of recognition continued—and even today. But you don't hear about it as often as you should. It's more common to hear about how Christians are "divided" or worse, how they commonly ignore each other.

Not so in the early church nor in those small communities that dared to live in Christian communion over the past 2000 years. But at least two things are needed for the bond of love to be so great. First, the center of the community cannot be political, or ethnic or the "youth" or protecting the elderly (each have merits, of course). The center must be truly *Christ,* the author of love, Himself. Those *in love with Him* will quite naturally be in love with others—it's unstoppable. But it seems that the modern Christian today looks far too much at humanitarian needs *first* and Jesus Christ, second—and ends up loving neither.

The second need for this bond of love among believers is persecution. And let me quickly say that only an ignoramus would *look* for persecution, yet it seems to me that the church has grown deepest and fastest where it is attacked, made illegal and not kindly regarded. In fact, it's been argued that Christianity might have covered the world had the persecution of the church not ended, to a large degree, in the fourth century.

In the USA, while no one would deny that we have religious freedom, we are mistaken to think that we are *not* persecuted. One need only look at Hollywood, the media (in general) and the manner in which our schools and governments are operated to recognize that an ardent follower of Jesus is treated with less respect and admiration than a nominal follower of Jesus.

So why don't we love each other like these folks loved Paul? Because we're not, by and large, in love with Jesus. We *like* what He says about the sins of others and we are *delighted* that He took our punishment on the cross. But He is not on the thrones of our hearts and we have not abandoned all to Him. The early Christians were paupers for the cause—they gave all they had to follow Him—total abandonment.

When we wake from our spiritual slumber and love as He loved we will be easier to identify in a crowd.

Open My Eyes

"Now for some time a man named Simon had practiced sorcery in the city and amazed all the people of Samaria. He boasted that he was someone great, and all the people, both high and low, gave him their attention and exclaimed, 'This man is rightly called the Great Power of God.' They followed him because he had amazed them for a long time with his sorcery. But when they believed Philip as he proclaimed the good news of the kingdom of God and the name of Jesus Christ, they were baptized, both men and women. Simon himself believed and was baptized. And he followed Philip everywhere, astonished by the great signs and miracles he saw.

When the apostles in Jerusalem heard that Samaria had accepted the word of God, they sent Peter and John to Samaria. When they arrived, they prayed for the new believers there that they might receive the Holy Spirit, because the Holy Spirit had not yet come on any of them; they had simply been baptized in the name of the Lord Jesus. Then Peter and John placed their hands on them, and they received the Holy Spirit.

When Simon saw that the Spirit was given at the laying on of the apostles' hands, he offered them money and said, 'Give me also this ability so that everyone on whom I lay my hands may receive the Holy Spirit.' Peter answered: 'May your money perish with you, because you thought you could buy the gift of God with money! You have no part or share in this ministry, because your heart is not right before God. Repent of this wickedness and pray to the Lord in the hope that he may forgive you for having such a thought in your heart. For I see that you are full of bitterness and captive to sin.' Then Simon answered, 'Pray to the Lord for me so that nothing you have said may happen to me.'" (Acts 8:9-24 NIV)

Peter "judged" this man's heart—at least that's what it looks like if you read about it in the book of Acts. (Acts 8:23-24 Paraphrased). Peter called it like it was; but note that it was not a *personal* attack stemming from jealousy or resentment or an injury to Peter. Peter's anger and incredible resentment toward Simon was because of what Simon represented: the suggestion that we receive gifts from God for *our own glory*. Peter did not suffer gladly those that attempted to take advantage of, or harm the reputation of, the church. I wonder how he would respond to manner in which we preach the gospel from pulpits today? I wonder what remarks he would make to those that announce, "Come worship and join us as you are—anything goes" or "God is happy with you just like you are right now." What would he say to the popular Christian authors whose faces are plastered on the front of their books—always grinning and often suggesting that there's a secret way to succeed and get God's favor"."

Yes, Jesus said, "Do not judge or you will be judged" (Matthew 7:1, NIV).... so what happened here? It seems that there *are* times when God's Spirit does give us the discernment to *see* evil or something "dark" within another and call it for what it is. And *within* the body of Christ we *are required* to call things right or wrong." Pity a society that has *no moral compass of up, down, right, wrong.*

It's risky to assume that you have the spiritual power to see another person's heart to be sure, but this man (Simon) received the rebuke *with the right heart* and he responded by asking for prayer! Peter did a great *service* to Simon by setting him straight! How grateful Simon must have been that Peter had the fortitude to speak out!

Paul's Confrontations - Our Gain

I have spent weeks reading and re-reading Paul's letter to the people of Corinth, Galatia, Ephesus, Philippi and so forth. What struck me for the first time (as is frequently the case as I re-read the bible) was that **all** these letters were written boldly, bluntly, and directly about some things that were wrong in the churches. And as I have read John's three letters and the apocalypse, I am reminded of the same thing. These were letters that were intended to upbraid and chastise congregants in the church—as well as some leaders—for doing the wrong things.

And then it occurred to me: We would not have some of the most beloved, quoted and memorized sentences in the world were it not for the conflicts that were being addressed by Paul and John! The naive, immature things that the early church members did ended up being a blessing to the church.

Now I am not saying this to suggest that we should do doltish things or seek controversy and conflict; peace, harmony, maturity and intelligence are to be desired. *No one* should look for trouble or attempt to stir up the dust for no purpose. But disagreements and conflicts *can* help us to get off our lazy behinds and get back to the primary and basic work as counselors, directors and church members. We are all followers of Jesus, not just men and women who worship a balance sheet or an attendance chart. Paul is the example of one who did not shirk or fade back from boldly pointing out those things that were theologically heretical, or items of Christian fellowship or behavior that were unacceptable and unbecoming.

Sometimes confrontations bring us back to the very place we should never have deserted.

He Really Does Want to Bless Us!

"'Ask and it will be given to you; seek and you will find; knock and the door will be opened to you. For everyone who asks receives; the one who seeks finds; and to the one who knocks, the door will be opened. Which of you, if your son asks for bread, will give him a stone? Or if he asks for a fish, will give him a snake? If you, then, though you are evil, know how to give good gifts to your children, how much more will your Father in heaven give good gifts to those who ask him." (Matthew 7:7, NIV)

- We have to *humble* ourselves and ask—like a child to his father
- We have to *look* if we expect to find it—it takes faith and taking the initiative
- We can't just stand at the door and expect it to be opened unless we knock—it requires action

How will God treat us if we ask, look for, and knock? *Better than our own fathers and mothers.* But do good parents give their children *everything they ask for the very moment they ask for it?* Of course not.

- Sometimes a child is not ready for it—e.g. a nine-year-old child asking, *earnestly and sincerely,* for permission to drive the car.
- Sometimes it is an inappropriate request—God has many, many times told me no, and now as I look back *I thank God with all my heart that He said no. He was right.*
- Sometimes the parent has something better in mind. If I, as a parent take *delight* in doing more for my children than they expect, how much more does God want to bless *me,* His, child, and provide for me over and above my supplications.

Throughout the Bible we are reminded to humbly, innocently and sincerely approach God as a small child gets in his daddy's lap and asks for help. If I am serious about my wants, needs and dreams, I need to climb into His arms and trust Him to do far more than I could imagine… and He will.

Love in the Highest

A friend once asked me how God could be a loving God and yet permit all the heartaches he had experienced in life. I could add to that line of reasoning, "How could God really love us and be so *slow* in responding to our prayers?" Another friend commented recently that it seemed to him as if God enjoyed watching us wait and suffer.

And all of this *is* true if our definition of God's love, or *real love,* is based upon a human, sentimental variety of love. That is, if love means that we *protect* those we love from pain and that we build a hedge around them to guard them from unkindness and hurt, and that we quickly respond to their petitions each time they ask, and that we rarely, if ever, say "no" to what they want—if these things mean love—then God is *not* love. He is something other than love. Actually, if we judge God on our standards of love, He is a very capricious God that seems to pick His favorites to bless and then treats rest of us like unloved stepchildren!

But what if our standards/definition of love is not the same as God's? What if His love is something *beyond our finite little minds to fully understand and can't grasp?* What if His love is, in fact, *a better love* than the one we know and we are *not* showing those we are very close to the best love?

And that, of course, is central to my misunderstanding of, and lack of greater appreciation for, God's love. His love *cannot* be fully grasped until we look at the cross of Jesus. *That* is the ultimate expression of His love—not a new car, or the perfect job or a chest full of gold. Neither are an easy life, excellent health, the ideal marriage/family, and a lack of conflict, expressions of God's love. *The cross is the symbol of His love.* And when I look at the cross I can *begin* to gaze into the very heart of God. Does He love me? Absolutely! Do I know how much? No, I cannot fathom it; I don't fully "get it."

God's love is not about Him doing things for me that make my life easier, nor does His love have to do with Him always giving me what I ask for, or answering my petitions as speedily as I demand or expect. On the contrary, His love is that *intense determination* to make me into the *whole son that He destined me to be me the moment I gave my life to Him.* That intense kind of love *requires* that He often says no to my requests, "not now" to things I think I must have, or, "wait, my timing is perfect." He says to me when I am anxious: "I will rescue you and you will not lose a hair on your head, but wait."

And so I really cannot compare God's love to me for the love that I have for my four boys, or the love I have for my parents or my best friends. But I can begin to love those I love like *God loves,* by saying "no," "not now," or "wait, you are not ready," without fear that I might disappoint the ones I love. I *am* going to disappoint people, annoy people and turn people off if I love them like God loves me. But I am loving them better and in the highest manner possible.

Even the Best of Us Are in Trouble

One of the most common questions I get asked at our home Bible studies from the campers is, "What happens to people that are good but have never heard about Jesus Christ?" Many of them point out that some people are really nice but have not placed their trust in Jesus. What happens to them? It's a great question!

We know that God loves these souls infinitely more than any of us. There are people that might appear to be really, really good when you compare them to me, a corrupt politician, a vain movie star, or a drug dealer. But when compared to God's perfect holiness, they are filthy and corrupt through and through. That's why God sent Jesus.

Solomon spoke 4,000 years ago, "There is no one on earth who is righteous, no one who does what is right and never sins…" (Ecclesiastes 7:20, NIV) Are we better today than the folks of Solomon's time? I don't think so, and in some ways, some of us might be worse. In fact, 2,000 years after Solomon spoke, Saint John said, "If we claim to be without sin, we deceive ourselves and the truth is not in us. If we confess our sins, he is faithful and just and will forgive us our sins and purify us from all unrighteousness." (I John 1:8-9, NIV)

This idea of being sin-free on our own is not a modern idea. Throughout history people have argued that mankind kind is basically good; but that's based on a comparison of really, really extreme examples of bad people (e.g. Hitler, rapists, serial killers) and really poor examples of good people (like billionaires who give away their money or good-hearted people who help the disadvantaged). The only example of good is God, and the only representation we have of God is Jesus Christ. Compared to Him, we're all in a desperate situation.

But something does change when a person comes to God and He opens his/her eyes to just how dirty, corrupt, and off-target he/she is. It produces the gift of tears, because it is then, and only then, that they can contritely say, "Against you, and only you, have I sinned." (Pslam 51:4, NIV) It's both sobering and heart breaking to be brought to the realization of how unlike God we really are and how totally dependent we are upon His mercy. No man or woman that God has allowed to see himself or herself as they really are is inclined to judge another soul, but rather they blurt out to Him, "*Forgive me,* because if I am judged outside of your renewing work in my life, I would be far worse than they are." We're all in need of a Savior – even the best of us.

Feet on the Ground

When I turn to God for an answer, protection, or deliverance, it continues to amaze me that He never responds to my petitions as I expect. It is *always* a surprise how He communicates to me His truth, His words of comfort, and how He sends the encouragement I need—but never like I imagined.

God speaks to me when it pleases *Him;* unexpectedly and through people or events I would never have suspected. That's part of the adventure and romance of my intimacy with Him. I can trust Him to hear me, respond to me, bless me, and protect me; but it's always a bit of a new dance that He teaches me each time.

I am ever learning that His purposes do not always mean I will experience success in the common ways man imagine success. I might have my mind set on how He must deliver me or justify my actions or my well-intended attempts before my brothers and sisters, but He comes and produces something much more far-reaching and incredible than I even dreamt.

When He does intercede, nothing He says, through His servants or means of supernatural revelation, is unknown or unheard to me; it's always something He is showing me that I have forgotten. I am guilty of *spiritual amnesia* and need to be shaken back to reality—His reality—on a regular basis.

Behind every rebuke, and even inside each unkind comment made against me, I am learning to see His hand and I find myself saying, "Speak Lord Jesus." It is never through the kindness of others or the compliments of my friends that I seek the higher ground, spiritually speaking; it is because of attacks or judgments on my motives or being chided for my imperfect attempts in Christian endeavors that I am called to take inventory on *where I am versus where I should be.*

I often see the photos of popular Christian authors on the covers of their books with wide grins, confident stares, smug smiles—some with arms crossed in apparent gesture of being comfortable in their relationship with God. But *for the life of me* I cannot imagine such a cover on the epistles of Paul, John, Peter or James, were they to be published today. If I am to honor Him, I must be forgotten, and Jesus Christ exalted. He allows the reprimands of people (some total strangers) and quite humbling events, to keep me near the foot of the cross and my head out of the clouds.

On Being Lukewarm

"Saul then said to his attendants, 'Find me a woman who is a medium, so I may go and inquire of her.' 'There is one in Endor,' they said." (I Samuel 28:7, NIV)

This is one of the creepiest passages in the entire bible. It represents the desperation of a man living in open disobedience to God. This entire chapter is about King Saul trying to find a witch so that he could find out what was going to happen when he went to battle the next day. He was *terrified of the future...* and he had good reason. He probably had a premonition that he would die in battle... and indeed he did.

Saul had already tried the traditional means of discerning God's will at this time, but when he threw the "urim" and "thurim" stones, he got no answers. (I Samuel 28:6, Paraphrased).The prophets had been driven away by him or were hiding from him, and God was silent when he prayed. His former mentor, the prophet Samuel, was dead. So in desperation he turned to the very ungodly thing he had outlawed and God prohibited—witchcraft.

Initially Saul was a good king, but he was guilty of half-measures; he soon disobeyed God and refused to prohibit some of the things that God told him were evil. But when Samuel confronted him he made excuses and then brooded. What a foolish response! Why not admit it, confess it, repent, and set things right? But wait, why don't I do the same? Why do I find it so easy to condemn the errors of others but yet "understand" my errors and think that they are simply a quirky part of my personality?

Saul drifted farther and farther from God because he would not admit his faults and stop disobeying God; soon he was doing the very things he would have not allowed others to do just a few months earlier. That's the slippery slope of disobedience. You one day find yourself doing things you never would have imagined.

If you read about Saul you will discover that his disobedience was not open defiance, nor was he worshipping Baal or desecrating the Ark of the Covenant. No, his sin was being lukewarm in his devotion to God and obeying God when it suited him and then disobeying him when it was to his personal advantage to things his way. Saul brooded, then schemed, and then made choices that caused God to cut Saul's dynasty off from *ever* ruling Israel. We're all free to choose our actions but we cannot choose the consequences of poor choices—duh.

We need to be careful of people who ignore the word of God and the warnings of God and are then faced with the consequences of their choices... they often become desperate and dangerous. Like someone drowning in a lake; if they get close to you they pull you under with them. Jonathan was a good son, but his association with his dad led to his death, as well as Saul's armor bearer and others.

Saul represents what happens when a good man, a king, chosen by God, gets it into his head that he is above God's laws or that he cannot fall. *Any one of us* could end up just as tragically as Saul.

Dictators and Despots

Every time I pick up the newspaper (or the Bible for that matter) there's always news about a dictator doing something evil. Historically speaking, there are rarely "benevolent" dictators, and more often than not, the longer they rule, the more corrupt, cruel and self-serving they become.

The problem with dictators like Venezuela's Maduro is that because of the depths of their corruption, the blood on their hands and the millions of enemies they have made, it's impossible for them to contemplate stepping down and going into exile. *Somebody* is going to find them and execute delayed judgment for their atrocities, or, worse, the international community will attempt to arrest them and bring them to trial for crimes against humanity. Even if a crony despot gives them safe haven, they're only as safe as that ruler permits and as long as that fellow dictator is in power! After all, his days are numbered as well. (I am using the personal pronoun "his" because I cannot think of one single female dictator in the present or past, Katherine the Great and the queens of antiquity notwithstanding).

Xi, Maduro, Castro (Cuba), Kim (North Korea) and Morales (Bolivia) all face the same dilemma, but then, so does any man. We're all a bit wired to be our own "emperor" or "dictator". By fallen nature *none* of us wants to submit to a higher authority, and today, more so than when I was growing up, youth are unabashedly educated and encouraged to challenge any "final authority" on *any* matter in life. For them, there are *no* absolutes.

The problem with dictators of one's souls and destiny—and we are all in the category of despots until we yield to Jesus Christ—is that try as we might, *we are never in absolute control.* Political dictators surround themselves with sycophants rather than the true friend that will speak honestly; dictators ignore and won't listen to rebukes or any narrative that contradicts their worldview; dictators believe that the only opinion that matters in this *own* opinion. In my lifetime I have never seen this more lived out on American soil than it is right now in our Capitol—what a sorry mess.

We might not be *individually* national despots, but all us are quite capable of being *spiritual* tyrants of our own destinies. We are all at risk of facing the ultimate consequence of tyranny—*judgment.* But then, that's why Jesus Christ came wasn't it?…to save me from *me own tyranny*….to save each of us from our own ultimate destiny as little despots. And as most of you know, I am committed to sharing the gospel at a summer camp with kids that are usually 21 years old and younger. But there's a good reason I feel that I have been called to this. Nearly *half* of all Americans who accept Jesus Christ as their savior do so before reaching the age of 13; two *out of three* born again Christians made that commitment to Christ before their 18th birthday; but only *one out of eight* born again people made their profession of faith while 18 to 21 years old. Once you're past 21, the chances are you will *never* come to Jesus Christ—the dictator is too firmly established by that time to yield to another Master.

The first sin recorded in the Bible was the sin of an angel that has become the archetype of tyranny—Lucifer, aka Satan. His temptation is upon each of us to be independent of God and to "create our own destiny" (as if that were possible). If history has taught us anything, it has taught us that the *longer* a man is a dictator, the *less likely* he is to humble himself and give his throne to someone else. The same is true spiritually speaking to the little despot within each of us. It's far easier to lead a child to the King of Kings and have that child trust Him than it is an adult.

Who Am I Trying to Impress?

"And when you fast, do not look gloomy like the hypocrites, for they disfigure their faces that their fasting may be seen by others. Truly, I say to you, they have received their reward." (Matthew 6:16, NIV)

Have you ever done something very special for someone you love—but only because you love them? Something that you and *only* the one you loved knew about? It creates a very special bond.

In the home I had that was destroyed by fire, there were many special items that had value to me because they were gifts given to me by special people: a smooth stone, a cross necklace, a Confederate $100 bill, a simple soap dish—worthless to most people but special to me because of the one that gave it to me.

Fasting is not the point of this passage but rather, what we *do* for God, secretly, because we love Him; that is the point. It's the secret things we do for Him, with Him, and the things that He does for us in secret that make the difference and that create the unbreakable bond and establish a dynamic relationship.

Fasting was practiced by the early Christians and Jesus *assumed* that His listeners would continue that discipline. It's a *good* thing. Denying the body what it *demands* and taking control over our appetites and instincts is a positive step in Christian sanctification. But Jesus' point was clear: Why are you fasting? For the adoration and admiration of others, or as an act of love and obedience to the One you love the most?

He goes on to talk about our appearance. Do we dress and groom ourselves to suggest we really *are* very godly, or do we *live lives that prove it*? It's much easier to fast and look like you are suffering for Jesus than to do it secretly, silently and resolutely. And yes, you will thereby encounter criticism, slander, and hateful accusation as you attempt to live for Him.

This represents a very simple and basic question: When you fast, or pray, or give money to charity or do any outwardly spiritual act, are you doing this out of concern for what you want people to think about you, or because it is a natural outflow of your affection and genuine adoration for Him?

Do I really *love* Him… or am I craving the admiration of others? If I really love Him I might find myself quite unpopular with humanity. If I want to impress and please others, the Christian life is *not* the best choice. But if I want to impress and please God, there is no other choice.

Las Vegas Murders

One of the worst mass shooting in U.S. history took place in Las Vegas recently. Over 60 people died and hundreds were wounded. I heard responses all day long from commentators on the radio, TV, social media, etc. Each opined about what *really* caused this to happen (lax gun-control, the NRA, congressmen, President Donald Trump). I don't mean to get political in these musings, but it appears that the folks in the media seem to think we're pretty oafish regarding what causes these things to happen. They're determined to find a cause that will allow them to attack an idea that does not sit well with their understanding of how the world ought to be.

One thing I have come to appreciate, as a follower of Jesus Christ, is that *no opinion or creed or political agenda* can undermine my faith, nor should it cause me to doubt my relationship with Him. Therefore, I can hear any cockamamie idea and not get my dander up. And *you* can believe anything you want and it should not cause me to attack you or treat you with any less compassion and gentleness than if you thought *exactly* like I do.

It occurs to me that I can say this for one reason: "*I know in whom I have believed and am persuaded……*" (II Timothy 1:12, NIV) It seems to me that those who get upset with folks that don't agree with them do so because they are *not* persuaded of what they claim to believe. Why should I care if you swear that 2 + 2 = 5 when I know quite well that it does not? Only if I were *unsure* of my math would I be tempted to get angry. Jesus never had verbal fights or personal attacks against those that railed against Him. *He knew the truth and was not agitated by those who did not.*

What was not said in the media was that this lone assassin did an *evil thing and that evil is ever present in our world.* His senseless murders remind me that this world is *not* heaven on earth… it's a dangerous place that is rife with evil. The word we don't use much from pulpits and editorials is *sin*. This event was sin incarnate, a man acting *against* God's command that we love one another. His sin snuffed out dozens of people's opportunity to know Him (if they did not already) or share their love of God with others.

Naturally, we will be told that he was "mentally ill," but it is the "spiritual illness" that will cause such senseless suffering to occur again, and again, and again. I am not sure about the cure for mental illnesses, but I do know the cure for spiritual illness… it's Jesus Christ. And until we recognize that it is the *spiritual sickness and dementia* of our nation that is causing horrific suffering and destruction, we are apt to see even more evil.

I pray for those that are spiritually ill to come to know Him, His forgiveness and the depth of His love—as well as for those who are grieving all over our country.

A Servant, Not a Boss

"Unless the Lord builds the house, the builders labor in vain. Unless the Lord watches over the city, the guards stand watch in vain. In vain you rise early and stay up late, toiling for food to eat—for He grants sleep to those He loves." (Psalm 127:1, NIV)

This verse kind of puts life into perspective. Why do some of us work harder and rise earlier than others? Why do some of us, usually the same people, often lose sleep worrying about our work, our time, and our sacrifice? I can attest that I work and rise early, and regrettably, I worry at times because of a preoccupation with my personal hopes and dreams. I understand that men are capricious and their affections can turn on a dime. Thus, whom can I trust? I also know that regardless of how long and hard I work, disasters, mishaps, and other bad things can happen. In my own little business, I can think of over a dozen things that could go wrong and ruin all that I've worked so hard for.

The Psalmist knew these *same* things, but he also learned that unless God is the architect and master planner of life, all our endeavors and enterprises are in vain. He keenly understood that God is the only true insurance and security and he rested in that fact.

Nothing is wrong with hard work, rising early, and toiling beyond the normal hours of others. In fact, there's a lot to be said about the dangers of not working diligently and with your whole heart—don't get me started on that! But I can be encouraged that if my work is solely for Him, His glory, and as He has planned, He will provide a place and a setting of His choosing for me to rest. It seems that it is only when we get ahead of Him, and think that we must make things happen, that we get frantic, out-of-sorts, and exhausted.

My purpose in Christ is to be so connected to Him and His kingdom's work that I stop seeing my work as *my work,* and instead see myself as His servant and my work as an offering to Him. This will surely divorce me from the megalomania that plagues so many leaders and bosses. But danger still exists for those who are dedicated to God's work because the human tendency is to worship the *work* instead of Him who commissioned the work. A routine evaluation of priorities is essential in this life.

My Son's Hero

The oldest boy in the house recently helped our nine-year-old in a remarkable way. The older boy is in college and likes his "space"; he keeps his room locked up to keep the younger boys out and in general maintains his privacy. He prefers to do his own thing on the weekends and at night and does not interact much with us during the week. But this time it was different. The elder son offered to spend two hours with the middle boy, and *it made the little man's day.* He was excited about it no matter what it was. It turned out that older son took the nine-year-old on a "basic training" regimen of running, sprinting, performing 200 sit-ups, calisthenics and weight lifting. The younger son never whined, complained, or asked for less. The older boy became my nine-year-old's *hero;* spending time doing *anything* with him was better than going to McDonald's for a Happy Meal. Yes, I was proud of younger son's determination to hold up for two hours of working out (he's not a very big nine-year-old) but I cannot properly elucidate the pride I take in older brother's forbearance and investment in younger boy's life. As I write these sentences I am still astonished that he gave so much energy and preparation into helping the little brother. He might forget about it, but the younger son will not. His hero became all—and more—than he ever imagined.

The youngest stayed with me all day that day but begged me to do with him what the other two brothers were doing. I could not because of phone calls, emails, and preparing dinner. But the youngest was with me the entire time, and after all was done I sat down to read the newspaper. The youngest, who cannot yet read, sat across from me, put on his glasses and took an old copy of a *WSJ* and attempted to read for the entire thirty minutes I read. He watched me fold the paper, drop a section when I was finished, and strained to understand what he was looking at. He mimicked my every action.

The elder son has become the example for these two young boys, just as I had hoped he would be. Honestly, my heart swells up in pride because his selfless investment in the young lives of these boys. *Eyes are upon us.* These boys watch *everything* and copy us! I am not yet at the place Saint Paul was when he encouraged folks to "follow my example" (I Corinthians 11:1, NIV) but I am aware that the boys *will* follow my example whether I request them to or not. What an opportunity in discipleship… but what a danger if the eldest son or I get sloppy, lazy, or indifferent in our walk.

It appears that as follower of Jesus I must accept the reality that people do copy us. And some might be inclined to copy my worst habits or attributes. God help me to be Holy….

The Big Lie

Today David seemed to be speaking to directly to me when he recorded in, "Cast your cares on the Lord and he will sustain you; he will never let the righteous be shaken." (Psalm 55:22, NIV)

The great thing for me to remember about verses like this, is that when I read them and choose to believe that they are as true for me as they were for David, I must also consider the condition of the heart of the one that wrote those words. When David said this he *believed it* because he was living a life that *was* pleasing to God, and he *was* humbly seeking God's favor.

I have seen that it is when I am obedient and humbly seeking Him that my faith increases, and conversely when I am avoiding Him or am prideful, my faith is diminished. There is a correlation between my confidence in His provision when I am obeying Him and how that obedience increases my faith—one leads to the other.

It's not that God is unable to give me all that I want or that He is conserving His resources. His pantry is inexhaustible! Yet I often pray about things cautiously, as if I might be taxing His ability to provide. If I am seeking to live a righteous life and humbly admit to Him my needs, *He will sustain me every single time—my cup will overflow.*

But let me confess that though I *profess* this to be true, and though I have *experienced* this to be true, I also suffer from doubts about what will happen *this* time around. I know it sounds absurd, but the enemy is ever trying to convince me that *this time* God might not be in the mood to help me, or perhaps that I have committed some "forgotten" sin that He intends to bring to light by allowing me to be defeated or humiliated, or that He wants to toughen me up by letting me endure incredible heartache and loss. You get the idea: Satan wants me to believe that *God cannot be trusted to look after me all the time.* That is the big lie that I fight. But I have found it helpful to ignore the taunts of the enemy and remind him (Satan) that he is where he is because he misjudged God in the first place.

My Father *is able* to care for me; He has called me His own; He sent His Son to secure my redemption (and many others) who would call Him Lord and Savior. If I am shaken, it's not God's doing—it's because of my short memory. He has always been there for me.

Hanging on every word

"Jesus was teaching at the temple every day, but the chief priests, scribes, and leaders of the people were intent on killing Him. Yet they could not find a way to do so, because all the people hung on His words." (Luke 19:47, NIV)

His enemies could *not* find a way to discredit Him because He *meant* what He said; He spoke with *integrity,* and *knew* what He was talking about.

I think about this when I offer vespers during the summer or preach on Sundays. Normally I talk for no more than five minutes because I appreciate the example of Jesus. Consider that He:

- did not waste His words
- did not chase rabbits!
- did not ramble, embellish or talk about Himself incessantly
- always had something *meaningful and profound* to say!

How many times during the day do I fail to communicate so nobly and responsibly? In Jesus' time the same folks that were guilty of babbling prayers and savoring the attention of the crowds with oratory—the same leaders of Jesus' time who spoke in haste and in arrogance and pride *knew* better than to silence someone like Jesus in front of a crowd. After all, the people were for once paying attention to a religious figure! Oh, that God would raise more men and women like this in America—and particularly in Washington, DC.

I get the idea that when Jesus spoke there were no personal anecdotes or references to His family, upbringing, or personal victories. He did *not* speak to impress people with His wit or accomplishments, but instead spoke about His *Father,* His *Father's* Kingdom and how His *Father* expected His children to treat each other. I cannot imagine that He told a joke or that He spoke a *second* longer than He needed. He spoke, in my opinion, with an economy of words and spoke with both *purpose and authority.*

Do I? How much time do I waste just gabbing or talking about things that do not matter or don't need to be addressed? How often am I just looking for a chance to show folks just how much how smart and informed I am? Do I really command attention when I speak because it's become my reputation to only speak when I know what I am talking about and to only speak truth?

And what about *your* priest or pastor? Some folks in the pulpit do speak, but *no one is listening.* Why? Because the one delivering the message *does not compel us to hang on every word.* There's either too much being said to win the approval (or laughter) of the listeners, or too little being said about the *Father,* or the one speaking lacks the credibility to be taken seriously. I pray that I am found to be worth hearing…

But here are the words for today, simple and short:

1. For those of us who know Jesus Christ as our Lord and Savior: We must obey His one command, that we love one another—it's a decision, not a feeling.

2. For those who are not yet a part of His family, know that God loves you, that Jesus died on a tree for you, that God miraculously raised Jesus, His Son, back to life to prove to the world that He is able to give us life eternal. He requires that we admit our sins, turn from our sins, believe that God raised Jesus, His only Son, from the grave, and trust that our sins have been removed eternally because of Christ's death on the cross.

This is good news worth listening to.

God's Precision

The single most frustrating thing about raising my sons is to get them to do their chores *well*. I have had lengthy and laborious lectures about the virtues of doing work with excellence, but my boys look at me as I have two heads on my shoulder when I tell them that doing the job right will make them "feel good" about themselves. Somehow we have conditioned children and youth to believe that as long as someone "does their best", it's okay if it falls short of excellence. But that logic falls short, of course, in practical life if you get a prescription wrong, or make a bad calculation on the design a bridge, or get the temperature wrong on the dinner you're cooking. No, doing things correctly, the first time, is quite frankly, intelligent, time saving and godly.

I was reading the book of Ezekiel recently and was astounded at all the details God prescribed about the dimensions of temple, the new city of Jerusalem, the altar, etc. God gave *very* precise instructions in the Bible. He made very specific measurements and was crystal clear about colors, the kind of wood to be used and so on. Consider: Noah' s ark; Genesis 6:13-22 ; the Ark of the covenant; Exodus 25:10; 37:1-9; the first temple that was built by Solomon in 2 Chronicles 2; God's commandments to His people in Exodus chapters 20-24. The regulations are precise and thorough. There are no "insignificant details" with God.

He cares about things being done right and with precision; He *knows* and cares when a sparrow falls to the ground! Mathew 10:30 (NIV) tells us that He even knows the number of hairs on our head.

God gives such precise measurements because it is His *nature* to do things exactly and correctly the first time with no margin for error, and perhaps to remind us that He not only *knows* every detail of our lives, but *cares* about every detail. Jesus told us this so that we wouldn't need to be afraid—God knows, cares and His arm is not too short or His stamina lacking. In short, with such an exacting God we have *nothing* to fear.

But what about you and me? How about our work and our thoroughness? There's no mistaking that He expects excellence from me. We are reminded that, "Whatever you do, work heartily, as for the Lord and not for men, knowing that from the Lord you will receive the inheritance as your reward. You are serving the Lord Christ." (Colossians 3:23-24, NIV) . In Ecclesiastes 9:10 (NIV), we're told, "Whatever your hand finds to do, do it with your might, for there is no work or thought or knowledge or wisdom in Sheol, to which you are going.". "So, whether you eat or drink, or whatever you do, do all to the glory of God." (1 Corinthians 10:31, NIV)

So what's my excuse for slovenly work or for not taking Godly pride in my work? Do I think it does not matter, or that doing it excellently is a task I can now avoid or simply put off? The Bible is *full* of counsel to explain the best way to live and how to enjoy a life that's pleasing to Him. My destiny is to be one with Jesus Christ in my mind-set, habits and the manner in which I do those tasks God places in my life. That requires that I give attention to all that I do, not only as a service to God, but because if has become, or is fast becoming, my nature to do work like my Father does. My sons are watching me—what I do and how I do it is the greatest sermon I will ever preach.

The Mind of Christ

We talk about having the mind of Christ, but how often, and with how many people, do you *see* the mind of Jesus Christ being lived out? Another saying of our time is, "What would Jesus do?" Again, do people see *in my life,* my living and doing as He would have? Can my family and friends look at me and honestly say, "He did just what Jesus would have done in the same situation."

-Forgive as *He* forgave. So why is that so hard for us to do? Why do we threaten to "forgive but not forget"? Aren't we glad God does not constantly remind us of our past indiscretions?

-Hold on like *He* held on. So why does common thinking, among Christians, suggest that we need to "let go" and not let someone else "drag us down"? Yes, yes, you can *enable* a person to live a compromised and sad life by not practicing "tough love," but never does God let go of our hand, no matter how irresponsible and naïve we may live.

-Invest in others like *He* has invested in me. But why do I we seek for others to invest in me but hesitate to support anyone that will not, in some manner, turn out to be a "good investment" in terms of how it comes back to benefit me?

The answer to all three of these questions is found in the *Christian* understanding of love. It is because I do not *love* others as He has loved me that I have a tough time acquiring the mind in these matters. It's love, and *only* love, that allows me to have a sustained heart of mercy, compassion and empathy to those that continually let me down, break my heart and take from my wallet.

It is impossible to find that we have exhausted God's love and it is impossible for His love within me to become worn out if my love is *established in Him*. But if that love is counterfeit or of a sentimental sort, I will soon succumb to the worldly counsel of telling people, "enough is enough," when they let me down, disappoint me or commit acts I disapprove of. I will simply cut them off and turn them out of my life—that's the way of the world. *But praise be to God, it's not the way of God or the disciple of Jesus Christ.*

Saint John Allen Chau

Many might recall the death of a young man named John Allen Chau. He was 26- year-old missionary killed on the North Sentinel Island (near India) by natives. As of right now, years later, his body is still buried on the beach of that little island, slowly decaying away. *No one* protested that he was murdered. No one seems upset that nobody has had the decency to recover his body for his family. The Indian Government announced today that they would *not ever* recover the body.

The problem is that John was a *Christian missionary* and he was illegally attempting to tell some non-believers of Jesus' love for them. So the common thinking seems to be (if you read every newspaper I've read), he kind of had it coming by going over there. There is *widespread* support for the Indian government's determination to allow these natives to remain untouched and uncorrupted by "civilization" (whatever that means). To most folks (at least all that are writing in the media) these people are better off *without hearing about Jesus' love and how He came to save them from hell*. Now why in the world isn't anybody reporting the obvious media bias *against* the Christian faith?

Why is no one *celebrating* the sacrifice of this young Christian *martyr*? He was brutally *murdered* for attempting to offer the good news of salvation to 100 or more souls and save them from *eternal separation from God*. Right? Do *you* believe that? Or do you think that these ancient people are really pretty good compared to other religious folks and if there *is* a heaven, they're probably going to be there anyway? If you think *that* way, you must be a reporter for the *New York Times*, because you *cannot* believe in the gospel and accept such nonsense.

The errors and abuses of missionaries in the past notwithstanding, the idea that civilization is somehow the enemy of a people that murder a slender, young, unarmed man is ludicrous. Saint Paul and the other apostles *broke the law and were executed* for their faithfulness to their savior. How is this young man any different?! It's shameful that this young man is not being recognized as a hero to his faith.

Count me as one of the cranks that believe the bible is the authentic, reliable and final word from God on man's depravity ("man" would certainly include these natives) and man's need of a savior. Christ died to save the savage as well as the polished and sophisticated.

In truth, it seems that a whole lot of Christendom does not believe that one must profess with their mouth that Jesus is Lord and believe in their heart that Jesus was raised from the dead. No, all you have to do is live like a savage and you will naturally avoid hell and go to heaven. Good grief. Read Romans 10:9.

God bless the memory of John Allen Chau. I have *no doubt* that others will come to Christ because of his sacrifice.

A Friend of Tax Collectors

"Now the tax collectors and sinners were all gathering around to hear Jesus. But the Pharisees and the teachers of the law muttered, 'This man welcomes sinners and eats with them.'" (Luke 15:1-2 NIV)

Once again, Jesus turns common teaching and behavior on its head. It was the sinners, not the religious, who were paying close attention to Him. It was the sinners, those headed to hell, who wanted to be close to Him, eat with Him and wash His feet—and who would die for Him.

Now why is that? Why were the bad folks wanting to be close Jesus and the good folks keeping their distance? Well, for one thing, He was kind to the bad people! They weren't used to that. They were accustomed to having religious folks ignore them or cross over to the other side of the street when they saw them coming. The good folks treated them like trash, reprobates or untouchables. But Jesus was different. He treated them as if they were worth the attention. In fact, He came to die for them.

Jesus also *listened to the bad folks—and He still does!* But how often *do I* listen to a beggar or a drunk or someone that's homeless? Is there anything kinder than to simply listen—and anything more inhumane than to ignore? Jesus *heard their pleas for help* and He *responded!* And He still hears and responds—praise be to God.

Jesus was also different in that He did not judge their hearts—as a future witness to you and me as to how we treat liberals, conservatives, socialists or communists! We cannot know where that person has been or what they've experienced. But *no one* wakes up one day and decides that they want to be poor, or a drug addict or felon (or a Democrat or Republican). It happens, over time, for a multitude of reasons.

These sinners were ignored and jeered by the righteous people and they never expected much from them. But then Jesus came, broke all the rules and by-passed all expected norms of behavior. May God use you and me to break the same rules and not "fit in."

Jesus came to become a friend of sinners, save them, and call them brothers and sisters. There's no other means by which *I* could have entered into His Kingdom. He came to the earth looking for people like me—folks who were in need of a hero, a friend, a protector and redeemer.

That's what I want to share to fellow sinners. Jesus loves you, hears, you, wants to be near you and He understands.

Have Your Own Way, Lord

I realize that sometimes my devotions must sound as if I were whining about how tough my life is, when in fact I am quite blessed and have little reason to ever complain. But I *have* experienced bathos and pathos in my life, and as I grow closer to the time that I will *not* be here, I am conscious of how He has ordained certain things to happen, for His good purposes, and how I have oftentimes *interfered* with His holy purposes. I am far too small and insignificant to stop God's hand from moving through history—I am keenly cognizant of this. But sometimes I find that I am my own worst enemy in the things He is trying to establish in *my life*. The very things my heart *truly desires* are often denied me because I chase after more base trophies.

This year He seems to be *removing* people from my life that I once counted on for support, friendship and to share my burdens. It's not that they are no longer my friends, but they seem to have been stripped away from me nonetheless—for various reasons—and I am in less contact with them than ever. The end result, of course, is that I find myself leaning more upon Him and seeking His company far more often than I normally did. I *needed* to have some of these influences removed.

He has also brought an end—or at least a revision—to some of my dreams and utopian hopes on this earth. That's not to say I don't see what I do (at our youth camp) as any less of a vision than it was decades ago, but some of the things I imagined and hoped for have been replaced for something more ethereal. I realize that it is for the Kingdom of God that I thirst, hunger, envision and dream—and I will never be truly satisfied until I am there with Him.

And finally, He has removed many things that at one time represented for me security, meaning and purpose. These were all, in and of themselves, *good things*! But the things I once reached for to provide meaning in my life I now see as illusory. It is in Him and *only Him* that I find safety, purpose, and meaning.

We sing songs about God having His way in our lives, and we recite Psalms about God being our Shepherd, but I wonder how many of us really are prepared to allow the God that loves us to have complete control. It's far more liberating than I realized.

Meaningless or Ultimate Meaning

As I read Ecclesiastes over two weeks recently, I was reminded again and again how truly *meaningless* all of my hurrying about is, as well as virtually *all* that I do when contrasted with the universe, eternity and the mere vapor of time that my life represents. The authors of the bible recognized this long before modern-era philosophers considered it. Life truly is without purpose and meaning when I consider how brief it is and how all my work is really merely a scratch on paper in terms of human history.

Solomon understood this, but he also understood that in his relationship with God—who is *absolutely meaningful and eternal*—life takes on a different intensity and utility. If He truly is God eternal, and if He truly does love me and call me *His own child,* then what I do not only matters *greatly*, it also echoes throughout the universe. I mean to say: if I matter so much to God that He suffered His one and only *begotten* Son to undergo humiliation, torture and execution for me, my life takes on a more profound existential significance. Obviously, I am more than a mere vapor.

It might appear that I have too much time on my hands as I ponder such things, but *if* my life really matters (to God), should I not, as Solomon suggests more than once, remember that "whatever your hand finds to do, do it *as unto the Lord?*" (Ecclesiastes 9:10, NIV)

More and more I find myself less satisfied with myself when I do something shoddily or incompletely. Sometimes I can't go to bed till I finish, excellently, the small project I began in my home. Yes, that might merely mean that I am OCD, but it might also mean that I am taking to heart the fact that *I matter because God has said so.*

And if I matter… if I am going to live forever… if what I do and say echoes into eternity… Perhaps I should take life and my short time remaining here quite soberly and with an appreciation for my opportunities to make my mark.

Is There a Time to Get Angry?

Is there a time to get angry and is it wrong to *not* be angry when certain things happen? Lately I think I am getting something backwards. I find myself very angry at my anger at the wrong things, and *not* angry at the right things.

The Bible tells us to "In your anger do not sin": Do not let the sun go down while you are still angry," (Ephesians 4:26, NIV) I tell my boys, "I don't need anger management, you boys just need to stop making me angry!" There are over a 100 billion nerves in the human body, and there are four people who have the ability to irritate *all* of them, and they *live* with me under the same roof.

So how can I know when to walk away from anger or jump into it? When do I show my disgust and rage and when should I measure my resentment and disapproval?

I've heard moms and dads often tell their small children just how *cute* they are when they get mad, to which a precocious four-year old little girl once quipped, "Well, you're about to see me turn gorgeous!" What are we teaching kids about anger—and how to show it?

What gets most of us mad?

> Being:
> laughed at
> patronized
> wrongly accused
> slandered
> ignored
> treated as an inferior

Self-control is a gift of the Holy Spirit—but that gift can be over-ridden if I am not connected to the Vine *all day long*. But this does not mean we can't or should not get upset at times. Anger is something that God Himself shows and that Jesus displayed, and *never* getting angry probably means that you've given up, don't care, see no solution; you're simply indifferent. Anger can drive us to abolish things that are evil and fight things that will never surrender until they are destroyed, and it can teach our children that there *is* right and wrong in the world that there *is* a time to burn with anger."

The therapists give us no help by failing to see that anger is not always a bad thing or something to suppress or avoid. The purpose of "good" anger is not meant to calm me down or make me feel better about myself. It is a God-given emotion that can inspire me to do the things that need to be done. It's discernment that I need. Not suppression.

No Regrets

Yesterday I had the honor of saying goodbye to an older friend that passed away a few hours later. He was one of the first people I met when I came to this mountain thirty-four years ago…. he has remained a steadfast friend for all those years.

I learned yesterday that he once guarded Adolf Hitler's top officials right after the fall of Berlin—yet he never talked about it to me until yesterday. But such was his generation—they didn't brag or toot their own horns. I am sure my friend had his flaws, but I was unaware of them. He remained faithful to one wife his entire life, raised a son and was constantly near to his three grandchildren and attended the same little church for as long as anyone can remember.

What struck me most about this neighbor was how quickly he volunteered to help someone in need. Again, his help was always unannounced and he acted as if it were a natural thing to do to help a neighbor—not a special expression of friendship, but rather the *only thing that a normal neighbor would do.*

As I talked to him yesterday and as I held his hand and prayed for him, I found it remarkable that the man had no regrets, no desires to correct something before he passed and no bitterness. Ah, to live to 80+ years and look back at your life and have *no regrets!*

Two other acquaintances passed away this week and my own mortality was brought to my mind. What will I leave behind? What will be remembered of me? Will the room be poorer because I no longer enter into it? Or will it be a more relaxed place? What things that I said (in anger, in jest, sarcastically, or in love) will be repeated? What will people miss about me—if anything?

The last thing my father said to me was, "I'm sorry" and the last thing I said to him was, "It's okay, don't worry about it." Praise be to God, our conversation was not an argument or an angry word or some past peccadillo resurrected! Truly, I do *not* want to be remembered for all my blunders, or all the harsh things I said at the wrong time and in the wrong way, or the things that I did *not* say, but should have said.

And so today I have been a bit more circumspect about what I say, how I say it and my facial expressions (which the seven-year-old *quickly picks up on)* and I am remembering my friend who lived a life with no regrets. I still have time to mend some fences and I can determine to leave behind a legacy that could be emulated rather than avoided.

When Business Gets in the Way of Ministry

Today was one of those days that I got *nothing* accomplished. That's not to say that I did not work or "do" something, but my agenda and plans where shot because of interruptions, surprises, visitors, unexpected problems with our on-line bank and every imaginable hurdle to me keep me from getting the things done that I felt should or "had" to do.

But now it's the end of the day and I am writing this little essay. Yes, I missed my workout, I did not answer every email and I did not return each phone call. I did not attain my personal goals with the ministry and I failed to take care of all the "punch list" of daily items. But I *did* prepare and feed the boys their dinner; we had a family devotion; I meet several guest visitors (twelve today); I shared the good news about God's love on two occasions; I prayed for those that called or emailed me for intercession and I kept my promises. But even then, I *wanted* to accomplish and complete more and I felt the poorer for not doing so.

Days like today are important, because they remind me that I am not the master of the day—things will happen that I did not expect and I need to be ready, in mind and heart, to not lose my wig when my little apple cart gets turned over. It's surprising to me that it is on days like this that I find myself doing more *ministry*—even though I am accomplishing less for the very *business* that makes this ministry possible.

What strengthens me in these "do nothing" days is the conviction that He is watching over me and is both aware of my frustration for not being able to work longer, more productive hours, but also of how *I know* that today's lack of meaningful accomplishments is nonetheless pleasing to Him. He knows that *I know* that it was His hand that upset my well-laid plans and caused me to lose my footing in my work, and yet maintain my certainty that He would be pleased with the end result. Ultimately, "some may trust in chariots, some in horses, but I trust in God." (Psalm 20:7, NIV)

And so tonight I have no idea of what lies before me tomorrow, but I do know that I gave my best today—even though I failed to reach the goals I set. He knows this...*He knows this!* And either He is a kind and gracious God that has compassion on frail children, like me, that are sincerely trying to honor Him, or He is an impersonal, indifferent, despot of a God—and Jesus Christ misrepresented Him. But of course, I know that the former is the case...and so I can sleep in peace tonight. He called me for a good purpose—regardless of how complicated and seemingly meaningless a day might appear, from time to time.

The Christians and Work

When I read in the Bible about a command or advice on what *not* to do, I realize that it was written because people were *doing* the very thing that was being condemned. Else while would the author have recorded that warning? That being said, it's obvious that some of the early Christians were just as lazy as Christians today. But it is instructive to consider the manner in which certain sins or errors were confronted by the apostles and Jesus Himself, as opposed to how we confront sin today.

Sometimes it seems that we are so careful to avoid hurting feelings that we do more long-term damage to people and the church than good. What strikes me in particular is our hesitation to talk in to children and youth about the four-letter word: *work.*

To some, the chief goal of man is comfort, pleasure, and relaxation. But in the New Testament it's made clear that we are to *work.* Even before the fall of mankind, man (Adam) worked—it's never looked upon as an evil or undesirable burden on man, but a positive and good thing. It's one of those things that actually draws us closer to our Creator. *God works.*

But in the early church some folks were taking advantage of the generosity, kindness, and brotherly love of the church by simply not working and enjoying the benefits of being a member of the body of Christ. Paul's words to those that did not work were bold and unflinching: *If you don't work, you don't eat.*(II Thessalonians 3:10, NIV) Imagine a camp or church or society that said that to its staff or members? That group would be following *basic* Christian principles. The ideal Christian community is comprised of people that work—there's no place for loafing around.

Paul commented to Timothy: "Now if anyone does not provide for his own relatives (that is, if he is not working for a living") he has denied the faith and is worse than an unbeliever." (I Timothy 5:8, NIV) Pretty tough words.

Paul was both being pragmatic and touching something that is essential for Christian growth—we must work if we want to *live,* and we must work if we want to experience the full *blessing* of a redeemed life. We were *created* to lead productive lives. If we don't work, we become idle and it makes room for the enemy to create discord and offers perverted alternatives—that's what he is good at. He takes good things like computers, iPads, cell phones, sports, TV and turn them into idols for us to worship.

Working throughout your life is what God intends. Getting your hands dirty and soiled is a *godly thing.* For his first 30 years, God's own Son learned to work as a carpenter—with His own Holy hands. If God found it beneficial in Christ's development to cause Him to labor, why do we shield *our* children and youth from work? Why do we allow ourselves and our children to avoid laboring, sweating or getting tired from the toil? If God Himself rested after creation, why is not proper for us to work so hard that *we* are tired and need to rest?

We are fighting a spiritual battle where the Divine One compels us to work and the enemy tempts us to avoid work at all costs. The enemy tells us to let someone else do the chores, pick up the trash, clean up the mess, work the long hours—better for us to eat, drink and be merry. But *work* allows Him who loves us to pour into us His joy and peace and sense of purpose that we can never enjoy by being lazy. The happiness we think we have by being lazy is a very poor substitute for the fulfilled life God wants us to enjoy.

A Christian community should expect all that are able to work, to work, and we should be teaching children and youth that work is good.

Do You Promise to Come Back?

I had to leave my home tonight for a two-hour meeting. As always, there was a major emotional meltdown with one of the younger boys. He begged to come with me, cried, pouted, threw a tantrum, screamed, and yelled. You name it … he did it. But I have never, not once, surrendered to his demands. Why does he do this?

Again, I was only gone for a couple of hours, but you would have thought I was being led to a firing squad by the way he behaved. Finally, thirty minutes later, he was exhausted, apologized, hugged me, asked once more if he could go with me, and then asked me if I would promise him that I would come back. That was the issue. Whether I would come back for him.

The boys that live in my home, my newly adopted sons, have on five occasions (and one boy on ten occasions) had their biological, step, or foster parents leave the house and never return. These boys have been fooled many times by adults that promise to come back but never do. Being placed in five and ten foster homes has broken their hearts more than once, and they are hoping that I won't break them again. It's heartbreaking for to think of it.

Whereas my oldest seems to have real fears that I might *never* die, the younger three live in anxiety each time I leave the house that something might happen to me and they will be placed in another home. God, please keep me alive until these boys are each able to live on their own and come to know the warmth of your all-encompassing love!

When I returned home there was great happiness and excitement from the younger ones (the older boy is far too "cool" to show his approval of my return). But I would dare say that the youngest was waiting in great anticipation for my return. Such is his love, dependence, and need of me.

Oh, what a witness of the Christian's anticipation of Christ's return – either on a personal level or in a great, cataclysmic event! Do I yearn for His return? Am I waiting, each day, for Him to come again? Could today be that day? What if He came before I finished this sentence? I would be the happiest I have ever been, but not because I have been the best example of one His servants, nor because I have lived a flawless life. It is because I have not only come to know His great love for me, but I have fallen in love with Him. He is the goal, the purpose, the light, the hope, and the joy. He is the source of all that I have always desired.

For the time being, my little sons look to me as the one that makes them feel safe, secure, protected, loved, and the one that will always love and look after them. Imagine their joy when they come to know the real source of security, purpose, and love. I pray that they will come to Him soon because I am a poor surrogate.

Mary and Martha

"As Jesus and his disciples were on their way, he came to a village where a woman named Martha opened her home to him. She had a sister called Mary, who sat at the Lord's feet listening to what he said. But Martha was distracted by all the preparations that had to be made. She came to him and asked, 'Lord, don't you care that my sister has left me to do the work by myself? Tell her to help me!' 'Martha, Martha,' the Lord answered, 'you are worried and upset about many things, but few things are needed—or indeed only one. Mary has chosen what is better, and it will not be taken away from her.'" (Luke 10:38-42, NIV)

The path to peace begins with one thing: "Martha, Martha, you are worried and troubled about many things. But *one thing is needed*, and Mary has chosen that good part, which will not be taken away from her" (Luke 10:41-41, NIV). Friends, the *one thing* is Jesus.

Mary wanted to sit at His feet and *listen.* That was the best thing to choose then and its still the best thing to choose. Martha wanted to *do things* for Him and get things organized. That might sound like more difficult and more important/essential, but it was not—and it still is not. It's far easier to do *work* for Him—or to do work and then *claim* it is for Him—than it is to sit at His feet and listen. Sitting at the feet of someone and listening is to assume the humble role and position of a child and *be taught. It's hard at first to do this. To admit you do not have your entire life and act together.*

Mary wanted the *essential* thing—a vital, living and personal relationship with Jesus Christ. Martha the extraneous and busy thing. There would be plenty of time in a few weeks to *do* things for Jesus, but there was precious little time to *be with Him. Jesus reminded Martha—and us—what to be "concerned" with, where to focus, and what should take a front row seat in our brains: our relationship with Him.* (Luke 10:41-41, Paraphrased)

Do You Know the Truth?

In Matthew 7:1 Jesus said, "Do not judge, or you will be judged." (Matthew 7:1, NIV) I don't think that Jesus was talking about ignoring the moral failures of others or just idly standing by when we see injustice occur in society. Rather, He was referring to my bad habit of thinking that I know another person's intentions when they act, i.e. the tendency to judge another person's heart.

We are all guilty of this and it's tough not to, at times, tell a subordinate or a child, "I know what you really meant by this!" In fact, we're told by Jesus that we do not know and to stop being so bold and negative, but to do quite the opposite. We should assume the best about the intentions and hearts of others!

Can you imagine a world where everyone thought the best about you and did not assume the worst? What a blessed place this would be if everyone we met always assumed we were acting for noble or selfless purposes, rather than to further a selfish or sinister agenda.

The Virgin Mary was once found to be mistaken when she assumed, wrongly, that the boy Jesus was being inconsiderate of His mother and father. She said, "Son, why have you treated us like this? Your father and I have been anxiously searching for you …" Jesus replied, "Why were you searching for me? Didn't you know I had to be in my Father's house?" (Luke 2:48, NIV). But Mary and Joseph did not understand what Jesus was saying to them.

Now, if the Virgin Mary can be mistaken about the motives of Jesus, I suppose that it's a given that I will also be wrong about the motives of children and friends. The lesson for me is that I must be careful, as she was, not to yell and threaten when one of my boys—or a summer staff—does something that I consider to be wrong. I should take the time to listen. As I read of the anger and wrong decisions of Luther, Calvin, Zwingli, and even of Saint Paul (in regard to his negative feelings towards John Mark), it is good to remember that all of us are at risk of being so sure we are right about someone or something that we become blind and can't see the truth.

What will bring young people to Jesus Christ at our summer camp is not an aggressive and dogmatic focus on our denominational doctrines or a focus on what we've been brought up to believe. But rather, it will be truth as revealed by the Holy Spirit. Sometimes I find that when I listen to the littlest camper, he or she will speak truth in the most amazing and God inspired ways.

The question is, of course, am I still young enough to learn and receive the facts about God and His plan for me, or have I become too old and too unwilling to be proven wrong?

What Would Jeremiah Say Today

Jeremiah was sent to Judah to warn the people of the coming wrath of God. The entire city of Jerusalem, the temple, the walls, all the buildings—everything would be destroyed. *No one* could escape the judgment.

Sometimes when I read the Old Testament I find the destruction of nations to be staggering and the total annihilation of people incredible to imagine. Just *how bad* could these people have been to bring about such punishment? But then I read a passage like this and get a better idea about why God was so grieved: "Go up and down the streets of Jerusalem, look around and consider, search through her squares. *If you can find but one person who deals honestly and seeks the truth, I will forgive this city."* (Jeremiah 5:1, NIV)

Now this got my attention for two reasons. One, if not a *single person* in this city of *thousands* was honest and looked for truth, something was fundamentally wrong with the culture, celebration, education, and lifestyle of these folks. *Not one person was honest?* Good grief... no wonder God was so dismayed with them. Is there *anything* so annoying in a family or band of friends as to have to deal with one that is dishonest and a constant liar? It eats at the very fabric of a family, club, fellowship, or office. Stealing you can spot, but lying is one of those things that only God can see—and He truly hates it.

Jeremiah does not say that God will punish Jerusalem *because* they are dishonest and do not seek the truth, but simply that it is *so* bad and *no one* is honest! Without getting political, I sometimes wonder if it is *possible* to run for a high office in the USA and also be a man or woman of *impeccable honesty and truth.* Please forgive me if those words offend a politician reading this devotion, but it's not only *honesty* that God demands, but also *seeking the truth.*

Secondly and paradoxically, I find it interesting that *no one* came to the salvation of Jerusalem. God, who cannot lie, would have saved the city if *one person of character* had come forward. But there was none. And what if **I** was there during that time in history... living and dwelling among people whose very habit was to lie, deceive, and avoid truth. Certainly, and sadly, I would have been no better. In fact, if it was not for the fact that Jesus Christ redeemed my life forty-five years ago, I could be quite comfortable right now, living as bad as or worse than these folks did. That is not to say, of course, that I am any better than the worst of them. No, but I was forgiven by the *One* who demands from me honestly and showed me the truth: Jesus, the Son of God.

One man could have saved all of Judah by simply having been an honest and trustworthy man. 2000 years later *another* man saved the world by meeting that requirement of being truly pure and holy man. He was the divine One from God, the One who could serve as the sacrifice for the rest of us.

In light of what He has done, ought not every one of us at camp, our churches, or in Washington DC, Paris, Bogota, Mexico City, Nairobi or Beijing *also* be people that cannot be corrupted and lower their lives to lying, deceiving, and defrauding? Many of us bear the name "little Christ", i.e. Christian, in a cavalier manner. I imagine Jeremiah would have something to say were he walking amongst us today.

Judged by our Works?

My Bible readings lately included John's Apocalypse, i.e. the book of Revelation. I am persuaded that nothing was recorded in the Bible without good reason; I am convinced that it represents the authentic word of God and was inspired by the Holy Spirit; I am of the opinion that many of us *routinely* ignore the things recorded in it that does not suit us or would cause us discomfort.

But, this passage from Revelation reminded me that just because I do not *like* what's written does not mean I can ignore it. Consider these words from Revelation: "Then I saw a great white throne and him who was seated on it. The earth and the heavens fled from His presence, and there was no place for them. And I saw the dead, great and small, standing before the throne, and books were opened. *Another book was opened, which is the book of life. The dead were judged according to what they had done as recorded in the books.* The sea gave up the dead that were in it, and death and Hades gave up the dead that were in them, *and each person was judged according to what they had done.* Then death and Hades were thrown into the lake of fire. The lake of fire is the second death. Anyone whose name was not found written in the book of life was thrown into the lake of fire." (Revelation 20:11-15, NIV)

What grabbed my attention were the words (in bold): "…the dead were judged according to what they had done…" We don't like to talk about "good works" and heaven in the same sentence because of the emphasis we prefer to place upon God's mercy and grace, and God's provision of His own Son to serve as a sacrifice, a "covering" for all our sins. We believe, according to scripture, that we are saved by faith in the completed work of Jesus on the cross. I hold this to be *absolutely* true. *But,* there's no getting away from the promises that John, Paul, and Jesus Himself made about *accountability* for what we said, did, or failed to do after our conversion experience. I am *not* suggesting that once you have received Christ you must work hard enough to earn eternal life, yet there's a clear warning here: We are expected to do good works and put away "living in sin" after we confess our sins to God and receive God's gift of eternal life.

Jesus gave a parable about how there would be some surprises in heaven, i.e. some would not be allowed in, even though they *knew* Jesus, but failed to "feed, clothe, visit, and have compassion" on other people—the "least" other people.(Matthew 25:35, NIV) Similarly, Christ spoke about a man who was *totally* forgiven of all his debts (billions) by a king, but then refused to forgive a friend who owed him a small sum debt; and how that one forgiven of much was basically *unforgiven* and sent away to be tortured. (Matthew 18:35, NIV). Yes, I know that this might sound weird, but I didn't write the bible, I just read it.

My point is merely this: By my deeds I will prove that I am heaven bound or not. Now, if my salvation is based upon the good things I have done versus the bad things I have done, I have *no hope* of attaining heaven; I am certain of that. But if my deeds are nothing but self-centered, deceitful, destructive, debilitating to the work of the Church, and callous and indifferent to the needs of others, I might be surprised when the roll is called up yonder; I might want to reconsider if I really know Him.

If I have received Jesus Christ, my life is *not* the same… I have become a new creature. If I have truly been born again my actual life, my altered reasoning is proof that I have been redeemed.

Negotiating with God

Every few days we have meetings with my family to discuss challenges, bad attitudes, weekend plans, baseball games, etc. Much of the time we talk about the *reasons* we did or said certain bad things, and at other times the boys try to talk me into something they really want. Their arguments can become quite convincing at times. At 8, 10 and 11 they are adroit at bargaining; as they put all their little skills of manipulation into showing how important it is that I see things their way, they put on an act that would win an academy award.

As always, the boys remind me how similar their struggles and antics are when it comes to the celestial struggles any Christian has. All of us in the body of Jesus Christ have dreams, burdens, fears and struggles with which to contend. As I progress in life, and perhaps more profoundly lately, I find that I am not afraid of dying—I am secure in my Savior. No, I am more afraid of the notion that I must continue living as I have had to for the past few years.

I think that if you live long enough you will probably experience similar sentiments. You love your family, your work, your friends; your life has been full and rewarding, but the present obstacles and trials have pushed you to the edge—and sometimes you see no way to pull back from the abyss that you are staring down at. These are the times we must, of course, surrender to God and call out, as David did: "Save me, O God, for the *waters* have come up to my neck. I sink in the *miry depths*, where there is no foothold. I have come into the *deep waters*; the floods engulf me. I am *worn out* calling for help; my throat is *parched*. My eyes fail, looking for my God." (Psalm 69:1-3, NIV)

Have *you* been there yet? In truth I *do* surrender my struggles to God (all the time), but *conditionally* (most of the time). What about you? When you're at the end of your rope *do you give up all your troubles to Him,* or are you still holding onto an imagination of how you expect Him to work things out?

It's easy for me to give control to someone else *provided* he/she will do things like I want, or the end result will be what I have hoped for. But I don't give control over parts of my business, ministry, family or personal life to someone that does things *contrary* to how I want it done—even if his/her way ends up being a better way!

But in my walk with Him, I have found that supreme peace only comes when I truly give it all up Him. That *perfect* piece comes from *totally* giving up with no thought of the what-ifs that often plague me during the night. I am tempted to muse: "What if He is late…what if He chooses to let me lose this thing that I want hold on to…what if His plans are inconsistent with mine…what if He makes a fool out of me…"

Have I already formed in my mind the method, time and manner in which He will rescue me or help give me hope? If I have, then I have not surrendered at all—I am negotiating with God. I am tempted to worry that perhaps He is not listening or that He is planning on harming me. And that thinking comes from a "works-righteousness" mindset. It's as if I am treating God as my equal, or an earthly father, where I attempt to scheme and play on His emotions so that He will come to my rescue and perform some sort of incredible miracle that will cause others to pause and stand in awe—awe *of me*, not Him.

When I negotiate, I am lowering God to the absurd level of a man. He is not a man; He is not in need of negotiating with me or even associating with me—let alone rescuing me. He is God—the only being totally pure and holy…epitome of love. So it comes to this every time I have a hard time letting go: Do I believe Him and do I trust in His goodness?

The Next Generation

If you read the book of Judges you will note that from the time Joshua led the Israelites out of the wilderness until the time he died, Israel was one nation under God: obedient and blessed. No nation or army could stand against them. Then Joshua died but those of his generation lived on a few more years, and the nation of Israel *still* flourished.

But then the last ones that knew Joshua, or that had been in the wilderness, passed away and the new generation knew neither Joshua nor God. In *one generation* the Hebrews turned away from God. It's only two pages in the Bible, but of course it represents more like 40 or 50 years—a generation.

One wonders: How could they be so blind? God's protection and deliverance were recorded for their posterity—for their benefit. The laws of God and His instructions were recorded to warn them about what would happen if they failed to obey and follow God—in fact *more* was recorded to warn them of the dangers of disobeying than the words to remind them of how He would bless them if they *did* obey! Their parents even set up stone markers as reminders, and they still had the Ark of the Covenant to *keep them aware* of God and His laws.

But they had *not* seen the miracles with their own eyes. They had *not* suffered and experienced the consequences of going down the wrong road. They had it rather soft. They had no *first-hand* knowledge of the Holy One and they quickly drifted away when those with a first-hand encounter died. In short, they did not love God like their parents did and did not know Him as pure.

The big question for me is this: As a parent, am I passing on my knowledge and intimacy of Him to the next generation? More importantly, do they *see* what I do as an expression of that primary love for Him? Am I representing and instructing my boys and the children and youth I help to come to know Him firsthand? The foundation of Christianity is a personal, passionate devotion to the Lord Jesus. The entire integrity of the faith depends upon that foundation!

The defining failure of the mainline churches today, in my opinion, is that we have devoted and passed on to youth pastors, weekend retreats, Sunday school or Christian camps that which *the Christian mothers and fathers should have been doing all along——i.e. raising their own children to follow their example of an abandoned love and devotion to Jesus.*

What will happen in forty years if we don't get our spiritual act together? The answer is the *certain* decline and elimination of Christianity in America. Just as in Israel, the next generation could turn their backs on God and follow the example of godless movie stars, attention-greedy professional sport figures; or simply turn to narcissistic agnosticism. You only have to look at Europe, the mainline Protestant churches, the YMCAs and other non-profits that began as ministries devoted to the salvation of souls and are now *primarily* fund-raising entities and *secondarily* "Christian" in focus and theme.

What about the next forty years? Our nation and the next generation will become apostate or atheist unless we somehow pass on to our young people the need to have a *first-hand encounter with Him.* Our intimacy with Him cannot be passed on genetically and it is not absorbed spiritually. It must be *experienced* first-hand.

Am I living for Jesus in such an obvious, and if you will, reckless and extravagant way that my boys yearn for a similar relationship with Him? Are they are spiritually envious of what I possess with God? Or am I perhaps so focused on keeping them happy and "in love with me" that I never show and enforce God's standards for right and wrong?

May God bless this generation with whatever is required to keep their eyes on God and their hearts tethered to Jesus Christ.

Kings of Judah

In the Old Testament there are many great stories about the Kings of Judah and Israel. Sometimes the stories are inspiring—good kings with great courage. But more often than not the kings did not measure up to God's intention or King David's example.

One of the kings, Asa, got my attention. He *began* as a very good king and did the right things. He honored God, removed the idols and always asked for God's counsel and direction before he declared war or did anything grandiose. And God blessed him with success, peace, and an extended kingdom.

But later Asa wandered away from God. Some trouble came his way (a nearby king declared war on him) and rather than turn to God, he turned to *another* man—the king of another land—for help. He even gave that king the gold and silver from God's temple as payment for helping him.

God did not like what Asa did and sent a prophet to make it clear to King Asa that it was wrong. But Asa foolishly put the prophet in prison for speaking the truth! Later, Asa's feet became diseased and rather than turn to God—the One who *created and shaped Asa's feet in his mother's womb*—he turned first to physicians. His feet were never healed and upon his death Asa's kingdom diminished.

That's a lot of narrative to take in, but I thought about Asa and myself. Am I Asa the "young" or Asa the "old"? Do I turn to God instinctively *first* when bad things happen, or to my own solutions, devices, friends and wits? *God desires that we remain dependent upon Him in our relationship as a small child is to a father.* It's not that Asa did evil things; it's that he "grew up" and no longer thought that he needed God. God has not called us to be teenagers or young adults in our relationship with Him but to be *children*.

Just because I am walking with God now does not guarantee that I will be next year. Am I "growing up" and drifting away from God? God *will* get my attention—with events, or something I read in the Bible, or perhaps with someone like this prophet coming into my life. I can pay attention to what God is saying, or get huffy and ignore it—but at my own peril.

Modern teaching tells us to constantly encourage and compliment children and youth. We are also urged to be very careful with their "self-esteem." But when we stray away from God we need people in our lives who give us the naked truth about right and wrong. We *need* people in our lives who don't always tell us what we want to hear, but the hard truth. Those people are called *brothers and sisters in Christ*—all the others that say what you want to hear are merely acquaintances.

The Priority of the Day

There's a certain pride to be found in the minds of those of us who work very hard, put in long hours at the office, achieve our goals or quotas. After all, if we put in 80, 90 or 100 hours of work a week at the office or on the road for our business (or ministry) we can look back and see what *we* have accomplished from the sweat of our brow. Frankly there *is* pleasure in seeing the fruits of our labor and sacrifice.

I am not very patient with people who are lazy, unmotivated to finish a task or slovenly in their work. But the danger in my life is trying to work harder and harder; staying up later and later; taking fewer days off and pushing myself to the point of exhaustion and *then* thinking that God must be *proud of* me.

It's not the work that matters, but my relationship to Jesus Christ. It's not the hours of toil that make the difference, but the *intensity* of my prayers. It's not the focus on the tasks to be completed that bring a smile to God's face, but my preparation to drop everything to help the "least" one of God's children when the opportunity arises.

I have found this year that the more I pray, the *easier* the day is. The more I sincerely seek Him, His will and His Kingdom, the more abundantly I am blessed. The best way to humble a man is not to ask him how hard he works, but how often he prays. Truly *prayer has made the difference* this year for me. I often find myself so caught up in my conversations with God that I am late to a staff meeting or forgetting an appointment. But nothing helps me navigate through the perilous, dark, and deep waters of doubt, or worldly challenges or concerns about my family than my ability to turn to Him in prayer *throughout the day*. In fact, I find myself wanting to be alone more and more just so I can be in fellowship with Him. I have discovered the joy of talking to God.

It is good to do work excellently for the glory of God. It's also proper to have a vocation and a skill that can provide you with an income and financial security. But it is *essential* to be in intimate communion with Him to enjoy the *abundant* life Christ offers.

"Rejoice always, pray without ceasing, **g**ive thanks in all circumstances; for this is the will of God in Christ Jesus for you."(I Thessalonians 5:16-18, NIV)

We Are Not Our Own

A book was recently published by Erica Komisar about the importance of a mother for her infant child. In fact the book argues that the mom's *intimate* presence with the baby is quite important for the first *three years* of the child's development, in a way a man or father could never equal.

More significantly, a neuroscientist, Dr. Nim Tottenham, has determined that not only are infants biologically dependent upon their mothers, but that babies are far more neurologically fragile than ever before realized. He remarked that babies are born *without* central nervous systems and that mothers *are* the central nervous system to babies, especially for the first nine months of life; but up until three years the mom serves an absolutely essential role for the baby's development. So every time a mother soothes or comforts her baby, she is actually *regulating* the baby's emotion from the *outside.*

Now you might wonder why I am bringing all of this up. I did not understand why this article caught my attention until it hit me while I was driving in the car one night on my way to a dinner: God chose the virgin Mary to carry His beloved Son; that same Son, Jesus, was born like all men are born, vulnerable and fragile, just like the babies described above. He was not born a "super baby" but was born into a very fragile environment. Jesus, like all infants, lacked this central nervous system and therefore was dependent upon Mary's protection, care, affirming words, and comfort for Him to develop as a young man. *What an honor* that God chose Mary to be that mother! But what a wonderful young lady Mary must have been to be chosen. *God trusted Mary with the emotional care of His Son—to see to it that He was properly loved, comforted, protected, and nurtured.* I don't think I have ever really grasped how incredibly *responsible* Mary was until I read this article in the WSJ. What an amazing task to lay upon a young mother and what a marvelous performance on her part.

What does that have to do with me, though? God has not chosen me to nurture the baby Jesus. But, I also considered that God has given me something just as holy as the baby Jesus. Paul told the Corinthians: "Do you not know that your bodies are *temples of the Holy Spirit*, who is in you, whom you have received from God? You are not your own." (I Corinthians 6:19-20, NIV) "I carry within me the Holy Spirit, a part of the triune God! Mary carried Jesus and was tasked with caring for that baby properly, *but I carry God's Holy Spirit within me and I am tasked with allowing nothing to cause Him (the Holy Spirit) disappointment, discomfort, or pain!* "I am not my own!"… is how Paul eloquently puts it. (I Corinthians 6:19-20, Paraphrased) I not only belong to God, but I am carrying within my soul a part of Him. *God forbids that my eyes, hands, mouth or imagination would see, touch, speak or conceive anything that would hinder His work within me." (I Corinthians 6:19-20, Paraphrased)*

I was born again or redeemed not to pursue my own agenda, career, pleasure, or personal enterprises, but to present my body as a holy sacrifice and to be a dwelling place for His Holy Spirit… no less than Mary presented her body as a proper dwelling place for the baby Jesus.

May God keep my eyes, hands, feet, tongue, and mind clear and clean for His Spirit.

The Liar and the Lover

One of my favorite books is <u>The Screwtape Letters</u>, by C.S. Lewis. As you probably know, it's a fanciful collection of letters sent by an "arch-demon" to an "apprentice demon." The book deals with how Satan's demons tempt us to doubt, or put aside our prayer time, or question the truth of the Bible and so forth. It's a *must read* for any believer, in my opinion, because it gives real insight into how real is the battle within us for the opinions we form in our minds.

Last night I had one of those moments when the demons seemed to be trying to "reason" with me and create panic. They suggested to me how hopeless my situation was, how undeserving my petitions to God were, how unlikely it was that God would respond, and how insane it was to expect my life to improve. And as I considered all those thoughts from 2 am forward, I realized that if I kept thinking about my life from *this perspective*, I would "curse God and die."(Job 2:9, NIV).

But *then* I began to think the opposite. I began to wonder, what exactly has the enemy suggested to me and countless other believers to keep us mediocre in our work, walk and spiritual assignments? What has he tried to do, countless times, to keep us away from the foot of the cross and to hamstring us in our pilgrimage? And it occurred to me that the enemy is far more predictable than you might realize. His common tactic is to remind me of my flaws, my failures, and all the areas where I am not what and where I want to be, and then suggest that *surely* I am going to fail and crash soon!

The last thing the enemy wants is for me to *cry out to God, "Abba father, please help me."* He is most concerned that I *do not* admit to God my need for *divine intervention* or that I *surrender my fears, concerns and apprehension to Him.* But of course that's what I did and that's when I am reminded that "Satan wants to devour us" (I Peter, 5:8, NIV), by suggesting that God has abandoned us, could not possibly love us, is tired of us, has given up on us or us no longer able to help us. *These* are the sentiments that the enemy desperately wants me to believe—-these are the very things I must fight the most.

And so I listed in my heart to what I *know* to be true about God—first-hand knowledge:

- He loves me
- He has led me to be where I am and has opened the way for me to do what I do
- He has never abandoned me
- Each and every time I have been in a crisis, God has eventually sent a miracle
- Then I listed what I *know* to be true about the enemy (Satan):
- He is a liar
- He twists and perverts truth
- He desires to handicap or paralyze me with fear
- He hopes for my destruction

How foolish to listen to him at 2 am each morning rather than *resist* his lies about God…and me. So I am learning to shut him down and to listen to the *other* voice. Those that live with me are far better off because of it.

Sometimes I Get What I Deserve

In Ecclesiastes 7:21-22 (NIV), Solomon counseled: "Do not pay attention to every word people say, or you may hear your servant cursing you—for you know in your heart that many times you yourself have."

Reality check: people talk and often do not think about what they are saying—and often speak misinformed… and I do the same thing.

This is one of the harder things I have come to apprehend: Good people often say the dumbest and most unkind things! But it does not mean that *they* are dumb or unkind. It's just a matter of fact that *all* of us say things we wish we could retract… and we often *hear* things we wish we had ignored.

Solomon is also right in that the very thing I dislike—being talked about abusively—I am guilty of doing to others. All of us speak about events and people about which we are ill informed—so I should not be so bothered when others do the same toward me.

But I also get the idea that there is a hidden lesson here about *not doing to others what I don't want done to me.* Have you ever noticed that the ones that tend to talk about others *the most* are the very ones that are also the subject of gossip *the most?*

Christ appears to have known what He was talking about (imagine that) when He said that we should do unto others as we would have them do unto us. And yet I find myself doing the very thing I don't want done to me *all the time!* The difference, I hope, is that more and more, I do *not* feel very proud of myself when I get through sharing something negative about someone else. I feel a bit weaker and a lot more vulnerable.

"…Whatever is of *good report*—think on these things…" Good counsel. (Philippians 4:8, NIV)

The Glory of God Filling Me

"Then the man brought me to the gate facing east, and I saw the glory of the God of Israel coming from the east. His voice was like the roar of rushing waters, and the land was radiant with his glory…... The glory of the Lord entered the temple through the gate facing east. Then the Spirit lifted me up and brought me into the inner court, and the glory of the Lord filled the temple." (Ezekiel 43: 1-5 NIV)

Some moments these visions of the glory of God remind me of where I came from (the mind of God) and my destiny (the eternal house of God). I yearn for this more and more, and I am more aware of *how real His glory is* as I humbly admit how *unlike God and His glory* the world is and how far *(how very far)* I am from being the man He redeemed me to be. Pitiful man that I am! Like Paul I *want* one thing but *live a* contradiction to it.

Two things pull me away from Him: (1) the disappointment of how very often I fail Him during the day; and (2) my concerns ("concerns" being a euphemism for "worry") of work, family, business, church and even ministry. Each of these things shift my focus from a steadfast trust and fixation on *Him.* And on these days when I am so far from where I *want to be,* and I read about the *reality of His presence and majesty—that is, the eternal glory of God—*I find myself thirsty for it. I wait with bated breath for the sound of those rushing waters—that time (soon perhaps?) when all will be set right! The coming of the God of Israel who will wipe every tear away from my face and will erase every disappointment I have ever experienced or caused.

What does this "imagination" of the glory of God do for me? It removes from my mind and heart *any* thought save Him and His indescribable beauty, grandeur, greatness and majesty. Truly, no man has seen, heard, tasted or imagined such an awesome presence. But the idea—or the pre-natal memory of it—is imbedded in our souls. We *know* that there is something greater for which we were made. We are *remembering(?)* that for which we were created. We are panting for the more awesome glory that our eyes were meant to behold. No matter what we experience with our senses on this earth, there we will always—*always*—have a yearning within us either to find that place of peace and rest.

In truth, we will never be satisfied—*never*—until we behold His glory. We get a glimpse of it as we read Ezekiel and Daniel and of the transfiguration of Jesus, and we feel, as in a movie preview, some of that awesomeness, as we lose sight of ourselves and we *sing* praises to God! That's why our souls are so drawn to *imagining Him* in praise! It's about as close as we can get to that sensation of *glory*!

But it's all still through a glass darkly. Something better is coming. As C.S. Lewis said, "If we find ourselves with a desire that nothing in this world can satisfy, the most probable explanation is that we were made for another world."(Mere Christianity by CS Lewis © copyright CS Lewis Pte Ltd 1942, 1943, 1944, 1952. Reprinted with permission.)

Amen.

Things Often Get Worse Before They Get Better

When the pressures of life start to fall upon me—or explode around me—I find myself crying out for rescue. I am reminded of King David seeing his life as if he were in a slimy pit and could not crawl out. Recently, while praying, I told God once again that I wanted to give up *everything* and let Him take total control. I wondered, perhaps, if *this* time God might respond, "No thanks, it's your mess, it's beyond impossible, fix it yourself". Thank goodness God is *nothing* like me—He never gives up and never tires of cleaning up my messes, nor does He get irritated when I ask Him to resuscitate me.

The Psalmist wrote in Psalm 42:11 (NIV) and again in Psalm 43:5 (NIV):

> Why, my soul, are you downcast?
> Why so disturbed within me?
> Put your hope in God,
> for I will yet praise him,
> my Savior and my God.

It's rather absurd to suggest that we *never* get a bit low or downcast. If David did, so will most of mankind. But he argued with himself that the *reason* he was disturbed and saddened was that he kept *forgetting to place His trust in God.* Against *all* common sense and the advice of others, put your hope in God…and soon enough you will find yourself praising Him.

Letting go—*really* loosening my grip on whatever it is that has become a burden to me—always brings an immediate sensation of His Holy Spirit and peace, and something tells me: "It's going to be okay." I know that He has taken over. But as much as I want to *permanently* "terminate my control" of those *things I can't control in the first place*, each time I do give Him total authority over something or someone in my life, it seems that the situation goes *really* wacko, and the very thing I had "released" gets *worse,* not *better,* later on in the day. And so there's that temptation of *trying to get my grubby little hands back around the thing again!*

The sustained peace comes in the morning… and I have to let things get worse before they get better.

It's the "holding onto" things that has always made me miserable—whether it's something I own, or something that I have neglected, or handled poorly, or that I want to manipulate—and this can be "things", emotions, people, and even good works!

I know that He *wants* me to let go and trust Him in *all* things, but there's a constant tug in my spirit to "get it done all by myself." There's that extreme on one side of me that does not want to become "lazy" about life and my work, and what I could and should be doing; then there's the other extreme that thinks I can't do *anything* right or good enough. *In between* is a Savior who whispers, "You can do *all things* through me, (Philippians 4:13, NIV)" but also, "apart from me you can do *nothing.*" (John 15:5, NIV)

Ring the Bells of Heaven

Last night we had one of our ritual "meltdowns" that seem to plague my family on the weekends. One of our boys got frustrated with his brother and allowed a tapestry of profanity to escape his mouth. When I confronted him, we had to go through about fifteen minutes of him denying, then admitting, then redacting, then admitting again what he did. While I am not *comfortable* with this, I am becoming more accustomed to it. Keeping promises, telling the truth, controlling tempers and keeping our hands to ourselves seems to be the common challenges of our home.

But after the meltdown, I spent some time with him to not only express my concern, but also to tell him that I *understood* his struggle. I shared with him my challenges when I was his age, and how those feelings of inadequacy and loss of control caused me to turn to God. For thirty minutes I explained how I felt when I was his age, how I attempted to *be good*, but all the while knowing that I was "acting" one way when my parents were watching, and "doing" another thing when they weren't around. Eventually, I explained to him, I got sick and tired of *me* and my attempts to be what I simply could not be.

It was strange how he instantly got very close to me and seemed to hang on to every word I was saying. It was as if he were thinking, "You had the same problem I have?!" I know that he was listening, that he wanted help and that he was unhappy with himself. Over the past month, I have heard him say on more than one occasion that he "hated himself." And so I shared the good news of Jesus Christ. This is something that he has listened to before, but last night he *heard it because he was hungry for it.* Last night he wanted to find redemption, restoration, newness and a fresh start. He was tired of the his own emotional outbursts and really wanted to know how to be the boy *he yearned to be.*

I explained God's love for him, his own responsibility for his sins and poor choices, God's gift of His only Son, the penalty of sin, and so on. He *heard* the gospel at a time when he urgently *needed to hear it.* He asked me to help him pray to God…and so we did….and my son became redeemed—born again. After he prayed I offered to pray for him. And with him next to me, I prayed and prayed and prayed—in a manner I don't often pray. But when I was through, he was sleeping soundly and quite peacefully.

I can think of no higher calling than the honor of leading a child to the open arms of our Lord. My son received salvation last night, while I received a double portion of joy. Sometimes we relegate things to a pastor or priest or youth leader things that *we,* as fathers and mothers, ought to be doing.

The Conclusion of Solomon

"Now all has been heard; here is the conclusion of the matter:
Fear God and keep his commandments, for this is the duty of all mankind.
For God will bring every deed into judgment, including every hidden thing, whether
it is good or evil." (Ecclesiastes 12:13-14, NIV)

I recall the day I finished Ecclesiastes, I was struck by how abruptly Solomon summed up the purpose of man and his evaluation of how to have a meaningful life in a "meaningless" world.

The *wisest man that ever lived* concluded that men should:

- *Fear* God
- *Obey* His commands
- *Remember* that we will be held accountable for what we have done—even those things in secret

Now, I understand that Christ's blood has redeemed my life and that because of His sacrifice I am able to stand before God free from the guilt and consequences of sin. Still, why do both the New Testament and Old Testament talk about how we will have to account for even the *idle words* we speak?

There's a blithe sense of security and cover, I suppose, as we consider that our debt to God is so enormous that naturally He had to come up with a plan (Jesus Christ's death) to redeem us. But what about all these passages about our responsibility to feed the poor and being required to give an account one day for what we *did* or *did not do* with the gifts and opportunities He afforded to us; as well as His commands—which clearly Christ did *not* come to abolish and to which the apostles made frequent reference?

Bonhoeffer coined the term "cheap grace" to refer to the idea that it cost God little and requires little back from us in order to receive it. But of course neither is true. I was redeemed by the *costly* grace of God—the precious body and blood of His beloved Son! And my redemption is *contingent*, according to Christ Himself, upon my preparation *to become a new man and see things quite differently* (e.g. "If you do not forgive your brother who sins against you, *neither will God forgive you*".(Matthew 6:15, NIV)

If I have truly been re-born, God's commands and requirements are not a burden on me, but a *privilege* to observe and dutifully obey. But if I find myself chafing under the burden of what God expects of me, and if I am deceiving others (and myself) into thinking that God does not care about what I do "secretly," something is woefully wrong in my relationship through Christ with God. Either I am evidently *not* a part of the redeemed, or I am far away from walking in time with Him. Either way: *He will hold me accountable.*

Persecuted or Practical?

One of the last things Saint Paul said were these words to Timothy: "…In fact, everyone who wants to live a godly life in Christ Jesus will be persecuted…" (II Timothy, 3:12, NIV)

These words we hold to be authentic, brave reflections of a life rightly aligned with a relationship and communion with Jesus Christ. But what happens in the church—i.e. the body of Christ—when one of its members seemingly lives a godly life and is attacked, persecuted or called "a failure"? Sadly, it seems that Christians too often "shoot the wounded" rather than recognize that their persecution and suffering might, in fact, be evidence of a life far more dedicated to God than those who are *rarely* attacked and never fail.

In churches, we tend to elevate office and give respect and admiration to those that are financially successful or "good in business"—as if those things have *anything* to do with the Kingdom of God. In fact, it might be those who are less educated, impoverished and suffering who better represent a mature Christian; quite possibly they are more familiar with prayer and trust and understanding God's ways than the well off.

I suppose the word that causes me the most pause, in Christian conversations, is when one person tells the other who is suffering (in relation to misfortune or disappointment, etc.) that "you need to be realistic and practical"—i.e. stop looking at life as if God were in charge and acknowledge that it is time to give up, admit you're not going to make it, or simply "curse God and die."(Job 2:9, NIV)

It is simply *not possible* to be pleasing and faithful to God in ministry and at the same time follow the practical advice of others—particularly those whose approval you do not want to lose. There are times and events when one has to choose whether to trust God and step off the cliff or listen to practical advice and throw in the towel.

I am learning more and more that challenges, catastrophes, and heartaches in life do *not* make me into a stronger man; they reveal the man I really am (or am not). Paul lived a righteous life and was persecuted far more than anyone I have ever known. What an honor to endure persecution if it is for *His* purposes.

The Most Powerful Muscle

The tongue. Think about it as you listen to people with strong accents. At the camp we hear accents today from Russia, Italy, Latin America, France, Belgium, South Africa, Jamaica, Ukraine and others… and just remember, when someone has an accent, it means that he or she knows one more language than you do.

The tongue: what a tool for good and bad. Think about how all the small things people say can make your day: *"One kind word can change someone's entire day."* But then, out of the blue, an unkind and unhelpful sentence can *ruin your week.*

Saint James addresses the challenge of the tongue best in the third chapter of his letter. He reminds us that the tongue might be small, but it is, ounce per ounce, the most powerful muscle in the human body and it is the cause of most of the world's heartache and discouragement. He likens the tongue to a small spark that can easily reduce a house or a forest to *nothing* in a just a few hours. Words we speak can destroy relationships, families, churches and fellowships such as ours at The Vineyard.

James poignantly remind us in that, "…no human being can tame the tongue. It is a restless evil, full of deadly poison." (James 3:8 NIV). Truer words were never spoken! And I am as full of that poison as any other staff, camper or member of a church. I say things I don't *need* to say but can't resist. I utter things that are utterly harmful and without purpose. What to do?

The best time for me to hold my tongue is the time I feel I must say something or explode. It took a contractor sixteen months to rebuild my home, but just two hours for former house to burn to the ground along with 40 years of accumulated furniture, art and beloved memorabilia; it is quicker to destroy than build, so be careful of what you say with your own tongue. You can destroy years of friendship and "building someone up" in a few words.

Ultimately there's only one answer for the Christian in response to the tongue: Totally submit it to the Holy Spirit and *keep quiet* when He tells you to hold back on responding or saying something. *Surrender your tongue, you pen and paper or your texts to the Holy Spirit.* You will find that you might be talking and texting less, and listening and understanding better.

Be careful with your words. Once they are said, they can be only forgiven, not forgotten.. So this week, think about this, "No matter what anybody tells you, words and ideas can change the world." - John Keating

Our Gift From God Today

"I know that there is nothing better for people than to be happy and to do good while they live. That each of them may eat and drink, and find satisfaction in all their toil—this is the gift of God." (Ecclesiastes 3:10-13, NIV)

These words are from the wisest man (Solomon) who ever lived. Truer words to live by were never spoken, especially in these very uncertain times. **Now** is a good time to think about how God "wired" us when He created us and what will truly make us "happy." From all that Solomon says, we should carefully rethink what *fuels* our souls. And it's pretty simple really; it has to do with being content with food and drink, and finding satisfaction (i.e. purpose and fulfillment) in our work. The other stuff that we've been snookered into believing is essential or will *really* make us happy, represents "junk food" for our souls. Perhaps this horrible pandemic we are now experience will wake us up!

We've been led to believe that happiness will come, by and large, if we make it our goal to get more or by having *a lot* more than anyone else; by working hard and saving for vacations and retirement. We've been taught that *not having to work one day* is the *reason* for doing good work now; we've been led to believe that we owe it to ourselves to "reward" our lives with more TV, movies, news and entertainment—after all, "we deserve it." We've come to the conclusion that work is bad, play is good, and that whining and complaining are evidence of our superior up-bringing—i.e. we can only be content with the very best life has to offer.

God's gift to us, unrequested and unwarranted, is *life.* What we *do* with our lives is our gift back to God. But now, more than ever, perhaps we should reconsider how marvelously He has made us and *what* we requires of us, what we need to add into our lives, and what we should be teaching our children.

Solomon would say that the basic things we need to remember are *to be content with what we have (drink and food)* and *be grateful for the opportunity to work!* Many of us this very hour *cannot work because of the virus,* and others are faced with uncertainty about food, drink and shelter. Perhaps we should remember the *blessing* of being able to work and being able to provide for our own food and drink—those things that give satisfaction and fuel to our bodies and our souls—and re-evaluate how much of the *other* things we really need—and perhaps, what we need to eliminate.

It seems to me that the "other things" I have acquired are the same things that take away my sleep and peace. It's the *simple* life that I am craving because it is the simple life that defined the life of Jesus, the prophets and the heroes of the church. They were unencumbered by possessions, debts, creditors and gadgets.

Think about it. Do the things you crave increase your laughter and happiness or is it the opposite?

'Tis a gift to be simple, 'tis a gift to be free,
'tis a gift to come down where I ought to be
When I am in the place just right,
I will be in the valley of love and delight
Joseph Brackett

The One Making the Biggest Noise

At the time this devotion is being written, the U.S. government has closed 33% of all government jobs. It's called a "government shutdown" because the President refuses to sign the budget that the House has presented because they differ on building a security wall on our border.

What seems to have been lost on politicians all over their world is that the common man (e.g. me) is not so much interested in the merits of their arguments when it comes to issues as we are with the *maturity (or actually lack of) they display—-they should be able to make peace with one another!*

Likewise, within the body of Christ, the true disciple of Jesus is not interested in the arguments from Christians that are unwilling to *listen* to the other side of the argument. The disciple of Jesus is interested in truth and in *listening to Jesus,* not the platitudes of the immature parts of the body that have too much pride wrapped around their convictions.

What *should* interest me is what God would have me do when I am challenged spiritually, intellectually, politically, or socially. Am I to strike back, or turn the cheek/walk the extra mile/put up with the weaknesses (and wrong way of thinking?) of others?

I was recently talking to a friend about the great intelligence and admiration of a Bible teacher we both know. I remain impressed with those that quote what he says and who follow his blogs closely. He's a very gifted man. But my friend reminded me that if this same, gifted and committed Christian is challenged or disagreed with, a rather surly and combative man comes out. It seems that his opinion is the only one that matters in spiritual matters and if you disagree with his monologue he can be quite dismissive of you *and* your opinion.

It's easy to look down my spiritual nose at people who act like that, but I *must* look at my own tendency to get frustrated with liberals, ultra-conservatives, spiritual folks that think they are God's gift to the rest of us, and so forth. Yes, I can become easily irritated with people that disagree with me, and how *revealing it is* of my immaturity in whatever area where they don't see eye-to-eye with me.

But what am I to do? Well, God does not expect me to "reduce" the gospel, deny *the truth* or deny the Lordship of Jesus Christ. But I would do well to "put up" with those that have not reached my "enlightened" conclusions, and should not demand that others to respect my opinion—as if I have some esoteric knowledge of God that others cannot grasp. The big challenge, for the bigwigs in Washington, DC, as well as the intellectually gifted in the Christian community, can be summed up in *one* word: *humility.* In the community of Jesus we're *supposed* to consider the needs of the other to be more important than *our* needs.

Imagine a world where politicians worked together like that. Imagine a place where every Christian author, speaker, pastor and camp director did the same…it would give us real glimpse of heaven on earth.

Serious About Prayer

"Then Jesus said to them, 'Suppose you have a friend, and you go to him at midnight and say, 'Friend, lend me three loaves of bread; a friend of mine on a journey has come to me, and I have no food to offer him.' And suppose the one inside answers, 'Don't bother me. The door is already locked, and my children and I are in bed. I can't get up and give you anything.' I tell you, even though he will not get up and give you the bread because of friendship, yet because of your shameless audacity he will surely get up and give you as much as you need.

"So I say to you: Ask and it will be given to you; seek and you will find; knock and the door will be opened to you. For everyone who asks receives; the one who seeks finds; and to the one who knocks, the door will be opened. "Which of you fathers, if your son asks for a fish, will give him a snake instead? Or if he asks for an egg, will give him a scorpion? If you then, though you are evil, know how to give good gifts to your children, how much more will your Father in heaven give the Holy Spirit to those who ask him!" (Luke 11:5-13, NIV)

If there was *ever* a time in our nation's history to be *serious* about prayer, *this is that time.*

Why don't we pray with such resolve and tenacity? Perhaps it's because we haven't had to! But "things-are-a-changing"… rapidly…and we'd better get serious about prayer and our future. We're facing things that our leaders, doctors and scientists cannot solve—at least not fast enough for *hundreds of thousands* of people that are going to be lost. Now is the time to pray, but not prayers from a prayer book or for the adulation of others that might be listening! Now is the time for those of us that know Him to get on our knees and *beseech God to protect us and heal our world.* He is more than able to restore us and give us back a future. So this is a time for *acknowledging* God, not denying Him; a time to applaud men and women of faith, not attack them for believing in a divine being; a season to see those that *do pray* and *do believe in "right and wrong"* as heroes, not someone we lampoon or mock. Salvation will *not* come from Oprah Winfrey or Jimmy Kimmel, or the newscasters, or the editors of our newspapers—*they* are part of the reason we suffer from such a lack of faith and prayer right now!

Turn off the movies, television shows and Netflix and tune in to Jesus Christ! Stop studying the political ads and debates and start reading God's love letter to mankind—the Bible. We must stop trying to "see things" from every strange and unmerited perspective that man offers in order to appear enlightened and in-tune with our times, and must yearn to see things from *God's perspective.*

Healing and restoration will come—and hopefully with them will come a healthier understanding of God and our need of a Savior and Lord. Horrible as it is, this virus might be the very thing that brings our nation and world back to God.

"For everyone who asks receives; the one who seeks finds; and to the one who knocks, the door will be opened." (Matthew 7:8, NIV)

Storms Have a Purpose

Sometimes I write these "thoughts" and then, after a few minutes erase everything and start over again. Such was my Saturday night. With four young men living in my home, there are days when I don't know if I am coming or going. Our house is full of bathos and pathos. But my work has become so much more enriched and tested because of it. I could write about *what they are teaching me and reminding me of each day.* But since the fire that destroyed all I owned in 2016, I have similarly found myself "remembering" things I once thought I knew quite well, but somehow forgot, gave up on, or turned my back on.

I never lost my faith nor did I take up a different concept of God, but conflicts, broken-heartedness, and, quite frankly, *suffering*, have brought me back to things basic in my walk with Jesus Christ. Suffering has a dual purpose, I now believe: (1) That I might be purified and (2) that Jesus Christ might be glorified.

This really does simplify it, doesn't it. And I am not suggesting that God *delights* in our suffering so that His Son is glorified, but rather that God chooses to purify me and *elevate me* by letting me be His instrument to draw attention to His Son, Jesus. God takes great satisfaction with me when I become a willing instrument, turning the spotlight and admiration to His only Son. And it seems that I am far more in tune to His intentions when things do *not* go my way, and I am forced to seek His face, His favor and His shelter. *Good times* never draw me to Him—they tend to drag me away.

And so today when one of the boys lost control when I refused to purchase him an expensive toy, and another boy forget his solemn promise that he just made less than a minute ago, and another behaved as if he could care less what I thought of him, I was reminded of what I have always known: that I have broken some of my vows to God; that I am ever asking for God's blessing but often shirk from *being a blessing back to Him;* that I often act as if I don't think He is aware of my inner and secret thoughts and intentions.

God gave me these boys, my ministry at The Vineyard, and my place in a local church for one sole purpose: That Jesus be glorified. *Is that happening* or am I acting like an adolescent? Am I glorifying Him by the way that I accept the disappointments of the young men in my home, as I endure insults, resistance, unkindness, disappointments, personal failures, and more?

He is *more than able* to provide for us a perfectly flawless life with no headaches or heartaches, but He works most profoundly in the storms and personal upheavals of life—not in the tranquil interludes. Has God allowed a storm into your life this week?—then glorify Jesus and watch God elevate *you.*

God's Creatures - Great and Small

I ran over a snake today on the way to check the construction of the new house. It was a small snake, probably less than two feet long—green with white stripes. I could have avoided the snake but something kind of urged me to run over it to kill it. And so I did.

On the way back to the office I drove by the snake again and I saw that it was not quite dead—it was in fact writhing in pain. The tires on my Jeep had crushed the snake but not killed it. It was in agony. I had immediate remorse that I was the cause of such suffering and pain. The snake could never survive with the injury I caused, so all I could do to remedy my carelessness was run over it two more times to be sure it was no longer agonizing.

That drama bothered me all day long. Why in the world did I harm that snake in the first place? It posed no harm to me and was probably keeping the mice population checked. But worse, I realized that I was the source of the great suffering of one of God's creatures—that little snake felt pain and was truly hurting for no good reason.

If I, mean-spirited and careless as I am, have compassion on a small snake, how much more does God have compassion and pity on people like me—reptilian though I might be at times. And if God has such compassion as I had today (and I know that He is infinitely more kind and compassionate than I can fathom), I know that He would never send agony and suffering on me for His entertainment or for no purpose. Unlike me, the suffering He causes or allows has a purpose for good!

But, I also wondered how many souls I have caused to suffer by my indifference, carelessness, or lack of thinking/planning. To be sure, I have caused others harm in my life; I take no pride in this and can offer no excuse or explanation. Sometimes I have done hurtful things simply by ignoring the obvious fact that I was causing injury to someone by not "letting up" or steering my actions a bit more circumspectly.

God's Word speaks again and again about "being careful"—i.e. thinking before acting or speaking. I need to be careful not only because of God's little creatures that cross the road, but also because of the precious ones that cross my path each day at work, the grocery store, at the stop sign, at the bank, on the phone. Being careful is to be "full of care" in the manner in which I do everything.

Proof of Repentance?

In the third chapter of Matthew we're told about Jesus' cousin, John the Baptist. The Bible says that, "In those days John the Baptist came, preaching in the wilderness of Judea and saying, "Repent, for the kingdom of heaven has come near." This is he who was spoken of through the prophet Isaiah: "A voice of one calling in the wilderness, 'Prepare the way for the Lord, make straight paths for him.' John's clothes were made of camel's hair, and he had a leather belt around his waist. His food was locusts and wild honey. People went out to him from Jerusalem and all Judea and the whole region of the Jordan. Confessing their sins, they were baptized by him in the Jordan River. But when he saw many of the Pharisees and Sadducees coming to where he was baptizing, he said to them: "You brood of vipers! Who warned you to flee from the coming wrath? Produce fruit in keeping with repentance. And do not think you can say to yourselves, 'We have Abraham as our father.' I tell you that out of these stones God can raise up children for Abraham. The ax is already at the root of the trees, and every tree that does not produce good fruit will be cut down and thrown into the fire."**(Matthew 3:1-14, NIV)**

I don't think I have ever heard an altar call like this! John was *brutal* with these religious leaders. Evidently he knew what they were *thinking* and he probably noticed how they carried themselves, and he surely noted their arrogant and smug faces. He was telling them, in effect: No! First there's got to be a *change of mind.* You must be answerable to an *amendment* in your life. There must be proper *evidence* that you are sincere and that there is a change of heart and will.

Luke recorded these words in Acts: "First to those in Damascus and Jerusalem, then to everyone in the region of Judea, and then to the Gentiles, I declared that they should repent and turn to God, performing deeds worthy of their repentance".(Acts 26:20, NIV). Likewise Paul said to the good people in Ephesus: "For you were once darkness, but now you are light in the Lord. Walk as children of light". (Ephesians 5:8, NIV)

There appears to be some responsibility in deciding to follow Jesus. Evidently we're supposed to *repent* and show that we are sorry and mindful of our need of a Savior. Jesus never begged people to come to Him and John the Baptist never cheapened the call to repentance and baptism. Sometimes I think we work within the church and Christian ministries as if there's some desperate need for us to drag people to the altar and into a relationship with Jesus Christ—as if the church will cease to exist if we don't. It's akin to offering discount tickets to the last of the unsaved to fill the empty seats on the Gospel Airline or the Almighty Railway.

Jesus taught us to make disciples—not beg people to joining the church. Christ's words pierced to the heart and many *did not* follow Him—at least, not at first. The church's explosive growth was not connected to persuasive oratory, but *preaching the good news* of Jesus Christ. Some will hear and obey, some will not, and I would suggest that if everyone does come, we're probably cheapening God's grace and misleading those who are truly seeking Him.

A follower of Jesus has repented—and that always involves remorse and sorrow. Pride and a sense of "I'm going to be a blessing to God" are never associated with Christian conversion.

Soot Covered Little Shoes

Oh, to walk in the other person's shoes for a few days before I make any assumptions. That's what I am reminded of quite regularly with my three boys in my home. I do *not* know what they are thinking, feeling, imagining, fearing, hoping or dreaming. Their pasts and multiple upbringinqgs (they've all been in several foster homes) are far removed from what I had.

In my family, my mother, father, and aunts and uncles cared for us, and we were *closely* knit to our church, friends and neighbors. My family never moved from the time my parents were married until years after my father died. We had roots and many, many people knew our names, our birthdays, our favorite gifts and, yes, our bad habits.

It is not so for these adopted sons of mine. They have no grandparents, aunts, uncles, old friends, or neighbors to turn to. Their lives are now centered on me, the staff at this camp and our new home. And when I am tempted to "guess" at why they do what they do, I must remember that I *do not understand what they have gone through.*

While my father was in the hospital, slowly slipping away from a massive stroke, my mother and my siblings and I *struggled* with what action we should take; he was on life-support and had specifically requested to *not* ever be kept alive in that manner. As we struggled, a young, well-meaning physician kept offering us encouragement and several times told us that he "understood what we were going through." About the fifth or sixth time he said that, I snapped and asked him, "Do you? Has your father died, or your mother, or a close friend? Have you *ever* had someone you love struggling to breathe on a ventilator?" He replied, "Actually, no I have not personally lost anyone in his life." And so I rather curtly asked him to please stop telling us that he "understood what we were going through," because clearly he did not.

But, with these boys I am committing the same blunder in assuming I know why they misbehave or why they don't pay attention. One Sunday before church, I was brought to a new level of humility as I made the same naive mistake. The youngest boy refused to wear the pants I chose for him, he did not like the socks, and kicked off the shoes I put on his feet. And that's when I "lost it." I was tired and I had to make sure all of us were ready for church, so I took the shoes (they were a bit worn) and I told him, "Fine, don't wear them ever again," and threw them into the fireplace. (Yes, I know that it was a bit dramatic, but please don't judge me, you're not living with these gentlemen.)

The house got quiet after the fireplace ordeal and I went to my room to get dressed. When I came back, just ten minutes later, the youngest one, contrite, *very carefully* showed me the shoes that he and his brother had rescued from the fireplace. They were covered with soot, but he looked up to me and softly promised that he would wear them and would get them clean.

I was, of course, struck in the deepest part of my heart by their act of contrition and restitution. I helped wipe off the shoes and thanked them both for their help. Then it hit me: the last thing these boys want is to lose their home, their "dad", their family, and their sense of security. *That* is what they have feared and have tried to block from their minds since they have been here: that I would be like all the rest and give them up when they did not meet my expectations!

God forgive *me* for treating them in such a way as to make them think that I would surrender them to another foster care family. My heavenly Father does not throw me away (or my shoes into a fireplace) when I disappoint Him. He keeps on loving me and forgives me now, tomorrow, and henceforth. *Nothing* I do can make me *not* His child and I need to let these boys hear that again, and again, and again. They are secure in my heart, just as I am surely in His heart.

Please pray for the dad of these boys—he has much to conquer yet.

The Allure of Money

"Who may live on God's holy hill?" (Psalm 15:1, NIV)

"…who lends money to the poor without interest; who does not accept a bribe against the innocent." (Psalm 15:5, NIV)

Some days my focus is on money. How willing are we to lend it and how eager are we to acquire it? Saint Francis of Assisi equated money to human excrement. He had no appreciation of it and thought of it as something that held a man back from enjoying the freedom of being in love with God and others.

I agree with much of Saint Francis sentiments. Money might be essential in our culture/modern world, but it certainly is the source of ruin for many lives. It's not the possession of money that can ruin people, but the love of it and the overwhelming need to have more and more of it. Several of my friends appeared to have loved God more and enjoyed a greater intimacy with Him *before* they "succeeded" in business.

The psalmist does not say we should *not* have money. Nor does he say that it's wrong to have *a lot of it*. But the proof of our "affection" with money is revealed in our ability to lend it to the poor with no intention of profiting from the loan. It's our willingness to do the *right thing*—even if there is no profit and we could profit from doing the opposite or wrong thing. Money has a habit of becoming an object of our love and devotion—and no one who wants to dwell on His holy hill can be in love with both God and money. We must make a choice.

The love of money is not the *source* of all evil, but it certainly is a major contributor to unhappiness all over the world.

Peter, James and John

At the transfiguration Jesus is seen by Peter, James and John with Moses and Elijah. Somehow the three disciples knew it was Moses and Elijah, so I suppose Jesus called them by name.

I have wondered *why* Jesus was with these two men. Why not with Adam, the *first* man, or Noah, or Enoch, or King David? But if you research this, the answer is interesting. First, Malachi, the last prophet to ever prophesy, said this in Malachi 4:5-6 (NIV) "See, I will send the prophet Elijah to you before that great and dreadful day of the Lord comes. He will turn the hearts of the parents to their children, and the hearts of the children to their parents....". This was the fulfillment of the *last* prophecy ever uttered about the coming Messiah. Jesus was the "bridge" between the old and new covenants, and the pillars of the church, Peter, James and John *saw this first hand.* Jesus was transfigured in front of them for a purpose.

And when God said, "Listen to him," (Luke 9:35, NIV)He made it clear that Jesus is His mouthpiece. His authority was *surpassing* the laws of Moses by virtue of his kinship with God!

Think of what else this proved to the disciples: Moses had been dead for 1000 years! Elijah was taken up in a fiery column 500 years later—but these men were *alive* and now live in the presence of the of God! Jesus showed them the truth of eternal life.

But what got my attention was God's admonition: "Listen to him." Earlier, at Jesus's baptism, God had proclaimed: "This is my beloved Son, *in whom I am well pleased.*" (Matthew 3:17, NIV) Those words are stirring, because both of these things reveal something I did not understand earlier in my life: The Father's profound *pride* in His one and only Son. *I cannot keep count of the times* during the day that all three of my young sons ask me, after performing a task, "Are you proud of me?" They perform small tasks, and diligently attempt to perform them in a manner that they assume will please me. But because of my attention to other matters (things that are *not* that important) I often fail to compliment them on their good work, and they must remind me with, "Aren't you proud of me?"

Praise be to God—Jesus never had to ask the question! His father, the perfect example of a Father, was quick to tell His Son. A **good** father tells his son, "well done!...I am proud of you!...You have once again done what greatly pleases me!"

Oh, to be the father that my heavenly Father is! God have mercy on me and help me see my sons—and other sons and daughters— *as you see them!* Help me to tell them how proud I am of them before they have to ask me...

So that God's Work Might be Displayed

"Neither this man nor his parents sinned,' said Jesus, 'but this happened so that the works of God might be displayed in him." (John 9:3, NIV)

So *nothing* happens, it comes to reason, without God's permission. It's encouraging to think that *everything that happens* has a purpose. Sometimes bad things happen *not* because we are bad, but so that God might be glorified and so that the one afflicted can be lifted up.

So what has God allowed to happen to me, or *sent to me,* today, or last week, or decades ago, that's supposed to result in "the works of God being displayed"? (John 9:3, NIV) How many times have I allowed my difficulties to become my opportunities to fall into self-pity rather than falling into my Father's arms and saying, "Have your way and do whatever it takes to give You the glory" ? Have my misfortunes and missteps been opportunities for *Him* to receive the attention and perhaps draw others to Him, or have I insisted on being noticed, pitied and the center of attention and become a stumbling block to others that *might* have found Him?

This man is not one we need to feel sorry for, but admired. He was *chosen, selected,* set apart for this event *so that he might testify to what God had done for him!* And if you read the entire narrative you'll see a man of courage who put the Pharisees in their place and clearly refuted their charge that Jesus was not the Son of God! Jesus set this man free to shake up the calcified religious thinking of his day—he rattled the Pharisees!

"One thing I know, I was blind, but now I see…" (John 9:25, NIV) So may it be with me! May we all come through this pandemic and all the economic and social tragedy that it's creating and be able to say, "We know this, our heavenly Father has been glorified in the manner in which we endured and we can see better than ever now!"

Lord, awake this nation and give us back our sight; give heart and soul back to our local communities, restore reverence and worship to our churches and Christian ministries. Please heal our world, in the name of Jesus.

My Existence... Why?

David asked this question in Psalm 144:1 (NIV) "Lord, what are human beings that you care for them, mere mortals that you think of them? They are like a breath; their days are like a fleeting shadow." This is the troubling existential question I have suffered with since I was a small child. "What" *am I* that God cares about me at all? Am I not, in reality, little more than something God *called* into existence out of nothing, and in truth little more than a vapor... a breath... a fleeting shadow. For whatever reason, that thought caused me to jump out of bed at night and walk around the house when I was very young. Something about the notion that I was merely God's imagination and not really "my own" still gives me anguish some evenings.

As I write this I must confess that I have never been successful in eloquently or properly articulating this struggle, but I think that David had the same question and doubt from time to time, because he speaks of it more than once in the Psalms. Why do we matter to God? What's the point of it all?

The answer to that question gives me peace in my inner struggle of my existence. The fact that He *does* care about me suggests that *something* about me is quite precious and unique to Him. If I were simply a vapor that could be re-created a billion times over until the perfect "me" were called into existence, why would God send His Son to suffer, endure humiliation on a cross, and die for "this" me?

Quite clearly, *I matter to God*—and so does every other soul reading this devotion. We matter not because God cannot do without us, *but because for some reason He does not want to do without us.* He loves me and that's what undoes all the false illusions of me being merely a breath or a shadow. God cares about me (and you) enough to have prepared something for us, from the foundation of the earth, which we cannot fully imagine, but which will be *ours* once we are brought into His Kingdom!

As so, like Paul, I can say that the pains and trials I undergo on this earth are *nothing* when compared to what He has prepared for those that love Him. This turns my existential queries into an exciting adventure of preparing for the unimaginable bliss in the soon-to-be eternal life that lies before me! Yes, every so often I have the same childhood existential attacks about my life, my soul, my very consciousness! But the closer I draw to Him... the more He speaks to me, the more He gives me glimpses of the glory to come... the less I am afraid.

"Satan Blocked Our Way"? (I Thessalonians 2:18, NIV)

Paul wrote to the good folks in Thessaloniki: "For we wanted to come to you—certainly I, Paul, did, again and again—but Satan blocked our way."(I Thessalonians 2:18, NIV)

Hmmm... if Satan can block the work of someone like Paul, one *commissioned by God to take the gospels to the nations*, can he (Satan) not also block my way? Yikes! *Has* he not done just that and is he not far superior to me in all regards? How am I to get anything done with him on the loose? Good grief, how can I possibly succeed when I am up against *The Prince of Darkness*?

Does this *really* happen? Is the Devil able to thwart our good efforts at times? (And I am not talking about a little red imp with a pointed tail and horns, but a spiritual being that wants to undo all God's good work.) Obviously he has *far* more power than we often ascribe to him. He can stop us at times, and harm us.

So how should I respond to all of this? I must admit that my best and most noble plans *could* be blocked by the enemy—it's a sober truth, but it also helps explain part of my struggle. Sometimes bad things happen and sometimes it's *his* fault.

What can I do about it? Surrender it to God! I am *no* match for Satan, but God, who loves me dearly, needs merely to speak *a word* and He can bring about whatever results He wants. Satan is far mightier than me, but he is a speck of dust compared to God's power and imagination!

This isn't a battle between two equal super powers. This isn't about Satan winning and stopping God. If anything, Satan's apparent "victories" are things that our God is permitting for a purpose. So in a sense, He is *using* Satan for His ultimate goals—even if that purpose includes some disappointments and postponements for me at times.

Paul went on to say in another letter, "For our struggle is not against flesh and blood, but against the rulers, against the authorities, against the powers of this dark world and against the spiritual forces of evil in the heavenly realms"(Ephesians 6:12, NIV). Paul's struggles, just like mine, are temporal and *permitted* by the One that can deliver us *in a split second*. But it is wise to remember that the enemy, Satan, will do all he can to stop any good we are attempting to start. If he's not attempting to stop me, discourage me, or block my path, I must not be much of a threat to his purposes.

On Facing the Lions

Some days I cannot imagine how things could possibly end up right. It's hopeless. Too many variables and too many irons in the fire. It would take *two* of me, working 24 hours a day to get it all done—and one of "me" would need to have a much larger brain. I cannot do it all—-I am unable.

He says: "Let not your heart be troubled"; (John 14:3, KJV) but what happens when your heart *is* troubled and you can't bring about the things essential to taking care of your children or your obligations to others that have entrusted to you? It does become *troubling* to your soul. It's akin telling a drowning person, "Now don't panic, you need to relax." When *should you panic when you're about to drown?*

When I am pressed upon and disappointed I wonder: What of *His* reputation and *my* reputation as one who tells others that, "God will deliver you in time of trouble"? From all appearances I have been abandoned and left to ridicule. Where is He *today*? Sometimes (a lot times lately), He seems so far away—almost indifferent to my cries for His Hand and His touch.

Yes, I know that He lives and that He is watching. I know that I must remain in Him if I am to bear the fruit of peace, joy, etc. But honestly, I feel that I am drowning at times with all that He has placed or allowed to be placed upon me. And yes, I realize that many of those things that stress me are self-inflicted—but the pain remains..

But to the point, "What do I do?" I am reminded of Paul's words in the letter to the Philippians, "Do nothing from selfish ambition or conceit, but in humility count others more significant than yourselves." (Philippians 2:3-4, NIV) *Those very words* are what help me when I am demoralized with self-pity or depression—the realization that it is often my pre-occupation with my troubles that gets *in the way* of His peace; whereas it is the focus upon the needs and hurts of *others* that brings about a change in my heart and mind. I have four young men that I am feeding, parenting, raising, and loving, for goodness sake! They look *to me* for stability, direction, encouragement and *as the example of how a real man should handle himself.* And strange as it sounds, the more I focus on their troubles in math, or how to tie a shoe, or how to grow muscles, et al, the less I aware of the troubles that were drowning me a few hours ago.

It is true, it is not good that a man should be alone—he tends to start taking himself too seriously. Praise God that He allows the needs and hopes of others to invade our self-centered orbits.

Rising Above the Rest

"Then I heard the voice of the Lord saying, "Whom shall I send? And who will go for us?" And I said, "Here am I. Send me!" (Isaiah 6:8 KJV)

Isaiah was a man in love with God *before* God called Him. This was a man *ready* to do whatever it was that God required—regardless of the assignment—great or humble, inspiring or dispiriting, noteworthy or quickly forgotten. It did not matter. His resolve was shown in his plucky response to God: *"Here am I. Send me!"* (Isaiah 6:8 KJV)

This, if you will, is what happens when one experiences the call of God in their life. And the call of God happens when we soberly consider, or take an inventory of, our gifts and talents, and humbly submit them to God's sovereign will and purpose.

Now these might sound like easy words for us to subscribe to Isaiah, Moses, or Saint Paul—but what happens if we apply these words to Ed, John, Kelly, Alice, Dean or anyone else reading these words. *If* I know Him, it is a certainty that I *love* Him. And if I love Him I am compelled to *be used by Him.* So that, my friends, is the question. If we *claim* to know Him and love Him, are we surrendered to Him? Have we accounted for the gifts, talents, time and environment in which we have received and have we allowed Him to "send us" to whatever place He chooses—or have we focused on something *good*—not the "best", but nonetheless "good"?

It's a lot easier to criticize the President of the USA than to *be* the President of the USA. The same holds true of being a pastor, evangelist or Christian speaker. It takes less preparation to disparage the message, delivery, or effectiveness of a man or woman in Christian vocation than to invest the time preparing, practicing and praying.

But *accepting* God's call to teach, preach, evangelize, or even to be a "sold out disciple" of Jesus Christ has costs and considerations as well. You don't have to be behind the pulpit each Sunday to be following God's call, but to follow Him, I do know that these things have to be present:

- You must be prepared to go it alone
- You must understand that you *will* be misunderstood
- You must give up any expectations of being celebrated
- You must daily rise above your fears, your doubts, and that urge to give up and go back to what you were doing before. No matter how dark it gets, no matter how many friends or members of your family turn their back on you, you must complete the mission He has given you—and that mission might take a lifetime to complete.

Living on the Other Side of the Boat

"Afterward Jesus appeared again to his disciples, by the Sea of Galilee. It happened this way: Simon Peter, Thomas (also known as Didymus), Nathanael from Cana in Galilee, the sons of Zebedee, and two other disciples were together. "I'm going out to fish," Simon Peter told them, and they said, "We'll go with you." So they went out and got into the boat, but that night they caught nothing. Early in the morning, Jesus stood on the shore, but the disciples did not realize that it was Jesus. He called out to them, "Friends, haven't you any fish?" "No," they answered.

He said, "Throw your net on the right side of the boat and you will find some." When they did, they were unable to haul the net in because of the large number of fish. Then the disciple whom Jesus loved said to Peter, "It is the Lord!" As soon as Simon Peter heard him say, "It is the Lord," he wrapped his outer garment around him (for he had taken it off) and jumped into the water. The other disciples followed in the boat, towing the net full of fish, for they were not far from shore, about a hundred yards. When they landed, they saw a fire of burning coals there with fish on it, and some bread. Jesus said to them, "Bring some of the fish you have just caught." So Simon Peter climbed back into the boat and dragged the net ashore. It was full of large fish, 153, but even with so many the net was not torn. Jesus said to them, "Come and have breakfast." None of the disciples dared ask him, "Who are you?" They knew it was the Lord. Jesus came, took the bread and gave it to them, and did the same with the fish. This was now the third time Jesus appeared to his disciples after he was raised from the dead." (John 21: 1-14 NIV)

Cast your net on the other side. It seems like a simple suggestion, but these young fishermen were tired, in no need of some amateur giving them direction, and keenly aware that there were no fish anywhere near their nets. But for some reason they complied—and they were glad they did, for the catch of fish was astounding. Have you ever obeyed and later realized how glad you were that you did?

Obeying—not reasoning or reckoning—is what God called His leaders to do. But we are so prone to ask "why" or to carefully ensure that if we *do* obey Him we protect ourselves from looking foolish, or failing, or appearing to have misheard Him and acting presumptuously. But these young disciples did not take any of that into mind! Praise God—it is the reckless abandon of Abraham, Amos, Moses, King Saul, Jonah, John the Baptist, and countless others that pleases Him and inspires us. The truth is, obeying God *might* make you look foolish, might lead to initial failure and might appear *very unwise.* But God smiles at those that are fearless and heroic in their love and submission to Him—it is what the heroes of old were celebrated for. Where are those heroes today?

If what God told you to do made sense and was totally logical, no faith would be required, and no character or trust in God would be engendered and kindled. Friend—what is God telling you to do that is reckless, dangerous, extraordinary?

So they did what they were told to do and they were astounded at their "catch" once they dropped the nets into the water—and in this case the result was instantaneous. They had so many fish that the nets began to burst and the boats almost sank!

But they would not have caught the fish if they were on land just idly hanging around or mending their nets or begging for fish…nor were they sitting down with folded hands just praying about it… they were out there *trying!*

Oh, that I would *listen* to Him like these seven men did in their boat! Oh, that like John, I could quickly *recognize* Him; oh, that like Peter I would fling everything aside and *rush to* Him and what He's doing when I see that it is He that is making preparations for something wonderful! It does not matter what He is doing—whether it's frying fish or sharing God's love with a prostitute—what matters is that I am *listening, recognizing and responding.*

He is talking to you right now. Am you—and am I—listening? He is on the shore waiting. Can we recognize Him? He's doing something and wants us to join Him. Can we throw everything else aside and join Him?

Oh, to Not Forget!

In the Gospel of Matthew, several times Joseph started to do one thing with his family, but was warned by an angel to do something else. *Each time* Joseph obeyed the angel, and the baby Jesus and Mary were protected because of it. (See Matthew 2:13, NIV)

Joseph, Mary's husband, obeyed and disaster was averted. Noah obeyed and an ark was built and humankind was saved. Abraham obeyed and the nation of Israel was born. Paul obeyed and the gospel was spread to the gentiles. These men obeyed and because of their obedience to God, His work was furthered. God could have chosen other men, but He chose these and they obeyed. But I wonder how many "would-be heroes" simply did *not* obey and therefore became forgotten men and women. Surely there are many—perhaps *most*—that merely ignore God's voice and disregard His direction. Count me as one of those at times! I know that I have not obeyed Him, that I have chosen my own "way" and that I have refused to do what I knew was the right thing to do. But where I am *ahead* is that I admit it… and God has been merciful.

No, I am not proud of my stubbornness or my pride in "doing it my way", but realizing that it is *my* fault, and not the fault of my parents, my "village" or my generation, makes it easier to avoid going down the same path day after day. God can work through a person like me if I am able to admit my error, repent of my ineptitude, and ask Him to use me anyways He wants for His Kingdom.

It is obedience to Him, when I am clear about what I should do, that draws me not only into a closer, more intimate relationship with Him, but it seems to establish me as being one He can count on more. I notice that as I am more obedient to Him, life does not become easier—in fact it is often the opposite—but rather, I can see His hand upon me (to rescue me and direct me) and His Spirit revealing to me more about *who He is,* all the more obviously and profoundly!

No one is ever brought into a higher spiritual existence by choosing to be obstinate and disobedient—they're crippled and developmentally stunted. It's only when I resolutely determine to trust and obey Him that I can live that abundant life Jesus promised. Why do I then fall back into the bad habits of disobedience that I *know* are bad for me and that hurt all those that are close to me? Because I have an *incredibly short spiritual memory!* I don't go to church, or a bible study, or a men's prayer group to learn *new* things—I go to be *reminded* of the very things I should *never forget.*

We all need fellowship with other believers to be reminded of God's commands, expectations and direction for our lives—particularly those of us who think we are mature in Christ.

Sickness and Health

"I have told you these things, so that in me you may have peace. *In this world you will have trouble.* But take heart! I have overcome the world." (John 6:33, NIV)

Today and last night I was sick… and I *never* get sick. But I came home (from a long trip) stressed, stretched and a bit weary—*before the real work had even began.*

But there are blessings to my maladies: I am alone (I don't like being fussed over when I am sick—just leave me alone, thank you), and I had the morning today and tomorrow morning to recuperate. *Praise God* I did not get this cold (?) on the plane or when I had a full day of meetings. Yet I have slept and slept and I am still tired! I have a low threshold when it comes to pain and sickness, so God has given me precious few days that I am ill, and I rarely miss work.

But for me, at least, when I run a fever (as I am right now) I simply do not function very well. I am absent-minded, easily confused and wobbly. I *hate* to be like this! But I pondered today about what I *did* that led to this cold. Was it not sleeping enough… skipping meals… letting the stress of our ministry/business get me down?

I am not sure if it was one or *all* of those things. But I do know this: It's a fight to live and grow no matter who you are, but if you are determined to work for the Kingdom of God, the fight is even *more* intense. There's no time to be careless or slow-witted with your health if you're doing work for the Kingdom of God—and each one of us who bears the name "Christian" is supposed to be involved with the work—and the fight.

If my body *is* the temple of the Holy Spirit, I am *obligated* to take care of it and maintain it for work. I am no longer my own, but a servant of Jesus Christ, with an obligation to take care of myself. A captain in the US Army once told me that he had two privates placed in the military jail for a weekend after they *got a severe sunburn* at the beach. Their crime was "harming US Army property."

How many times have I harmed "Kingdom of God" property by not watching what I eat, drink, watch on TV, etc.? Yes, I will get sick from time to time, and eventually some small virus or bug will cost me my life—I have long had that premonition. But I can still have peace—even on days like today when my whole body is aching—because *He has overcome the world.* And with that victory I can have peace—He is in control—even in my weakness, my sickness and my confusion. *Nothing* that is going to happen to me has caught God by surprise. The great Physician is able to keep me right where He wants me—regardless of my opinion.

Pity King Saul

In First Samuel, I read where God *chose* Saul to be the first King of Israel, and then God *regretted* that he made Saul King just a couple of chapters later. Can God make mistakes? (See I Samuel 15:11, NIV)

Could God have been "unknowing" or "misinformed" about Saul? Obviously God *cannot* make a mistake, He is *all knowing*, and He is in *total* control of His creation. So *why* then? Why would God *publicly* choose Saul with great acclaim and then, shortly thereafter, abandon Saul? And more important to me existentially, will God one day "regret" that He chose or redeemed me?

I would suggest that *disobedience* is a much bigger spiritual matter than we imagine. It always seems to be the little, seemingly insignificant acts of rebellion that bring about tumultuous consequences! God said, "Go to Nineveh and preach"(Jonah 1:2, NIV)…"strike this rock and water will come" (Exodus 17:6, NIV)… "You are free to eat from any tree in the garden; but you must not eat from the tree of the knowledge of good and evil, for when you eat of it you will surely die." (NIV, Genesis 2:16-17, NIV)

Saul was disobedient, just like Jonah, Moses, Ananias and Saphirra, and Adam and Eve, but he did something *very common* that all my sons also do; when confronted with blatant disobedience he made excuses, belittled the extent of his waywardness and out-and-out lied. He did his best to minimalize his insubordination by playing with words and arguing the point. That really irked the prophet Samuel and probably God even more.

God expects obedience, not excuses or whining, and now that I am raising four young men I understand why. My boys' lives would be *infinitely* more pleasant and far less painful if they trusted me and *obeyed*. But they typically don't obey the first time around and suffer because of it.

What is it that we don't understand about obedience? Why are we so bent on *breaking* laws—both of man and of God? Why are we so wayward?

When it comes to God, I think that these four things come into play:

1. Despite what we *say, w*e really don't trust God. We think that He might not be the best one to turn to and we therefore question His rules.
2. Although we don't tell Him, we don't think that He really understands our need/situation. It's as if we think that God is for children and their fears and needs, not an adult's needs and wants.
3. In our naive way, we think that somehow we are above His rules: "I don't need to obey, His rules don't apply to me…"
4. We fool ourselves into mistaking His long-suffering patience with our waywardness as His apparent blindness or disinterest in our obedience.

We need to become children in heart again and turn back towards trusting and obeying—regardless of whether we like or agree with His direction. Pity Saul for not having a heart set upon pleasing God. But anyone of us can start out committed and find ourselves drifting from our first love…

On Remaining Put

This past week, my boys asked me if they could once again visit a friend of mine in Raleigh. She and her husband are very kind and generous to them and they love going to visit her. But when I pressed them and asked them if they would perhaps prefer to just move away from me and live with my friends *forever*, they *instantly* and with *great enthusiasm* said, "*Yes, can we go upstairs and pack now*?" They followed this joyous outburst by reassuring me that they would still like to visit me every other month or so for the weekend. They were ready to move forward with their plans that very hour.

So much for the notion that I have created a safe haven and happy home where the my four boys feel secure and have a sense of "belonging." For me, *it was heartbreaking and depressing.* Then I began to feel some genuine *annoyance* that they were exhibiting such a profound lack of loyalty and appreciation for all I have done and all that I have given up for them! It ain't easy taking care of these four little men!

I was once warned, in a foster care course I took, about the danger of "EGO" (i.e. expecting "Eternally Grateful Orphans"). It's the erroneous notion that because you adopt a child, he or she will be forever appreciative of your altruism. The truth is, they are *not* grateful at times. But after all, they did not ask to be adopted, or abandoned by their parents. *It's me who needs to be eternally grateful for God's gift to me of them.* If I see them from that side I don't get depressed when they are ungrateful.

It hurts, though, to care for someone that does not appear to reciprocate that love and affection. But pity the children (and adults) who are *unable* to respond. Some of us are so hard in heart, so wounded and disaffected with humanity we are unable to be vulnerable—and some of us are only eight years old.

But mankind is *not*, by its fallen nature, "eternally grateful" to its Creator and Redeemer, so why should my boys be to me? My gratitude to God comes from a deep awareness of how utterly dependent I am upon Him and how desperately depraved I would be without Him. Yes, this is something of which I am cognizant.

But there are times when I make promises and vows to God of my loyalty and love—and yet my heart wanders. He is my first love and I have no intention of abandoning Him, yet my behavior is *not* as consistent as I *know* it should be. He blesses me, restores me, prepares a table before right before the noses of those that don't like me; He shields and shelters me and calls me His own—and yet, time after time, my heart is not as loyal and my head is not as "one-minded" as it should and could be! What is wrong with my boys' loyalty to me is also what's wrong with my loyalty to Him. None of us are there yet.

Each time I wander away from what is *essential* (i.e. my relationship to Jesus Christ) I wander back to Him—for nothing and no one satisfies the longing of my soul as He does. And each time I ask myself—-why did I take my eyes off of Him in the first place? (My boys will come to the same conclusion in time.)

But before all else, three things are essential:

- maintaining my intimate time with Him each morning, before I do anything else;
- giving Him the best part of my day rather what's left over;
- having accountability and fellowship with men and women who share my passion for Jesus Christ.

These three keep those devilish suggestions that I wander away from Jesus at bay.

The Very Same Thing I Cannot Stand in Others

I have "watched" myself react to things that my sons do that *really* irritates me, and I find myself, more and more, retreating to a private place to ask God to show me how to respond. I have lately become *furious* at some of the unkind, irresponsible, and ignoble things that they do, and find myself at a loss at how to properly explain why they should stop living like this.

The *common* faults are dishonesty, disobedience, a lack of respect, selfishness and *not listening*. One of them is quite lazy, one is not able to empathize with others, one complains and whines about *everything,* and one is never satisfied with what he gets—he *always* wants more or better.

Now if you are reading this and you are a parent I am sure you understand what I am talking about. I am *not* the perfect or ideal father and I sometimes wonder if all their issues are a result of my idiocy as a parent. But when I think of *each boy* and what it was that irked me the most, I realized that whereas there were some similarities, each one had something unique that "pushed my button." And then, as I lay there thinking of those bad habits, it hit me: *These are my bad habits as well when it comes to my relationship with my Lord.* In *every case* the things that got my dander up *the most* were the very things that I confess to God each morning! The very things I cannot abide in these children represent *my* spiritual battlefields with God: Broken promises, a lack of compassion, selfishness, whining and complaining—these are all things that God *must get sick of with me!* And yet (praise be to God!) He does not get as angry at me as I get with these boys.

God has every reason to turn His back on me, give up on me, ignore me or punish me for choosing the same bad behavior towards Him that my boys show towards me. But for some incredible reason He loved me *so much* that He allowed His Son to be the recipient of His displeasure—and not me. He does *not* ignore me, give up on me, punish me or get angry with me, <u>because </u>Jesus Christ has taken the punishment in my place. Praise be to God that He does not throw in the towel when I fail Him again and again…

So what should my response be to God? What can I offer Him in *eternal thanks and praise for His incredible love?* I can treat my boys with the same love, forbearance and compassion. They will one day come to know that their rebellion is against God—not me. And, God willing, they will come to experience the same salvation and forgiveness that He has to offer through Christ. And perhaps they will be further along in the process of being made holy ("sanctification") than I am, when they reach my age.

Rise and Shine?

There are some mornings that I am not necessarily ready to "rise and shine." More lately I am wishing I had *one more* hour to sleep, other mornings I wish I could just stay in bed all day, but lately I am not so eager to "seize the day." It's not only that I feel a bit worn out: it's also a certain lack of excitement about all the drudgery that lies ahead: waking the boys up, getting breakfast ready, making sure everyone has the right backpack for school, and so forth. Then there's my *personal* tasks of reading the emails, texts, voicemails, and "messages" that came in overnight, checking my personal and business accounts, making the credit card charges, planning the day, checking my calendar and on and on and on…

It's not that I *dread* the work, but rather I don't get terribly motivated about the boring and non-stimulating things that I simply *must* do each day. But *this is life,* and while it might not always be "happy work", it's what is required if I am going to be the man He wants me to be. I don't know of any saint that has accomplished great things in his/her life and *always* had a smile on his/her face.

I really don't think that it is the spectacular moments or heroic events that make a man what he is, but the ability to rise up in the morning and do the same boring, unrewarding tasks, day in and day out, and not "check out", run away from it, or become a curmudgeon when things get gray. This is the challenge for not only moms and dads who want to be Godly, but even more so for youth and children. Someone, somewhere, must have suggested that it is the parent's job to keep a child entertained (I am assuming this) and today a parent's life seems to revolve around how to keep junior happy and to help him avoid boredom. But a *good* dad or mom has the duty of explaining and showing kids that dull work and drudgery is an expected and *rewarding* part of life on this earth!

It might depress my sons should it be revealed that drudgery, common tasks, cleaning toilets, and washing the car does not get "easier" as we get older, but it can become our *nature* to become creatures that accept the common chores and mundane living as something a *holy* man (or *holy* woman) does. I am trying to teach my young men that it doesn't matter so much about how I "feel" as it does about how *I have purposed in my life to live.* Some things require prayer, but some things, like bad habits, laziness, whining and procrastinating, God leaves to *me* to conquer, either by neglect or getting personally fed up with it!

Yes, rising *and shining* is not always what I *want* to do, but it is what I am *going to do.* It is my destiny even if it is not yet my completed nature yet.

Pure in Heart?

"Blessed are the pure in heart, for they shall see God."(Matthew 5:8, NIV)

We think of the heart as being the center of our emotions, but in the Bible it is used to also describe the "will" or the choices. And so to be pure in heart means that the *decisions, the desires, the thoughts and intentions* of the will, are "pure"—i.e. consistent with what God wants us to decide, desire, think and do. *If* we are truly pure of heart, good things, acts of love and mercy, desires for righteousness and justice, decisions that please God will *naturally* flow out of us.

But the heart is not only for good things. Jesus said that from the heart come those things make us mean: evil thoughts, perverse notions, etc. And this is our "default" will. Having a pure heart cannot happen to us by simply *wanting to have a pure heart.* This is where Christianity parts ways with other religions and philosophies. Jesus taught that nothing short of a *new* heart will bring about a pure heart. If I am to see God, I must have this new, *transplanted* heart. And the promise for me is that I *will* see God. The Bible says that "no man has ever yet seen God", (I John 4:12, KJV) so what an incredible statement!

One aspect of this promise is here and the other is for eternity: I *will* see God in the events and happenings of my life because of this new God-focused and God-oriented heart; one day in heaven He *will* be visible to my new, transplanted eyes and heart. And I will realize that I was waiting for *that* moment more than anything else in my life—-no matter how long I live.

How can I gain a pure heart? It happens when I encounter the living God and He gives me a "new" heart; it continues through the process of sanctification as I follow Christ; walking in the light and learning to live by the word of God. In time, He will change the way I think so that my heart will grow more and more pure and I will "see" Him as He is.

Yes, I need a transplanted, new heart to be pure. And only God, through the Son, can give it to me.

The Ugly Face

Today I became angry, *again*, about something insignificant that occurred at the camp. I was right, I suppose, to be "unhappy" with what happened, but what made me a sick to my stomach was how I allowed the actions of others to set me off and how my anger was expressed (facially and verbally). This has happened two times now this summer and each time I get enraged, I feel sicker and sicker because of it.

It's not a matter of *what* annoys me, but rather of how I allow that irritation to take control of my emotions and my mouth! Though I realize that there *is* a time for anger and perhaps even an outburst of wrath, my anger always seems to be out of place once I walk away from the setting.

I *hope* that the sick feeling I get when I become incensed occurs because of the process of my becoming more like Him (Jesus). There simply is no place for the "old" me—the one that would get angry and say unkind things. But as I struggle with the disgust I feel when I lose my temper, I realize that frankly, I am *powerless* to *not* get angry. At this point in my spiritual pilgrimage the only thing I can do when someone does something wrong and I get angry is get out of the setting, breathe, hold my tongue, and ask God to help me!

On days like this I realize how very far I must still travel. The thing I want to be, I am not—and least not yet. And the things I don't want to be, I still am—but only presently. But praise be to God that I am more and more intolerant of what I know *does not belong* within me, even if it still raises its ugly head from time to time.

The World Needs More of This

"Blessed are the meek, for they will inherit the earth." (Matthew 5:8, NIV)

"Meek" does not mean weak, or cowardly, or lacking a backbone. It means something more refined, I believe. Jesus was instead referring to those who have a spirit of *gentleness* and *self-control* and at the same time are free from meanness and a condescending or spiteful spirit. The meek do not take advantage of others; they are not violent; they do not try to take over a conversation for their own agenda. They are people that have emulated the nature of Jesus in their lives and learned from Him.

Their promise is that they will "inherit the earth" (Matthew 5:8, NIV) —whatever that means. And while I am not totally sure of what Jesus was referring to, it's obvious that it's a big deal! He's saying that they get it *all*—the whole earth. It's common in our world for the powerful, the arrogant, the despots, and dictators to get as much as they can... at the expense of the weak. Consider, for example, what is happening right now in Venezuela, North Korea, and Syria. *One man* has absolute power and ruthlessly eliminates anyone that gets in his way or causes him to worry about what he thinks is essential to make *him* safe, happy, and secure. The *only one* that matters is him (Manduro, Kim, Asaad). These dictators and strongmen are the *antithesis* of the meek. They will one day inherit what they deserve, but the meek will inherit far more than any dictator could ever have imagined. *That* is a promise from God's Son.

Meekness, gentleness, and goodness do not come naturally; they are *supernatural* extensions of God, given to the man or woman, who is living a life connected to Jesus Christ—they are fruit of the Holy Spirit.

Do I want to be meek? He (Jesus) alone can teach me, and His Comforter, the Holy Spirit, can produce it my life. But I have to remain connected to Him.

Rocking or Rowing

"But Elymas the sorcerer (for that is what his name means) opposed them and tried to turn the proconsul from the faith. Then Saul, who was also called Paul, filled with the Holy Spirit, looked straight at Elymas and said, "You are a child of the devil and an enemy of everything that is right! You are full of all kinds of deceit and trickery. Will you never stop perverting the right ways of the Lord? Now the hand of the Lord is against you. You are going to be blind for a time, not even able to see the light of the sun." Immediately mist and darkness came over him, and he groped about, seeking someone to lead him by the hand." (Acts 13:8-11, NIV)

Saint Paul became quite irritated and impatient with the one that was slowing down the good work. *"Get out of the way,"* 9Acts 13:8-11, Paraphrased) is what Paul appears to be saying. He knew that this "sorcerer" wanted to hinder the gospel so he prayed that the man would be *blinded* for a while—and it happened. It's one of the few occurrences of a prophet or apostle praying for something *bad* to happen to someone else. But Paul was fed up; he had a job to do and this man was in the way of the salvation of lost souls.

Do you notice how the men in the book of Acts were *bold?* I have many friends in full-time Christian ministry, and I mean nothing unkind by this, but I don't know many pastors with the fire and backbone of Paul and Peter. For the apostles, preaching the gospel was *all that mattered.* They did not care who was offended, cut off or upset. They put their very lives on the line to preach about Jesus Christ's Lordship.

One of the greatest coaches of all time (in my opinion) was Vince Lombardi. But in leading his football teams to victory, he was relentless in his demands for excellence and a superior "mentality" of *playing to win.* From what I have read, he, like Paul, had a focus—and it made him into a great coach and mentor. *He wanted to win and he removed obstacles (and even star players) that stood in the way.*

Saint Paul, Coach Lombardi, and anyone serious about their work/calling would tell you to: "Lead, follow, or get out of the way!" The older I get, the more I appreciate that counsel. So many folks seem to want to rock the boat rather than *row the boat.*

Are we *dead serious* about the gospel and the resurrected Christ? Are we sure—totally sure—of the power and presence of the Holy Spirit? *Do we believe it? Then ask yourself this question:* What causes *you* to get quite agitated and impatient?

Struggles Included

Camp closed its 38th season this past weekend. It was, again, a blessed summer with wonderful memories and experiences. Many youth will look back at this summer and be reminded that *this* was the summer they gave their heart to Jesus Christ…or *this* was the summer they learned to appreciate people from other countries…..or *this* was the summer they finally came to understand the meaning of forgiveness.

Some folks think that I should not share too much of my personal challenges, doubts, frustrations or fatigue, but this summer, unlike any other, taxed me in all the before mentioned ways. There were many, many days I just did not want morning to come at all. It was not depression, just a general dread of having to contend with so many things I simply could not "solve" on my own. And whereas I trust God far more now than I did twenty years ago, it is still hard for me to not accomplish my tasks, realize my hopes and achieve all my personal goals. It seems the *more* I have come to trust Him, the more challenges I face and the more tempted I am to give up and choose another line of work!

Why is God doing this or allowing this? In truth, *if* I can be sure it is God's hand at work, I can rest and let go—but it's always a temptation to wonder if all my troubles and shortcomings are not self-inflicted or a result of inferior spiritual DNA, etc. And if I am honest, I lose the most sleep and have more stomach pains in knowing (thinking) that I have let *others* down by not being more adequate in all my efforts and attempts. Truly if I focused more on being sure that *He* was happy/proud of me I would rest better—I know this.

Some days I feel like if I get *one more* angry email, phone call or text from someone "disappointed" with me, I will *explode* (such are the challenges and responses I am receiving of late. But that's what happens when you are transparent and share your weakness—some folks just jump all over you and push you lower and lower into the pit.) But what did Luther, Calvin, Saint Paul, and thousands of other heroes of the faith due when they were attacked, insulted, threatened, imprisoned, beat, tortured, exiled, abandoned or murdered? They gave praise to God, whispered, "Speak, Lord Jesus," or admitted that God had allowed the dirt to fly for a good reason. Clearly I am not there yet.

And yet…I think I am getting closer and I believe that He is having His way. It's worth the journey—struggles and hurt included.

Who's Afraid Of...

Are you afraid of something? Snakes…spiders…deep water…flying…Donald Trump….Joe Biden… getting old…living beyond your retirement funds…death..?

Most all of us would have to admit that we have a "phobia" or two. And some fears can be good, of course. We're afraid to go to jail or get pulled over by the State Trooper so we obey the traffic laws. Children are afraid of losing some privilege or getting spanked so they avoid misbehaving. The "fear of the Lord" (Proverbs 9:10, NIV) is spoken of throughout the Bible as a *positive* thing—something that was used to rescue Israel or bring people to their senses. The fear of God is a positive, helpful thing. On Fathers Day I would confess that my "fear" of my biological father was based 100% on my corresponding *love* for him. I was never afraid of him when I was doing the right thing at the right time, but I had a fear of his response to me if I was doing the wrong thing at the wrong time. Friends, my fear of him kept me in school, out of jail and employed. We should be grateful for our fathers' focus and determination to raise us into gentlemen and ladies rather than foolish or lazy slugs.

But I am talking about the kind of fear that can paralyze you and lead to depression. Fears can leave us unable to function. When I *attempted* Judo I was taught to make a loud yell before I started to throw someone because the yell would startle them, and that made them stiff and easier to throw to the ground. Fear can do that—it can knock us out, emotionally speaking.

Do I live my life in *fear* …or do I live upon God's promises? Do I boldly say that, *"(You) God are my refuge and protector"* (Psalms 91:2, NIV) or do I live in doubt and anxiety? That's the challenge to consider today.

And to give be clear, *regardless* of my failures, sins, obstinacy and ineptitude, God cannot and will not fail me! So I do not *have* to fear. It's the devil's lie that He no longer cares for me or that His arm is too short. John says in 1 John 4:18 (NIV), "There is no fear in love. But perfect love casts out fear, because fear has to do with punishment. The one who fears is not made perfect in love." The context here is important: verse 17 says, "This is how love is made complete among us so that we will have confidence on the day of judgment: In this world we are like Jesus."

This does not mean that we will never *tempted* to fear, and only a fool would never have *reason* to be afraid from time to time. Yet It's only when we *face* our fears that we can experience the nobler things of life like courage and tenacity. You can only be shown to be courageous when you have good reason to be afraid. "Superheroes" have nothing to fear under their armor or super powers; it's the mortals, the ones made of flesh and blood, and only the mortals, that are able to display heroic courage.

Jesus understands fear, first hand, and He knows how debilitating it is. No, I don't think that He was ever afraid—but He was tempted with fear at the garden of Gethsemane. But this temptation to fear was not in reference to failure or pain or humiliation. His struggle had to do with carrying upon His very body the consummate sin of all mankind… and then to hang on a cross, abandoned by God as He took upon Himself the penalty of mankind's rebellion. (If you are ever tempted to think that you don't matter, meditate upon the Jesus suffered for you. You are not a piece of trash, a mistake or a non-essential man or woman—-you are precious and the focus of His separation from God for a season.)

Jesus was clear. There's really only one thing to really be afraid of—God. He said plainly, "Don't be afraid of those who want to kill your body; they cannot touch your soul. Fear only God, who can destroy both soul and body in hell" (Matthew 10:28, NIV). And yes, we can water this down any way you want, but ultimately God is in total control—-it's best to remember that before we attempt to manipulate Him, argue with Him, expect Him to excuse our mistakes and poor choices and tell God that it's not fair for Him to hold us responsible. He is God and He will do what He wants when He wants.

And yet throughout the Bible we hear in both the Old and New Testament this same refrain: "Don't fear, for I have redeemed you; I have called you by name; you are Mine." (Isaiah 43:1, ESV) God actually commands us **not** to fear, or worry. The phrase "fear not" is used at least 80 times in the Bible, most likely because He knows the enemy uses *fear* to decrease our hope and limit our victories. And He knows that we are inclined to fear because of the violent and uncertain world in which we life *breeds* fear. He knows that that fear leads to helplessness and depression. But He provided a rescue for me from fear and depression: Jesus Christ, who is able to show me how to let go of fear and depression. I can rearrange depression and spell out "I press on" by rearranging the letters! What a difference in perspective! And in Christ, my friends, *I can press on and not live in fear or the oppressive attacks of Satan himself.*

Today I have reasons to be depressed, anxious, fearful. It's ludicrous to say that I don't. It's a scary time to live, quite frankly. And if you listen to the enemy he will whisper to you that you *could* be destroyed…you *could* fail…you *could* be wrong about God…you *could* be convicted about the wrong understanding of God and the wrong religion…you *could* be wrong about "god" even existing. Those things could make you worry and go to bed at night in fear!

But *His love* dispels not just a few fears, but *all* fears. *If* we experience His love, first hand, we will *want* to keep in His love—because we won't want to return to a life ruled by anxiety. *If* we have His love in our heart there's no room for fear—He drives it out. His Holy Spirit will *not* permit a spirit of fear to co-exist with Him. He is more than able to extinguish anxious thoughts and the pestering attacks of those little demons.

Though He Slay Me (Job 13:15, KJV)

I have received more emails this fall than I can ever recall before from former campers and staff, all hurting because of broken or wounded relationships. The common theme was: "How could my friend treat me like this?"

Sometimes I too am hurt by one I thought would *never* let me down, and wonder the same thing. All of us that live long enough have been scarred by the wounds and stained by the tears that *were only possible* because we were very close to someone we loved incredibly; then one day, inexplicably, that beloved person stopped loving us or hurt us so deeply that we had to let go of that relationship. During those times you have a hard time breathing; your hurt so much you never want to ever be close to another soul again; you find yourself walking as if in a trance or a bad dream; nothing seems to matter anymore.

To love someone is of course to take the risk that someday the beloved will break your heart by rejecting, ignoring, or deceiving you. But I would argue that painful as all of this is, it still serves the point of directing our thoughts and ideas *back* to God. *Where* did the idea of "that's not fair" come from? How did the notion that, Love should be pure and faithful, come to be a part of our nature—when it obviously is *not* our nature? *Why* do we keep thinking about, praying for, caring for, and *loving* the same ones that seem to no longer love us?

The answer, of course, is God. *God is love* (I John 4:8, NIV). He is the creator of love and all those sublime aspects of love that cause our hearts and our imaginations to race! We were created both to love and to be loved… that's how He engineered us. Praise God when your heart is breaking about something that was unfair, unkind, unfaithful, or ignoble; it is precisely because there *is* something or someone that *is fair, kind, faithful and noble* that our hearts pine and are lost. We *know* that a broken heart is *not* the way things should be! We *know* that life should *not* be about the things that break hearts but rather the things that cause a heart to sing. *He is the author of that idea.*

So, when we think we have no reason to live another day, or we decide that we will *never* fall in love again, or we question, "How can there be a God when He keeps letting my heart be broken?"… remember that He is not only the "inventor" of that which we crave the most… love….but also the one that can heal that love-starved heart.

He promises to give us "the desires of our hearts", Psalm 37:4, NIV, but He never suggested that our hearts would not be wounded in the process. Do I trust Him? Is He able to give me the love for which my soul pants? Is He, truly, the ultimate lover of my soul? Then I must wait and allow Him, *in His time*, to answer my prayers as I exercise my faith in Him. "Though He slay me, yet I will trust in Him." (Job 13:15, KJV). May Job's words become the words of my friends that are suffering.

Tempted After 40 Days

According to the fourth chapter of Luke, Christ was led into the wilderness *for the* purpose of being tempted by the devil. And then, AFTER 40 days with nothing to eat, He was tempted. (See Luke 4:1-13, ESV).

It's one thing for me to be tempted when I am in church, or surrounded by my Christian friends, or when I am at the "top of my game" mentally and spiritually, but what about the other times? God help me when I am not functioning at my peak when I am tempted! And that of course is part of the point here: We'd better have God to shelter and protect us when we are at our weakest and Satan attacks us the strongest. We're not match for him.

There are good reasons Jesus taught us to pray, "And lead us not into temptation" (Matthew 6:13, KJV). We're weak and fail surprisingly easily! We don't need to be looking for trouble. This is also why God said that "It is not good that man should be alone" (Genesis 2:18, NIV). We need the support of others (true brothers and sisters) when we're weak, and others need us when <u>they</u> are weak.

When I think about it, the times that I have failed succumbed to doing what I *knew* was wrong (i.e. after I was tempted), in each instance, was when I was:

- alone
- feeling sorry for myself
- in the "wrong place" or with the wrong people, and/or
- at a point and time when I am exhausted

But Jesus was alone, hungry, thirsty, tired, worn out and yet He did **not** give in to temptation. Surprisingly it was God, His Father, that set all this up! He **wanted** Jesus to be tested; He planned for Jesus to be hungry and desperate for food and water; He allowed Satan to tempt His beloved to fail by means of compromise and taking an easy path.

But the difference is that Jesus as *not* alone—-He and the Father were one. He did *not* feel sorry for himself or fall into self-pity...*ever.* He was here for **<u>His Father's</u>** divine purpose and was never swayed from that vision. Yes, He was in a bad place, but He was in the place God called Him to be—-and therefore God delivered Him. And yes, He was exhausted, yet He trusted that God would, in His time, restore Him and provide the nourishment He needed—-and indeed God did at the end of this narrative.

Friends, you're not alone in this present pandemic and national lock-down. God is there—more now than ever. Deny the enemy the pleasure of you falling into self-pity—rise above that childish emotion and remember that He has redeemed you to rise and shine for His glory. God *will* restore you, your family, this nation and His children all over the world if we determine to trust Him and not trust our own instincts.

Nothing that happens to me—or to you—has caught God by surprise. Let us look, in great anticipation, to the time when God will send His angels to tend to our needs us just as He did Jesus after His ordeal with the deceiver.

The Old Testament—A Treasure

"For everything that was written in the past was written to teach us, so that through the endurance taught in the Scriptures and the encouragement they provide we might have hope." (Romans 15:4, NIV)

Hmm, I find it interesting that Paul wrote this to Christians at a time, of course, when the New Testament did not yet exist. He was *clearly* talking about the Old Testament. So why do some of us cast off the Old Testament as being insignificant or even *inferior* to the New?

Jesus quoted from the Old Testament, the New Testament writers used the Old Testament as proof of Christ's messiahship (the fulfillment of prophecy, et al) and at no point does any scripture in the New Testament suggest that we should merely focus on Paul's letters or the gospels.

The Old Testament was *inspired by God's Holy Spirit* and therefore can be counted upon to not only be true but also *essential* in teaching, encouraging and giving hope to us (these are Saint Paul's words, not mine). The Old Testament scriptures *validated all that Jesus said and did.* They're *essential* for a proper understanding of who Jesus is and why He came.

So why am I am making all of this "noise" today about Old Testament scripture? Just to remind *all* of us to ask the Holy Spirit to use those God-inspired records to inspire us, teach us, encourage us and give us hope. By reading both the New Testament and Old Testament each day I gain a greater understanding of what Jesus meant when He taught, why He did what He did and to remind me to see that during those 2000 years that the Old Testament was written *mankind's habits, conditions, proclivities and nature have not changed a bit.* Were it not for the blood of Jesus we would be living no different than the folks of Sodom, Gomorrah, Jericho or at the time of Samson and the subsequent King of Judah and Israel.

The Old Testament does show, at times, what a woman or man dedicated to God can accomplish, but in each case, after the demise of that woman or man, the people were constantly lacking direction and never seemed to get the full picture of who God is and how much He loves us.

Read the Bible my friends—every book in the Bible was written to teach us something.

This Is a Marathon

When things begin to stand still and I don't see the change and progress I think is required—despite my best efforts and most earnest prayers—I begin to wonder:

1. Am I doing enough? (After all, no matter how much I do, it won't be enough.)
2. Have I somehow missed something? (Because no matter how thorough I try to be, there's always something I could have overlooked or could have addressed better.)
3. Why is He so quiet of late? (I know that He is often silent, but is it a sign of His displeasure or Him waiting on for something from me? Does He simply not *need* to say anything?)

I tend to measure my value to God by my "success," my ability to complete a task, or how I excel others or "win" at the things I do. Paul saw it differently. He saw his work for God as his response in love because of his salvation through Jesus Christ; his life was more like a "race" than a series of successes or attempts to hit personal goals. (See II Timothy 4:7, NIV).

And that "race" is not a "dash"; it's a life-long marathon. "Winning" means that I complete the race, not that I complete my "bucket list" or achieve those marks of "having arrived" that I have created in my own mind based on what others have accomplished. I am called to keep pace with Jesus Christ…..and not attempt to keep up with a televangelist (may God forbid!), an accomplished author, a gifted speaker or even the most humble man or woman I meet. His pace seems at time relentless and impossible (!) and yet I find that if my eyes are set upon Him, I am somehow able to keep up. But if I lose the focus on Him and begin to realize just how dark, deep and ominous that water is below me I immediately begin to sink.

Ultimately all my anxious thoughts are not really about me being good enough to warrant His attention (I am not good enough), or wondering if I have worked hard enough and been faithful enough (again, I fail in both); my anxiety is related to my lack of faith that He will protect me. That's the truth. What makes me doubt? Why do I not think back to the times He has always caught me and kept me from falling?

Well, the answer has to do with why Christian fellowship is so essential. We need to be reminded that we all are struggling and we need to return to the very things we were once certain we would never abandon. The essential question for each of us to ask about the fellowships we attend is simply this: Are we being *reminded* about the truths about Him that are irrefutable? Each day, am I seeking Him and His Kingdom work with all my heart—and then truly trusting Him to take care of *all* the rest?

When People Join Together and Pray

I read the story about how Peter was put in jail by Herod and subsequently how the Christians prayed for Peter. The background was that James, the brother of John, was just *killed* by Herod, so these folks were praying *mightily*.

And then, of course, the miracle happened. God *answered* their prayers and Peter was miraculously freed from prison by an angel and walked to the house of the folks that were praying for him. He knocked on the door as they were praying for him, and the girl answering the door was so shocked that she left the door locked, and Peter outside (!) as she ran to tell the fellow believers that Peter was outside—no longer in jail.

But the people *praying for his deliverance could not believe it and told the girl she was out of her mind.* It's reassuring to know that even the early Christians had moments when they were spiritually dim-witted. They *prayed* for Peter's deliverance, Peter *was delivered, and they could not believe that their prayers were effective!* Why am I also so slow to believe, trust and understand, when, just like these early believers, I have seen God do the impossible *many times before?* (See Acts 12:1-19, NIV)

Peter would one day be arrested, and tradition tells us, crucified up side down—regardless of those prayers that were being lifted for his deliverance. There are times when God answers "no" to our requests—just as He answered "no" to His own Son's request that "this cup pass" (Matthew 26:39, NIV). But there are far more times when He answers in the affirmative and our lives are blessed beyond expectations.

I have learned *never* to pray for what I merit, or to wallow in self-pity before God about what I think I *don't deserve.* Peter and Paul certainly never did this. They were resolved to allow Him to have His perfect will in their lives—even if it meant jail, banishment or martyrdom. I talk about being abandoned to Him, but it's surprising how quickly I squeal when things get difficult or He fails to answer me in the time and means I think most efficient!

Peter was delivered, I believe, because *the people prayed for him. God heard their prayers and it pleased God to answer their prayers.* There is power in the prayers of men and women who *believe that He hears them and is pleased with their petition.*

Shroud of Turin

The shroud of Turin, the burial cloth that is believed to bear the "negative photographic" image of the crucified Christ, is something I have wondered about since I first heard about it. And from what I have read, seen and heard to prove its authenticity, consider me a believer.

But I never saw the *under half* of the shroud, which showed the *back* of Jesus, until last night at a friend's house. It was horrible to behold, and I now believe, more than before, that this is no hoax or medieval attempt to fool the faithful.

The image of that back caused me to put my hand to my mouth in shock, and haunted me so much last night that I could not sleep. The one whose body was represented in that shroud had a back that was *torn to pieces* by whip that must have been tipped with metal pieces or broken pottery. The flesh was mutilated and cut in a way that caused me to wince and turn away from the screen. It looked like a field that had been dragged over with a deep plow. That man suffered incredibly *before* He was crucified. In fact, I am told a man was rarely, if ever, scourged with the whip as Jesus was *and then* crucified! It was one or the other, but not both; even for folks as cruel as the Romans, enough was enough.

I suppose the angst that gripped me for hours was the *reality* that "the man" Jesus of Nazareth suffered incredibly for *my sins and my restoration* (and the whole of mankind) to His Father. The enormous price He paid! The humiliation, pain, blood, suffering, separation and absolute torture He endured *for sins He never imagined*, caused *me* to suffer last night. Too often, I think lightly of the things *I choose to do* that I *know* are inconsistent with what God wants of me, and quite honestly of what *I* want with me. Somehow, after seeing that shroud, I became a bit more convicted and concerned about the things that I do that I do not want to do and the very things that I hate and keep on doing. Like Paul, I feel like a wretched man at times! And yet He chose me, loved me, gave His life for me, is cheering for me, and will never abandon me!

But thinking about the cross and how that Man suffered…that is something all Christians must brood upon; maybe we don't do it enough.

B. B McKinney wrote these words many years ago:

> I am satisfied, I am satisfied,
> I am satisfied with Jesus,
> But the question comes to me,
> As I think of Calvary,
> Is my Master satisfied with me?

…The question comes to me *as I think of Calvary…is He "satisfied" with me?* For certainty, I am not.

Helping versus Enabling—Which Am I Doing?

I heard that one day that the renowned C. S. Lewis and a friend were walking down the road and came upon a beggar who reached out to them for help. While his friend kept walking, Lewis stopped and proceeded to empty his wallet. When they resumed their journey, his friend asked, "What are you doing giving him your money like that? Don't you know he's just going to go squander all that on alcohol?" Lewis paused and replied, "That's all I was going to do with it."

In many ways that story sums up my dilemma. To me, "helping" means that *my heart* is set on making another person's life better, somehow. It's an act that gives me hope that what I am doing is going to cause the recipient to have a better life.

On the other hand, "enabling" seems to refer to me doing something that *keeps a person on their present track but does nothing to help them rise to a higher level.* But with that definition, C.S. Lewis was an enabler, not a helper, but I just don't think that this was the case. The question for me is: How can I know the difference?

By the end of the day, I have determined that I really cannot be sure that my "helping" might unintentionally be "enabling"—such as giving money to a beggar to buy more beer. The real danger I see in ministry is that the warning of "not enabling" someone might be a hidden excuse for simply not helping or caring *at all*. And while it is true that my helping might indeed do more harm than good, I believe that this is the exception, not the rule.

The truth is that Christ commanded us to be kind, compassionate, forgiving, forbearing, and charitable *to the least of those we come into contact with*. Whereas I cannot always tell if my intentions help or hinder someone, *God certainly is able to know the difference and judges me on the intentions of my heart. He* looks at the true reason I try to help or why I show mercy and grace when it might not be wise. If I wait for proof that what I am doing will help a person and not become a crutch to that person, I probably will never help another soul!

So I pray for discernment, guidance and the wisdom that God alone can give. And if I err in forgiving too much, or trusting too often, or helping in a way that really *does not help*, God is able to work through my mistakes and bring about good regardless. But we're called to have compassion, to try to make a difference and to show the love of God—even it at times we're taken advantage of.

"He Must Increase and I Must Decrease." (John 3:30, ESV)

These are the words John the Baptist spoke when his disciples complained that people were leaving him (John) and going over to Jesus. What an incredible statement from a man who *knew His place* in God's work! He was, in effect, telling his disciples: "It's not about me, it's about me being of use to God. And if it suits God for me to decrease so that Jesus may increase, let me start deflating right now."

So many inspirational books are splashed with the photos of their authors nowadays, and I wonder: who is increasing and who is decreasing? The task of those of us in ministry is to do the planting, cultivating, watering, or harvesting, or whatever else He has gifted and equipped us to do, and then, quite frankly, *get out of the way and let the Holy Spirit take over.* God did not call John the Baptist to establish a new religion, but to prepare the way. He did not ordain Paul to create a new church order, but rather to preach about *the church of Jesus Christ* to the gentiles. Even now, God is in no need of men or women rescuing His endeavors, but rather He beckons us to be servants of the risen Lord, willing to do what they are asked to do even if it means being *forgotten.*

John recognized his place in God's work and in his relation to Jesus. He said: "He who comes after me (that is Jesus) ranks before me, for he was before me; …among you stands one (Jesus) whom you do not know, even he who comes after me, the thong of whose sandal I am not worthy to untie." (John 1:15, NIV)

John simply refused to envy Jesus' popularity. His call from God was to faithfully prepare the way for Jesus, not to claim the top prize for number of souls baptized or to vainly enter into some popularity contest.

Here's the point with John; It was his *mission* to see Jesus Christ increase…*end of story.* But is it *my* mission to see Jesus increase at my camp and in my home? Is it *our* mission to see Jesus increase in our churches—or are we looking for something else? And could that "something" be our own reputations, our denominations? God forbid…

If He *increases* in a church, or our community, it is a sure sign that those of us doing the preaching and teaching and discipling are doing a good job. But if people are being drawn into devotion to any one of us or our pet projects and never get to Jesus, we're doing a pitiful job and need to reconsider our call. If people are being drawn closer and closer to me—but never any closer to Him—I am a fraud as a Christian. My hope, my goal, my dream must be to see Him increase in the hearts and lives of those I love, as my own influence and their attentiveness to me *decreases.*

Am I ready for that? Am I praying for that? Am I preaching, teaching and discipling with that in mind?

The Day God Changed His Mind

A good King named Hezekiah was informed by a prophet of God that he would soon die. God told the prophet plainly to warn Hezekiah that he needed to get his house in order; death would be soon. (See II Kings, 20:1, NIV)

Hezekiah was ill. He turned his face to a wall, cried bitterly and begged God for more time. Something noteworthy followed. God heard his prayer, saw his tears **and** *changed His mind*. Now I don't say that to cause alarm or to suggest that we need to fear that God is capricious and that He might break His *good* promises to us in the future. But, I find it *incredibly* encouraging to know that He *sees* our tears, *hears* our prayers, and is able to not only reconsider some negative consequences in our lives, but also even alter the *laws of physics* to prove His love to us! (As a sign that God would give Hezekiah fifteen years to his life he caused *the sun to stop and then go backwards ten steps, or ten hours!*) (See II Kings, 20:5-6, NIV)

Have I cried bitterly about things in my life? Have I sincerely sought God's intervention and humbly admitted my total dependence upon Him for my deliverance? Hezekiah did, and God *delivered* him from the Assyrian assault on Jerusalem, *healed* him of a deadly infection, *added fifteen years* to his life and caused *the earth to change its course for ten hours to prove the point!*

Is anything too difficult for God? No! Then why am I not laboring more at prayer and less at attempting to make things happen on my own?

> *What a Friend we have in Jesus, All our sins and griefs to bear!*
> *What a privilege to carry Everything to God in prayer!*
> *O what peace we often forfeit, O what needless pain we bear,*
> *All because we do not carry Everything to God in prayer!*
> *Have we trials and temptations? Is there trouble anywhere?*
> *We should never be discouraged, Take it to the Lord in prayer.*
> *Can we find a friend so faithful Who will all our sorrows share?*
> *Jesus knows our every weakness, Take it to the Lord in prayer.*
> -Joseph Scriven

Hearing and Doing

"Then his mother and his brothers came to him, but they could not reach him because of the crowd. And he was told, "Your mother and your brothers are standing outside, wanting to see you." But he said to them, "My mother and my brothers are those who hear the word of God and do it." (Luke 8: 19-21, **NIV**)

What does this mean? What is "hearing and doing"?

Hearing: It means more than just noticing noise or listening to a person give a lecture. It has to do with focused attention—giving heed to, and deciding to believe in, what's being articulated. Have I *heard* the words of Jesus? Is my preacher or priest *speaking the words of Jesus*—i.e. the "word of God", or is it just noise?

Doing: It's not admitting that I *need* to change or give up on the way I am living, it's *doing something about it*. It's one thing to be sorry about the way I live (or that I got caught) but quite another to turn around and walk in another direction.

But "doing" *what?* The "doing" seems to refer to first seeking, asking and knocking—i.e. an earnest pursuit of God—a yearning and a passion for *Him*. And following that, the "what" is entering into a new life of *obedience and love*. They go hand in hand. If I *obey Him* I will love Him and I will love His creatures—i.e. mankind; and if I *love* Him I would not want to enter into any kind of behavior that would interfere with that love relationship. True obedience to God is an *extension* of love, not my anxious reaction to the oppressive demand of a despot.

Who then are the true children of God? Those that live lives of love. How can you see that a man or woman loves God? By the manner in which they love others. It comes to reason, then, that a person who is *not* loving others does not know the love of God and is not living a life of obedience to God.

May we hear more than noise from those that lead us spiritually and may those we turn to for counsel give us the "word of God" in these times of trouble.

The Little Donkey

I am still working on areas of my life in which I need to be more charitable and forgiving, and one area where I am not so charitable is when I am around people that wilt when they feel they have been ignored or just "give up" when they feel that their efforts are not fully appreciated. I hate being around Christians that act like babies and I want nothing to do with them.

Yet, as I honestly assess my own responses to people who whine when they feel like that are getting a lack of appreciation, I realize that this childish behavior still shows itself in *my* life. Yes, I see it clearly, at times, and I am at a loss to explain *how* it can still be in my heart after all I have seen and been through.

Isn't it these things (pride, anger at being ignored or not properly appreciated) that cause most of the problems within our churches, families and ministries? At the heart of the problem is simply this: *Secretly* I think more highly of myself than I should. *Without telling anyone*, I am annoyed that my ideas, work, or suggestions are ignored. *I would never admit it*, but I have this aggravating idea that people don't appreciate just how smart and talented I am.

Mankind has *not* really "evolved" or improved in these matters. And though I find my own pride and petty whining *disgusting*, the same vices are common to all of us—particularly to those that think they are "pretty good people."

So what am I to do? First, I need to stop getting so bent out of shape with others' pride until I can bridle my own. Next, I must remind myself each day that *every man is in some way my superior* and to *consider the needs of others more important than my own*. This leaves very little room for pride and sets me up to live and learn (from watching others).

It's said that Francis of Assisi always referred to himself as a donkey and, as a result, never really took himself seriously (who takes a donkey seriously?) but never hated himself either (who could hate a silly little donkey?). We once had a donkey at camp and one of staff named it after me. It seems quite fitting.

It Is a Holy Day

I had been in France more than two weeks and I was truly, *sincerely,* ready to come home. I rose at 4:00 am and got to the airport in Paris in plenty of time, but then I had a connection in Brussels with a three-hour layover. Then that layover ended up lasting *five* hours because of snow and ice. Finally we boarded the plane, but I was in a foul mood, because I was *sure* I would miss my connection in Dulles. So I was less than polite, perhaps, as I walked down the ramp and onto the plane. Then I saw a poster from the airport authority that caught my eye: "Relax—if something goes wrong. we'll make it right. After all, you're on holiday." And as I took my seat, I thought, "It's true. I need to relax. Everything *is* going to work out. And besides, my trip was work for God—I was not on a holiday, but every day at work for Him is a "holy day." And in a real sense, if we are in love with Him and if He shines in all we do, aren't *all* days "holy days"—i.e. *days set apart to be sacred for God?*

Anyway, that epiphany changed my attitude and I relaxed and began planning how I would get another plane from Washington to my home. And I relaxed and relaxed and relaxed—for *four hours* as the plane sat on the tarmac and accumulated more and more snow and I slept. To make the drama short, let me simply say that by the time the plane *was* ready to take off, the flight crew's policies would not permit them to fly because we had stayed on the plane too long. The flight was cancelled.

We had to de-plane, claim our luggage and re-book our flights. We were told that the hotels were *all* full, because *all* flights were cancelled at the airport. *It was a mess!* People waited for two hours for their luggage and four hours for taxis, but most slept a miserable night in cots at the airport.

I was *not happy* and confess that I lost the whole idea of "every day is holy day" for a few hours. I had to *first* re-book a flight, *then* find a connecting flight and *then* find a hotel somewhere in the center of the city, *then* find an Uber driver, and *then* contact the camp to let them know of the fiasco.

The point of this little message is not to give all the details, but let me simply say that the next day—the day I wrote this devotion—the plane was *again* delayed and I arrived in Washington, DC too late for my connecting flight—or *any flight.* So I had to rent a car and drive home from Washington to the camp late at night. This is not something I enjoy doing so late at night and for six hours.

So, what's the spiritual lesson? This happens to business travelers every day—and worse. Yes, I had a hard time *getting* to France, I got *sick* in France and now I wasted money I cannot afford to lose purchasing new tickets, renting a car, paying for a hotel, etc. *It's not supposed to happen to me.* At least, that's how I am *tempted* to think. But again, either God *does* orchestrate these things or He is indifferent and uncaring. Friends, *I know Him and I am persuaded that He loves me.* And *that's enough for me to know.*

I am raising four young men now. What an honor… but what an *obligation to their heavenly Father.* They could all tell you that I am constantly telling them to *trust* my judgment, rules, demands, and so forth. *Frequently* they question my wisdom and experience when I try to pass on the reasons for what I want them to do, but I *know what I am doing—and so does God when He allows these things to happen to me.* He is teaching me, reminding me, or preparing me for something—or He used my misfortunes for His greater purposes. That's enough. I trust Him, I relax. Everything is going to be okay. It's a holy day.

Get Out of the Boat!

In the gospel of Luke we are told that, "Shortly before dawn Jesus went out to them, walking on the lake. When the disciples saw him walking on the lake, they were terrified. "It's a ghost," they said, and cried out in fear. But Jesus immediately said to them: "Take courage. It is I. Don't be afraid." "Lord, if it's you," Peter replied, "tell me to come to you on the water." "Come," he said. Then Peter got down out of the boat, walked on the water and came toward Jesus. But when he saw the wind, he was afraid and, beginning to sink, cried out, "Lord, save me." Immediately Jesus reached out his hand and caught him. "You of little faith," he said, "why did you doubt?" And when they climbed into the boat, the wind died down. Then those who were in the boat worshiped him, saying, "Truly you are the Son of God." (Matthew 14:25-33 NIV)

This same passage was read to a Bible study group by a friend of mine, and he asked each person to re-state the story in their own words, *as if they were there watching the narrative.* One member, to the surprise of my friend, assumed that when Jesus said, "Why did you doubt?", (Matthew 14:32, NIV) He was *not* looking at Peter, *but around and behind Peter at the eleven disciples still safely and comfortably sitting in the boat.*

Many people in my life claim to be "behind me" in my determination to follow Him, yet appear to be only watching me make the move of faith as they remain within the safety of the boat. While saying that they have faith in me and what I am doing, and agreeing to pray with me and for me, most are not ready to "step out on faith" and work hand-in-hand.

But what about *me?* How many times have I done the exact same thing? How often do I see a man or woman of God doing the *right thing,* the *very thing He has called him/her to do,* and all the while I lack the faith, the pluck, the determination and the discipline to join with him or her. I stand condemned if I hear Jesus telling *me* to "come also".

James said, "What good is it, my brothers, if someone says he has faith or if he *believes* in how God is leading another brother or sister but does not have works." (James 2:14, NIV) I hear so many folks talk about promising to pray for this person or that ministry, but I do wonder (1) If they *really are praying with resolve* and (2) if the promise to pray is tantamount to "staying in the boat" so that the one praying will not get his/her feet wet or have to *actually exercise belief by taking action.*

I certainly ought to pray for those who are courageously serving Him, but I ought to also get out of the boat more often, and perhaps be willing to step out in faith *away from those* who are merely watching from a comfortable perch.

Not Everyone That Calls Him Lord Knows Him as Lord

"'Not everyone who says to me, 'Lord, Lord,' will enter the kingdom of heaven, but only the one who does the will of my Father who is in heaven. Many will say to me on that day, 'Lord, Lord, did we not prophesy in your name and in your name drive out demons and in your name perform many miracles?' Then I will tell them plainly, 'I never knew you. Away from me, you evildoers!'"" (Matthew 7:21-23, NIV)

Some folks claim to be followers of Jesus (i.e. they *call* Him "Lord") but are not going to be in heaven. Some will *speak* about Jesus convincingly and with great passion and will even do *incredible things* in His name. They will be pastors, priests and camp directors —but some are frauds. Some are *not what they claim to be—and Jesus is not fooled.*

Man looks at the outside, God looks at the heart. You and I might talk about how much we love God or how strongly we believe in Him—and many folks might be impressed. But God knows the truth—even if we try to fool ourselves. One day the game of pretending will be over and we will stand before God—and the acting and illusions will be over. According to Jesus, some will be shocked to hear Him say, "'I never knew you; depart from me, you workers of lawlessness.' (Matthew 7:23, ESV) I cannot imagine any sadder sentence to be said in all eternity.

This is not a "feel good" thought. It's serious: The *proof* that I know Him is my inclination to do His will and my disgust at doing the wrong things I used to do. If my life is *not* any different than it was before I came to Him, something is wrong. Either I am not in intimate fellowship with Him—and something needs to be corrected—or I never was one of His and I need to get things right between Him and me at once.

If I know Him and He knows me, my life will shine in a way that proves and illustrates that relationship. If I am merely talking religious and nothing I do gives evidence of my new nature, I need to consider His warning.

L. DEAN BARLEY

The Fear of God Leads To...

I was reading Psalm 103 today—what a beautiful passage! It describes a life that is blessed and covered by God. But in this Psalm, as often in the Bible, the blessings, coverings, protection and forgiveness are connected to person's humble life and his/her *fear of God*.

As I grew up I was always told that the "fear of the Lord" (See Proverbs 10:9, NIV)just meant a healthy respect and reference for God. But "the fear of the Lord" (See Proverbs 10:9, NIV) is mentioned over *300 times* in the Bible. Have we watered down what the Holy Spirit meant when He inspired these words to prophets, kings and apostles?

As I read the Word, it's obvious that the fear of God is a *good and positive* thing. Those who fear God aren't wimps or cowards or folks that are unsure of God's love or approval of their lives. Throughout the Bible it is the *God fearing* men and women that became our heroes! But they all had a healthy respect for God as being "wholly other"—not like us, but rather absolutely pure, holy, righteous and removed from anything that is evil, wrong, deceitful, etc.

Jesus drove the point home *even more strongly* when He said, "Don't be afraid of those who want to kill your body; they cannot touch your soul. **Fear only God**, who can destroy both soul and body in hell" (Matthew 10:28, NIV). Obviously, fearing God is good because it reminds us of life outside and against God. A life opposed to God is a lost cause. Who do we look up to and trust the most? For me, at least, it's those folks that are *God fearing! Those* who *fear God* keep their word and their promises.

What does the fear God *do* for me?

- Checks my ego
- Reminds me to keep my promises
- Sets me free from chasing rainbows and instead sets me to following God
Reminds me that He will judge me—and then forgive me because of the blood of Jesus

And where does the fear of God *lead* me? To the indescribable love of God. But I cannot come to understand and experience that sublime love unless I understand and see the need to "fear" life here and life everlasting *without* Him. And *that* love leads me from fear (which is the beginning of getting to know God) to a relationship with Him that fulfills all my hopes, dreams and yearnings.

> Psalm 103 Of David
> Praise the Lord, my soul;
> all my inmost being, praise his holy name.
> Praise the Lord, my soul,
> and forget not all his benefits—
> who forgives all your sins
> and heals all your diseases,
> who redeems your life from the pit
> and crowns you with love and compassion,
> who satisfies your desires with good things
> so that your youth is renewed like the eagle's.

The Lord works righteousness
and justice for all the oppressed.
He made known his ways to Moses,
his deeds to the people of Israel:
The Lord is compassionate and gracious,
slow to anger, abounding in love.
He will not always accuse,
nor will he harbor his anger forever;
he does not treat us as our sins deserve
or repay us according to our iniquities.
For as high as the heavens are above the earth,
so great is his love for those who fear him;
as far as the east is from the west,
so far has he removed our transgressions from us.
As a father has compassion on his children,
so the Lord has compassion on those who fear him;
for he knows how we are formed,
he remembers that we are dust.
The life of mortals is like grass,
they flourish like a flower of the field;
the wind blows over it and it is gone,
and its place remembers it no more.
But from everlasting to everlasting
the Lord's love is with those who fear him,
and his righteousness with their children's children—
with those who keep his covenant
and remember to obey his precepts.
The Lord has established his throne in heaven,
and his kingdom rules over all.
Praise the Lord, you his angels,
you mighty ones who do his bidding,
who obey his word.
Praise the Lord, all his heavenly hosts,
you his servants who do his will.
Praise the Lord, all his works
everywhere in his dominion.
Praise the Lord, my soul. (Psalm 103:1-22, NIV)

In the Secret Place

"And when you pray, do not be like the hypocrites, for they love to pray standing in the synagogues and on the street corners to be seen by others. Truly I tell you, they have received their reward in full. But when you pray, go into your room, close the door and pray to your Father, who is unseen. Then your Father, who sees what is done in secret, will reward you. And when you pray, do not keep on babbling like pagans, for they think they will be heard because of their many words. Do not be like them, for your Father knows what you need before you ask him." (Matthew 6:5-8, NIV)

I grew up hearing "babbling" prayers. They were religious *sounding* prayers, but as a young man I never felt that the prayers had *power* or that they were really intended for God's ears in the first place. I realize that I am in no position to judge the intention of those men that offered up those prayers in my church, but truly, most of those prayers did not inspire or encourage me to pray or to draw close to the One to whom the prayers were directed. They sounded more like something from Shakespeare.

The words from Christ in this passage haunt me because I realize that it is what is done in *secret* that is authenticated in *public*. *If* I have spent hours alone, in seclusion, sincerely and genuinely seeking Him in my prayers and imagination, it will quite naturally spill out from me when I pray in public. But if I have not had my "secret time" with Him, my prayers are a charade in spiritual piety. More and more I am understanding that what I *think, ponder upon, dream about and commit in secret* is the same that gushes from my soul, speech, temperament and language when I am required to give an account in public.

The battlefield is my mind and my wandering thoughts. Those things that consume my conscience and idle imaginings during the day are, in fact, my "god" or my "God." He has saved my soul, but He will *not* do for me what I am able to do for myself—i.e. discipline my time, thoughts, and secret times with Him in prayer.

Open Heart—Open Mind

"One thing I know: Once I was blind but now I can see." (John 9:25, NIV) What a great response to the hectoring questions of the Pharisees from the young man who was *born* blind—then healed on the Sabbath by Jesus. The religious folks could only focus on a narrow understanding of the law, of how things were "supposed to be done" in religious activities, and simply could not explain something that was *clearly* outside their own limited experiences.

It's convenient to look back at these proud Jewish leaders and shake your head in disbelief that they could be so "block-headed." But the spirit of Pharisaism is quite alive and active in our churches, Christian communities, and my *own* mind. It's often said that the last seven words of a church are, "We never did it that way before." Just like the boastful Pharisees, sometimes we're afraid of change, surprises, or God doing things "differently" than we think He should.

How do I respond to things that He does that are obviously *His* doing? Jesus healed a man BORN blind, something unheard of and obviously not "from Satan" as some suggested. So how do **I** deal with things like that? Most appropriately, it appears, by humbly admitting: "One thing I know. I was blind, but now I can see." (John 9:25, NIV). It's hard to argue in the face of the miraculous, intervening hand of God, unless one's heart is so hard and so decidedly against Him that one is unwilling to hear, see, or feel Him when He comes.

God is *going* to do things, great and small, His way, in His time, and in the manner He chooses. If I am wise, I will get used to it, and recognize it, and remember that He *never* (at least in my life) does things the way I think He should; He always does things far better.

The danger is "catching" the "hardened-heart" disease that seemed so common in Egypt, ancient Israel, and with the Pharisees. This spiritual malaise evidently caused men to turn a deaf ear to what was true, pure, beautiful, of good report, praiseworthy and in a word, "of God." As with all diseases, the best cure is to take protective measures against it in the first place. I must ever beware of assuming that I understand His ways, or that I deserve an explanation, or that He is obligated to gain my approval of what He does. Maintaining a humble position of a *servant* and remembering that He knows what He is doing is good medicine for anyone wanting to keep the heart soft and teachable.

Lord—teach me and keep my heart tender!

Am I Really His?

As I read the gospel of Luke, I am mindful that Jesus never really asked people to "do the right thing" or "do what is expected in life," but rather to do what was *unexpected*. Usually, this was far beyond what simply seemed "right" to them. For example, He did not tell people to love their friends, but to love their enemies. (Matthew 5:44, NIV). He did not tell folks to simply forgive an offender once or even seven times, but to forgive an offender seventy times seven. (Matthew 18:22, NIV) He taught His listeners that people of His Kingdom should not be vengeful, should not demand their rights, should not look after their own needs first, should not focus on money or possessions, and should consider their mothers, fathers, brothers and sisters to be those that did the will of God.

Jesus' teachings were neither common nor self-sustaining. If you live as Jesus taught, people will take advantage of you, you could end up destitute, you will never defend yourself, and you won't see people as they are, but rather, you will see them as how God hopes they will be. In short, you will live a life that's full of scarcity and self-inflicted abuse … or perhaps not. Perhaps, if Jesus is who He says He is, He will become your "all in all," your defender, your redeemer, your supplier, and your focus throughout the day. Maybe if you live as He taught, you will come to see that He is in fact quite able to care of all your needs, and give you far more than you had ever hoped for or imagined.

Yes, what He taught is not common and quite frankly not often followed even by those of us who profess to be Christians. But like Saint Francis of Assisi, I for one believe that His teachings can be lived—*if* we abandon our fight to get noticed, admired, respected, secure, and "common," and instead determine to be anonymous, forgotten, despised, vulnerable, and "uncommon."

"Wherefore by their fruits ye shall know them" (Matthew 7:16, KJV)—those are Jesus' words. People should be able to see His fruit in me by the manner in which I speak, respond, react, and order my life. Is that the case?

Amazing Jesus..

Jesus was amazed at the Centurion's faith.

There's a story of a Roman Centurion approaching Jesus after He had just spoken. The Centurion had a sick servant and he *knew* that Jesus could heal that servant. Why? Because he had *heard* about Jesus from others and then He must have **seen** Jesus do the impossible. From what He had seen and heard, Jesus never failed.

"Jesus said to him, "I will go and heal him." The centurion replied, "Lord, I do not deserve to have you come under my roof. But just say the word, and my servant will be healed. For I myself am a man under authority, with soldiers under me." (Matthew 8:8, NIV) Jesus was astounded at the man's faith——and was quite impressed I think. "Then Jesus said to the centurion, "Go! Let it be done just as you believed it would." And his servant was healed at that moment." (Matthew 8:13, NIV). But this happened because of the man's faith in Jesus.

Jesus was happy then, and now, it seems, to help those that trust Him.

Do I make Him happy trusting Him when it seems totally impossible?—do you trust Him? Is He amazed at me for my faith, or dismayed by how thick-headed and quick to forget I am. I have seen Him do the impossible and turn a tragedy into a triumph time and time again—-so why do I doubt Him now?

"Just then a woman who had suffered for twelve years with constant bleeding came up behind him. She touched the fringe of his robe, for she thought, 'If I can just touch his robe, I will be healed.' Jesus turned around, and when he saw her, he said, 'Daughter, be encouraged! **Your faith has made you well.**' And the woman was healed at that moment." (**Matthew 9:20-22**)

Again, it was the faith that moved the mountains—-it was faith that led to incredible miracles—it was faith that opened the door to a new life! The little old lady mentioned above may not have seen Jesus heal before, but she trusted with just the little faith she had. She trusted Him, and because of this, her faith in Him led to healing.

Lord, heal me....heal my nation......heal your church.

The Little Man

"Jesus entered Jericho and was passing through. A man was there by the name of Zacchaeus; he was a chief tax collector and was wealthy. He wanted to see who Jesus was, but because he was short he could not see over the crowd. So he ran ahead and climbed a sycamore-fig tree to see him, since Jesus was coming that way. When Jesus reached the spot, he looked up and said to him, "Zacchaeus, come down immediately. I must stay at your house today." So he came down at once and welcomed him gladly. All the people saw this and began to mutter, "He has gone to be the guest of a sinner." But Zacchaeus stood up and said to the Lord, "Look, Lord! Here and now I give half of my possessions to the poor, and if I have cheated anybody out of anything, I will pay back four times the amount." Jesus said to him, "Today salvation has come to this house, because this man, too, is a son of Abraham. For the Son of Man came to seek and to save the lost." (Luke 19:1-10, NIV)

Zacchaeus was a chief tax-collector at Jericho, mentioned only in the Gospel of Luke. A descendant of Abraham, he was an example of Jesus' personal, earthly mission to bring salvation to the lost. Tax collectors were despised as traitors (working for the Roman Empire, not for their Jewish community), and as being corrupt.

Because the lucrative production and export of balsam was centered in Jericho, his position would have carried both importance and wealth. In the account, he arrived before the crowd who were later to meet with Jesus, who was passing through Jericho on His way to Jerusalem. He was short in stature and so was unable to see Jesus through the crowd (Luke 19:3, NIV). Zacchaeus then ran ahead and climbed a sycamore tree along Jesus' path. When Jesus reached the spot, he looked up at the sycamore tree, addressed Zacchaeus by name, and told him to come down, for he intended to visit his house. The crowd was shocked that Jesus, a religious teacher/prophet, would sully himself by being a guest of a sinner.

So Jesus came into the home of a man who was despised by his neighbors and countrymen. Can you imagine! The most important man in the city (and in fact the universe) asks to come into his home. Consider the joy and feeling of worth that must have come across Zacchaeus!

How does Zacchaeus respond to this surprise of a celebrity visit? He inexplicably announced that he would give half of all that he had to the poor and pay back *four times* whatever he took improperly in taxes. Could you *imagine* that after all of this Zacchaeus would return to a life of stealing or cheating? No, nothing in this narrative leads us to doubt that he did in fact follow through. Jesus told those watching that "salvation" had come to this man…. (Luke 19:1-10, NIV)

Here's the whole message today: *Jesus came into this man's home and that man was changed forever.* Again, consider his *joy*! Jesus is coming to *my* home! Once He comes in you are never the same and others will eventually see it.

Has He come into your heart and house? If not, why have you not invited Him in?

What are our resolutions to Him? Are they so magnanimous and profound?

What would you say to Him, right now, if He said that He was coming to *your* house right after this service—and for the sole purpose of being with you?

Being Made Into a Man for God

Paul told the Corinthians in his second letter, "We do not want you to be uninformed, brothers and sisters, about the troubles we experienced in the province of Asia. We were under great pressure, far beyond our ability to endure, so that we despaired of life itself. Indeed, we felt we had received the sentence of death. But this happened that we might not rely on ourselves but on God, who raises the dead." (II Corinthians 1:8, NIV)

Paul succinctly explained why we face pressures as Christians: That we may depend upon God and not on ourselves. He also offered us great consolation in knowing that we are not some sort of "stunted" Christian if at times we've had enough and want to give up. Paul also despaired of life, and yet he persevered. He did not capitulate to self-pity, and neither should we.

Lately God has done wonderful things in my life—things that I didn't see coming. He surprises me each day. His tendency to not act, or rescue me, in the time and manner of my choosing, does not mean His plan is not accomplished. This is the life of faith I was called to live; a life shared with all who claim Christ as their Lord. It is not a natural, safe, or stable life—quite frankly, it is a wild ride most of the time.

But I realize that He puts challenges, obstacles, frustrations, setbacks, and heartache into my life for divine purposes. These are things that He knows full well that I cannot endure, but in retrospect they have drawn me closer to Him. It is because of the desperate situations in life, quite honestly, that I trust Him. He provides a better solution to my seemingly hopeless odds than I can find alone or by relying on others.

Even now, this very day, I have good reason to be perplexed and downcast. Things just haven't gone the way I had hoped and prayed they would. Despite this, I have an indescribable joy of knowing that He has orchestrated this circumstance for the very purpose of pulling me closer to Him, only because He loves me, and despite how desperate and precarious my life is today!

I know that some folks seek a high from adrenaline, sensational thrills, and breathtaking adventures. But honestly, nothing reveals who, what, and whose I really am as when I call upon Him and say, "Have your way with me Lord, no matter what it requires and how long it takes." That's when the real adventure begins that separates the men from the boys (or the women from the girls).

Dear Lord, make me into one of those men.

A Spontaneous Kind of Love

After dinner tonight, something drew all of us (the boys and our guests) outside. Maybe it was just to enjoy the warm evening and the coming of summer, but before long we began throwing a Frisbee around, and within a few minutes, everyone was playing with the Frisbee, competing to see who could catch the most, who could throw the farthest, and so on. For thirty minutes we were all engaged in a spontaneous time of running, laughing, showing our athletic prowess (or lack thereof), and in general just enjoying each other's company.

It was totally spontaneous, an event for which no one gave any advance thought or preparation. It just happened because a Frisbee was nearby and we all felt like playing together. Aren't those the *best times* in our lives, as compared to the events we carefully plan, meticulously organize, and fret over? Those events tend to be a bit of a let- down once they're all over, but the fun times that we just fall into are the most memorable and satisfying.

It's been said that love is like this. If you have to plan and prepare to love someone, it's a sure sign you really don't love them. But if you do love someone, you find 1,001 spontaneous ways to show it, and it just happens. Likewise with God, if I must make myself go to church, a prayer meeting, or force myself to recite a prayer, but don't find myself doing the same things unexpectedly and off-cue, the love may not be real. If it is forced and required, it may not be authentic.

I wonder, at times, if the way we teach children to love God leads them to think that loving Him has to be planned, rehearsed, memorized, and recited. Real love to God (and to anyone else) must be spontaneous and natural—something we just can't keep bottled up within us! Saint Francis of Assisi was known to break into songs of love for God for no apparent reason. They would just leap out of him!

How can I come to love Him and have this urge, this hunger, to just be with Him, and like Francis, break into unrehearsed songs of joy? I'd have to do at least two things:

1. Realize that there is no greater thing for me to do for myself, and for those I love, than to spontaneously display my love for God. Truly I am a better man, and all those that I know are blessed, because of my decision to remove those barriers that restrain me from shouting out my love for God!
2. I must find time to be alone so that He can tell me things that can only be said one-on-one. I need to be alone with Him so that I can tell Him about my day, my challenges, and my hopes and dreams. But I also need to hear Him, the love of my soul, remind me of His great love and approval of who I am, where I am going, and what I will one day become!

There's a place and time to formally proclaim our love for God and others that are important to us. But I think that it is the unplanned expressions and acts of love that touch His heart, and the hearts of those we love, the most profound way.

The Work to Be Done

Why did God redeem me and then leave me on this earth? Why did He not simply redeem me and take me on to glory? Why leave me here for all these years when I am so "homesick" for my ultimate and eternal home?

In a word, God left me here to *work*. Many of us spend the better parts of our lives working so that *one day* we can stop working and "retire"…whatever "retire" means. For some, retirement means chasing a little white ball across lush green meadows. For others it means fishing or hunting for something we could more easily and economically purchase at the market. For many, like my father, retiring means living your last years wondering *why* you retired in the first place.

Count me as one of those that does not think, hope, or plan for retirement. I believe that I was created to be productive, and I am most content when I am creating—and most irritable when I am idle. Jesus once remarked that, "The work of God is this: to believe in the one He has sent." (John 6:29, NIV) That is what I have been called to do; the very work of God. And the work entails just one thing. It's *not* about me being a perfect Christian specimen to display in a museum; it's *not* about me establishing "heaven on earth" in my summer camp; it's not even about me being resolutely religious and free from sin. The work and purpose is to *believe in the one that God sent — i.e. His Son, Jesus.*

What does it mean to "believe in" Jesus? *To confess, admit and live my life as if He really is a part of the Triune God; the only Son of God.* He lived and spoke and taught not as a mere sage or godly prophet, He spoke as God Almighty. His words, His teachings, His demands, His expectations, His warnings, and His proclamations—*they all carry indescribable power and truth because they emanate from the mouth of God!*

My "work" is to believe this and by association, *live this.* Do you see many people "working for God" living the very life that Jesus urged and taught the disciples to live? Believe me, it's work. To give up worry, envy, anger, hate, and ungodly living is not as simple as *saying* you're sorry and you want to stop sinning; it means *stopping a way of life and starting another…. One that is not common.*

I am *so* drawn to the men and women who truly have taken up this truth. They *believe in Him* and are markedly differently from those that just "talk the talk". So where am I? Do I *believe in Him?* And if I do, is it omni-obvious to the world that I am His? Do the things I say, the responses I display, the way I accept offenses, the ultimate focus of my relationships and the transparent desires of my heart cause others to want to believe?

The Foolish One

"Why don't you judge for yourselves what is right? As you are going with your adversary to the magistrate, try hard to be reconciled on the way, or your adversary may drag you off to the judge, and the judge turn you over to the officer, and the officer throw you into prison. I tell you, you will not get out until you have paid the last penny." (Luke 12:57-59, NIV)

We will all one day stand before "The" magistrate—God Almighty. Better to be reconciled *now* (i.e. "on the way") than to stand before God guilty. Our adversary is Satan himself and he would love to see us stand before God *guilty* as charged; after all, "misery enjoys company."

And that's the good news about Easter. We *can* be reconciled before we meet the Judge. Christ is our Defender; He has gone before us and has already made restitution for our crimes, sins, errors and even our corrupted nature. We stand before God innocent because of the blood of Jesus!

There is an old story of a king and his clown or "jester" who sometimes said very foolish things. One day the jester had said something so foolish that the king handed him a staff, said to him: "Take this, and keep it till you find a bigger fool than yourself."

Some years later, the king lay on his deathbed. His courtiers were called; his family and his servants also stood round his bedside. The king, addressing them, said, "I am about to leave you. I am going on a very long journey and I shall not return again to this place, so I have called you all to say goodbye."

Then his jester stepped forward and, addressing the king, said, "Your Majesty, may I ask a question? When you have journeyed abroad visiting your people or paying diplomatic visits to other courts, your heralds and servants have always gone before you, making preparations for you. May I ask what preparations, your Majesty has made for this long journey that he is about to take?"

"Alas!" replied the king, "I have made no preparations."

"Then," said the jester, "Take this staff with you, for now I have found a bigger fool than myself."

Am I smart enough to realize that I need to be reconciled with God *before* I stand before Him on that journey I too must take one day…. or am I a fool?" Friend, ignorant as I am, I *am* smart enough to know that my goodness and my feeble attempts to make things right before a perfect Creator are *not* enough to put the scales of justice in my favor! My sins and shortcomings are colossal and have placed me in an untenable situation with the Judge. My case is hopeless unless *someone* can reconcile my sins for me. *I have therefore made preparations and I have been reconciled with God through Jesus Christ*! Have you? Will you be able to stand before the ultimate Magistrate one day with no fear and no apprehension about the outcome?

Am I Up to the Challenge?

For the past few years I have permitted the pressures of running a Christian ministry and business to create quite a few sleepless nights. The details don't really matter, but the fact is that I have struggled like never in my life to do all the work required to operate this little summer sports camp. Many, *many* weeks I simply don't know how I will make it. At times the challenges for me, a man limited in every way, seem insurmountable—and this has been going on for over ten years now.

Am I on the right path? That's what the enemy keeps suggesting to me. It's the "second guessing" and his attempts to cause me to bring into question God's goodness or personal approval that really eats at me during the wee hours of the morning.

Am I listening to Him? Am I carefully watching for His signs? Am I reading the events unfolding in my life circumspectly? These are the taunts of the enemy—the very things that steal sleep and peace. It is the *unknown* about why things are happening and the question of whether I am properly reacting that grieves me. Am I being a simpleton for not giving up on all that I am doing, or am I a "mighty warrior" that will one day be vindicated...or am I something else—perhaps "a *foolish warrior*"?

Should I (were it *possible* to) listen to all the advice and criticism that my friends (some descended from the lineage of Job's friends) throw upon me? Or at my own peril do I *ignore* their well-intended counsel? And how to know the difference between *godly* advice and the unhelpful sort?

But then I wonder: Isn't this what faith is? Am I not a living witness of a disciple of Jesus precisely because I do *not* know what will happen next in terms of the details and timing? Does not living such a life of blindness prove that I do *trust* that He *does* know what will happen as well as all the details and timing?

Have I *surrendered* all of this to Him? That means giving it *all* up with no suggestions to God as to how I think He could/should handle this, but 100% abandonment and yielding to whatever He wants.

Yes, yes, I know this and have "re-learned" it many times, so why can't I *remember this? Because I am living in a fallen world where it is uncommon and uninspiring to live by faith.* We talk about how much we admire and appreciate those that steadfastly believed in God, but few of us are ready to be thrown into a lions' den, a fiery furnace, the belly of a fish, to wander about the wilderness for years or stand in front of a tyrant and not flinch! We want to hear about such heroes—but what if He determines to use you——or me—to inspire? Are we up for it?

The Small Gate

"Enter through the narrow gate. For wide is the gate and broad is the road that leads to destruction, and many enter through it. But small is the gate and narrow the road that leads to life, and only a few find it." (Matthew 7:13-14, NIV)

The road less traveled is the road to the Kingdom of God. It's not that it is impossible to walk through that little gate or walk that narrow road, but because it is so small and narrow, most folks choose the bigger gate and broader road. After all (or so the rationale goes), everyone else is going this way so it must be okay.

That is the manner of thinking that Jesus came to challenge. If He were present today, in our world of democracies and parliaments, He would probably remind us that, "The majority may rule, but the majority is very often wrong." Be careful of assuming that doing, thinking, acting or living a particular way is acceptable to God because "everyone else is doing it"—such was the thinking of the Germans during WWII, and the citizens of Jericho and Sodom and Gomorrah...

Jesus was clear: Choose the path that most folks choose *not* to take. Walk through the gate that might require you to bend a little. Don't follow men and the common way of thinking, living and being...but rather be prepared, to learn to think, live and "be" a new way—God's way. And His way does not rely upon the approval or accumulation of men. In fact, following God can at times be incredibly lonely. But if I examine the heroic men and women of God in the Bible I am astounded at how lonely and bereft of companionship they often were. Following God and seeking His Kingdom will *not* make me popular or a celebrity—but it will draw me closer to the heart of God Himself.

Jesus said that, "Unless you become as a little child, you will never enter into the Kingdom of God." (Matthew 18:3, NIV)

One week at camp, a few years ago, all the devotions examined what Jesus said about the Kingdom of God (heaven) and what was required to enter into it. And we began by acknowledging that the most *important question* in the universe is, "What will happen to *me* when I die?" Every other question pales in comparison. Christ came to not only *answer* the question but offer an incredible alternative and indescribable gift.

What is surprising to me, as I talked to both campers and staff, is how many had no idea of the very *specific and precise* things Jesus said about the gift of eternal life and about how to **know, for sure,** that they were going to heaven.

Three things are clear:

- Eternal life is a gift—we're not entitled to it.
- Jesus said we have to "become as a child" (Matthew 18:3, KJV)—whatever that means—to receive it.
- We're told again and again that some folks will be surprised that they are not a part of the Kingdom while others are surprised that they *are.*

So it's free. We have to become as a child. And some folks have mistaken ideas about what it takes to get it. Again, Jesus said that God wants *all men (i.e. mankind)* to be saved. But it's only given to those who are willing to become *like a child.*

I will tell you what I *think* that means.

I enjoyed a wonderful childhood of playing games, building tree houses, boating in the lake, riding my bike, etc. All that I did or experienced was possible because of my parents who taught me, provided for me, and protected me.

Never in my entire childhood did I have trouble sleeping at night; I don't ever recall being anxious over any future events; I laughed a lot more than I do now and thought I was very gifted and special—because my parents kept telling me how wonderful and bright I was.

I can still recall as a toddler hearing my dad come home and running down the hallway to have him pick me up and usually stumbling, hitting my head on the terrazzo floor! I could not *wait* for him to come home and pick me up.

But as I grew up I began to doubt that I was smart, or special or gifted. I *learned* to worry about grades, being accepted at a new school, being cool enough to be a part of the most admired groups in my classes, etc. And I began to get stressed! The truth is I *never* lost sleep over stress till I began The Vineyard Camp and Retreat Center.

Becoming as a child in order to enter into His Kingdom does not mean that I never worry or have doubts. It means that I have come to a place, at some point in my life, where I realize and admit that I *am* in need of a father once again—someone that can look after me, give me rest and be the delight of my soul. And I have to acknowledge to this Eternal Father that I not only need to be taught *a lot*, but that I also need to *unlearn* quite a bit. Becoming a small child means that I humbly admit to God that I do *not* have the answers and I am *not* able to make it on my own! I need a dad to help me!

But I also think that coming to God as a child means that I am, in my heart, looking forward to all that He has prepared for me. I am ready to chase rainbows, collect stones from creeks, and run to His arms. This is becoming a child.

If we are too mature or independent or proud, the Kingdom will not be ours, according to Jesus. We have to humble ourselves and allow Him to be our Father…

…and what a wonderful Father He is.

A Magical Sentence?

Are there magical words in the world? The Psalmist seems to say so when he states clearly, "If you say: 'The Lord is my refuge,' and you make the Most High your dwelling, no harm will overtake you, no disaster will come near your tent. For he will command his angels concerning you to guard you in all your ways." (Psalms 91:9-16, NIV) This seems almost like some sort of enchanted spell! Just say these words and all will be fine. Count me in! But of course there's a point here that needs to be made: You have to mean it when you say it—faith is required.

What does it mean to utter "the Lord is my refuge?" (Psalms 91:9, NIV) Simply that He is my hope, my salvation, my security, my shelter. It represents a condition of the heart. It means I choose Him and I desire intimacy with Him over anyone and anything else. To say these words requires that I place my confidence in Him first, second, and third. I do not place my hope in men, horses, or chariots.

Success, financial security, popularity, admiration, and good health are often the very things that keep me away from Him. As counterintuitive as it may sound, failure, troubles, and sorrow are the only things that can bring me back into the shadow of His wings.

It's been said that when faced with personal struggles and the stress of daily life I have three choices: I can have a second, secret life (e.g., an affair), I can turn to drugs or alcohol, or I can just learn to live with stress. As wise as this counsel may seem, the Psalmist would disagree, because in the presence of God there is no stress. When I make my dwelling the Most High I have no fears or anxiety. It is when I am trying to accomplish, complete, or solve things all on my own that I become saddened and stressed. But if I attend to His work, His tasks, His projects, His appointments, then can I be at peace. Only then can I find a respite from the things that try to steal my sleep, my peace, and my joy.

Jesus was clear when He said, "seek *first* God's delights (i.e. His kingdom) and He will add to your life those things that delight you." (Matthew 6:33, NIV) He's not trying to hold them back from you and me! But He is trying to prepare us to properly appreciate them.

Who Will Prevail?

"Many are the plans in a person's heart, but it is the LORD's purpose that prevails." (Proverbs 19:21 KJV)

These are the words I hold to and live by when things don't go as *I have planned*. I lay my days out each morning; I set daily, weekly, monthly goals. I prepare budgets and targets for where we need to be in enrollment, donations, etc. But ultimately the question is, "What is God's plan in all of this?" "What is it that HE wants to happen?"

And so, when my schemes and well-intended preparations don't bring the results I felt they should have produced, I must remind myself that it is the Lord's purpose that prevails—not mine. If I am working diligently for Him I can leave the final results to Him and know that He will win the battle.

My purpose for most of my traveling might be "success" and to increase camper enrollment, but *His* purpose might be far more profound and have reverberating consequences. I cannot know what His precise purpose is on my journeys or as I operate the camp, but I can choose to be at peace when He upsets my goals and agenda and uses me for other purposes. The question is merely: Am I willing to be used anyway He requires? It is a matter of humility as well as the sober recognition that His ways are not my ways, and His thoughts are not my thoughts. I am clay—He is the master potter.

In truth, He has consistently not only allowed my plans to go forward, but He has re-defined some of my earlier dreams and expanded them. I thought, in my heart, that I was "called" to do this or that—but He has purposed that I do far more. My own heart could not contain or perceive the good things He had prepared for me. And as I look back on the former things I had planned on my own, how *grateful I am* that many did not come to fruition. Praise God that He has His hand on the steering wheel *and* the gas pedal.

I don't think that any of this means that I am to do *nothing* until I can see clearly His purpose. If that were the case I would never accomplish anything. But it does mean that I must be careful to remember the *journey is more important than reaching the destination* in God's plans. It's not a matter of achieving a goal, but rather what you did, who you blessed, what souls were drawn to Him, and what barriers were removed by the manner in which you did your work.

If I look for Him in all of life's challenges and my struggles I can be sure to find Him and feel His hand upon my shoulder. But if I dictate to Him what He *must* cause to happen and how it *must* occur, I will find that I am on a very lonely path indeed.

The Camp's Summer Ends Today

"Let the peace of Christ rule in your hearts, since as members of one body you were called to peace. And be thankful. Let the message of Christ dwell among you richly as you teach and admonish one another with all wisdom through psalms, hymns, and songs from the Spirit, singing to God with gratitude in your hearts. And whatever you do, whether in word or deed, do it all in the name of the Lord Jesus, giving thanks to God the Father through him." (Colossians 3:15-17, NIV)

One summer, a few years ago, we had a truly "golden summer." We had our challenges and troubles, to be sure, but the peace and joy that permeated the camp was obvious. I asked one of our long time staff (a ten year veteran) what was so different that summer? What was it, I asked him, that made everything "feel" better? He bravely responded that it was *me*. He remarked that **I** was "less" angry, more positive, easier to work with and live with, and less stressed than in previous years.

On the one hand I was glad to hear that I had *something* to do with the peace that was felt at the camp, but also ashamed that I was the reason for a lack of peace in summers past. What is true of a church, or camp is true of any spiritual organization: Each takes upon itself the *character and personality of its pastor or director.* Like it or not, the camp's outlook and "spirit" reflects *my outlook and spirit.* And the humbling fact is that I had to find peace from God in order to dispense peace that summer. We had financial struggles like never before that summer; we had challenges with parents, staff, volunteers and campers as much as any year; our boats, horses, vans, trucks, jeeps and equipment gave us MORE trouble than ever. But *I was different this year in how I responded.* Again, I am not here tooting my horn. I am confessing that I *should* have been a lighthouse to God's peace in the past, and I was not. The troubles of the camp I wore on my face and exploded in previous years.

The change that year came from my meditation upon the verse just quoted: *His peace ruled in my heart and I was thankful.* I discovered, afresh, the peace that is mine when I abandon my ambitions, my agenda, my concerns and my needs to Him and then go about His work with all my heart. I realized the joy that comes from singing to Him in the morning and desiring Him throughout the day—instead of constantly seeking *what He could do for me.*

Those of us who lead must ever be mindful that our peace and joy—or lack of it—is absorbed by the flock that we tend. Am I feeding those I am caring for with His peace, joy and love—or am I feeding them my doubts, frustration, prejudices and personal disappointments?

I am praying for many more golden summers.

I Am…

"What is mankind that you are mindful of them, human beings that you care for them?

You have made them a little lower than the angels and crowned them with glory and honor." (Psalm 8:4-5 NIV)

It's a great question! And within *the answer* are the existential answers to what has bothered all of us from the very beginning. All of us wonder about why we are here, what it is that will really satisfy us, what will happen to us when we die, if we are *merely* creations and why He made us in the first place.

Why does He care?! Why did He call us into existence? Why did He make "me" as He did? I am not able to properly answer all these questions, but I have come to a place of peace knowing this: I am *more* than a mere creation. Obviously when God breathed life into man and when determined to create me in His image, something was given to me that was not given to other creatures. Somehow I became the object of His incredible love—a love so outstanding that He intervenes in my life and throughout the history of mankind to keep me from falling off the edge! While He could have simply wiped all us out and started a new, better kind of creature, he's determined that we will one day become His Sons and Daughters—in fact, because of the Christ's sacrifice for you and me on Golgotha, we have become redeemed through Jesus Christ and *are* children of God now!

So here's what I have come to believe: I am special…He loves me…He does not want to lose me…I am important and unique to Him. This is what <u>fuels</u> me when I am down, dejected or unsure of tomorrow. Others might scoff at my abilities or ambitions; some may question my motives or my heart, but God has called me His own and sees something within me *worth* redeeming. I have value and am special *because God says so.* Nothing adds such vigor or gives me strength more than that assurance. And when the enemy whispers to me at night that I am nothing more than a creature, I remind Him that my Creator says that I am far more important and valuable—He knows my name and has a plan for me!

A man or woman finds peace in the most penetrating and haunting questions of life when he or she realizes that it is in God, and God alone, that the answers can be found.

Number One

For the past few days one of my sons set up a lemonade stand in front of our home, but he is actually selling orange juice. He has made $78 in two days and is on his way to launching his own company! And yes, most of the customers are my friends and neighbors that want to reward him for his entrepreneurship; they're not really interested in the product he is selling, but they all have generous hearts.

But the other two boys have watched him make money and they're jealous. So this morning the youngest woke up early and interrupted my Bible study to share with me his plan on how to make his own fortune. Then the next son greeted me his own plan of how to make a million dollars in my front yard by selling hamburgers and chips. It appears that I am raising three Elon Musks—they're nothing like me.

But the competition between the three of them is exhausting. The fights to see who is better results in tears, unkind words and occasional sabotage. And every time they see me, it seems like they want me to do something special for them that will allow them to rise higher than their brothers. Jealousy…. sibling rivalry…boys just being boys? Whatever you want to call it, it creates a lot of waste and anger and I am ever on my guard for being scammed.

But then I think about my own approach to my heavenly Father. I hope that I am coming to Him because I genuinely desire Him—and for no other reason. But the temptation is to always ask and ask for His blessing (as if the gift of being with Him is not quite enough!) and even though I know He is God, I wonder if I sometimes attempt to scam Him by asking for things that I don't need, but rather things I *want* so that I can be envied? God, purify my petitions!

It's part of our fallen angel to compete, in a negative way, and to always look after "number one"—i.e. me. But Saint Augustine once said that: "It was pride that changed angels into devils; it is humility that makes men as angels." It's the determination to think others, and their needs being more important than mine, that will keep me on the right path.

I hope to have three *angels* in my home soon. But it takes one to know one. The battle starts with me and how I see my relationship to my Father. I am happiest *not* when I seek to acquire more, or garner more attention, or even when I pragmatically make sure that I am safe and secure. No, the greater joy comes from giving others the extra recognition, making certain that my family is protected, and feeling the joy that comes from being surpassed by those I love.

Create in me a new and extraordinary heart God—one that is always looking to you and ever devoted to helping those I love. Forgive me for competing with the very ones I want to help.

An Insatiable Thirst

I found peace today after I struggled with some things that were not going my way. No need to go into detail; we all have things in our work, lives, and families that disappoint us. But I wanted to be right before God, both in my petitions and my complaints. And so, as I lay in bed at about 3:30 a.m. this morning, I prayed for peace for my soul and a return to the joy I so deeply want and have experienced in the past. After being totally honest (and why not, since He knows all things anyway), I believe that I came to understand why I am not more full of joy.

First, I sensed that I should stop asking Him for the things that I think will make me happy and at peace, and instead ask Him, without naming anything, to give me the things that He knows that I want and need.

But then, a small voice reminded me to ask for His help, i.e. to help me desire the things that he wants me to desire. That changed the whole dynamic of my prayer and focus. My "wants" are often provided for, but I am most frequently left with an empty feeling. "That's it?" I say to myself. After all the longing and striving to get something I really, really want, I am left with the understanding that my desires are out of balance.

And so I am praying, even now as I write this, "Lord remove from my heart, mind, and memory the things you do not want me to desire! You and you alone know what I desire deep inside my soul. When you knitted me together in my mother's womb you established a desire deep within my heart for the holy and perfect things that reflect you. Remove the plaque and calluses that have hardened my heart and change my heart for you."

My prayer is that He will help me let go of wanting the wrong things and give me an insatiable thirst and hunger for the things He wants me to desire. I cannot imagine that God will not answer this simple prayer over time. The older I get, the wearier I am of looking for satisfaction in the temporal or illusionary things this world has to offer.

…As We Forgive Others…

"Forgive us our sins *as we forgive those that sin against us*". (Luke 11:4, NIV)

Few remarks of Jesus seem to be glossed over or ignored as much as the last phrase in this prayer… "**as** we forgive those who sin against us." (Luke 11:4, NIV)

Our forgiveness is based upon the blood of Jesus—not our own merits, or our attempts to make up for our mistakes or even or acknowledgment that have sinned. It's all about Jesus and God's mercy—*based upon Christ's death for our sins.*

This is very important to understand: God did not forgive us because He is simply kind and good-natured. He forgave us because His Son paid the penalty for our sin.

But in more than one situation, Jesus is very, very direct about the absolute *demand* that we, in turn, are merciful and forgiving towards others that hurt, wound or offend us *in light of what He has done.* In fact, in one parable the forgiveness is *nullified* if the one that was forgiven of much did not forgive others of small matters.

But try for a moment to imagine this:

1. God can bless you *far more* than you can bless Him or any of the children He has placed in your path. Imagine the good way you treat others *magnified and increased exponentially*! That's what we are told that He has done and will do for us.

2. God can forgive you of *far* more mistakes, broken promises, lies, and just plain *mean* things you have done and *will* do than *anyone* could ever do to you. *But*, if He forgives you He demands that you forgive others—every time they offend you.

He also talks about "forgiving from the heart," (Matthew 18:35, NIV) which means, I think, you give it up, you don't hold a grudge, *you forget about it.*

Our human history is littered with the catastrophic results when men could not let go and forgive. Imagine how happy our homes, our camp, our churches, our nation and our world would be if we forgive others as He has forgiven us.

How do you want God to forgive you? For *all* your sins, or just part? And what about God *reminding* you of your sins? Would you like Him to forgive you but constantly bring up your sins and mistakes whenever you started to begin a new adventure?

"Forgive us *as we forgive others.*" (Matthew 18:35, NIV) I, for one, plan on forgiving and letting go of grudges, not attempting to keep score.

Do not let the attacks and hurts and offenses of others hold you back from enjoying the full measure of being forgiven by God! Let go of the anger or fear or resentment you have for someone else and see how God fills you with unspeakable joy, peace and His unfettered love!

We *have* to forgive or we will not enjoy abundant living.

A Living Sacrifice

"Therefore, I urge you, brothers and sisters, in view of God's mercy, to offer your bodies as a living sacrifice, holy and pleasing to God—this is your true and proper worship." (Romans 12:1 NIV)

"In *view* of His mercy", i.e. *because of* the blood of Jesus, I am *forgiven* of all my offenses against God... *and* God is blessing me. (Romans 12:1 NIV) *That* is mercy! I am getting a total "get out of jail free card" *and* He has determined to give me the desires of my heart and bless me!

In view of this, He asks that I "offer up myself", or "surrender" myself for *Him,* (Romans 12:1 NIV) over the next few decades, so that others might come to receive the same mercy. What a magnanimous, purposeful and fitting request. I can hear Him whisper to me, "In light of what I have done for you—i.e. forgiven you of *all* your mistakes, blessed you, prepared a mansion for you in heaven, named you as my own for *eternity,* etc.—I want you to surrender your rights, your goals, your personal agenda, you aspirations, your very right to life... and become a living, walking and talking sacrifice for me. In response, again, I want to remind you that I am going to give you those things your hear really pines for *and make you a joint heir in heaven with my Son for all of time."* Only a blockhead would say, "No, thank you," to such an offer.

But let me point out a challenge that a brother once mentioned to me about "living sacrifices." They have a tendency to crawl off the altar. You see, if Christ required us to *die* and become a *dead* sacrifice it would be a far easier. But He is asking us to be *living sacrifices* (See Romans 12:1, NIV). And that means that every day of our lives we have to make that conscious effort to give up our rights and serve Him in whatever way He chooses for that day.

This is both glorious and humbling. Some days He abases me, some days He lifts me up—but every day He gets the glory *if* I relinquish my rights to have a say in how He uses me. *That* is being a living sacrifice. So I must think of my "life" as being over; He has absolute command over what happens to me.

But the more I know Him, the more I understand His abounding love, the more I can say with all my soul, "Take over and do what You want! I am yours—and I will never be at peace until I know that you are in total command."

Being First

"Sitting down, Jesus called the Twelve and said, "If anyone wants to be first, he must be the very last, and the servant of all." He took a little child and had him stand among them. Taking him in his arms, he said to them, "Whoever welcomes one of these little children in my name welcomes me; and whoever welcomes me does not welcome me but the one who sent me." (Mark 9:35-37, NIV)

I thought about our little camp and how we strive to do these three things:

We celebrate ambition. There's nothing wrong with wanting to be the best, or desiring to lead or wanting to stand out as the winner! Paul talked about running the race *and winning the prize.* It's okay to want to make your mark and be recognized as one that won the trophy and leads.

We celebrate serving others. In the Kingdom of God the *greatest, the "leader', the "winner"* is the one that succeeds in "out-serving" all the others. The real leaders are those that lead in their example of putting themselves *last.* The "winners" are those who discipline themselves to joyfully help others without whining, complaining or demanding time for themselves.

We celebrate children. Those that are the "great ones" in God's Kingdom recognize not only the worth and value of even the small child, but the need to treat them with dignity and respect because they *represent the heart and freedom of one that dwells in God's Kingdom.* Children are singularly celebrated in Christ's ministry because of their parallels to living lives free of worry and devoid of chasing after possessions or position.

We celebrate hospitality. Again and again we're reminded to welcome strangers, to be kind to the foreigner, to show hospitality to the alien, the poor, to the widow and the orphan. Because, you see, *we* are the alien, the poor, the foreign, the widowed, the stranger when it comes to God's Kingdom! Treat others as you want *Him* to treat you.

Search My Heart, Lord

"Search me, God, and know my heart; test me and know my anxious thoughts. See if there is any offensive way in me, and lead me in the way everlasting." (Psalm 129:33, NIV)

What a perfect prayer for the man or woman who is serious about God. David wrote this Psalm and surely meant what he said. He did *not* trust in his own thoughts, habits, or self-evaluation. He wanted for God *to have His way in his life.*

What is in my heart? That is to say, "What is the *true and underlying purpose* for the things I do and say?" I can agree with David here: "God, please search my heart *and make it right.* Give me the opportunity to choose the right thing and see if I make the right choice. Then look at what it is in my life that makes me anxious. Is it not the *fear* that I might be found *hindering* the gospel of your son and being a drag on the progress of your Kingdom?"

I understand what David meant when he sincerely asked God to "check me out... am I doing *anything* that is offensive or contrary to what a man seeking everlasting life should be committing?" There's more than one reason that David prayed this prayer and that I pray the same thing. For one thing, I truly want to make Him happy with me. I want to live and shine like *I was His "favorite."* But the other reason is that I want to be 100% sure that *I am where I ought to be* in my work, relationships, and decisions. If I can be sure of this, my prayers are far more powerful because I am praying *with great confidence and belief.* I am, in fact, praying *in His name* and have acquired the mind of Christ. That means there is nothing and no one in relationship to me that causes me to stumble, nor am I causing another to stumble because of my behavior.

But do I truly *want* to be placed under His microscope and evaluated and tested? *Absolutely...* and for the same reasons listed above. The *ultimate reality is God. Why on earth would I want to put off hearing God's opinion of my life thus far?* Better to know where I come up short *right now* and focus on it *now* than to wait to when I create damage by not begging for God to "search me" while there is still daylight.

Imagine a community of believers that prayed like this, or a government full of men and women that held this to be true. "*Yes, Lord,* search the hearts of *all* those that apply to work at our camp; show us their *real* hearts; test us and know our anxious thoughts. See if there is any offensive way in them, and lead us in the way everlasting." A summer camp composed of such dedicated young men and women would reverberate around the world.

He's Never in a Hurry—Get Used to It

When Jesus' good friend, Lazarus, became *deathly ill,* Jesus waited at least five days before He went to see him and the sisters Mary and Martha. His love for these three siblings is unmatched in any record of the Bible. He loved all men, but His love for these three was exceptional and mentioned more than once. (See John 11:1-34, NIV)

Those that loved Lazarus *suffered* as Jesus delayed in coming to the rescue—they *suffered.* Some would argue that there *cannot be* a "good God" if He sends or permits all the suffering that occurs in the world. And I suppose that would be true if all suffering is bad. But what if suffering, viewed from an "eternal perspective", is not bad, but perhaps even the best thing that could possibly happen to us at the time? What if suffering were the *only* way God could redeem mankind and get our attention to save our very souls from an eternity of suffering?

Hearts were broken in this narrative, and Jesus could have prevented it. He knows about death and heartache and tears—and yet He allows them—all the time. To the family of Lazarus all seemed lost. They did *not* know that Jesus would come in five or six days and bring their brother back to life. They rightly assumed that he was gone for good. From *all appearances,* Jesus let them down—at least for five days. He did not hurry…He did not jump and take action. He took His time despite the pressure from *others* to hurry.

But this I know:

- *Nothing* that happens to us catches God off guard. He is control of time, space and the future.
- *God will not be pushed or hurried* despite how desperate we might think things are.
- *Lazarus* became more than a hero—he became the efficacy of the Jesus' Lordship.
- *Mary, Martha* and many others had their horrible sorrow, pain and suffering turned into indescribable joy and entered into a new understanding of who Jesus *really* was.
- Jesus loving me does not mean He will not allow suffering in my life; but I can be certain that He is aware of the suffering and that it *will* be turned into indescribable joy if I trust in Him. Things might not turn out like I expect…when I expect…in the order I expect, but He takes no pleasure in my hurts or broken-heartedness.

A Friend Loves at All Times

"A friend loves always and a brother is born for times of adversity." (Proverbs 17:17.NIV) Today, I was reminded again of how blessed I am to have genuine friends who are not mere "acquaintances." These are people that know most of the bad things about me and still consider me their friend. These are the same men and women from whom I have had to borrow money to establish and maintain this ministry. They are the people who support my work, pray for me, encourage me, believe in my dream, appreciate my presence, and give me courage to hold on when I am inclined to let go.

We all need friends, and yet I do know some poor souls that have very few friends. Some of these people were at one time my friends, but they got married (which is a good thing) then slowly pulled away from all their friends and clung only to their spouse. This is sad. That's not God's plan for marriage and is certainly never encouraged in the Bible. Frankly, I would challenge anyone to find an example in scripture of a man or woman getting married and then turning their back on their friends. There are no *good* examples. Friendship and the love between friends are celebrated in the Bible, and examples such as David and Jonathan, Ruth and Naomi, Jesus and John, Barnabas and Silas, drive home the point.

But my sons are saddened about their lack of friends. More than once, each son has come to me crying and asking me to adopt a new boy so that they can have a friend. It's heartbreaking that some folks don't have friends, but I remind the boys that if they want a friend, they have to *be* a friend. I am not the perfect friend, but I do invest in my friends and I do attempt to maintain friendships. These two things are essential: the willingness to give *my time*, and a determination to do what is required to *maintain communication* and a strong bond. It takes work! Friendships are not common among lazy or selfish folks. You have to give of yourself and work at friendship.

Please do not assume that I am suggesting that I am the ideal friend, because I am far from it. But despite my faults, I have been blessed with many friends. I consider myself "wealthy" in terms of people who care about me despite my faults. My point is that I can see *the face of God in the face of my friends*.

To my friends: you have no idea how much your passing compliments have meant to me. And not only your compliments, but also your *belief* in what I am doing, your support of me when I have been hurt and felt like quitting, and your forgiveness when I was less than what I wanted to be. You kept me going! You have served vicariously as the voice, smile, and touch of God. I sincerely thank you

A Man of His Time

I recently read a book about the reformation, and specifically learned about a man from France named Servetus, the heretic that did not believe in the Trinity. Since the word "Trinity" does not exist in the Bible and there are few direct references to it in scripture, he denied its existence on the grounds that it was not biblical.

John Calvin and others opposed him in court and had Servetus convicted of heresy. *He was burned alive at a stake.* Calvin was largely responsible for this—*John Calvin!* If you go to Switzerland, a plaque to Servetus acknowledges Calvin's hand in the execution but then explains that, "Calvin was a man of his time." That suggests, I suppose, that at this time in history it was acceptable to burn alive those disagreed with what the church or ruling religious majority believed. Thus, Calvin was only acting as any other man of his time would.

Foolishenss. I can't think of anything else to say. To suggest that a man of God, like Calvin, could one day argue the *eternal* truths of the faith and of regeneration based upon God's mercy and grace, and the *next day* calmly watch another child of God be burned alive "because it was the practice of the day" causes me to wonder just how intimate a relationship with Jesus Christ, Calvin had. Me saying *that* is heresy to my Presbyterian and Reformed friends, I suppose, but are we to believe that the mind of Christ, which we are all urged to acquire according to Paul, is a mind that is conditioned "according to the historical setting"? Would Jesus Christ have been a part of another man's death—and in such a hideous way? Could you imagine Paul, or Peter or John taking part in lighting a fire to extinguish the life of one that disagreed with them?

But here was a *colossal* figure in the Reformation, John Calvin, doing something unthinkable to the apostles 1500 years earlier, and he was <u>excused</u> because he was "a man of his time." We're redeemed not to be merely men and women of our time, but rather to be Sons and Daughters of the Almighty God that are able to prayerfully discern mercy, grace, kindness, forgiveness and compassion *in a timeless manner.* Surely one who walks intimately with Jesus is not bound to accept the mores, norms, and values of the *present* generation but is taught from *Him who is Holy what is pure, proper, just and pleasing to God.*

This all causes me again to look in the mirror and ask myself, "What am I doing right now that represents a man of my time but *is inconsistent with the Son of God's timeless expectations of a true disciple?"*

May God give us leaders, preachers, camp directors and cabin counselors who are not limited by the pressures and prejudices of their own generation, but live, act and respond to others as citizens of the eternal Kingdom of God—one that eschews indifference, hatred, intolerance and cruelty.

Shout to the Lord!

What do you "shout" about? A referee's bad call at a basketball game? Your favorite team just scoring the winning goal in soccer match, or maybe a touchdown in football? Do you shout at the clueless driver that just pulled in front of you and then hits his brakes? Do you shout at your friends, co-workers, spouse… your children? Sadly, I have found the effectiveness of "raising my voice" when the boys do something that *really* irritates me .

I get loud when I speak for my country, my favorite celebrity, or about things that anger or annoy me; but do I raise my voice for my God, for that baby in the manger, for the joy of the Lord? When you think about it, the things that cause me to yell, scream, or shout are really the things that bring out the passion within me. But what am I *not* yelling about that says volumes perhaps, about where I need to direct my server and zeal.

When Christ walked in Palestine there were many beggars. But I've been told that the most pathetic of the beggars were the blind beggars. With no hope of employment or careers and with *no one* sympathetic to their plight, they were the poorest of the beggars—truly, they were ones to be pitied the most. They got only what was placed in their hands and only went were they were led. It was commonly believed that they were blind because, somehow, they deserved it. It's heartbreaking to think about. We still think badly about the poor, the blind, and the orphaned, but in a more repressed way.

The blind man named in Jesus's story was Bartimaeus. He heard about this man Jesus. Because he was blind, he tended to *listen and pay attention* more than those that had good eyes. He had picked up these stories of how Jesus performed incredible, *unheard* of miracles. "He must be the One—the long awaited Messiah! Jesus must be this 'Son of God'," Bartimaeus must have mused. (See the Luke 18:35-52, NIV)

And so, when he heard that Jesus was passing nearby he *yelled*, "Jesus have mercy on me!" (Luke 18:38, NIV). It was his chance to be made into a whole man. And when those around him told him to be quiet, he *screamed at the top of his lungs*: *"Jesus, Son of David, have mercy on me!"* (Luke 18:38, NIV)

Jesus heard the yelling—the loud voice—the hollering… and He stopped and healed a man born blind. *Something that had never happened before and never recorded before in all scripture.* Jesus did something that no one had ever done—all because He heard the shouting of a blind beggar. *Bartimaeus believed and shouted out to God …and was healed.*

Friends, Bartimaeus inspires me. Perhaps I have been shouting about the wrong things. *No one* has a right to shout at God, or to scream at Him. But to raise my voice to *praise Him, to cry out to Him, to shout all the louder—"Jesus have mercy on me"* (Luke 18:38, NIV)—is not only acceptable to God—it gets results.

What could I shout about to God? *My blindness! My emotional sickness! My failures as a father, brother, son, friend, and boss! My inabilities to reach my goals, keep my promises and be the witness for Him that I desire to be!* "Jesus, have mercy on me!" (Luke 18:38, NIV)

Send me?

Why don't we "take the call" and do what He whispers to us that we ought to do? Answer: *We make excuses.* My personal heroes are the Abrahams and Saint Pauls: those that *immediately* obeyed God. They're giants because of their non-whimpering, abrupt compliance. But most of us find evade with arguments like:

1. We're too old. But what about Abraham, Moses? He was *as old as dirt* but Abraham quickly surrendered, and Moses eventually did the same. It's not a matter of years behind you *but the years He has set aside ahead of you.*

2. We've got too many other things going on right now. But what's more essential and what will matter the most when you're gone? How can I stand before God and offer any suggestion that there were *more important things I had to do and He would have to find someone else?* What an insane defense. "I was too busy with my family, my career, my hobbies, my retirement, my garden, my investments…" Those things might be significant, but can we stand in the presence of God and assume we can recuse ourselves?

3. We're not qualified. Perhaps not, *but all the qualified folks are gone so He's calling and preparing to qualify you!* It's nothing short of impertinence to suggest that God cannot equip us *beyond any other man or woman's qualifications to complete His tasks!*

4. We don't really love Him as much as we hope others think that we do. And that, my friends, is the real reason we don't harken to His call. We are deceiving ourselves when we say that we are surrendered Him, that "Jesus is Lord" (Romans 10:9, NIV) or that He is my "All-in all" but fail to take up our cross and follow.

But what can we expect to receive if we listen to His call?

*   Renewed energy and the power of the Holy Spirit—e.g. Caleb and Jacob. The divine One that created us is quite capable of renewing your strength, mind, stamina and heart.

*   More time than we realized—the One that can stop time can also help you to accomplish far more if you put Him first. Try it.

*   He qualifies us with extraordinary insight and sublime gifts. God does not tease us or lead us into frustration—He is more than able to open our mouths, minds, imaginations to complete the assignments He tasks us with and He is prepared to tax the last star for the resources we need to faithfully execute the commission He gives us. In a word, God *blesses us* when we obey and follow.

*   We find ourselves falling into love with Him more, as well as with those He sends us to care for. But isn't that the way it is in life anyway? I mean, you *talk* about liking someone or respecting them, but then, after you are *decide to work with them, very closely, or you share a trench with them in war, or you go through a heartache or loss with them, you come to love them—because you really start knowing them.* You cannot draw closer to God and not be energized and set on fire by His love!

Haven't you heard about how Jeremiah, Isaiah, Daniel, Peter, John and countless others acquired this astounding devotion and love for God that caused them to be willing to walk around Jerusalem *naked* for months, or endure absolute rejection from *every other human being* and yet remain full of the ultimate measure of love and joy! *How?* Because of their connection to this unimaginable power source of love—God Himself. And all because they answered His call to be poured out wine and broken bread—they gave up their rights and careers and their choices of priorities and exclaimed: Here am! Send me…..

A Fairy Tale

I have discovered that the times when I am writing and I am *empty* and have absolutely nothing to share, God blesses me in my ignorance, weakness, and journalistic dearth, and finds a way to speak. He does His work best when *I* get out of the way.

As I am writing this, as you can probably surmise, my day was a spiritual and personal fiasco. I did not live up to my expectations and goals as a pastor, camp director, father, or boss. I am not happy with my responses to the challenges I faced, the manner in which I responded to difficult phone calls, emails, and meetings, or my attitude in particularly awkward moments.

All day today, it snowed, but the School Superintendent failed to let parents know that school was cancelled until after we got up and got the children ready for school. So rather than relax and enjoy a little respite from the Monday morning madness, we hurried up so that we could wait and be told the obvious—the roads are impassable and school is canceled! As an aside, yes, I know that I am not sounding very "Christian," but I am responding honestly nonetheless. There are days that I am weary of the "race" and "the good fight" (II Timothy 4:7, NIV); I feel rather ignoble and am not ready for the next task at hand.

All the boys were home today because of cancelled school, all the office staff were sick or unable to come to work because of the ice, and everything fell upon me. It was the perfect environment for a "feel sorry for myself" day, and I felt that it was my right to claim this sentiment for the entire day. Again, I am not happy with how I handled this, and I hope and pray that we will have no more snow days. I pine, more than ever in my life, for a time, place, and state of mind when I can stop being responsible for the business, family, ministry, and operations. I long to simply enjoy the snow, solitude, sunsets, and quietness in life.

But of course this is not the reason I was redeemed by Jesus. It was for these very days that I was purchased by His blood, i.e. to live as His example in the common, everyday, rat-race existence that we call life. The notion of "living happily ever-after" is indeed a fairy tale for real people. But I am certain that I am walking on a path traveled by other men and women, many much further along in their faith than me, who met greater challenges, frustrations, and "snow days" than I have, but maintained their composure, focus, determination, drive, and zeal.

Being a Christian is not a fairy tale existence; it's an odyssey.

A Sheep of His Pasture?

"I lift up my eyes to the mountains—where does my help come from? My help comes from the Lord, the Maker of heaven and earth. He will not let your foot slip—he who watches over you will not slumber; indeed, he who watches over Israel will neither slumber nor sleep. The Lord watches over you—the Lord is your shade at your right hand; the sun will not harm you by day, nor the moon by night. The Lord will keep you from all harm—he will watch over your life; the Lord will watch over your coming and going both now and forevermore." (Psalm 121:1-8, NIV)

We would all like to live knowing that He protects us, shades us, and watches over us. But what is required for us to enjoy this peace of mind? According to this Psalm, it is that we are looking to Him for our security, not our own wits, resources, friends, or possessions. These words found in Psalm 121 were uttered by one who constantly looked to God as His "all in all" and "Jehovah Jireh."

This is what He desires from me. My surrender, yes, but also a childlike dependence on Him, placing my hand in His and trusting Him to lead me to green pastures, quiet and still waters, and to an abundant life, a life I could never imagine or attain on my own. This is what He truly wants for me, and truly wants for you too.

So, do I really want this? Do I truly desire for Him to direct my paths, or do I prefer my own wandering excursions? Do I want Him to protect me from harm by keeping my eyes, feet, and mind from places that are dangerous, or do I merely want Him to rescue me once I've had my fun? We all want a superhero to rescue us out of a bad situation, but if I am following the Good Shepherd there are certain things, places, and people that He would never lead me to in the first place.

I've learned that you can't have it both ways. He can be your shepherd and lead you, but He can't be a good shepherd if you keep jumping over the fence and looking for greener grass. Either He is your shepherd or He is not. The Psalmist was a sheep of His (Jesus') pasture, and I want to be and remain a part of the same flock.

Trying to Keep Everyone Happy

"Am I now tryin to win the approval of human beings, or of God? Or am I trying to please people? If I were still trying to please people, I would not be a servant of Christ." (Galatians 1:10, NIV). How true! The two (pleasing people and serving Jesus) are incongruous. *Not* because serving Jesus is not *good for people,* but because serving Jesus will eventually and *inevitably* make you unpopular with people.

For those that disagree, I would suggest this: Try to please people *and simultaneously* be a *genuine* servant of Christ. Some things can only be experienced in life—we can't just "accept it as true" or believe it by reading or hearing about it—we have to jump in and try it out for ourselves. I have tried to walk that fine line of pleasing others and serving God, and ultimately I had to ask myself: Do I want to make Him proud or someone else proud—because I can't do both. Nothing is gained, of course, by deliberately annoying others, but following Jesus *is* annoying to the masses; anyone that is not an irritant to the world is not walking very close to God.

In general, to be pleasing to others requires compromise, saying things that are pleasing to the ear, not challenging the other point of view (unless your acquaintance enjoys being challenged) and above all, never suggesting that there are absolute "right and wrong" things in the world. Following Jesus means at times, and *in love*, saying things that are "hard" and might even appear unkind. If we serve the King of Kings, it means that we are *compelled* to speak the truth, even if we know that our associates might take offense at it.

A servant of Jesus is never rude, but never afraid to offer the truth; a servant is never unkind, but never shirks from standing up for His Lord; God's servants never judge another man's heart, but are fearless in support of God's commandments and expectations for mankind; their first concern is the approval of God—not men. No wonder, then, a servant of God is not very popular.

Pity the man that tries to live in two worlds or serve two masters.

Is Our Work Sustainable

One part of my job as a camp director is to raise funds for campers that can't pay full tuition, or in many cases, for those that can't pay *any* tuition. And so I "beg" for support. Presidents of universities do the same ("beg") as do pastors (though they might call it "development efforts"). Begging might not be a very professional term, but that's what I do—I plead for help. Saint Francis was a beggar—and the world is a better place because of him and his witness. We love Francis because he really lived the beatitudes; he was one of the most beloved beggars in the world.

But lately, in my fund-raising efforts, I have come across people that have made it clear that they only support "sustainable ministries." I know it's not polite to say things like this, particularly when only one side (mine) is being presented. But the question, "How can I be *sure* that your ministry, or your church, or your orphanage is 'sustainable'?," really burns me up. I've been trying to remove "my pride" from this and have prayed about how to respond when people say things like this.

This "sustainable" line of thinking, i.e. that you only support something that will continue, is suitable for a bank focused on stock holders or a financier determined to have a very positive bottom line—but not for a Christian that's giving freely from the abundance from which he/she has been blessed.

1. John the Baptist's ministry was *not* sustainable—he lost his head and his disciples were dispersed; based upon "a sustainable ministry criteria" no one should have supported him.
2. Jesus Christ's short work on this earth was not a very bankable investment—it was just a three year ministry with zero assets at the time of His execution; clearly He not qualify as a "sustainable" enterprise.
3. All seven churches mentioned in Revelation are gone—*all of them.* One would have been foolish, if you are a devotee of Wall Street, to have made an investment there.
4. George Muller and the Ashley Down Orphanage saved the lives and souls of thousands of children in the 19th century, but a few years after he died the orphanage was closed and the children were moved to a foster care kind of existence. All he worked for passed after he passed, but thousands of people know who Jesus Christ is because of the time that that ministry did function.

One Christian leader once remarked that he had "never seen God's children having to beg for bread or being forsaken by God." The suggestion, of course, is that if we *are* beggars (as I am) or *appear forsaken* by God (as I am sure I do to some), we're *not* a part of the "chosen" or "elect" or somehow we deserve our hardships. That's biblically perverse. After all, was Job not forsaken, for a season, by God? What about Jesus on the cross when He cried out, "My God, my God, why have you *forsaken me?*" (Matthew 27:46, NIV) And what of the *millions* of Christians that begged for food and *starved under Stalin, Lenin, Pol Pot and Mao?*

I have witnessed the mega-church growth in the USA and heard *so much* of the "feel good message" and "God wants to bless you" canard that I *have to say something!* God did not save me to *bless me,* He *blessed me by saving me.* And when the New Testament talks about the "abundant life" (See John 10:10, NIV), and God "giving us "the desires of our hearts", Psalm 37:4, NIVs." it is *not in reference to making us prestigious prigs in the community, or sending us financial security in a fat portfolio, or producing a life protected from disease, heartache or financial ruin.* Why do we read into scripture such sophomoric spiritual dreaming! In fact, following Christ might lead to the precise *opposite* of the above-mentioned "promises."

We're called to faithfully preach the gospel and make disciples. Dietrich Bonhoeffer did that till the day he was lead to the gallows to be hung by piano wire by Hitler's henchmen. *People were praying for Bonhoeffer's protection and release…* but his death might have done more for the church than 30 more years of his preaching. May God raise up more such men and women who are focused on God's Kingdom, not sustainable earthly substitutes.

Start Doing It Now

Many times, more lately, it appears that the Holy Spirit is directing my morning Bible reading with precisely what my soul is thirsty for. The Word becomes nourishment for my heart and reminds me that I am not the first man to face challenges and obstacles beyond anything I could have imagined.

David said this 3000 years ago—but it was perfect spiritual sustenance for me today:

"The Lord is my light and my salvation— whom shall I fear?
The Lord is the stronghold of my life—of whom shall I be afraid?
When the wicked advance against me to devour me,
it is my enemies and my foes who will stumble and fall.
Though an army besiege me, my heart will not fear;
though war break out against me, even then I will be confident." (Psalm 27:1-3, NIV)

The Lord is my "pilot" and he will provide my rescue—not the federal government or my governor or the W.H.O. If that is the case, then why be afraid? Do I trust the UN and politicians more than God? What a ludicrous comparison! But of course this virus is not a small matter. Some are saying that it might be more deadly than the 1918 Spanish flu and that our economy could take years to return to where it was just a few weeks ago! We will never be the same.

But when David offered the words above, he had good reasons to fret and panic—events were happening that were even greater worries for him than ours. People were hunting for him, his son wanted to murder him, his most trusted friends had betrayed him and the armies that surrounded Israel had a bounty in his head. David knew the reality of intrigue, betrayal and murder. He had lived through more personal loss, through the deaths of his best friends and precious sons and the consequences that God sent upon his nation for his own foolish choices, than most any other man. And yet, he was confident of God's love, forgiveness, restoration and favor.

How is this? He had *experience with God* in matters of catastrophe and he _loved God and knew that God loved Him._ Because of this, at the end of this Psalm, David could write:

I remain confident of this:
    I will see the goodness of the Lord in the land of the living.
Wait for the Lord;
    be strong and take heart and wait for the Lord. (Psalm 27:13-14, NIV)

Do we have the same experience with God… the same confidence…the same courage? If we don't, it's our own fault. Experience the power and presence of God in your life now—don't wait for the next worldwide catastrophe. Choose *today* to give Him the *best* part of your day; seek Him, praise Him, confess your failures to Him and lift your petitions to Him.

As with planting a tree, the best time to get to know God was ten years ago. The second best time is now.

Am I Drifting Away From or Towards Him?

In the Old Testament there are many stories about the Kings of Judah and Israel. The stories are inspiring when they are about the good kings that had great courage. But more often than not the kings were not courageous and did not measure up to God's intention nor King David's example.

One of the kings, Asa, got my attention yesterday. He began as a very good king and did the right things. He honored God, removed false gods, and always asked for God's counsel and direction before he declared war or did anything grandiose. God blessed him with success, peace, and an expanded kingdom.

But later Asa wandered away from God. A nearby king declared war on him and rather than turn to God for help, he turned to the king of another land. He even gave that king the gold and silver from God's temple as payment for helping him.

God did not like what Asa did and sent a prophet to make it clear to King Asa that it was wrong. But foolishly, Asa put the prophet in prison for speaking the truth! Later, Asa's feet became diseased and rather than turn to God, the One who created and shaped Asa's feet in his mother's womb, he turned to physicians. His feet were never healed and upon his death Asa's kingdom diminished. (See II Chronicles 16:12-13, NIV)

That's a lot of narrative to take in, but recently I thought about myself and Asa. Am I more like Asa earlier in his life, or like Asa in old age? Do I turn to God instinctively when bad things happen, or to my own solutions, devices, and friends? God desires that we remain dependent upon Him like a small child is to a father. It's not that Asa did evil things, it's that he "grew up" and no longer thought that he needed God. God has not called us to be teenagers or young adults in our relationship with Him, but to be children.

Just because I am walking with God now is no guarantee that I will be next year. If I start drifting away from God, He may get my attention with events or perhaps through someone like a prophet coming into my life. I can either pay attention to what God is saying or ignore Him at my own peril.

Modern teaching tells us to constantly encourage and *compliment* children and youth. We are also urged to be very careful with their self-esteem. But when we stray away from God we also need people in our lives who give us the naked truth about right and wrong. We need people in our lives that don't always tell us what we want to hear but give us the cold, hard truth. Those people are called *true* brothers and sisters. All the others that say what you want to hear are mere "acquaintances" in comparison.

Courageously Walking Right Back

Paul was stoned in Lystra, assumed to be dead, dragged unceremoniously out of the city like a dead animal, revived, and then walked back into the city. *What was going on?* It's incredible that he survived the stoning, but remarkable that he went back to the same town! (See Acts 14:1-20, NIV).

On other occasions he "fled" to avoid being caught, but here he is walking right back into the hands of the same folks that just tried to kill him! I am not sure about the wisdom of running away from a lynching and walking back to the same folks, but I am certain that he returned to the city because he was *inspired* to do so by the Holy Spirit and he was fearless about men could do to him. *He saw himself as ready to be sacrificed for Jesus Christ!* What love! What devotion! What admiration this man had for Jesus Christ. He had met Jesus and could never deny Him or fail the test of absolute love or loyalty again. What is wrong with the rest of us?

He was now really a problem for the Jews. He was earlier a mere trouble maker and was stoned because of it—the assumption being that this would either scare him away or kill him. But now he showed his true mettle and proved that we was not going to simply "go away"; the man had no regrets for what he had said and done in the name of Jesus and no regard for men could do to him. My opinion is that his critics were now speechless and dumbfounded. This guy was trouble!

He was now an apostle that stood above most of the others. No one was a fiercer defender of the faith, a more determined and adamant evangelist or more of a threat to Satan's work against the growth of Christianity than Paul. It's one thing to perform miracles in the name of Jesus Christ, but this man was beaten nearly to death with rocks and got right back up and walked straight back as if to tell them, "Is that all you can do?" Paul was courageous, zealous—and on fire for Jesus! It must have given great strength and hope to those that were also being persecuted, but really riled those who were determined to stamp out the new "religion."

Why have I written all of this about Paul today? I realize that as a father, friend and pastor, I am no Paul, and my sons and friends are the worse off because of it. As I write this, I am cognizant of my shortcomings and can see that members of my church, the parents of campers that entrust their children to me, and my friends are all reading this. But it's true about me—to my shame. I go to bed every night, keenly aware that I have been far too concerned about my sons loving me and being happy with me than I have been about loving them regardless of their approval of my parenting. I have courted the favor of those I love far too much and have remained silent, or motionless, when I should have "…got up and went back into the city." ? (Acts 14:20, NIV)

May God give me the courage and intensity of Saint Paul so that I can be finally empty of me (a glorious departure!) and filled with His Holy Spirit.

A Time Even to Die

In Ecclesiastes, Solomon talked a lot about topics that examined the purpose in life and the inevitability of death; he pointed out that most of our ministries, careers and enterprises will be short-lived and forgotten after we've gone. Few of us will do things that will cause us to be celebrated in a history book a hundred years hence; we'd be blessed to be found in a footnote! While it is true that a few notables leave their historical impressions for several generations, usually that is not the case. You can walk through the cemeteries of any city and see row after row of headstones that mark the graves of forgotten people. The epitaph on many a gravestone, "Gone, but not forgotten," unfortunately is not true. The point is, one needs to exert his influence now; he should use his talents, energy, money, and personality to do good while he is living, for the day is coming when his earthly opportunities will be over. We're all actors on a stage—but the final act comes for all of us.

Lately the uncertainty of *everything* has come upon me more profoundly. I might have escaped the dreaded result of my concerns at this same time last year, but this new year has new concerns as potent and mind-boggling as the former. Coincidentally, I was awakened early this morning by an inability to swallow and noticed a large swelling-about the size of a golf ball-on the right side of my neck. Clearly, something was wrong with me and I wondered about my last performance on the stage. Was it coming?

These things cause anyway to stop for a moment and consider: "Is my house is in order?"; because death is inevitable for me and everyone reading this devotion. Surprises as I had Saturday morning put life in perspective. If I leave this world today, or next month, will I leave my community a bit better because I was here? Will I be missed? What will *really be* said about me what I am gone? Will folks say, "Well, he was a nice enough fellow, buy you know he really was a '_____'"; or will others say, "I don't mean to be uncharitable, but now that he is gone I really think it should be said that he was '_____.'"

How will the sentences about me be completed when I am laid to rest in the ground—and what can I do about it *now* to save my family and my close associates embarrassment and chagrin? Far more important, when our time is up, will we have finished the tasks He has given us? Will we find that our last act on the stage is our finest, or will we find we missed too many rehearsals and made far too many excuses for not memorizing our lines? And regardless of my performance, will the things people repeat and copy from my life draw them closer to Him or push them farther from Him?

Either some antibiotics will clear up whatever it is that has my doctors confused, or a biopsy will show that I have cancer. Regardless, I still have a race to complete; I have a legacy and performance that I can still effectively hone to be one that others will want to copy, not eschew. But there's no time to waste thinking that I will live forever on this earth and I have a second life in reserve to live! The curtain is going to fall one day on my play (and yours)—ready or not.

A Poor Reflection, But a Reflection Nonetheless

There is nothing more heartbreaking than having your child tell you that he does not want to go to school, church, or camp because, "no one likes me," "nobody will play with me," or "no one will be my friend." I have heard these comments a few times from my boys and it burdens me. But today the youngest told me very quietly, softly, and painfully that he did not want to go to school tomorrow because he had no friends and no one wanted to *become* his friend. He begged me to allow him to stay home with me from now on. It brought tears to my eyes to think how unkind children can be to other children, and how much I wanted to shield him from that hurt.

I have watched my boys literally wilt when adults casually accuse them of errors they did not make, or mistakes they committed accidentally. These little boys lack the cognitive skills to defend themselves or explain why they did what they did. So they simply give up and accept that they will never be trusted.

When they feel that they are under attack, the two younger ones run to me and want to bury their faces in my chest, or hide in my arms, or to find shelter behind me. Children are incredibly afraid of rejection, abandonment, or of offering someone their trust and having that trust broken. My boys have carried these fears far more intensely than others. Now, more than at any time in my life, I truly understand how important my life is for the emotional and developmental health of these young men. I need to be here for them.

In truth, I suppose that all of us are like these boys even in our adult lives. We've learned to mask our fears and call our sorrows by a different name. But deep down we dread being disliked, ignored, having no friends, or being alone and unnoticed. In my own life as a "mature" adult, I still struggle with the reality that some folks do not like me and never will. I know that no one fully understands me or appreciates my good intentions, and ultimately, I am alone in the world. My boys struggle with these same things, but in me, they have found someone who will never give up on them or abandon them. That's what I once had in two loving parents. I still miss their touch, their support, and their love. I miss hearing their words, which gave me such hope and instilled confidence in my life.

But I have found in Jesus Christ all that I yearn for and more. There are many days when I want to hide behind the shadow of God's wings. Days when I need my Father to pick me up so that I can hide my face in His chest. And, days I need to listen to Him as He reminds me that I am the apple of His eye.

For the time being, I hope that I can be to my boys what God, through Jesus Christ, has become to me. Soon, I want to introduce them to a far better Father and Protector than I can ever be.

A Breath of Fresh Air!

If I were asked to point to one thing that a redeemed man should be doing that unregenerate men are often not doing, it would be "telling the truth." Dishonesty is more destructive to a relationship with a friend, a mate, or your Savior than anything else. I would dare to say that it is impossible to be walking closely with Him and also be "living a lie," or in general, to be known as a liar. Why? Because the Holy Spirit is not going to provide the fruits that are essential for a holy life if a man refuses to confront his own dishonesty and put that part of the former self to death.

I write this because the more time I spend in His word, the more I see "a lying tongue" (see Ephesians 4:25, NIV) referred to as something that God absolutely hates. There is no place for it in the community of God. I ask myself the question: If lying has never been accepted by the Christian community, and is soundly condemned throughout scripture, why don't we talk more about it from the pulpit, in devotions, and in our national discourse? And if you ever wonder *if* lying has became an established part of our culture, just listen to a politician speak for a few minutes.

Where is the outrage when our elected leaders lie? Where is the disgust when those we trust or admire are found to be lying to us? There are a few people that I can trust to never lie. These people, I believe, have become so *unaccustomed* to lying that being untruthful would never enter their minds. They have unlearned the devil's tongue. Far more of us are comfortable with telling a lie if we are fairly certain that no one could ever prove that we are being dishonest. But of course *we* know that we are lying, and we know that God knows. Hopefully, that sin eats at our conscience, as it should, and we find that we cannot live with it any longer.

As a Christian, I am responsible for speaking the truth even if I am hurt by doing so. And often, telling the truth requires the discipline to think and reflect on my words before they are spoken. I remain a creature of my culture and I'm still haunted by the memories of "original sin." It's only when I am determined to be completely honest that I can begin to take on the mind of Christ and develop the habits of always speaking the truth. Soon, that habit will become something I am comfortable with and through God's grace it will become my very nature.

I often wonder if someone could *ever* get elected to congress or the presidency without telling lies or misleading others. I am certain that only an honest man or woman can enjoy a sustained life of intimacy with Him. For my life, I want that more than anything else.

Oh, to Be Loved by God!

"'Because he loves me,' says the Lord, 'I will rescue him; I will protect him, for he acknowledges my name. He will call on me, and I will answer him; I will be with him in trouble, I will deliver him and honor him. With long life I will satisfy him and show him my salvation.'" (Psalm 91:14-16, NIV)

I want to be rescued by God—I need a hero. I need a bodyguard and one that can protect me from all those things out there that seek to pull me down. I am desperate for One that I can call on that will not let me down when I am in trouble!

And here is God Almighty! The One far greater than Iron Man or Superman who is not only able to rescue me, protect me, answer me, but also give me a long life with honor. *What could be better to hope or pray for?!*

And what does He expect from me? Why is God going to do this for me—or any other servant that desires what I desire? Simply that *I love Him*. Because if I love Him, God will rescue, protect, be with me, deliver me, honor me, and give me a blessed life.

Is this true or just poppycock? Did David know, *first hand*, what he was talking about, or is this just a lot of sentimental/metaphysical blather? David, and millions of other men and women that worship the living God, not only *believe* this to be true, they have *experienced it*. But here's the *key—the one item that cannot be ignored:* The thing required of me is simple, yet direct and immovable: Am I willing to *love Him*?

It seems absurd to not be willing to love God as a reaction or response to His great love and who He is! But even more so now, in light of this testimony from David: Because we love Him, He is prepared to move heaven and earth to bless us!

So the big question is this: *Do you love Him?* And if you are thinking, "Of course I love Him", then ask yourself, "How am I showing it?" We are clearly told that if we *love Him*, we will keep His commandments. Yes, I could argue that the laws of the Old Testament are numerous and difficult to follow; I can also point out that through the sacrifice of Jesus all my errors, sins and broken laws have been wiped clean. But this is not a matter of salvation—but of sanctification and blessing. If I want to be blessed, I must ask the simple question: Am I loving Him and *showing it in my obedience to Him?* It is in *obeying* Him that I enter into a greater faith and experience the fullness of the Christian life. *Am I living an obedient life? That's how I show how much I love him.*

What does He command and require of me:

1. "To act justly and to love mercy and to walk humbly with (my) your God." Micah 6:8 (NIV)
2. Obey Him—especially when He "whispers" to me
3. Bury and treasure His word in my heart—i.e. read the word and put it into practice. If I do these things, I can expect blessings.

A Toss of the Dice

"Then they cast lots, and the lot fell to Matthias; so he was added to the eleven apostles." (Acts 1:26, NIV)

It's a funny way to choose the twelfth apostle—the most important leaders in the history of the world's greatest religion. Jesus chose the twelve based upon His perfect discernment of people and His complete clarity into God's will. So the remaining eleven disciples decided to throw dice to see who the next disciple/apostle would be?

Casting lots—in this case, probably one stone representing one candidate and another stone representing the other candidate—was used to render an impartial, unbiased decision on a very important matter. Once the lot was cast, no one could argue that the decision was the result of human intervention. They only cast lots, it appears, when there was no other means of determining who it should be—or in some cases in the Old Testament, who was guilty!

But what I see being emphasized is the idea, all things being equal, that there should no partiality in making weighty decisions. So if both candidates were approved, the idea of throwing the dice is that "we›ll accept either choice." Kids do the same thing every day in games—they draw straws or flip a coin. It's "fair" and cannot be manipulated. In the Bible, the point seems to be that no one should get the advantage because of family, connections or politics.

There's also an element of trusting that God is going to see the sincerity of our efforts to make the right choice and that He realizes that we simply don't know what else to do but ask for a "sign." God understands that there are times when we just need a vision or epiphany—like right now in our fight against this virus.

Finally, it looks like even with the disciples, there was a keen awareness of the danger of leaving important decisions to one person. Peter—the one Jesus chose as head of the group—never "laid down the law", but rather he presented his case to the other leaders and let them decide. Power corrupts, and absolute power corrupts absolutely. The early church recognized this and tended to make their decisions after much prayer, and complete presentation and examination of the facts (or merits of the one being considered, as with a deacon or elder), and if needed, after God provided some means of pointing out the right choice.

A Goal for the New Year

"The fruit of the Holy Spirit is love, joy, peace, patience, kindness, goodness, faithfulness, gentleness, and self-control….." (Galatians 5:22, NIV)

These are the traits, virtues, and the proof of His seal. These are the things that I should be showing if I am truly born-again. So how can I produce this outgrowth of His Spirit and prove that He is present and working in my life, i.e., that I am truly His? I would argue that whether you're a Christian or an agnostic, it's a good and sobering exercise to be patient, kind, good, faithful, self-controlled, full of joy, and gentle. But the more I *try* to act this way and the harder I try to bear spiritual fruit, the more frustrated I become and the more annoying I am to those with whom I associate. And yet that frustration, just like other personal failures, can lead to the best possible outcome.

We are told that we should naturally bear spiritual fruit, and here the nine fruits are plainly listed in black and white, but I would suggest that it's unfair and impossible for a *natural* man to achieve that goal. To find success, we must discover a supernatural means of becoming a kind of a "miracle" human being. I cannot bear the spiritual fruit for which I yearn through my own discipline, education, and efforts. And, that of course, is what the gospel is all about.

The beatitudes and the list of the fruits of the Spirit describe an ideal life that is impossible for even the best of us to acquire. It is beyond our grasp and outside the realm of our possibilities. The failure to live that kind of life may lead you to despair, or it may push you to the source of holy living as described in the Jesus' teaching and expressed as being the "fruit of the Holy Spirit." All of this points to a life-changing encounter with Jesus Christ. He did not come to improve my character or sharpen my understanding of how to be holy, nor did He come to merely fertilize the fruit I was already bearing. He came to totally change my heart, mind, and soul. He came to re-create Himself within me so that my natural life can be lived supernaturally day-to-day through Him. In short, He came to plant a new tree within me.

Saint Paul concluded by stating that if we are producing these fruits, "... against such things there is no law." (Galatians 5:23, NIV) In other words, there is no need to fear that our lives are offensive to God or that we have become a stumbling block to others because of our witness. If I am "connected to the vine," bearing these nine fruits, and am in intimate communion with Jesus Christ, there is simply no room, time, or desire to sin. I have chosen to allow Him to be re-born within me and I simply don't have to sin anymore. There is no longer a place or a longing for it in my life. I have tasted the heavenly fruit and no longer hanker after the substitutes this world has to offer.

Personally, I am not there yet. But with God's grace I will be closer in the year to come.

A Reason to Say No

I am learning more and more of the need to be able to say no. I once heard a very successful businessman remark that he had made more money saying "no" than saying "yes". As my family has grown, I can see that saying yes brings instant smiles, but saying no more often brings stability and a firmer foundation.

When it comes to shopping, such as going to the mall or a hardware store, the more I say no, the more I save and the less I have "buyer's remorse." In Christian fellowships and Christian camps, saying no seems to bring about more blessings than saying yes all the time.

The early church offered a moral code for members that was clear-cut and easy to grasp, and they practiced discipline on those that would not accept no for an answer. And the church grew! It seems today that more Christian denominations and charitable foundations find it expedient to say yes—and it's far more politically correct. But I wonder, more and more, if it is honoring to God. God's commandments include eight no's and two "honors" (the Sabbath and your parents). (See Exodus 20:-1-17, NIV)

Now why all of this talk about no's in this little devotion?

We are all bound by our fractured and broken nature. Often, when we are told "no", we refuse to comply unless given a good reason why. We don't like being denied the things we want to do when we want to do them. It is in our fallen DNA. Hearing and obeying the word "no" stands in the way of us being our own god. So what should we do?

The answer is not to fight the noes, but to submit and say yes to Jesus Christ and His lordship in my life. I can no more resist the things I really want to do than I can stop the sun from rising. If I try, I will certainly fail. Only Christ can cleanse me from the perverse desire to say yes to every compulsion, hidden passion, and resistance to submitting to God in my natural spirit. But through Christ I can say "no" with no regrets.

The Button

Have you ever stopped and considered what it is that really makes you angry? What is it that "pushes your button"? I have buttons and I am embarrassed to admit that some pretty silly things push my button: e.g. borrowing my stuff and not putting it back; breaking a promise to me; someone texting on his iPhone while we're eating a meal or carrying on a conversation and so on.

But some people I have come across are simply covered with buttons! No matter what you say or do they seem to find a way to be offended, or annoyed, or itching for a fight. I have learned this about bad moods: they only go away if you *starve them of attention*. I have to let go and go on and stop thinking about those silly things that aggravate me and realize that it's *not* a big deal.

What I *truly* need to consider is what pushes *God's buttons*. What was it in Jesus' ministry that got Him upset—what about Paul, Peter and the prophets of old? You see, these men were closer to the heart of God than I am. They had an intimate understanding of what was essential and what was inessential. All their "personal" buttons had been removed, one by one, as they grew closer to God; and the *new button was God's hot button*. And what was that button? What was the thing that quickly caused them to become angry: *God's button is* actions, words, conduct, or indifference that causes one seeking Him to not find Him or to give up the search.

God forbid that any of us pushes that button.

Joy Comes In The Morning

"Though the fig tree does not bud
and there are no grapes on the vines,
though the olive crop fails
and the fields produce no food,
though there are no sheep in the pen
and no cattle in the stalls,
yet I will rejoice in the Lord,
I will be joyful in God my Savior.
The Sovereign Lord is my strength;
he makes my feet like the feet of a deer,
he enables me to tread on the heights." (Habakkuk 3:17-19, NIV)

Somber and sober words from one of the last prophets: Habakkuk. He knew that the "end" of the nation of Israel was at hand, but in the middle of that ruination, he was looking to his Savior, not to the inevitable tragedy, or the annihilation of all those things he loved. His joy, in the midst of the oncoming destruction of his beloved nation, was God, and he was full of joy (joyful) at the thought of his Redeemer.

We're not the first people to have troubles and we won't be the last. It's been said that if you want to be *happy*, get a bottle at the local liquor store and happiness will come quite easily; others find it by gorging themselves on some other appetite of the body. But joy is not happiness. Joy is caused by elation at a moment in time. Joy may not always be about oneself but be about others' contentment also. Happiness is about the self's pleasure. Happiness dwells on materialistic, worldly pleasures while joy is derived from soul satisfying, emotional well being. And for the follower of Jesus, the *source* of joy is Jesus Himself.

My joy comes from abiding in Him—it is the by-product of staying with Him and not seeking any other source for purpose or peace. It happens when I reflect on Him and find myself quite naturally looking for Him in all of life's happenings. Dwelling upon Him and training my mind upon Him and His kingdom, and then trusting Him to fill in all the rest, creates a peace and joy that confounds the world.

Yes, I do sometimes allow the emails, phone calls, family matters and petty squabbles to get my eyes off the goal (Jesus Himself), but—praise be to God!—He does not get His eyes off of me! Oh that as a father, pastor, friend and an employer I could be known by the manner in which I become a small source of joy for those that look to me!

Lord, help me to find the joy of keeping my eyes upon you and establish in my heart that sublime joy of helping others find contentment in you.

A Better Father Than Me

Moses begged God for the chance just to see the Promised Land. As I read this passage I thought, 'After 40 years in the desert, with all the rebellion and bellyaching that Moses had put up with, why not let him go into and at least spend a few days in the promised land before he died?' But God said, 'Enough of that! Speak no more to Me of this matter", (Deuteronomy 3:26 NIV) and in a few verses God told Moses to basically prepare for death!

This is one passage that is hard to understand, because after an initial reading, God seems far too rigid. Why couldn't He extend some grace to Moses? After all, Moses begged God to give the Hebrews grace when they rebelled against Him, and God was merciful and patient with the Hebrews. It doesn't seem fair that God was unwilling to give His favored one, Moses, a second chance. I have never fully grasped what Moses and Aaron did that made God so upset with them. In the narrative, Moses and Aaron struck the rock that produced water; but they did the act wrong, somehow, and they knew it.

I have to remember that God is the perfect Father and I am far from it. When Moses is recorded begging God for what he wanted after God already told him "No," Moses adopted a stubborn rather than humble posture. Moses was a great man of faith, but he did not always do the right thing. As we look at the heroes of the Bible and our Christian heritage, we should never put our total confidence in a single man or woman—only One is truly good and totally worthy of trust.

With God, "no" means "no". A good parent does not waver in regard to his or her standards of what is best for the child and the family. They place their love for their child above the child's begging and temper tantrums. Why do my kids beg and beg after I tell them "no"? Sometimes, I think it's because they feel I may not love them enough and am therefore easy to manipulate. I am weak and vulnerable to their pleas and they know it. In a word, they sense my "guilt" for not being a better dad.

However, I want my children to trust me. Teaching them to accept "no" and to trust me for their well-being is preparing them to one day accept "no" from their Heavenly Father, and trust Him in accordance with His will.

There is a point when God says, "that's enough," and then we must stop asking for that about which He has already said "no." From my vantage point, I don't know what is best for me. I don't know what is going to happen tomorrow that might totally upend all of my life's detailed plans. My heart does not always pine for the best things and I sometimes change my mind!

I thank God that He is a better Father than I am.

L. DEAN BARLEY

Raising a Son

I took my middle son to Florida for a family gathering recently. It has been a year since most of them had seen him and I was very heartened by what they said. Yes, he was a year older and a bit smarter. He was taller and had a little more muscle on him. But what surprised them was his new self-confidence, his laughter and smiles, his gregarious and friendly demeanor, and the obvious joy he got in being with his uncles, aunts and cousins.

All my children were adopted, and the middle child was brought into my home when he was nine. The difference now is that *he belongs.* He knows that he will never again have to pack his suitcase and move into another foster home or go and stay with a distant relative again. He is now relaxed and at peace *knowing* that his is where he can be safe and protected. He has a home.

But there's another thing that has made him "fit in," I think. I have told him "no" far more often than I have told him "yes." I have required that he, and his brothers, *work* for thirty minutes to an hour a day. He has been told that he is expected to excel at school and not look for excuses for being a bit behind in his classes. I've reminded him that I am not overly concerned that he is "happy", because that's a choice he makes, but that I will give him every *reason* to be happy.

He's also been told that he is *not* the center of the universe, that life is not fair, that I cannot be counted upon to always be right, but that he must nonetheless comply with my rules and expectations.

My sons do not have a very modern or "cool" father, but I am trying to raise sons that *the rest of the world* can appreciate and endure—and that means that I am quite unpopular half the time. I also recognize that I am training my sons against the grain of the common understanding of parenting (they are the only ones they know that do not possess a smart phone, for example).

But the closer I am to them, the more I hope they know that they can mess up, fall down and disappoint me. But they are yet secure in my relationship with them—no matter what, I will not give them away. I hope that throughout the chores, denial of PG13 movies, and those lofty expectations that run counter to how their friends behave, they continue to feel secure, safe and confident.

I expect more of them because I *believe in them and their ability to overcome those things that others have offered as an excuse for living mediocre lives.* But then, that's the same way my heavenly Father treats me. I am a far cry from expressing God's love, but I understand, a little bit better, the depth and mystery of the Father's love now that I have sons to love.

A Pity…

At the end of one the gospels Jesus had just "reinstated" Peter as the leader of the disciples and described how Peter would one day be led away, against his will, to his own death. Peter motioned towards John, and said, "What about him?"(John 21:21, NIV) Christ reminded Peter that Jesus' plans for John had *nothing* to do with Peter. We each need to look after your own walk and work and stop worrying about "John's" walk and work. (See John 21:22, NIV)

I suppose that many of us are like Peter. We are always looking at the circumstances of others, comparing them to our own situation, and wondering if we get less than we deserve. I can unequivocally attest that I am *not* getting less than I deserve! And I *praise God* that I do *not* get what I deserve. I have been receiving His grace for 60 over years—*not justice or what is fair or what I deserve.* I thank God that He has given me far more than I could hope for, dream of or ever expect to attain on my own merits! But sometime people like Peter and I forget this—and we whine.

The single most insidious, dangerous, spiritual-life-evaporating sin is not sexual depravity or greed or even violence—it's self-pity. In my opinion, *nothing* destroys a person's potential, hope for personal triumphs and pursuit of spiritual excellence like self-pity. When we go around feeling sorry for ourselves and blame others, or events, or things God has permitted or withheld from us as the cause for our "shallow" unfulfilled life, we end up living an endless existence of pointing to events in our childhood, or college, or our first job, or to an ex-spouse, etc. for being the *real* reason why we did not "succeed."

What a waste and what a pity to go through this *adventure* on earth nursing what we have determined were undeserved wounds and slights in our life. How sad that so many people *allow* the errors of others in their lives to dictate a life of mediocrity rather than allowing Him to heal them and give them the unlimited power of the Holy Spirit to overcome every obstacle life throws in their paths.

God holds us accountable for the good things He has given us *and* how we allow the bad things to push us into His arms… or into a pity party.

I prefer His arms.

Praise Him in all Situations

Of all my tasks at the camp, traveling long distances, like Asia or Africa, is what I appreciate the least. And yet I know that I must go on these trips for the life and health of our "international" camp. I look forward to the day when someone else handles *all* the foreign travel.

My last trip was a bit more complicated and stressful than normal. I now have young sons that depend upon me. Each has his needs, challenges, gifts and peculiarities. As I prepared to leave, the youngest made it abundantly clear to me that he did *not* want me to go. He is quite attached to me and is fearful that I will die, not come home, abandon him, etc. *It breaks my heart to leave him.* The older sons are more independent, but I understand their need to be affirmed, encouraged, and given "grace" when they get out of bounds. *I need to protect them. They all need to be heard.* The fourth and eldest is already a man and would never admit that he wants to be approved of; but he most surely does—perhaps more than all the others.

So I left full of hope that all would go well, but after being gone just a few hours "meltdowns" began to occur with two of the boys and my iPhone began ringing and the texts descended upon me. I was not there to solve the problem, referee the fighting, or put an end to the quarrels... *and I felt more hopeless than I have in a long time.* Not only could I not solve the dilemmas for them. I could not even evaluate *what the problem was.* I have learned in these desperate moments to do one thing: *Praise the Lord.* Its seems counter-intuitive, I know, but when I can't fix it, stop it or help it; praising Him *always works.*

Why praise Him in these troubling situations? Because that's what He told us to do and it puts me at ease. I *praise* Him because He is worthy of it 24/7, regardless of my little disasters; I praise Him because I was *designed* to function *at my best* when I praise Him; I praise Him because His supernatural power and intervention is released, it appears, when I *praise Him in all places, in all situations, regardless of how much I hurt, how hopeless the matter is, and how much I am despaired.*

And again, let me say: It works.

That Ugly Word Little Word

If you know my sons you also probably know of the drama in our home that seems to occur each time I use a word that the boys find unsettling... *"No."* I am finding myself saying it more and more as they ask for iPhones, iPads, motorcycles, pocketknives, fireworks, video games, etc. It was so much easier when I *told* parents the importance of telling their kids "no", but it's a different matter having to do it yourself to your own kids... *and do it all the time.*

The truth is, these boys would *really* love me more if I said "yes" a lot more, and I would not feel like such a Scrooge all the time. We would have *a lot* less drama, tears, pouting, and attempts to transfer "guilt" to the head of the household (me) for being so "mean."

Of course, I know at least two things about all of this. One, it's not a matter of them loving me, but of me loving them *and doing what love requires me to do to help them and protect them.* And so I must say "no" to the things that they do not need and that will not help them. Secondly, I know the danger of living for the approval of men... or sons. Some of the greatest men and women that ever lived had their walk with Christ compromised or destroyed because they fell into the trap of not wanting to disappoint anyone or hurt someone's feelings *by doing the right thing and saying no.* King Saul was afraid of the approval of his men, so he allowed them to keep some of the plunder after battle rather than give it all to God; he failed the test and lost his crown (See I Samuel 15:1-24, NIV). Peter was more concerned about the consequences of admitting that he knew Jesus so he denied Christ-three times in public—and then wept bitterly for not saying "no" to his fear. (See Luke 22:59–62, NIV)

In my Christian walk, "yes" is easy to justify in my mind, but it represents a lack of courage and character. "No" takes fortitude and often leaves me lonely and unliked... but I do sleep better standing tall and saying "no."

To go forward with these boys and not give in and tell them "yes" each time they get tears in their eyes, I try to remind myself that God treats me just like I *should* be handling these boys. He does *not* always answer my prayers in the affirmative. I must never give them a rock when they ask for a piece of bread, but I have to also be prepared to tell them (as He tells me), "No"... "not yet"... and even sometimes say, "I can't believe you are even asking me that."

Honorable?

"Jabez was more honorable than his brothers. His mother had named him Jabbed, saying, "I gave birth to him in pain." (I Chronicles 4:9, NIV)

Many people pray the prayer of Jabez every day (as I also do) expecting the "miracle prayer" to *cause* God to bless them and make them successful.

But as is often the case with bible verses, we quote them out of context or we forget the preceding or succeeding admonitions. This is a good example.

Jabez's prayer is as follows: "Jabez cried out to the God of Israel, saying, 'Oh that you would bless me indeed and enlarge my territory! Let your hand be with me, and keep me from the evil one.' And God answered his request." (I Chronicles 4:10-11, NIV)

But *before* God answered the prayer, please note that Jabez was a man of honor. The word *honorable* has to do with people and actions that are honest, fair, and worthy of respect. God answered the prayer of Jabez *because he was an honorable man.* Not a *perfect* man, but a man who choose to seek God and His Kingdom first, which includes being honest, fair and *worthy* of respect.

Am I honest? Do I not only tell the truth, but do I also paint a picture with my words that *represents truth?* Am I fair? That is, do I do what is right no matter who is watching and who is involved, or am I always looking out for my best interests? And, Am I *worthy* of the respect of others? Some respect is innate, to be sure, but there is a respect among my neighbors, fellow workers and associates that is *earned* by the way I live, the way I treat others, the way I keep my promises, the way I do what I say and the way I mean what I live and preach. It's called "character."

Yes, God answered the prayer of a man *rightly related to others and rightly related to God.* Am I as honorable as Jabez? If I am, I can pray expecting the same response from God! But if I am not, there is a Savior that is ready to make me honorable and show me the way of becoming a new man, set apart and holy, as Jabez was.

The Seven Churches

Since the beginning of the church there have been divisive ideas, bad theology and problems within Christian fellowships. As I read Revelation, I am reminded that the church is supposed to be what few fellowships really *are*. The first three chapters of Revelation talk about the seven churches in Asia Minor along with their strengths, weaknesses, challenges, and the warnings that Jesus placed on the doorsteps of each.

What is obvious is that Jesus intends to bring each church to absolute holiness; He does not hold back in telling them the truth; even if the church was doing a pretty good job, Jesus pushed them to a higher standard! It appears that He had no intention of ignoring the errors, mistakes, laziness, misplaced "tolerances" etc. of His bride, the church.

Typical preaching and teaching in our churches today seem to have little of the fire and "surgical strikes" that you find in Revelation or that are so common in the New Testament. Paul named names, spoke of specific places, and aggressively addressed what was right and what was wrong. John, in the book of Revelation, does not accept excuses, nor is he lenient in reminding the churches that they needed to get their act together.

It seems to me that we focus far too much on attendance and too little on *attention* in our churches. If we are attending for the primary purpose of the church and if we are allowing Him to bring us to holiness and purity, we *will* grow in attendance.

The same of course holds true for me. He has not called me to be a good man, but to be pure and holy. His call is to bring me into such an intimate relationship with Him that there is no room for sin, so that I am drawing others to Him by the manner in which I reflect Him. If I am serious about the cost of discipleship, I must remember that He does not coddle, make excuses for me, or ignore my shortcomings and moral ineptitude. He wants me *on fire* for Him, not lukewarm; He demands me to remove the relationships in my life that pull me away from Him; He expects me to maintain a steadfast love for Him that is primary in all that I do.

I have been like each of the seven churches described in Revelation. "Listen" is what He says again and again. *Speak, Lord Jesus.*

The Only Command

When Jesus told us to follow a "new" command, it was, "… Love one another. As I have loved you, so you must love one another." (John 13:34, NIV) This was the *only* commandment He ever gave. All the other things He said and taught were basically, "*If* you do this, you will receive this," and so on. But the *command* He gave to His followers was that they were to love each other.

Two things are obvious. First, if we do love each other—as He loved us—we're going to stand out and be noticed as a unique group. And secondly, if we love others as He taught, our lives will be far less complex and burdensome and our hearts *lighter.*

When I love someone—in every sense of the word "love"—I am more charitable towards his/her bad habits and shortcomings. I display more patience and understanding and I want to believe the best about him/her. Even when I know that the one I love is taking advantage of me, lying to me or being unkind to me, somehow I am able to tolerate it precisely because *I love them.*

But when I receive bad behavior from someone I *don't* know and love (as today with a banker from NYC), I am far less sympathetic and kind. Those kinds of run-ins (with unkind folks I don't know) tend to ruin my day and I have a hard time letting go of my resentment. The result is that my load becomes heavy, I feel tied to my angry feelings and I have a hard time not brooding on the disappointment/resentment; I even refrain from loving those near to me. In effect, I am corrupted; my soul is polluted by the *lack of love* I have for the stranger or one that I have difficulty loving.

So I have come to understand the truth of His command (or His "yoke") making my life easier. It works! When I determine to love others—even strangers—*as He loved*— I am a happier soul! I cannot remain bitter, weighed down, plotting my revenge or hoping that he gets what he deserves if I love him—it's not possible. He might not be better because I love him (as Jesus loves me), *but I am better!* This is the yoke Jesus was talking about. It *is light and easy.*

Try it.

The Need to Be Alone

The Bible says that it is "not good that man should be alone," (Genesis 2:18, NIV) but it also says that it is better to be "alone in the desert than together with a contentious woman." (Proverbs 21:19, NIV) The point is, I suppose, that there's a time to be alone and a time to not be alone—all things in moderation.

I *do* think that being alone has many benefits, spiritually speaking. In the scripture the angels, and God Himself, tend to speak to people when they are alone. Of course the same could be said of Satan—he prefers to tempt us when we have no one to come to our defense. In fact it might be argued that the real person, the one underneath all the pretensions, is recognizable for what he really is when he is alone doing things that he would only do when he is alone.

Every summer my life changes as 70 -100 staff descend upon our holy little hill—The Vineyard. Before they arrive I am both excited and at the same time counting the days until I can enjoy some solitary moments again. Be sure that is quite difficult to be "still and alone" when 300 youth fill your facilities.

I understand why Jesus rose early and sought lonely places to pray. It's not that He wanted to be apart from people; just that He craved an uninterrupted conversation with the One He loved above anyone else. And as I fall further in love with Him, the more I "pant for" lonely times and places with Him. I don't want those times diminished or crowded by other things or people. In a sense, I have a certain "selfishness" in my time with Him—I need it.

We are hoping to bring staff and campers to a better understanding of the need to be alone with the Master and Savior each day. We want to show them that only on their own can they come to an intimate understanding of His approval, love, and expectations. Craving community and also lonely intimacy with Him allows me to enjoy the horizontal and perpendicular life I have been redeemed to relish.

Please pray that I can encourage others to desire the same each summer.

On Being Reminded

On a recent trip to Africa I was reminded how far I have to go in my adventure with Him and how simple my needs really are. For the past many years He has been teaching me essential things but I am still learning about discipleship, listening, and obedience. Yet what He is showing me are *not* new spiritual concepts or new codes to live by, but gentle *reminders* of things He has already taught me—the very things I promised myself I would never forget.

Friends, how patient He has been with me. And how I need to *copy His patience in dealing with others!* This past week I found myself saying things (via email and face-to-face) to the ones I love the most, that are absolutely true, but totally unhelpful and unnecessary. I *knew* this before I opened my big mouth or typed the message; so why don't I remember to *not* do these hurtful things? Do I really need to chastise and correct people that might well "deserve it"? Do *I want* to be chastised and corrected like that by God?

The entire trip I planned and prepared to "make things happen" (as I often find myself trying to do) and to press for the results I expected; rather than living and enjoying life *knowing* that He has gone before me, prepared a table for me, and most wonderfully, that He *loves me* far more than I can appreciate. I *know* about love, but I must remember that God, the creator and epitome of love, can teach me more if I submit to His hand and His timing. I was in Africa by His design, but truly I tried to get out of going and was hoping it would be canceled! Sixty hours of flying and waiting for connections in airports is something I dread more than a visit to the dentist.

The other, more pressing issue, is that for the past four years I have been living "on the brink" because of multiple challenges in my ministry, business, and personal life. With God as my witness, I wake up *every morning* unsure how I am going to "make it." The pressures are just too much for me. I cannot carry the weight and I wonder if I can take much more. I sometimes think that if I have to address *one more issue* I will break. But for four years He has sustained me, sent miracles, and looked after me. Yet my *tendency* is to forget these divine interventions and deny that His arm is long enough and that His hand is strong enough to sustain, protect, and defend me.

The *historical experience* I have had with God is that He does far more than I expect or hope for *when I abdicate my will to His.* Why do I keep forgetting this? And so, I returned home determined to "let go and let God… be God." I committed to pray more and be troubled by the demands upon me less. I promised to love, forgive, and be more like *Him* when I see the boys, the staff, and my neighbors; also to stop speaking or typing first and then asking God to forgive my impatience later. That makes these trips, wherever I go, worthwhile even if not a single thing goes "my way."

It's an Adventure, Not a Fairy Tale

As I look back over the past four decades of ministry I recognize that Christian work is not a "happily ever after" fairy tale, but an adventure; it's fraught with dangers, losses, sadness, incredible events, and the *absolute unknown.* Truly, I have never had a *single summer* when I was certain that I would have *another summer!* There are so many variables in operating an international, non-denominational, co-ed sports camp that it is *constantly* an act of faith to start the next season.

Being in ministry is not for the faint of heart, I suppose, but I don't recall being taught that in seminary. Sometimes when you apparently do all the "right things" (and always seem to miss something), life can still be an amazing challenge for your very survival. But I am aware that it is not what I have *accomplished* that matters, but instead how He has used me… albeit with my self-inflicted wounds, errors and blunders. Somehow He uses all of this to draw attention unto Him. The greatest danger for the ones called to pastor or lead camps is to lose sight of Him and focus too steadily on "accounts payable", attendance, the annual tally of contributions, etc.

As I look back I would *never* have chosen to have a career of such incredible uncertainty, frustration, disappointment, and vulnerability. But I cannot imagine any adventure that I would have been able to look back upon, when the journey is over, that made better use of my God-given gifts, talents, and preparation than what I am doing right now.

The Christian journey is not a fairy tale or made for one that prefers to stay far from the "front lines" of battle; it is an adventure of highs and lows, breathtaking beauty, and almost unbearable desolation. The Christian minister, pastor, camp director, priest, or missionary can feel at times absolutely abandoned, totally misunderstood, and unfairly judged. But those are the very times when He reminds you that He will never leave you, that he completely understands and He esteems you as His own.

L. DEAN BARLEY

His Indescribable Favor

My most recent trip to France was the antithesis of the last time I tried to fly to France for my meetings. *Everything* happened just as planned and all things progressed incredibly smoothly. Pity that I allow the things I *cannot control* to often set my tone and tempo. Surely He *is able* to do infinitely more than I can imagine if I merely give up *my* desire to be in charge and let Him set the calendar and setting for His Kingdom work as He pleases.

But, as I was waiting for the 4:15 AM alarm to sound at the hotel today, I prayed earnestly for the trip, the meetings, our needs, our hopes, our plans, etc. There is much for which I *must* be grateful, but also many things that could cause me to fret. As I was praying, I felt the presence of the Holy Spirit in a very sublime way. I was encouraged, emboldened, and strengthened for the adventure that lies ahead of me. Suddenly my heart leapt as I sensed that not only would things "work out" but that our ministry and I would be blessed beyond measure.

I don't get these "revelations" often. In fact, for the past *many* months I have suffered with His silence. But when He speaks, when His Spirit moves and whispers, there is nothing you can do but bask in the lightness of the moment! He *moved* my heart with the reassurance that, *yes,* He was still aware of my challenges, frustrations, embarrassments—and He was going to take care of me.

That is what the Savior is to me; my Redeemer; but also the lover of my soul! The enemy attempts to plant and nurture fears in mind of how humiliated I would be if suddenly I got all that I *really* deserved. Satan is the master of taking *some* truth and pulling God's children away from Him. Whereas he is right—I do not deserve the love, protection, favor, blessings, and smile of God—I am nonetheless the grateful receiver of all of this and more. What I must do when the enemy whispers doubts and fears into my heart is *quickly* confess the fears and doubts to God and ask Him to remind me of His love! It is His *love* that dispels the darkness and spiritual cobwebs of my mind; dwelling upon His unmerited *favor* rather than just what a weasel and fallen creature I am is what allows me to go through my front door each morning. Without His arms about me I would be a most miserable creature.

And this, of course, leads me to treat other men and women such as myself as my true brother and sister, regardless how far they are from the cross… because, "there, but by God's grace, go I."

The Rudder of the Ship

"...whose tongue utters no slander, who does no wrong to a neighbor, and casts no slur on others;" - (Psalm 15:3 NIV)

Why is it so hard to hold my tongue when someone does something that *annoys* me? Why do I find it so tempting to "educate" someone else about the *real* character of a person we both know? What makes it so pleasurable to cast doubt or an unflattering innuendo about some other soul that has wronged me?

I think that the answer is simply because it makes *me* look superior and allows me to feel better about my own flawed existence as I compare myself to someone who is apparently *more* flawed than I am. This way of thinking reminds me of the "relative argument" teenagers often use. When caught doing something wrong, the "relative argument" occurs when the teenager compares his/her offense to someone who has committed a far more egregious sin. "Yes, what I did was wrong and maybe even bad, but look at how bad Hitler was!"

When I slander people, gossip about someone else, or attempt to make someone doubt the goodness of another soul, *all* that I say may be true, but it is a lazy attempt to diminish my own failures, weaknesses and faults. It might make me feel good for a short time, but eventually the reality of who I really am and my need to humble myself before God will catch up with me.

The Psalmist here is once again painting a masterpiece of what a man or woman of God *should* look like, and if we look at that painting and don't see ourselves reflected in it, perhaps we need to talk to the Master Artist and ask him to "re-paint us."

In fact, the more aware I become of *His* mercy and grace, the more easily I can forgive my neighbor, rather than slander him—or even speak the unflattering truth! The more *He* reminds me that it is against Him—*and only Him*—that I have sinned, the less bombastic I tend to be in arguing that another man is contemptible.

I appreciate people who are able to tell the truth from the pulpit, on talk radio or from the Senate floor. And yes, there *are* times we need to rebuke a brother or sister or confront what is patently wrong. But there's also a need to esteem others highly and to always *want* to believe the best about the other. Christ has not called us to be naive or innocent of truth, but rather pure and free from a burning desire to hurt or offend others by our words.

As I think about my own words today, I wonder how many were kind, positive, persuasive, uplifting, and encouraging; and how many were snide, unneeded, unhelpful or mean-spirited. There's more than one verse in the Bible that warns about the destructive power of the tongue.

Lord, take *possession* my mind, tongue and motives—I am not where I hope to be yet.

The Thought of Thee

What is it that causes my soul to rest and be at total peace? It is not an edifice, or a place, or a possession. It's not even the closeness or intimacy of someone that I love. No, it is a thought ...the thought of Jesus. That sounds so strange as I read what I have just typed, but what Bernard of Clairvaux wrote almost 200 years ago *stirs my heart: "Jesus the Very Thought of Thee".* I have sung this song since I was a child, but the lyrics have taken on true meaning as I have lost confidence in the many "good" things that prevented me from taking hold of the "best" thing... Jesus Christ Himself.

Why does this thought give me peace? Because *He knows me* and yet approves of me and loves me. He sees my every movement and is aware of my thoughts, motives and hidden purposes, and yet He does not cast me aside or allow the destruction I deserve to befall me. He has called me His own! And as I am coming more and more to recognize His voice and bask in His approval, the more I find myself approving of others and ignoring the urge to "set them straight" or point out their errors.

You can't really appreciate this until you've experienced it. It would be like me trying to describe the taste of chocolate to one that had never tasted it before... you have to taste it! How can one begin to explain the confidence He gives me when I hear Him whisper encouragement and rest: "Relax, I've got this under control... take courage, I am going before you... don't worry when folks fall on your right or left. I am your shield."

I would not deny that I do not always feel His hand upon me. Some days I forget to look to the cross and to the Savior to embolden me and lead me. But He allows the right things to happen, at the right time, to bring me back into joy. Praise be to God for challenges that cause me to return to Him.

> Jesus, the very thought of Thee
> With sweetness fills the breast;
> But sweeter far Thy face to see,
> And in Thy presence rest.
> Nor voice can sing, nor heart can frame,
> Nor can the mem'ry find
> A sweeter sound than Thy blest name,
> O Savior of mankind!

The Heavens Declare Your Glory

I don't normally quote an entire chapter in the Bible, but Psalms 19 is so special I thought it appropriate:

"The heavens declare the glory of God; the skies proclaim the work of his hands.
Day after day they pour forth speech; night after night they reveal knowledge.
They have no speech, they use no words; no sound is heard from them.
Yet their voice goes out into all the earth, their words to the ends of the world.
In the heavens God has pitched a tent for the sun.
It is like a bridegroom coming out of his chamber,
like a champion rejoicing to run his course.
It rises at one end of the heavens and makes its circuit to the other;
Nothing is deprived of its warmth.
The law of the Lord is perfect, refreshing the soul.
The statutes of the Lord are trustworthy, making wise the simple.
The precepts of the Lord are right, giving joy to the heart.
The commands of the Lord are radiant, giving light to the eyes.
The fear of the Lord is pure, enduring forever.
The decrees of the Lord are firm, and all of them are righteous.
They are more precious than gold, than much pure gold;
They are sweeter than honey, than honey from the honeycomb.
By them your servant is warned; in keeping them there is great reward.
But who can discern their own errors? Forgive my hidden faults.
Keep your servant also from willful sins; may they not rule over me.
Then I will be blameless, innocent of great transgression.
May these words of my mouth and this meditation of my heart
be pleasing in your sight, Lord, my Rock and my Redeemer." (Psalm 19:1-14, NIV)

Two things struck me about this chapter. First, these are not common words from a "religious" man, but a letter from a man *in love with God;* and may I fall under the same intoxicating love.

Second, I had to ask the question: Am I leading and living a life that is a *revelation to who God is and what He has done for me?*

The sky and heaven are inanimate objects that *give glory to God;* they have no spirit, soul, or mind. Yet even these things *shout out* God's incredible *glory;* why in "heaven's name" don't I? If something as expansive as the *sky* was designed to attest to how incredible God is… why am I not also?

Funny how I get so focused on my petty enterprises and projects and forget that the foundational and most important "witness" for my God is the manner in which I live my life; "pre-evangelism" as it is often called. And of course, God is there (as He always is) to *help* me be a natural reflector of His glory by giving me the rules, standards, and steps to take to acquire the wisdom that will allow me to be the creature of *natural revelation* I could be if I got my priorities, each day, sorted out.

Oh Lord! Help me to be a blameless man whose words, acts, reactions, and focus gives glory to you… and you alone…

How Can You Tell I'm A Christian?

It is interesting that Jesus told His disciples that what should *distinguish* them from other people was the *manner in which they loved one another. Not* their personal devotion, or fanaticism, or preparation to be martyred, or ability to perform miracles, or superlative knowledge of the Bible—but how they loved one another. That was the sign of following Jesus. We should preach and illustrate this in our lives more.

What has happened to us? Why is this not *still* the distinguishing sign that a person is a follower of Christ? It was said that in the early years of the Christian church the Roman soldiers would comment that you could tell certain folks were Christian because of the love they showed for one another—and this was purportedly said as an insult, not a compliment.

But few commentators would suggest that this is what sets Christians apart from the other people of the earth today. It might even be argued that Christians are *unloving* to Muslims, atheists, homosexuals, or others. But the life of Christ, and the example of the disciples was one of *love.* Jesus did not condone Judas' betrayal, Thomas's lack of faith or Peter's denial, but no one would ever suggest that He did not love them!

Paul might have had harsh *words* for the Christians that incorrectly taught one had to first experience circumcision before he could become a follower of Jesus, but we also know that he would quickly have given his life for the salvation or benefit of that same soul.

Jesus's point is that He expected His *true* followers to *love as He had loved them.* This was not some sentimental love and certainly not a romantic love, but rather the love that contends with *making a decision to love—and sticking with it!* And that, I think, is what is lacking today. We love when we *feel like it*—which is no different from any other religion or society. But in Christ we have been taught to love each other in such a way that it is obviously a *determination* to love and not give up, and also that it obviously flows *supernaturally* from us (because of our connection to God, the ultimate source of love).

To *not* love means that we are not connected to Him and/or that we are unwilling to act as He acted. It's not a matter of loving the lovely, or those that will love back or because it feels good—but because it is our *choice* and our *reborn nature to love.*

The Roman soldiers did not understand this when they saw it—*but they saw it consistently among those who claimed Christ as their Savior.* Should it not be true of us today as well?

The Ideal

"I will be careful to lead a blameless life — when will you come to me? I will conduct the affairs of my house with a blameless heart." (Psalm 101:2, NIV)

I read this today and asked myself three things:

1. Am I being *careful* about how I lead my life? Do I really remember that I *am* a witness for Jesus Christ—I have no choice in the matter! I can choose to be the best possible witness for Him… or something less. But if I call upon Him as my Lord, I have been identified with Jesus Christ, and I *must be careful of how those outside the body and those struggling within the body* see what I do and hear what I say.

2. When He *does* come for me, do I want to be found doing the very things that I am doing right now? Is it my resolution to *never do anything* that I would not want to be found doing the very second that Christ returns?

3. If I want to be useful to God, I had better get *my own home in order first.* If I want Him to expand my borders and give me greater responsibility I must first be a godly master of my own home. How do I treat those in my family and those that live with me? How do I conduct my *personal finances and affairs?* I am living in such a compelling manner that those who work for me, beside me and with me are inspired to a closer walk with Him?

The present political and social climate of our nation seems very fixated on the sins and shortcomings of the *other* party, nation, race, etc. But the Word reminds us that until we begin to see that the source of our problems is within *our own skin* and the solution is within *our own confession and resolve,* we will never advance His Kingdom.

It's been said: "The Christian ideal has not been tried and found wanting. It has been found difficult; and left untried."

Am I Plumb?

We were getting one of the bathroom showers ready this past weekend with a new piece of glass that was to shield the shower from the rest of the bathroom. I called the glass company and asked them about installing it and they assured me that *anyone* (i.e. I) could install it.

It was simply a piece of glass with two pieces of metal channeling. You simply glued the bottom channel piece onto the floor and long piece onto the wall and then slipped the glass in. Simple! Or so they said.

After *an hour* of fiddling with the silicone caulk and a level, I was finally ready to let it dry and then install the glass the next day. It was *perfect!* So the next day the eldest boy I and carefully picked up the glass and slid it into the bottom piece of channeling and then slipped the glass towards the long piece of channeling attached to the wall. It did not work. The wall was not "square" so there was a full *inch* gap between the wall and the glass. It was a *total* waste of time. I now had to call in professionals to do what I should never have attempted by myself. I have no idea how to make an un-square wall, "square."

But two things did occur to me. The wall *looked* straight and square. I would never have guessed that it could have been one full inch off plumb with less than six feet of height. Second, I should have made *sure* it was level, plumb and square before I began my work! And as I thought about all of that, I had to laugh at myself and say, "No wonder God has not cut me loose to change the world yet!" In my own mirror, I look pretty straight, "righteous," spiritually plumb and morally "in square." But that's *only* if I compare my life to the lives of others—particularly those that I know I am a little ahead of in these matters. But there's only one "level life" that I can compare my life to if I want to be spiritually plumb—and that life of course is Jesus Christ. And the more I dwell on *imitating Him* I will be less impatient with God giving me "great" assignments, and the less I will question why He doesn't make my life easier or do things as quickly and abundantly as I think He should. If I am honest, I would admit that I know I am not yet where I desire to be in terms of being "straight", "level" and "plumb."

But the good news is that He is able to complete the job within me. And He *will* bring me to that place if I yield to Him to do the wrecking, re-building and shaving required. Nothing on earth or heaven can prohibit Him from completing this "sanctuary" for God within my life… except for me. Do the work required, Lord Jesus. Make me whole and complete.

Really Dead

"Pilate was surprised to hear that he was already dead. Summoning the centurion, he asked him if Jesus had already died. When he learned from the centurion that it was so, he gave the body to Joseph." (Mark 15:44-45, NIV)

Jesus was really dead…gone…not coming back. That's what death means. It's over. That's how I felt when I got a phone call that my mother had passed away a few weeks ago. She had departed from this earth, was not coming back, her body already on the way to the funeral home. The curtain came down.

Death means the end of dreams, hopes, expectations. It's *horrible* and even if you know that someone you love is going to die, as with my mom, it's riveting and life changing. I realized that my mother would die soon, but the finality of that dreadful phone call is unnerving nonetheless.

Pilate was "surprised" that Jesus had died so fast; but after the beating He took and the weight He carried, it should not have surprised someone as callous, indifferent and accustomed to death as Pilate. Of course He was dead!

And yet Pilate had to make sure that Jesus was really "gone for good." It really "hit" me as I read this passage, that the man, Jesus, this charismatic, incredible speaker, miracle worker, humble man of God was really *dead*. And his death must have rattled His disciples, family and friends. Imagine the shock of learning that a young man so wonderful, gentle, intelligent and well loved *was dead*. There's something surreal about hearing about the death of someone you love. You feel like you are walking slowly in a dream…you are not sure you heard it right…you ask person telling you the sad news if they are *sure*.

My young sons keep asking me if I am going to die. The Covid 19 news is all anyone is talking about and everyone is scared—but especially our children. They are completely dependent upon us as parents, and they are not only vulnerable to the disease but they also are considering the possibility of their parent(s) being lost. One of my boys has asked me several times over the past few days who his new parents will be if I die. Death is scary and we need to be able to share with our children and those who do not know Jesus Christ *why* there is no longer a reason to *fear* death.

Jesus conquered death and the reason for death on the cross. That's why "Good Friday" is a good day. Jesus was *really dead*, but *really* did rise from the dead. My mother is *really* gone—and one day I will be gone also. But my sons and I can be *absolutely certain* that a grand reunion will take place, and my mom, dad and I will be there to greet each of them. Death has not won the victory. There, at that blessed, eternal home, there will be nothing but smiles, laughter, joy and unrestrained love.

We have nothing to fear—death has been defeated….the days of the Corona Virus are limited as well. Our God reigns—let's tell our children.

The Truth Is

One of challenges with my adopted sons is how to react to the *constant lying* they became so accustomed to while in foster care. It's been said that you can tell when the North Korean government is lying—it's *anytime they print or say anything.* In some ways that makes it easier to work with them—you know from the starting point that they can't be trusted. But my boys *do* sometimes tell the truth. And while I don't want them to know it, I just can't tell when they are lying and then they are "truthing." But nothing, *absolutely nothing,* eats at the fiber of our home like dishonesty does.

God tells us in Proverbs that he *hates* these things: "A proud look, a lying tongue, hands that shed innocent blood, a heart that devises wicked plans, feet that are swift in running to evil, a false witness who speaks lies, and one who sows discord among brethren" (Proverbs 6:16-19, NIV). Please note that at least *two* of the things God hates are involved with deceit—a "lying tongue" and "a false witness who speaks lies." (Proverbs 6:16-19, NIV). God hates it, and that's enough for me to know that it's bad.

But having four young men in my home I have a greater appreciation for why dishonesty is so evil and *worthy* of being hated. It destroys our unity, steals our peace and wrecks the security of our home. We end up not trusting what the other says and begin to even question motives. Even the *kind* things that are said and *apologies offered* become suspect.

The second recorded sin of man was deceit—it's a part of our DNA. We try to wiggle out of accountability for our mistakes or bad choices by, well… lying! And yet I would tell you that my first-hand experience is that I am never *more* impressed with a man or woman than when they *admit* to something they did that should diminish their reputation rather than lie about it. I can work and associate with someone that's always honest—even if that honesty sometimes results in he/she telling me something I had hoped was *not* true.

How are we to share to the Good News of God and of Jesus the Redeemer if we don't have integrity? How can a person be convinced that what we are saying about our eternal home (heaven)—a home that could also be theirs—is true if we are known to lie, exaggerate, embellish or deceive?

May God hold us accountable for the *truth* in all matters at our little summer camp and may He give me the wisdom and grace to teach my boys to be honest and trustworthy.

Persecuted for Good Reason

"Blessed are those who are persecuted for the sake of righteousness, for theirs I the Kingdom of Heaven." (Matthew 5:10, NIV)

You might decide to follow Christ, become a pastor or priest for the good purpose of promoting peace, become a champion for righteousness, or live a life of gentleness and meekness—but you will find opposition. *That's the promise.*

John the Baptist called for righteousness and went to an early death; Amos spoke of justice and righteousness and ended up being cut in two; Stephen merely spoke the good news of God's love and was stoned to death!

This beatitude is for those who suffer persecution for the sake of doing and saying what is right, pure, true and just. They are the ones suffering for Christ's sake… and they will find anger, resentment, and hatred in their lives. Nevertheless, they should rejoice, for their reward in heaven will be great. God will bless them many times over what they have suffered.

Genuine righteousness is offensive to many, and so I must be prepared for opposition. But here is how I can most persuasively communicate the gospel and prove that I know Him and that Jesus Christ reigns in my heart: The *manner* in which I endure, accept, and prepare for persecution. My act of giving water to those that hate me, or sincerely praying for those who have taken advantage of me, or truly turning the cheek, or *not* seeking to justify myself, prove my good intentions, and defend my character and integrity.

That is where I am blessed! In *allowing* attacks, insults, slander, and persecution, however it may come, to illustrate my intimacy with Him. In doing this I behave as one who is already *in* the Kingdom of God. I am close to the very heart of Jesus when I accept persecution without responding in anger, self-defense or complaining.

Remembering the First Time I Loved

I think sometimes of the first time I realized His amazing love for me and how I first loved Him. It was a time of incredible peace and joy and a sense of unsurpassed certainty that He was in control… I had nothing and no one to fear. All things were possible! I *loved Him*—and therefore, quite naturally, I was drawn to "copy" His love towards others. I *saw* by His actions of love what *real love is,* as well as the cheap imitation or the lesser sentimental expressions of affection, fondness, preference or appreciation of others that I had mistaken for real love.

There were times associated with these deep revelations of His love when I told Him I would do anything for Him; truly I laid down my career and my hopes to earnestly and sincerely seek whatever it was for me that He wanted. And each time He gave me back what I already had with more than I had dreamed of—those times were overflowing moments of His sublime love.

There have been more than a few times that I have re-dedicated, afresh, my life to Him. We all tend to "drift," and as things become for a while routine and we establish ourselves in society and life, living is less "scary"; it's easy to begin to think that perhaps I can do things "my way", or that I need to be more like the people I come across who "appear" happy, successful and respected, but don't seem so tightly tied to God and His expectations.

So why must I re-dedicate my life to Him routinely? Why do I personally, and we as churches or a nation, have need of a "revival"? As I look through history, it's surprising to note that it's the times that God blessed a nation or a people or an individual, that nearly always also eventually brought spiritual demise and decay. But when a man like Saint Francis embraced poverty *his entire life,* or Paul was persecuted *his entire ministry,* or the early church in Rome hid in catacombs under constant danger of arrest, torture or death, that they were each able to maintain an intimacy and primary love for Him that never seemed to fade or waver.

And although I do *not* desire poverty or persecution or danger, a realization of how temporal, fragile and hostile life can be me reminds me that without His love I am nothing, and with His love I am more than able to *live, love and be at peace with myself and others.* I am *beloved*—therefore I am able to treat *others* as beloved.

To be a beggar, it appears, means that I am left with no one to trust but Him—-there's no competition for my heart! (Also, there's no overhead, payroll, maintenance, repairs, depreciation on the property, professionals to pay, etc.)

To be persecuted, it could be argued, might mean that my Christian associates are reduced and our ranks may thin, but those that are left standing with me are the men and women that share my primary love of Jesus Christ!

And to be in danger, would result in the conclusion that ultimately He is the only assurance and insurance I have against life is this hostile world—better to know that now than to be lulled into spiritual slumber by assuming "nothing can happen to me now."

It is the manner in which I have both experienced His love and responded to His love that defines who I am, in my witness for Christ and how I see myself. Do I remind myself of this when I am pressed, squeezed and caught up in modern life? These "bad" things are really essential.

The closer I come to Him, the more I am "revitalized" in Him, the more I hope for a simpler life—one with less, not more…one with more fellowship with fellow "lovers"…one with more who have experienced a reason for hopelessness and yet have never had a given up hope—those are the real heroes.

To Listen to What We Don't Want to Hear

"Then the Lord said to me, 'Go; I will send you far away to the Gentiles.' "The crowd listened to Paul until he said this. Then they raised their voices and shouted, "Rid the earth of him! He's not fit to live!" (Acts 21:21-22, NIV)

Eventually, if we live long enough and speak loud enough, the common man will be offended by us. That seems to be the lesson of the New Testament. I wonder, then, what is to be made of me if I never cause consternation or draw the ire of the common man. Could it be that my message has become to accommodating and "watered down"? Have I become like a "mega-church" pastor, far more interested in being the darling of the lukewarm Christian rather than a lion of Judah for those truly sold out for Jesus Christ?

Paul did not try to please the crowd. Yes, he used his knowledge and skill to win as many as he could, *yet* he spoke boldly and *stepped on toes.* To me, that's authentic preaching! Paul would not leave a crowd *comfortable* but rather either wanting to hear *more* or ready to kill him.

If my teaching, preaching and challenges make a person feel good about herself/himself, what's the point? When the good news of Jesus Christ is preached, it brings a person to the realization of the truth that has been denied or suppressed (sin in my life) and the acknowledgement that I am in great need of someone *outside my life to bring order, purpose, purity and hope.* Preaching should never leave a person thinking that all is good with nothing to worry about, but rather that *only God is good and without Him I have much to worry about!*

And yet even if I am within the fold and a genuine member of the body of Christ, I am still in need of being challenged, reprimanded, rebuked and corrected. *None of us has fully arrived yet* and it is the purpose of the church to call and send out pastors and priests to offer a clear vision of where we need to go as well as a sober assessment of where we are.

God, give us men and women of courage who are able to offend us in order to call us to higher ground! And may God give me the grace to receive those blows and thank Him for the ones He sends to produce them.

The Idolatry of Routine

I have a habit often "worshipping" my routine. I get up at a set time, have my coffee, Bible study, prayer walk, breakfast, at specific hours; and then there's my office routine, time to work out, time to read the paper. My daily agenda is divided into four-minute blocks for calls, emails, letters, etc. Or at least that's how my life used to be.

When I adopted three boys I had *no idea* how it would turn my "idol" of routine upside down. The boys recently came with me to the gym to work out, and as they do each time, they fought, quarreled, and caused me to have to depart from the workout early. That day I was fit to be tied because they *promised* they would behave but were worse than ever. And, so I entered into one of those "out of body" experiences where I saw my entire world starting to fall apart. I become anxious that, "what if" I can never work out again because of these boys? What if they keep waking up early (as they have been doing lately) and interfering with my set time for prayer? What if these confounded meetings with psychiatrists, therapists, and social workers (weekly!) continue to squeeze my time?

But then it hit me: Why not work out at 2:00 pm when the boys are still in school? Why not move my devotional time an hour earlier or wait until after they've gone to school? And why not plan my other errands in town for the same days I have meetings with the boys' professional therapists?

The point is, of course, that all I have to do to keep from having a nervous breakdown is remind myself that my schedule was made to be interrupted by more important things. Three of those "things" are my three sons—and they're more than worth the effort to rearrange my schedule.

All of this is probably entertaining to those of you who are accomplished parents, but it's all new to me—and I truly have relied upon my routine and discipline of handling my time carefully to get things accomplished! These boys are pushing me to become far *more* efficient with my time than I thought possible, and a *lot* more dependent upon Him for patience and clarity of purpose.

God knew what He was doing in allowing them to enter into my family.

The Fireflies

On Wednesday evenings I can be alone each week during the summer. The campers go camping with their cabin-mates, a pastor friend offers to provide vespers message after supper, and I retreat to my home to rest and refresh. I've been taking this midweek break for many years now and it helps me pace myself for the entire summer.

Nothing I relate in these little devotions is profound or particularly noteworthy, I suppose, but tonight as I drove the old jeep up to the site where the new "Eight Gables" (our new home) is being built, I felt a bit lonely and despondent for no apparent reason. Within seconds I received a phone call from a close friend; he was just checking up on me and offered the precise amount of encouragement required to get me out of my melancholy spirit. I thanked God for that call and for that friend *listening* to the Holy Spirit when He whispered to him to call me.

On the way down the hill the sun had just set, but I could still see the grass on the sides of the road…light green and lush from all the rain… and then out of nowhere the fireflies began to gently shine their soft lights… hovering all over the grass and mountainside. How can a person behold such an *unexplainable* pleasure one gets from seeing something as inspiring as the silhouette of the Blue Ridge Mountains in the background and the green grass and hundreds of floating fireflies in the foreground? The God that made these creatures and imagined these settings did it for a purpose. They speak of His peace, His glory, His unspeakable beauty—and His presence when people like me feel alone.

I had to venture out of my home tonight night to see those fireflies and I must remember that it was not simply a friend, but God Himself on the end of that phone call tonight. He is sovereign. These good things happen for a good purpose. I was encouraged… I sat in awe of the kind of beauty that one cannot create or orchestrate, but simply see and experience.

God reveals Himself to me every day; but sometimes I need to be alone to hear Him and see Him.

Our Raison D'être

On a recent trip to France I had to catch a train from Lille to Paris, then navigate the Paris subways and take smaller trains to get to Versailles. From there I had to present the camp to more than a dozen *very* polite French parents, then rush back to the train station in Paris to get back to Lille, very late. All the while answering phone calls from the USA and France, responding to texts and emails from parents, campers, supporters and so forth.

I am *glad* to be busy and honored for the work I am able to do for His Kingdom, but for 40+ years I have felt, quite frequently, that I was "living on the brink." I have also always had this feeling of transience in the work I do at the camp. And it is not that the *work* that I do does not have lasting—eternal—value. But for four decades I have wondered, "Is this my last year doing this?" Again, I am not saying I don't like what I do, nor am I looking for "greener pastures," but there's *always* "something" that challenges my ministry's very *existence!* 9/11, the banking crisis, the great recession, the fire that took my home, the most recent Presidential election—these are all things that have *absolutely* had a negative financial impact on the camp and our ability to continue.

Every time, however, miraculous and wonderful things happened. *Every single time.* But it is because I cannot *immediately* see the answer or solution or means of rescue that I sink and fall into despair and often depression. Sometimes it's the assumption that He is waiting for me to *do* something… but what? That's my fear, I suppose… that I have somehow failed to do everything I could have done to protect the camp and its future for the campers and staff.

It is human to want to give up. I do not, but the temptation is ever lurking. I am *not* tempted to give up *on* Him or His work; I *am* ready to fight for the Redeemer of my soul and to humble myself before Him. But the temptation is to give up the passion, the heart, the drive, the dream… And that, I am guessing, is precisely the plan of the enemy. To lure me into such self-pity and a perpetual state of whining that I fail, by my *own example,* to *further* the cause of Christ.

I was never called by God to create an institution to myself or to establish an eternal camp. I was called to follow Him with such passion and single-minded devotion that others might also want to experience the joy and peace I have. The camp is a *tool* to bringing other souls to Christ…this little camp's continuation is *not* the goal…sharing Jesus Christ, and Him crucified, resurrected and seated art the right hand of God the Father is.

Sex—In the Christian Sense

In the fourth chapter of I Thessalonians Paul wrote these words: "As for other matters, brothers and sisters, we instructed you how to live in order to please God, as in fact you are living. Now we ask you and urge you in the Lord Jesus to do this more and more. For you know what instructions we gave you by the authority of the Lord Jesus. It is God's will: that you should be sanctified: that you should avoid sexual immorality; that each of you should learn to control your own body in a way that is holy and honorable, not in passionate lust like the pagans, who do not know God; and that in this matter no one should wrong or take advantage of a brother or sister. The Lord will punish all those who commit such sins, as we told you and warned you before. For God did not call us to be impure, but to live a holy life. Therefore, anyone who rejects this instruction does not reject a human being but God, the very God who gives you his Holy Spirit." (I Thessalonians 4:6-10, NIV)

In the Christian community a woman (and a child or man) is to be *respected*. They are not to be viewed as objects of lust or abuse. And in sexual matters we are called to be chaste and seek *the one* that we are prepared to spend the rest of our natural lives with. So why are we so afraid to touch the subject of appropriate sexual behavior and monogamy today? Have you *ever* heard a sermon about these things? If Paul were speaking today, at *our church or our camp*, would people take him seriously? Would the elders, deacons and leaders of your church *accept* such a sermon?

Bill Cosby, Morgan Freeman, Matt Lauer, Harvey Weinstein, *to name a few,* illustrate the problem of men doing just as they want, sexually speaking, without regard to God's plan. I cannot attest to any of these men's faith, nor am I suggesting that I have a right to judge them, but a man or woman of God (i.e. a Christian) is supposed to be far better than this, with their eyes wide open and set upon the hearts and souls of the other, not just the physical allure of the other's body.

The argument *seems* to be: "It's my body and it's none of *your* business"; but if it is God's will that we be sanctified, that is, made holy, how can we ignore this topic in our churches and Christian ministries? It's not *my body anymore* when I come to Jesus Christ—I become a vessel that carries within me the Holy Spirit.

Others might say that these words of Paul and Peter were written only for the first century listeners—not for us. But throughout the Bible, God's children are told to avoid sexual sin, and sexual sin, as I understand it, is using God's gift of sex in *any way outside of marriage*. These aren't my words or ideas, but I would challenge anyone to find scripture that suggests the opposite. Sex was God's creation and marriage was His idea. He *does* hold the upper hand in these discussions. Consistently, predatory and abusive sexual relationships are condemned— *everywhere in scripture.*

Another complaint has been that you can't attract folks into church if you start telling them what they can and can't do. And that might be true and it's also true that we're not told to "save" people from pornography or inappropriate sexual behavior; we're told to simply bring them to Jesus Christ. *But,* when they come to Christ and are taught how to allow the Holy Spirit to begin that process of "sanctification," it does involve giving up those things that are impure—and you can't, we can't, shy away from teaching this.

The weakest of all arguments is, "Well that's (i.e. chastity or faithfulness to a life-time partner) just your opinion and interpretation of scripture." But could anyone honestly examine scripture and find any support for the way sexual activity is commonly portrayed in our media today? We're told to live lives *pleasing to God*. That's the litmus test. Is it pleasing to God? Are you prepared to argue your point of view with God Almighty? Do I really think that God's expectations for how I care for my body, and respect the bodies of others, has evolved and that somehow He will eventually come to better understand mankind and sexuality?

Peacemaking

"Blessed are the peacemakers, for they will be called the sons of God." (Matthew 5:9, NIV)

We, i.e. mankind, have been at war with God since man first walked on the earth. We've rebelled against God's intentions and directions and have told God that we don't care about His opinion and expectations; yes, we've basically taken up hostilities against *God*. How foolhardy—it's a war we can never, ever win. And the only way there can be *peace* is for one of the warring parties to surrender. That's what is required for me to have peace with God, and that's what I must teach and proclaim to any camper, staff or volunteer that wants peace: You must surrender to God.

Fortunately, our God is not vengeful nor does He choose to humiliate us in our surrender. Quite the opposite—He not only establishes peace in our hearts and souls, but He declares us, the very ones who were formerly His enemy, as His sons and daughters—His own children.

How can there be peace *on earth*? Only when all of us at war with Him seek His Beloved Son by laying down our arms and declaring that He is Lord. And what does He give us? Infinitely more than we could ever hope to gain from a war against Him!

The kingdom of darkness and hell quakes and shakes each time a boy, girl, man or woman sues for surrender and accepts God's terms for peace, which is simply a confession of our rebellion and an acknowledgement that all reparations have been paid by God's own Son on the cross of Calvary.

What an incredible ending to a fruitless war! We surrender to God, God pays the price for the war, and He makes us into joint heirs, sons and daughters, to the Kingdom of God.

As I wrote this devotion, there were *forty wars* being fought all over the earth. Oh, that the men that win the wars and accept the surrender of their enemies were as compassionate as our God.

Surrendering in a Valley

Recently I experienced "delayed jet-lag" from a trip to Africa, as well as the consequences of breathing stale airplane air for 60 hours. I lost my voice, became congested, was fatigued and in general felt rather "puny." I am not a good patient when I don't feel well. What serves me best is sleep, not sympathy. I went to bed early and immediately fell into deep, deep dreams. But this dream seemed to keep on repeating itself.

I realize that some dreams are our subconscious replaying events of the past, while other dreams might have more to do with bad tuna fish for supper. But sometimes dreams are epiphanies or visions from God. There are times I do *not* want to wake up and at other times I wonder if the dream is reality, and waking puts me back into "make-believe."

This dream was *pure and holy*—it did not come from my "suppressed desires" or some sort of imagined fantasy. The dream gave me instant peace and I know that it was Him talking to me. God speaks through visions, dreams, events, His word, His church and His prophets. That dream, or rather the *series of dreams,* caused me to look forward to the following night's sleep.

In the dream I was walking through a valley of some sort. Everything in the valley was purple, dark blue, black and gray; it was not a pretty valley. The vegetation was about a foot tall and as I said, dark colored. Each plant represented a fear or object of anxiety that was keeping me from being at peace. I remembered how sad I was to see all those vexing concerns, the very things that haunt me during the day, strewn all over that expansive valley.

Then, without anyone telling me to do so, I began to call out, "I surrender" to the "problem plant" and it immediately fell to the ground and wilted. It was dead. For the entire dream, which seemed to go on for hours, I walked about that valley surrendering those torturous plants to God; I knew that it was God I was surrendering them to. I knew that I was giving Him full control over those "things" that were controlling me, and each and every time, without the slightest interlude, the plant withered and ceased to live. As I walked I saw every trial, every cause for fear, every matter that caused me to be anxious, wither and die as I surrendered the plant to God.

"Let not your heart be troubled: you believe in God, believe also in Me." (John 14:1, KJV) Those are the words of Jesus. They took on new meaning to me. As challenges, fears, or personal "terrors" try to grip my heart, I remember to surrender it to Him and I am at peace.

Our Father

"This, then, is how you should pray: "'Our Father in heaven, hallowed be your name". (Matthew 6:9, KJV)

This is how Jesus began his example when his disciples said to him, "Teach us how to pray." (Luke 11:1, NIV)

a. He is *our Father*—not just *my* father. Don't think for a second that God does not love people in other lands or of other religions or ethnicity. Jesus' prayer begins by reminding us that there is only One God and One heavenly father—*our Father*. It is sad to say that many don't know Him as their Father and many who claim to know Him disavow any family ties to Him by the manner in which they live. But when we pray we are all lifting our voices to the one, same and only God.

b. He is holy. His very name is holy and all that He does is holy and altogether perfect. His timing, His answers to prayers, His solutions to the problems that seem *beyond salvation,* are *perfect, holy and pure.*

When I begin my prayer to God it is good to keep two things in mind: I can talk to Him because He is my *Father.* Praise God! I don't have to be timid or afraid or to worry that He is too busy to talk to me or hear my whining or complaining. He *knows me* and loves me anyway! He takes delight in the time I give throughout the day to talk to Him. I am not an irritation or interruption to Him; I am the apple of His eye. He is my Father.

But I must ever recall in prayer that He is altogether holy and totally without sin, and that *He intends to make me holy and without sin* as I grow closer and closer to Him. Praise be to God—He is not going to indulge me and spoil me; He will not look the other way when I mess up. He will remind me that He expects more and better of me. Our Father is *not* our heavenly "Grandfather", but our heavenly Father. He believes in us—but expects us to be proper sons and daughters.

The Hurricanes of Life

A few years ago there was quite a scare in the southeastern part of the nation because of an *enormous* hurricane that was projected to hit the Florida coast. The entire state was warned about the possibility of catastrophic winds and rainfall. It was called the largest hurricane *ever* recorded. And this was happening just a few days after *another* hurricane hit Texas and dropped more water than has *ever* been dropped on the continental USA at one time.

Does this mean the "end" is coming? Well, the end *is* coming, and we're closer today than we were yesterday; but these natural disasters remind me of how frail, unprotected and un-guaranteed life really is—*not* that the eschaton might be upon us. I might be healthy and in total control of my life right now, but in a *split second* I could find myself fighting for my life or watching it slip away. I am promised nothing from this world or "mother nature" except the certainty that all forces outside me are working to destroy my physical existence.

Although my walk with Him is far from exemplary or without slips and missteps, I cannot imagine walking out the door of my home (or any door) without having absolute confidence that my Redeemer lives and has called me His own. That does not mean, of course, that the redeemed will not suffer in storms, floods and hurricanes, but it *does mean* that we can confidently rely upon Him not to allow any harm or misfortune to call upon us without His permission or plan. Either way, I can be assured that He does *not* waste suffering on His children—there's always, *always,* a reason that He permits setbacks and pain.

No sane man sets out to encounter trauma or pain, but no follower of Jesus Christ can avoid it either. There is a certain winnowing I am seeing in my life lately. Whether He is preparing me for something special or is merely removing the chaff that should have been separated years ago does not matter. What does matter is that He is having His way—and I know that He loves me throughout this process.

Praying and Doing

Think about the verses in the Bible that reflect on the power of prayer:

1. "If my people, who are called by my name, will humble themselves and pray and seek my face and turn from their wicked ways, then I will hear from heaven, and I will forgive their sin and will heal their land." (II Chronicles 7:14, NIV) (If we humbly pray *and* turn away from disobedience.)
2. "Therefore I tell you, whatever you ask for in prayer, believe that you have received it, and it will be yours." (Mark 11:24, NIV)
3. "*Devote* yourselves to prayer, being watchful and thankful." (Colossians 4:2, NIV)

I have been praying more in the past few years than I have at any other time in my life. The challenges, trials, and struggles that God has permitted have caused me to pray immediately when I rise; I am also praying throughout the day; I pray as I fall asleep and I pray when I awake in the middle of the night. Although I am still not praying enough, a prayer always seems to be on my lips. In all those hours of prayer I have come to understand many things about myself (some not so good), but far more about *who* God is and how He answers prayers.

In the first place, I have discovered that the more I am praying and *looking to God*, the less I have any need to look at myself. What a relief! Or as Tozer once said, what a "blessed riddance!" The more I pray to Him, the less I think of me—and the world and I are better because of it.

Secondly, I found that prayer is connected to my *faith*. The more I earnestly seek Him in prayer, the more of a man of faith and resolve I become. And as I consider men and women of strong faith in the history of the church, they have *all* been men and women of intense prayer. *Always*.

Thirdly, I learned that the more I pray, the more I realize that prayer is not merely preparation for work, or laying the foundation for the work that needs to be done, but prayer is the one *essential thing that I must do in my work*. Prayer has become the ends to the means.

But finally, and most lately, I am coming to a better comprehension of praying *and* living the Christian life. Prayer is absolutely essential before, during, and after anything I do that is worthwhile or essential—at the camp, in my home, or at church. But prayer alone, when there is repentance, or sweat equity, or getting my hands dirty with the work to be done, is not enough! I can pray all day about God blessing my camp with enrollment, but if I am not following that up with marketing, planning, responding to inquiries, my prayers will not suffice. I had *better be on the phone, sending out emails and visiting homes*.

God has blessed me beyond my expectations at The Vineyard—but not because I simply prayed and left the work to someone else. God has responded to my prayers *as I have gone out and addressed the work that had to be done*.

Paul did not merely pray about the lost Gentiles—he *went to them;* Jonah did not only pray for the salvation of the Ninevites, he also travelled there and preached repentance; Jesus did not only pray that God would forgive those that did not know what they were doing—He died for them.

I can work as hard and long as I want and never accomplish the tasks He has placed before me; and I can pray all day and fast all night for some noble venture for God and be equally ineffective. It requires both to be of use to God.

On Receiving

Tonight I took my three boys "trick or treating." It was the first time I have ever taken kids to collect candy, and I must say that I was amazed at how many children and families walked the streets of Pilot Mountain collecting candy, greeting each other and taking candy from total strangers! It was something I have not seen in many years and I was touched.

What caught my attention immediately was how *appreciative* the older folks were to invite the children and youth into their homes to receive the candy. Porch lights were on, jack-o-lanterns were lit, and there was a festive spirit of goodwill and generosity. I have not seen such kindness in my little community, even at Christmas!

But on the way home from Pilot Mountain I was moved almost to tears as we passed by the country homes in the rural part of our county. Our camp is twenty minutes from town, and the homes between town and the camp are spread out pretty thin. But to my surprise many of the small homes had their porch lights on—just as in the little village of Pilot Mountain. I passed by several homes on the drive home thinking that I had never knocked on any of those doors in my 30+ years here and was not about to do it tonight! But something within me urged me to stop at a very small home that had a porch light on so that the boys could ask for treats. So we stopped, the boys ran to the house, and I could see a slight, older lady hurry to the door with candy for the boys. She talked to them, *invited them inside*, gave them double portions, and then we continued our drive. But I felt inclined to stop again…and then again… and for the rest of the drive home we stopped at *every* lonely home that had a porch light on.

Every home we stopped at (save one) had *only* an older lady at the door. Those little ladies were *delighted* to see the boys race up to the front porch. One said that we were the only ones to come by for trick or treat this year, and another told us that we were the *first* to come *in five years*.

Yes, the boys have huge sacks of sugar-laden candy, but in a very tangible way, my boys gave twenty-plus widows and a very old couple something those folks desperately needed—the ability to give. These old women know the blessedness that comes from giving and they have been denied that joy, it appears, for months and even years.

We were made in the image of God, and our destiny is to be *conformed* to the image/mind of Jesus Christ. *God is a giver, Jesus is a giver, the Holy Spirit is a giver and all who have grown in His image delight in giving.*

Paul said in the book of Acts: "…ye ought to support the weak and to remember the words of the Lord Jesus, how he said, *It is more blessed to give than to receive.*" (Acts 20:35, NIV)

Tonight my three boys experienced the excitement of *receiving*—and praise God, they did receive! By receiving from these sweet people, the boys gave those widows joy, purpose and the fulfillment of knowing that they had done a selfless and blessed thing—they had given with no expectation or means of "getting back."

I need to be a *gracious receiver* for those that want to give and to teach the youth and children that it is truly more blessed to give than receive. But being a courteous and excited *receiver* made a lot of little ladies quite happy tonight.

The Biggest Hypocrite in Our Home

At the end of the day I sometimes take an inventory of where I "won" and where I "lost" in terms of my witness for Christ. By that, I mean to say: "Would others have been *drawn* into wanting to know more about Jesus Christ based upon how I handled myself?"

It's obvious that an *atheist* can be kind, gentle, and compassionate if all things go perfectly for him each day. For me, there's no real challenge in shining for Jesus if there's nothing but sunshine all about me. But how I radiate His love and humility when things are "overcast" or dark can make quite an impression on those looking for the *confirmation* about God and His love.

Oh, how I have failed to be that radiant light in my own home lately. I realize why Paul said that a deacon or elder should be able to "manage his own family well" (I Timothy 3:4, NIV) before being considered for the office. Oddly enough, I *am* a deacon in my own church, but I was invited to be a deacon (and approved) before my adopted boys came into my home.

One of the greatest blessings of living with others is that the conflicts and "grinding" of sharing your home with others sheds light on where each of us needs to grow and face our own inadequacies. These boys in my home have shown me just how selfish I am about my private time, my "space," my routine, my schedule, etc. Just this morning I lost my temper with the two youngest boys because they interrupted my Bible study and quiet time. After I raised my voice and told them to put an end to their silly games, loud laughter and running about the house, I had a small epiphany: Here I am, yelling at my boys and demanding that they shut their mouths and be still… so that I can pray to God and become more holy! What a hypocrite I am. God sent those boys into my life for a good purpose—primarily, it appears, to push me to the daily recognition of *my* need to abide in Jesus Christ *that I might bear the spiritual fruit of patience.* It has taken these young boys to open my eyes: I need annoyances and interruptions *in order to bear spiritual fruit and bring others into fellowship with him.*

It is God's love, bursting into my life through the very things that annoy me (when it would seem most appropriate to *blow up and lose my temper*), that will bring these boys to experience a relationship with Jesus Christ; not my frustration, temper, anger, or disappointment. Nothing, *nothing,* happens in my life without His hand causing it or His permission to allow it. If I can *remember* this, I stand a better chance of shining for Him and allowing myself to laugh a bit more at how ridiculous I must look when I throw a temper tantrum for not being allowed to read my Bible.

The Biggest Decision to Make

In the Book of Acts I read the following narrative about Paul when he preached to the Athenians:

"When they heard about the resurrection of the dead, some of them sneered, but others said, "We want to hear you again on this subject." At that, Paul left the Council. Some of the people became followers of Paul and believed." (Acts 17:32-34,NIV)

And that is the history of mankind when it comes to responding to Jesus. *Either Jesus did arise from the dead or He did not—there's no middle ground.* If He did, everything He said about Himself and all the prophecies about Him are valid, fulfilled and He is Lord. If He did not, nothing we say about Christianity really matters and we that preach about Him have misled people and misrepresented God!

All of this first came to my mind when I graduated from Seminary. I was brought up to *believe* all that the Bible said was true and to take all that the preacher spoke from the pulpit as valid. But when I turned twenty-six I went through a crisis of faith and began to wonder if I *really* believed *any of it.* How could I be sure that Jesus even existed? Who is alive *today* that can testify to His miracles, crucifixion, resurrection, ascension and so forth? What if all I have been taught is no more than a fairy tale or "myth"?

What brought light and drove away the clouds of doubt was my "discovery" of the truth. And here's what I came to believe: That Jesus of Nazareth really did live, teach, and walk the earth. He also talked about His death and subsequent resurrection, and He did die a cruel death on a cross. Most importantly, I also came to see, without a doubt and unequivocally, that *Jesus rose from the grave. No man has ever claimed to be God and to have power over death and then proved it.* That is what changed my ministry and life. I was so sure of it that I determined that there was *nothing more important in my life than the reality of the resurrection of Jesus Christ.*

I could explain the way I came to know this and talk about the Christian apologists that helped me come to this conclusion, but that's not the point if this devotion. My point is that *until you believe in the resurrection you will always be secretly sneering at the suggestion that Jesus rose from the grave. You will never be sure that you will also be raised to reign with him forever!*

Who do you really believe? If not, what *do you* believe in that you've not witnessed first hand?

If you do not believe, but could somehow be *brought* to believe, how would that change your life?

Blessed to Have Her as My Mother

Those that attended our camp prior to 2010 surely remember my mother, Nan. She made thousands upon thousands of her special chocolate chip cookies, helped in our kitchen, and headed up transportation for a few summers. She played in the camper/staff tennis tournaments and even won one year! Her mirth, laughter, faith, support of our ministry, dedication to her children and love of God were inspiring. I don't know of anyone that knew her that did not love her.

For the past ten years Nan battled Alzheimer's disease and has not been able to return to the camp or enjoy a conversation with her children, grandchildren or friends. But today heaven is a happier place today and Nan is once again able to be with those she loved; she passed away a few days ago, surrounded by three of her daughters as they sang, prayed, loved and wept for her.

I can only hope to become *half* the self-sacrificing parent my mom was for me. As I shared with my sons that she had passed, I realized that they had no recollection of their mothers or fond memories of them. They were unable to identify with my loss. All three were given to the state by their mothers when they were quite young, and none of them knows where their mom is or what she is doing.

What a pity they did not have a mother like mine—one that taught me how to play tennis, hold my tongue, act like a gentleman and even control my temper. She showed me how to behave in friend's home, how to do what I did not *want* to do, but *needed* to do, and how to worship. I am not saying that I have always followed her directives, but she did *teach* me and *show* me how to live. Sometimes I got it right.

To this day I can still recall how it *grieved me* to disappoint her! She expected great things from all of us and demanded that we lived up to our God-given abilities and the privileges to which we were born. To my knowledge she never asked for help but always was ready to give it. She was not one to gossip, but could quickly put the lid on it if her kids attempted to throw mud at others. Never one to try to impress others and quite confident in who she was, she associated with others in our church and with neighbors who shared her understanding of humility; yet she combined this with a clear understanding that we are *all* marvelously made by a God who says we are precious and unique. She believed that we all have a purpose and value in God's eyes.

To a large extent, I entered the Christian ministry because of *her* ministry to me. Within a few years of graduating from college, in fact, all three of her sons became ministers of the gospel. Her legacy lives on. God blessed my siblings and me with a wonderful mother.

The Battlefield

Sometimes when I am trying to understand why a seven-year-old, nine-year-old, ten- year-old and eighteen-year-old *do what they do*, I try to think back to when I was their same age. And as I do, I find myself tempering my frustrations and aggravations towards them. It is good to reflect back on what was going on in *my* little brain a few decades ago.

Recently, for example, school was *cancelled* because of the cold. *Cancelled!* That meant that *all* four boys were at the house or my office *all day long.* For most of the day all I could think of was how "cancelled school" would affect *my* day; but later I tried to think about how I would feel if *I* was seven or nine years old and school was cancelled. How can I *possibly* ask the boys to "calm down" when there's no school? How could I expect them to *not* be excited and ready for fun! If I was one of them I would be bouncing off the walls with excitement! And yet, for an inexplicable reason I asked them to act like nothing had happened and behave as if it were just a normal day.

So the boys came with me to work today excited, looking for adventure and ready to experience the fun of being a Camp Director. I kept reminding them that I had to get my work done, answer my emails, return my phone calls, keep on schedule and so forth. The two youngest boys really did *try* to maintain their composure, but the fascination of all the books in my office, all those desk drawers, the papers, the doo-dads in boxes all over the office was too much for them, and I had to give in and let them explore. It's funny how a small child can find such pleasure in a colored piece of broken glass, or an old photo album, or some dated credit cards. But these boys had more fun plundering through my junk than they could have had watching movies all day long—and they learned a bit about their new father by looking at my worthless stuff.

I don't claim to be a perfect man—far from it. But fortunately, there *is nothing in my office or my home* that I would be ashamed for them to find—because they would surely find it. A friend once remarked to me that if a movie was inappropriate for a child, why should it be appropriate for an adult? I have never forgot that and have excluded DVDs from my home—along with *anything else*—that a child should not see. The point is that I can rest, knowing that there is nothing "questionable" to find in my home or office—unless it's found on the Internet.

Again, I don't mean to be bragging or presume to be a hero, but why should I allow anything in my life that might cause others to pause as they considered a life devoted to God? But it's one thing to *easily* remove or destroy those physical things that could cause a child to stumble or think twice about my faith in God and my devotion to His Son, but quite another as I considered the *real* battlefield—the place where no one sees, i.e. what goes on in my mind. And that is the real place of the fight for any man (or woman) of God. It's what I *meditate upon* and *imagine* that I must surrender to Him each day—not so much what I purchase or put on my walls. *Only* by His grace and power am I able to maintain that fight! My struggle is not against "flesh and blood" but truly against the spiritual darkness that wants to consume my thoughts.

The answer for me is to keep my mind and thoughts on, "whatever is true, whatever is honorable, whatever is right, whatever is pure, whatever is lovely, whatever is of good repute, if there is any excellence and if anything worthy of praise, dwell on these things." (Philippians 4:8, NIV) Otherwise I am consumed by things that have no place in a boy's mind—and certainly not mine either.

The Dream

I know that some folks give dreams a lot of spiritual attention, while others suggest it's all about "repressed" emotions, and some prefer to ignore them altogether. But count me as one of those who does believe that dreams are means whereby God speaks to us—at least on some occasions. Last night, *I think*, was one of those times. And as background, I should explain that I remember my dreams each day. Since I was a young child I have woke up remembering my dreams, often quite vividly.

But the dream last night was out of the ordinary, and it as far too bizarre for me to make up. I dreamt that I had traveled a long distance to visit a friend and his family. I stayed at this "best friend's home" and was preparing to share the camp video to a large group at the church he attended or pastored—I can't recall that detail. I recall that his house was a single level home in a nice neighborhood in a suburb. Sunday morning I rose earlier than my host and headed into town looking for a Starbucks. At 7:15 am I called him to tell him that I would there soon to drive with him to church for the camp presentation.

But he told me, "Your suitcase had been packed and is beside the road, the church meeting was cancelled and you should come and get your suitcase as soon as possible." I asked him, "What happened?" After all, I had traveled very far for the meeting and had done nothing wrong, but he responded, "I have just discovered that you were using me and my church to promote your camp. I am very offended." And I thought, "Well, that is in fact quite true—but so what?"

I got so angry that I woke up and *could not go back to sleep.* And then I prayed for discernment. *What did the dream mean? Why did I dream this?* I have been praying to God and asking Him this question all day. *Speak, Lord Jesus!*

One of the greatest personal sorrows I have experienced in ministry is rejection from friends, members of my own family and even camp alumni who disagree with what I am *attempting* to accomplish for His Kingdom. And whereas I truly do try to please everyone, it's just not possible. I might have a noble goal of living at peace with everyone, but as soon as work for the Kingdom of God is involved, the attacks *will come*—and normally not from non-believers, but from those within the Kingdom. The Christian community has been guilty from the very beginning of the establishment of the church of rivalry, improperly judging the motives of brothers and sisters within that "family", and worst of all, "shooting the wounded."

Praise be to God that He judges—*perfectly*—our hearts, and not our clumsy actions and efforts. Thanks be to God that smiles upon my desire to do the right thing, even if I appear to be an utter moron. O God, please help those that don't know you to become good children, and help your good children how to be kind and nice to each other.

On Telling the Story

Paul, Peter, John and the early church leaders *never* talked about or celebrated their personal challenges, families, experiences; they never reminisced about how they overcame some emotional trauma or made any mention of hobbies, pet peeves, etc. They talked about Jesus—all the time. In fact, Paul clearly remarked that this was all he was interested in knowing and sharing. It's the theme of the entire NT. The apostles rarely mentioned the merits or strengths of the *other* apostles or the importance of the faithful—again, it was nearly always about Jesus and the power of His resurrection.

Many of us spend far too much time talking about ourselves and precious little time talking about *Him*—at least that's my take on it. We talk about the Christian life, about Christian saints and heroes, and we go on and on about Christian causes (*good* causes) and about church buildings, fund raising, youth retreats, and, yes, Christian summer camp for kids—like mine. But do we talk, with the single-minded devotion, as *all the authors of the New Testament did*, about *Jesus?*

The ones that knew Him intimately and wrote about Him passionately and testified fearlessly were *not* interested in having folks walk away saying, "Wow, he's a great speaker", or "Didn't her dedication inspire you." The folks came to the apostles "seeking" something that was missing in their lives and they departed having "found" the fullness of Jesus Christ—and Paul, Peter, John and the others *could have cared less if they were remembered or not.*

To be blunt, sometimes the things I read or hear from Christian speakers, authors and musicians make me wonder if they really know *Him.* It seems that a lot of what is written addresses our curiosity about Biblical geography, history, language and alternate meanings of scripture, et al, but do *we* speak out of a genuine love relationship with Him? *Is what we are doing* communicating the gospel and does it cause others to seek Him…or us?

The atheists, agnostics and other non-believers typically base their lack of belief on things they have read about God that they disagree with, or some examples in history where Christians did not act very Christ-like. But the *power of the good news of Jesus Christ can cause ears to hear and eyes to see*, e.g. Saul's conversion, 3000 souls being saved after hearing Peter present the gospel right after Pentecost.

Paul argued passionately and persuasively till the day he died—and many came to Christ. But it's also true that many *refused* to turn to Jesus and perished. I do not have an answer as to why some respond and some don't, but our focus must be to preach Jesus Christ, to faithfully tell the story, and not get discouraged over those that reject God's Son. He'll handle the rest.

Stained Glass Examples

In his first letter, Peter states that he is well aware of how those that followed Jesus *suffered*. (See I Peter, 2:21, NIV). It's funny how we have all seen these priceless stained glass images of Peter and the disciples but sometimes forget that they were men and women just like you and me. And yet unlike you and me, they walked and talked in the flesh *with* Jesus and lived lives that reflected that association; they lived like people who were witnesses to the resurrected Son of God—because, of course, they *were*.

So Peter says in the fourth chapter, "Don't be ashamed if you are suffering" (See I Peter 4:16, NIV) (be ashamed if you never suffer). These folks were Spirit-filled, were walking totally in line with what God wanted and yet they were *still* suffering. I am *certain* that some folks within the church were thinking, "This is happening because of some un-confessed sin," or "Somebody here has ignored God's voice." But Peter reminds them that suffering is not a sign of God's displeasure but rather something He allows to happen to bring glory to Himself and His Son. (I Peter 4:19, NIV)

And so Peter proclaims: Praise God in the suffering! (See I Peter 4:13, NIV) Yes, give Him thanks when there's apparently no reason or explanation for why you're going through a tough time or event—*He knows what's happening to you* and He is receiving glory in the manner in which you turn to Him and cry out, "Abba, Father! Have mercy on me!" There is *an indescribable joy and sense of peace released when we praise Him as we suffer through things that seem to have no end in sight and no meaningful purpose!* When we rejoice and praise Him, we're telling the world, "It's all going to work out and be okay, and even if it does not, my suffering is going to bring glory to God and is going to be used to bless His children to repentance and salvation! Let the suffering go on!"

Peter goes on and says, "When suffering comes, commit yourself to God and continue to do good." (See I Peter 4:19, NIV) That is, do not wallow in self-pity or give up because you are hurting, or appear to be losing the fight or see no way to come out ahead….*commit it all to God and keep on doing what you set out to do for Him! This* is what defined the true men and women of God and this is why we see them portrayed in stained glass windows: these folks never gave up and never gave in to self-pity.

Idle Talk

I commonly get asked what "gossip" really is and what to do about it. It seems that gossip is a problem not only in Hollywood, but in churches, camps, gyms, among friends, etc. We all know what gossip is when the remarks are about *us*, and we don't like it, but what do we do about it?

I confess that I say things about others that I don't need to say, but the remarks just seem to blurt out before I *think* about what I am saying! I can tell it's gossip because of the sick feeling I get in my stomach after I have said it. By then, of course, it's too late and the damage is done—and *my* reputation has also suffered.

Whereas I don't have the last word on what it is, I can tell you what I have learned about "idle talk": I should always ask myself, (1) is it *true,* (2) is it *helpful,* (3) is it *necessary,* and (4) if *I were the subject* of the conversation, what would I *want* others to be saying. If I would always take those four considerations into mind, I would refrain from gossiping. It's a certainty that Christ did not gossip and that it does no good *at all* in building up the body of Christ.

Reprimands, rebukes and a tough word might need to be said from time to time, but it should be said to the directly to the offender, and *to him/her alone or not at all.* It's the talk behind my back or me speaking behind another friend's back that destroys unity and focus in Christian endeavors.

One interesting point to end with: Have you ever noticed that the very people who gossip the most are the very ones that are also gossiped *about the* most? What goes around seems to come around.

A Friend Was Lost Today

This morning I got up early to organize my day, shuttle the boys to their schools, prepare for our staff meetings, and so on. I had a full day planned by 9:00 a.m., had just finished our staff meeting, and got a text from a friend asking me if I lost our long haired dachshund, "Biscuit." Then it hit me that I had taken Biscuit to school with the boys and I left my car door open when I walked the youngest boy to school (he was having one of his "I hate school" tantrums). Biscuit must have jumped out and the leaders at the school were calling around trying to find out who the irresponsible owner was.

I called the school and rushed pell-mell to get there hoping that he was still safe and sound. But he was gone. The receptionist had seen him just ten minutes earlier, but despite all my calls, whistles and prayers, Biscuit was gone. For an hour I drove around looking for him, and totally forgot about all of my agenda items and the "essential" matters of the day.

When I returned home I was dejected, defeated, and had no stomach or willpower to do much of anything. If you don't have a pet, particularly a *dachshund*, you probably don't understand. But that twelve-year-old dog was a member of our family, and his personality, playfulness, and gentleness with the boys was endearing. He was gone and I knew that I would not be able to find him. He had no collar or tags on him and it was four miles from my home to the school. The road, Route 66, is curvy and treacherous for a man in truck much less a ten-pound canine trying to get home.

I immediately asked folks to pray for me and that little dog. It seemed childish, but it was breaking my heart to think that I would not see that little dog again, and I was dreading the boys' response when they found out. When you're grieving over something like this it's nearly impossible to think about anything else, and any business you attempt to transact is less fulfilling and purposeful. The sadness was overwhelming, which I understood intellectually, but could do nothing to prevent.

So, I prayed and prayed for my little dog's return and then realized how impossible it must be for the parent of a kidnapped or missing child. How angry and disillusioned a parent must become towards God and all of humanity when their pleas and searching leads to nothing. I felt all of this as I waited and prayed. Finally, I lifted my hands to heaven and said, "Okay, Lord, I give this up to you and I surrender Biscuit to you. Please let him be found if possible, but I abdicate my will to yours."

I lowered my hands, turned around and there was Biscuit! He had run four miles back from the school and had returned home, pushed the door open, and sauntered in as if he had just returned from a stroll in the park. At that moment, nothing mattered but the celebration of his return! All the work and challenges of the day lay ahead of me, but our little hero had returned home and we played on the carpet in celebration of his return.

Yes, this is only a pet, but I can imagine how much more emotion must be displayed in heaven (according to Jesus) when one of His beloveds returns home after being lost. Biscuit was God's natural revelation to me about the sadness of one being lost, and the joy of one being found. I understood it a bit better today.

Thank you, Biscuit.

About Heaven

What most people call "heaven" is actually an eternal city that the Bible calls the *new* Jerusalem. (Revelation 21:2, NIV). It will be spectacular. As a sampling, here is what the Bible says heaven will look like:

> *"A river, clear as crystal, will flow from the throne of God down the middle of the city. On each side of the river there will be a tree of life, yielding twelve kinds of fruit every month. The streets will be pure gold, like transparent glass. The walls of the city will be adorned with every kind of jewel, emerald, onyx, amethyst, topaz, etc. There will be no need for a sun or moon, and no need for a temple or church. The presence of the Lord will be its light." (Revelation 22:2, NIV)*

However, the real beauty of heaven is this:

"*Now* the dwelling of God is with men, and he will live with them. They will be his people, and God himself will be with them and be their God. He will wipe every tear from their eyes. There will be no more death or mourning or crying or pain, for the old order of things has passed away...I am making everything new." (Revelation 21:3-5, NIV)

Heaven belongs to Jesus. He created it. "For by him all things were created, in heaven and on earth, visible and invisible...all things were created through him and for him." (Colossians 1:16, NIV)

But He says *this* in reference to "getting into" heaven: "If your right eye causes you to sin, gouge it out and throw it away. It is better for you to lose one part of your body than for your whole body to be thrown into hell. And if your right hand causes you to sin, cut it off and throw it away. It is better for you to lose one part of your body than for your whole body to depart into hell." Matthew 5:29-30 (NIV)

These sound like very scary ideas, but Jesus is talking about what is required if a person really wants to avoid hell and live with God eternally. He spoke often about the idea "counting the cost" and "not turning back" and having a new mindset. (See Luke 14:25-34, NIV)

What He demands is that *we turn our backs on and give up certain things*. It is a *permanent* removal of some things. There's *no going back* to the old way of doing things—it's being "born again". And He promises that we *will* be "complete" or "perfect" if we come to Him.

Do I want to be in heaven? Am I willing to renounce those things that I *know* are wrong? Am I willing to cut off my arm and gouge out my eye, so to speak, if they stand in the way for me giving Him my life? Or on the other hand am I unwilling to kneel and call Him Lord? Am I determined to hold onto things that have *nothing to do* with God and His Kingdom, and yet still want to escape hell?

To the woman the well He said, "Go and *sin no more*." (John 8:11, NIV)

To the rich young man He said, "Go *sell all you have and follow me*." (Matthew 19:21, NIV)

…..and what is He saying to me—and to you?

Parts of the Body of One Body

"For just as each of us has one body with many members, and these members do not all have the same function, so in Christ we, though many, form one body, and each member belongs to all the others. We have different gifts, according to the grace given to each of us. If your gift is prophesying, then prophesy in accordance with your faith; if it is serving, then serve; if it is teaching, then teach; if it is to encourage, then give encouragement; if it is giving, then give generously; if it is to lead, do it diligently; if it is to show mercy, do it cheerfully." (Romans 12:4-8, NIV)

Our summer camp is not that large in terms of a community; on average we have about 250 campers and staff here each week. But the 100 that operate the camp—from Leaders in Training, to Program Heads and Dining Hall Managers—are *essential* for the smooth operation and tranquility that can only exist when everyone does his/her job.

And so it is in the *body of Christ*—i.e. His invisible church. Each of us is unique and each holds special skills and gifts that others do not possess. Some of us have many talents, some a few, and some (such as myself) only one. But it does not matter whether we are multi-talented or simple, we all are able to contribute to the work of the Kingdom of God by *using the gifts, talents, and jobs that He gave us to glorify Him… and we should not attempt to diminish the gifts and jobs of others.*

Christ was clear, *the greatest in the body of Christ is the one that serves the others—not the one that leads the others.* My task at the camp is to be the Director and Leader, but the greatest one here, the one that is celebrated in God's eyes and in His Kingdom, is the *hidden* one who secretly serves others all the time and never seeks, receives, or requires recognition or applause.

I have spent the past 42 summers at camp—*42 summers.* But I am quite certain that the greatest pleasure and satisfaction I *ever* had was serving as a cabin counselor for six campers 42 years ago. My tasks were simple, I was at the bottom of the organizational totem pole, but no one had a grander time than I did at camp. I was unknown to the leadership, unrecognized at ceremonies, and totally obscure to the camp director; but by pouring my life, talent and time into my campers, I was filled up, I *increased* and I was never in need of encouragement or compliments. It was truly a glimpse of what living in His Kingdom must be all about.

But I must ask myself, am I serving Him as sincerely and simply today as I did back then?

Suffering That Leads to New Life

Upon my return from a trip to Kenya I experienced three small physical challenges. First, my ankle was somehow injured as I walked through the terminal in Frankfurt. I don't know what I did or how I did it, but by the time I got on the plane my ankle was so swollen I could hardly walk and only with pain and an awkward hop could I get up or down the stairs. My shuffle was so pathetic that the attendants at the plane offered me a wheelchair when I got to the Dulles airport!

The ankle healed in 24 hours, but the next night, while at home, I experienced the most painful cramp of my life in my left calf! Sitting in a plane for 60 hours over four days took its toll on my circulation, I guess. But it was a day and a half after I left Kenya, lying in my bed, that this cramp hit me, and it was so excruciating that I yelled out in pain—and that's something I just don't do. And whereas I realize that this was nothing like passing a kidney stone or giving birth, it was horrible for me. I am in the "minor leagues" when it comes to pain. What was worse was that I knew that there was *nothing* I could do about the cramp! I had to simply wait for it to pass…

Then the next night I woke up again, turned my head the wrong way and with what felt like electrocution, I had a major crick in the neck. The pinched nerve was, again, *excruciating*, and I began to wonder: "Is my body just going to break down this weekend?" I've commented before that the frailty of our bodies is astounding to behold. We can be alive, healthy, happy, in total control of every muscle, and then, in a matter of seconds, a stroke, or the viral infection, or heart attack can change *everything*.

Of course, the memory of these painful episodes in my life causes me to be quite *grateful* that the *longest* chapters of my life have been totally free from physical pain. I am, in fact, quite sheltered, it appears, from harm to my body, and I thank God for it. I do not think I am so "saintly" and pure that God shields me from pain, but rather I am not able to stand up to much physical pain yet. The suffering of Jesus, the pain-filled lives of the true heroes and heroines in the Bible and within the church, remind me of how sequestered and "held in reserve" my life has been thus far.

True followers of Jesus should never seek pain or persecution, but no one worthy of bearing the name "Christian" should shrink from it if it is placed upon him/her. My puny, short, insignificant moments of pain are nothing… truly *nothing*. But my short bouts with suffering *might* allow one who is seeking affirmation that the Christian life is truly different from the common man's (as was the case, I hope, when two of my new sons heard me yell two nights ago and asked me what had happened) to place his/her faith in God. Then, obviously, suffering is a very blessed state in which to minister.

As I think about those men and women that have been dearest to me and who have represented who Jesus is more than any others, I realize that their faces showed evidence of pain and heartache, not of exuberant laughter and gaiety.

The prophet Isaiah prophesied that the coming Messiah would be… "despised and rejected of men, *a Man of sorrows*, and acquainted with grief. And we hid as it were our faces from Him; He was despised, and we esteemed Him not. Surely He hath borne our griefs and carried our *sorrows*; yet we did esteem Him stricken, smitten of God, and afflicted." (Isaiah 53:3-5, NIV)

If God would allow sorrow, grief, and pain to be an essential part of His Son's purpose, why should I be surprised when the same tools are used upon me for His Holy purposes?

Worth the Hurt

I have been writing these little devotions for a few years now, and I am so *honored* that some people write to me and comment on my remarks about the Christian life. Truly, I have wondered why I have had to struggle in my own ministry so much for the past 42 years. I have experienced setbacks, and I have had doubts and disappointments that I think would cause most men to give up their mission. And I am not saying this to brag, but to confess that I wonder at times if He *has* told me to "change course" and I was simply too bull-headed and arrogant to alter my plans. Yet, sharing my fears along with what He has taught me appears to have helped a few people in ways the musings of a more successful man might not.

At times I have found that God is incredibly quiet at those *very moments* I thought I needed to hear His voice the most. Many, *many* nights I have come to the conclusion that I was totally alone in my quest to create this summer camp for children. *I felt like an absolute hermit and abandoned even by God.* I have suffered through these doubts and have had a few existential moments where I wondered about my own call, salvation, belief, and sanity. Do these confessions cause those that read my thoughts to pull away from me and my ministry or do they evoke something else that offers some comfort?

That question is the point of this little devotion. It *appears* that my failures, challenges, doubts, and fears are not unheard of. And I have found that I am perhaps "uniquely" able to appreciate those that are "living on the edge" or struggling with understanding why they have had to fight so much to keep their business or ministry open, or are wondering how to be cordial and kind to those that have been anything *but* considerate to them... *I understand because I have been there and am there even now.* And that is what has changed *me* so much of late: The knowledge that the insults, failures, false-starts, lost friendships, and questions of His approval have all prepared me to *listen, show compassion, and pray for people in a way I could never have done if my life were "easy."*

Also, let me say emphatically that *no one* should choose a Christian ministry as a vocation! In the first place, it's not a vocation, it's a marriage and life-style. But more importantly, "ministry" is something a person is either *called, equipped, or qualified to do*, (and it is *God* that does the calling, equipping and qualifying) or it becomes a profession that drains, debilitates, and diminishes one's life. You simply cannot perform your role as a pastor, priest, missionary, or Christian camp director and not be able to look back to the time and place that *you knew* He called you to do what you are doing! If you lack that "event," you will eventually give up the vision and dream and choose another line of work, or you will become a cynic or spiritual charlatan. Either way the work of the Kingdom has become compromised.

So I write these thoughts not as one who is incredibly successful, wise, learned, gifted, or enabled, but as one who has been called and commissioned. If my words bless you and cause you to have hope, then my suffering, humiliations, failures, and wrestling have been well worth the occasional sadness and doubts.

Try This for a Month and You Won't Be the Same

I began reading today the longest chapter in the Bible—Psalm 119. My favorite part of this is at the beginning where the Psalmist asks: "How can a young person stay on the path of purity? By living according to your word. I seek you with all my heart; do not let me stray from your commands. I have hidden your word in my heart that I might not sin against you." (Psalm 119:9-11, NIV)

Two things came to my mind. One was the memory of the last USA Presidential debates. All of us who watched it on TV were clear about what we heard and we were clear on how we determined the candidates performed. But at the end of the debates, the network reporters, who were listening to the exact same debate we just heard, began to explain to us what was really said, as if the rest of us were first graders and that only their sophisticated opinions mattered. In my opinion, we really *don't* need reporters to explain to us what we can plainly see and hear.

Why, then, do we read books about people that have read the Bible and listen to their opinions rather than read the Bible for ourselves? Why do we trust others with what God has clearly said? Anyone of us could easily pick it up and read it. On the other hand, why do we listen to those that *condemn* the Bible but have *not* read it? We accept the authority of agnostics, atheists or non-believers when they disparage the Bible and then find out that these experts rarely, if ever, read the Bible.

The second thing that came to my mind is the real truth about the Bible: It is God's living Word—that should mean something not just to me, but to all mankind. If it *is* God's Word, why would I not spend time in it—daily—so that His Holy Spirit might speak mightily and appropriately to me? I have found in the Bible a powerful tool, ally and weapon with which to fight the enemy—the "one" that desires to discourage, confuse and hamstring me. Truly, His word is *light* as well as a love letter from God…to me.

And so, without sounding too "preachy", I wonder if you read the Word of God…or do you allow someone else to read it for you? None of us would ask for another adult to read to us a novel or the newspaper, so why are we so hesitant to read the very words of God Almighty or listen to the words of Jesus as He told parables?

My mornings begin with an espresso and the Bible—seven days a week—and I *know* that I am a better man because of it. Try it—you'll like it.

To Be Lost in His Love

As my life with four boys continues, I am made aware, day after day, that it is far easier to *counsel* parents about raising kids properly than it is to actually complete the task yourself. As with many things in life, it's wiser to not offer counsel where you have no experience.

I have seen the gospel come alive, that is, "lived out," as I have tried to counsel these boys and deal with their young development. For example, I know that God loved me so much that He gave His Son to die for my sins. I have quoted John 3:16 more than any other verse in the Bible. But now that I am raising a eight-, ten- and eleven-year-old (the fourth boy is 20), I realize that *if love* comes first for these boys, what follows is raising them into becoming the kind of gentlemen that God desires. What I mean is one follows the other; I love them and *therefore* I am not permitting them to watch TV, have an iPad, drink sodas, neglect their chores, ignore their homework. The love that I have for them *compels me* to not turn a blind eye to the bad things they do, the good things they avoid, or their inclination to show indifference about all things good and praiseworthy.

That is the same way God loves me. I am no different from these boys in my tendency towards indifference, doing the wrong thing, and avoiding the right thing. Adults (at least the ones I know) don't always act like mature humans—just sneakier children. And so, when I pray for these boys and complain to God that they are ungrateful, disobedient, lazy, requiring my constant attention so that they don't do something really foolish, etc., He smiles at me and tells me that they remind Him of someone He is very fond of who does the same thing… Ouch.

For me to really allow the work of the Holy Spirit to transform me into a mirror of Jesus I have to stop trying to *be* holy, and stop thinking about myself *in particular* and simply *be lost in Him*. As long as I am demanding to be seen, heard, appreciated, understood, felt sorry for… I am not much different from an ill-mannered child. But once I let go and allow Him to have His way, I am a child at heart… and a man after God's own heart.

The Foot of the Cross

As I was reading in I Corinthians today, this verse caught my attention: "For whenever you eat this bread and drink this cup, you proclaim the Lord's death until he comes." (I Corinthians 11:26, NIV)

It's strange how my attention is oftentimes drawn to scripture that I have read *hundreds* of times, yet today, when I read these words it took on a new, more profound meaning. The focus of communion ("The Lord's Supper"), is His death…until He comes again. (See I Corinthians 11:26, NIV). It seems that we talk about the resurrected and ascended Jesus *so much* that we forget about the death of Christ on the cross. Paul was quite clear: The Lord's supper is about remembering His death (and of course the suffering), the *reason* He died, and how He took our place.

What struck me is how often we (meaning me and those close to me) seem to forget the Crucifix and focus solely upon the empty cross ("the resurrected"). And whereas the empty cross has *great* spiritual and theological significance, it is the Christ *on the cross* that we're told to remember—not the empty cross.

I wonder if we have sanitized the story of Jesus too much or perhaps found that it's easier to market the "happy Jesus" that is often depicted, talking to children and holding a little lamb. You don't see many paintings in a Christian bookstore of Christ on the cross—suffering, bleeding, bruised or dead. And yet suffering on the cross was *always* God's plan for His Son. So why do we cringe at the thought?

Death and suffering are things we try to forget or ignore, and many assume that God would not want His saints to suffer. But why should any of us that bear the name "little Christ"—i.e. "Christian"—not see the purpose and plan of God's permission of suffering in our lives?

When I look at the dead Savior on the cross I recall the suffering that one man endured because of His love for man. The Christ on the cross is God's commentary both on how precious we are to Him and how much He hates sin. It's hard to remain in sin and remain at the foot of the cross of Jesus.

What If We Have It All Wrong?

I wonder if we teach and preach enough about how to understand disappointment. Do we talk enough in our churches about what to do when we face imminent failure, or what to do when we cannot hear God for a long time, or if we are confused as to what He is telling us? Many people talk to me about these things because they are experiencing it—and I so am I—and so did King David, the prophets, Mother Theresa, and every leader in the Christian faith. It's not uncommon, but talking about it appears to be taboo.

In everyday life, sometimes quiet is *needed* in order to prepare for, and to be able to appreciate with all our senses, the sensation of an incredible finale of a play or movie, or a sporting event or musical performance. Sometimes being still is a prelude to an eye-popping explosion of unexpected events! The Psalmist learned the importance of being still and counseled himself to, "Be still, and know that I am God" (Psalm 46:10, NIV).

What if we have it all backwards in this spiritual matter? What if *a sign of God's favor* is the amount of pressure and stress He permits us to endure; what if a carefree, casual and pain-free life is a sign of a *lack* of God's favor or confidence in us? What if His favorites, His "heroes", are the very ones who are always near the brink of disaster and are frequently abandoned by the world, and the "light-weights" in God's kingdom are those that coast through life as if they are charmed and insulated from despair and heartache?

Strange as it may sound, I don't know of a *single* man or woman whom I highly regard who is not now, or was at some point in the past, in great pain, turmoil, danger, disappointment, or intense persecution. It seems that it is the things our culture calls "unpleasant" (i.e. hurt, deprivation, injustice) that produce giants, heroes and legends, and it is the easy and charmed life that produces apostasy and a lukewarm church.

There's a difference between having God's peace and an ease of mind, with being *free* from the winds, hail, scorching heat and numbing cold of life. Bad and sad things, along with long winding paths that appear to lead nowhere, happen routinely in the life of a saint—there's no avoiding or denying it.

So do not think it strange or a sign that God is disinterested in you or that He has forgotten you when times are tough and you can't seem to find any answers. It might in fact be that He is far more interested than you ever imagined in what you are doing, how you are handling your apparent failures and the manner in which you hold up to the contempt and insults of others. He might be orchestrating and allowing all these things that the world calls "defeats" for a divine purpose; the conclusion of what you are going through is not going to be a disaster, but instead a miraculous and inestimable victory for Him and the work of His Kingdom.

Angels are watching and little "saints to be" are all around us hoping that we are the warriors He calls us to be.

Use Me!

"He restores my soul: he leads me in the paths of righteousness for his name's sake"(Psalm 23:3, NIV).

He restores my soul, i.e. He adds back into what has been taken out and what I cannot receive on my own. The idea here is that *something I am doing* causes my soul to be exhausted and depleted (perhaps "kingdom work") but that He is able, happy, and prepared to refuel my engines.

We remind staff at our camp that their purpose is to be used, drained, broken and poured out for Him (and the campers) each day…and that He is able to re-fill and restore us each evening.

He leads me! … For His own glory He is leading, using, and employing *me.* And this is what causes me to be in need of being restored. I am blessed, honored and grateful that He, the King of Kings and the Good Shepherd, would *choose* to allow me to follow Him, represent Him as I do my work and experience the favored life of serving Him. But following Him is at times lonesome, tear-filled, and exhausting. There's simply no denying it.

And yet, is the life of *any* ambassador any less demanding? It's sad to admit that almost *any one of us* would happily agree to be the Ambassador to a country for our king or President, and we would also accept the lonely nights and difficulties that are associated with being an ambassador. But when God seeks us to represent His Son, we demur and suggest He find another more "qualified." As the prophet Isaiah exclaimed, "Here am I, send me!" (Isaiah 6:8, KJV)

That must be our response when the Shepherd calls us to follow Him down a path of service: *Use me, Lord!* And at the end of the day, exhausted and depleted, we can faithfully trust Him to restore us… and He will. I've been experiencing it in ministry for over 40 years now.

Who is Being Preached and Who is Being Glorified?

Jesus said: "Very truly I tell you, whoever believes in me will do the works I have been doing, and they will do even greater things than these, because I am going to the Father. And I will do whatever you ask in my name, so that the Father may be glorified in the Son. You may ask me for anything in my name, and I will do It." (John 14:12-14, NIV)

Jesus was, of course, talking to His disciples, not to *me. They* had seen His miracles, things *never* seen before in the history of mankind. And they would soon also witness something never heard of: An innocent man would be executed but prophesied that in three days he would be resurrected from the dead. Heavy stuff was happening 2000 years ago in Palestine—and these men *saw it first hand. When they prayed they knew of whom they were speaking.*

And as I read in the books of Acts and the epistles, I can see the record of how these followers of Jesus certainly *did* perform incredible miracles and how they did *"wow"* the crowds with their teaching and defense of the good news of Jesus Christ. But *two things* caused them to have such power: They *believed...* and *the Father was glorified in the Son.*

So, is that the manner in which I perform my work here at the camp, at my church, in my neighborhood and with my family? *Am I* believing in the *resurrected Son of God* with *first-hand conviction*, or is my faith based upon what someone else told me that I should believe? *Am I* doing what I am doing to *glorify the Father through the Son?* Or am I seeking to elevate someone else (me?) or something else, (my work/ministry) instead?

"Blessed are the pure in heart"...(Matthew 5:8, KJV) because they don't struggle with ego and pride and concerns about "reputation." They are purely devoted to Him—and that makes life and ministry *so much easier.* I do not claim to have arrived there yet. My day *begins* with a determination to live every moment 100% for Him, but somehow that ugly "self" raises its head from time to time during the day and I forget for Who and for What I am striving. I have often thought that it would be far easier to serve as a pauper or beggar than as a pastor or camp director. "Blessed are the poor" (Matthew 5:3, KJV)—they focus on one source (God) for all their needs and are not pressed upon by others for sustenance.

Forgive me if my words sound a bit melancholy, but sometimes I need to wake myself up to the real call of following Jesus and not maintaining an operation, no matter how noble. He is more than sufficient but I sometimes lose focus of the ultimate goal.

Transformers

"Do not conform to the pattern of this world, but be transformed by the renewing of your mind. Then you will be able to test and approve what God's will is--his good, pleasing and perfect will" (Romans 12:2, NIV)

Have you ever tried walking *up* a swift stream? It's not easy—it's a workout! It's far easier to simply relax and float downstream and not resist the power of the current at all. Floating downstream is "conforming" to our environment; being "transformed" means walking upstream. You *do not* see many people walking upstream but you can watch a lot of folks floating *aimlessly* downstream—at river parks…and in life.

Let me tell you what I am learning and re-learning every year: To live the transformed life of allowing Him to renew and refresh my mind is far more difficult than just conforming to the customs, culture, opinions and shared wisdom of my society and friends. It's a *fight* to *live* the Christian life— *don't ever think it's easy.* Salvation is easy—Jesus did all the work and suffering. But living for Him is a fight that we must fight until we leave this life.

And if you are not fighting for your spiritual transformation—if you don't feel the attempts of the enemy to discourage you or his subtle suggestion that you "give up", it's because you are not in the fight of transformation—you're in the fog of conformation.

Ask Him to bring all your thoughts, dreams, and aspirations under His domain—subject to His leading and direction—and you will be able to discern what is good, pleasing and in line with His perfect will. But allow yourself to be drawn into living the expected, common, current and acceptable life and you will always be unsure of what He wants, expects and has prepared for you.

Dreaming About a New Camp

At a time like this, when everything is topsy-turvy and upside down, I think more and more about how I would like to do things *differently* at my little camp, if the time *and* resources were available. After all, everything *is* going to be different after this virus—that's a certainty. Maybe we can open the camp, "resurrected" in a brave, new way! So I have been thinking about what I would *ideally* like to offer for campers and our community (and what I would eschew).

First, I would like to offer to campers and families *free*. I would also like to offer our visa program (we help foreign staff acquire a J1 summer work visa) *free*. Yes, I know it's insane, but I am *dreaming* right now. But wouldn't it be wonderful if our camp (with fees at $1350/week) offered children the most exciting time of their life free of charge? And the same for staff. What if each staff we accepted did not have to contend with a $500 charge for the visa fee? After camp was over, the parents and staff would be invited to offer any kind of "gift" they wanted that represented their satisfaction with the camp, and those funds would pay for the next summer. This makes sense to me, but my friends and board members would be quick to tell me that most people (no names, nationalities or political parties to be mentioned) would probably pay zero. And some would, but I believe that people are often more generous than you realize and that *most* parents and staff would be honorable, and some might even pay *more* than expected.

But there are also some things I would not do or allow, that we have permitted in the past and is constantly being requested. This list might appear to be too fanciful or prejudiced towards *my* understanding of worship, but I am merely dreaming.

a. I would *not* adhere to the notion, prevalent among mega-churches and youth ministries, that youth and children have to be entertained and stimulated in order to hear the gospel. So I would not allow, or allow others to use our camp, if they wanted to turn *worship services* into mini "pop concerts."

    It appears that we are pandering to young people when we use gimmicks to share the truth about God or when we complain that they will not sit still unless you have a rock band on a stage along an expensive sound system, videos and a laser show.

b. I would not focus on large church retreats but instead upon opening the camp on the weekends for individuals, couples, families or small groups seeking God in nature, the solitude of the mountains or a group looking for a "Trappist" environment to be alone with God.

c. Finally, I would like to create a chapel on the property dedicated to God's glory and the elevation of Jesus Christ, but devoid of anything that would take away from a simple focus on the Trinity. No loud speakers, projectors, TV monitors *and no wifi or internet access*. I dream of a quiet and holy place where the focal point is the spoken word and the community of the redeemed raising their voices in honor of Him and His beloved Son.

In my new "dream camp" I would be sure that *He* was the focus—not activities or events or celebrated speakers. What I yearn for, I suppose, is "heaven on earth." During these times of reflection I am "homesick" for how things could/should be.

I know that this is a rather soap-boxy kind of thought today, and as former youth pastor of a large metropolitan church, I appreciate the challenges that youth pastors and youth leaders face. But more and more it seems like we're begging youth to come to events instead of carefully "setting the table" and inviting young people to meet the King of Kings. Youth need God and should be reminded that He is Holy. There's nothing wrong with demanding that those entering into a "holy haven" have reverence for the God to whom it is dedicated and to stand in awe of *Him.*

We don't need technology, padded pews or air-conditioning to worship the Lord.

Abandoned to God

Right before Christ was betrayed, tortured, humiliated, and executed, He talked about what was coming and said, "Now my soul is troubled, and what shall I say? 'Father, save me from this hour?' No, it was for this very reason I came to this hour. Father, glorify your name!" (John 12:27, NIV) And God did and also glorified His Son.

Jesus was born to be slandered, beaten, ridiculed, stripped naked, and nailed to a tree. God's only Son was born for that very purpose. But instead, why didn't God allow His Son to come and destroy the evil Roman Empire and establish a theocracy on earth right then and there? Why not let Jesus emerge as a superhero, some sort of "Ironman Messiah"? And why does God seem to allow His favorite people to rot in prisons, waste away on remote islands, and have their lives cut short by an executioner or a fatal disease? God's favored often suffer severely.

God does not do things the way that Hollywood does. He does not let His messengers "live happily ever after." In fact, many are not happy endings at all. Millions of followers of Jesus have been martyred and forgotten. The Lord does not act like a very rational man at all. And that is what I have to keep remembering as I face challenges and obstacles throughout my day. God does things the way a holy and pure God does them, not the way a mere man would. I don't understand why He does what He does, but I do know that He would never waste the pain and suffering on His children. There is a purpose in His ways. I am grasping, more and more, how it is only through the humiliation and suffering of those He loves, that others can receive a true appreciation for who He is and their need for Him. God could easily bless and endow His favorites, but that would only draw those to Him that wanted to have more *from Him*, instead of more *of Him*. He is trying to show us something that is far more important than His blessings. We are told repeatedly that it is "the great I am" (Revelation 22:16, NIV) that He wants me to seek, thirst for, and find, not His gifts or even His protection. It is Him alone.

As I consider how the true giants of the church have been so abused and neglected by their own, I understand that only a higher reward and relationship could cause these rational men and women to abandon what might have been an easy and rewarding life. Instead, they dedicated their entire existence to a God that was prepared to send them into a gauntlet of suffering for His glory. These folks tasted and experienced something far greater than fame, popularity, or earthly delights. They came to know the depth of God's love and nothing else. No manner of suffering could deter them.

And so, I understand a little better that when my occasional humiliation and pain might give me reason to give up or change course, I can follow the spiritual example of these true disciples of Jesus. They willingly endured anything so that Jesus might be exalted. They exhibited a profound love for Him that caused them to consider it *pure joy* that they were considered worthy to suffer for Him. They knew that something better was coming. Do I share that robust confidence in Him?

The Covid 19

As of right now the world is in a panic over the Covid 19—the new deadly virus that was unleashed from China at the end of 2019. It's funny how nations, adults and our leaders very often act like little children when they do something wrong or foolish. My sons tend to look for an excuse, try to blame someone else, or even point out something positive that might have happened because of the bad thing they have done.

I don't know all the details, and because the communist leadership of China is so secretive, opaque and dishonest, no one will get the entire truth until the present dictatorship is dead and gone and people are free from the fear of telling the truth. But the Chinese leaders, primarily President Xi, initially *denied* it was a problem, then downplayed the issue, then blamed it on someone else (the present canard is that the US army somehow *planted* the virus in China to hurt the country), and now, most recently, proclaimed that they are not the culprits of covering it up or hiding the truth, but really the heroes for showing the world how to defeat the very disease they unleashed on the world! Admittedly these words will never be seen by my friends in China, because despots, just like the devil and those within his camp, eschew and fear truth more than anything else.

As I am writing this, our nation has shut down all schools, restaurants, bars, athletic events, large events and even churches. And yet most of us realize that God is still *God* and that He is able to rescue, restore and redeem our nation and the other nations regardless of how dire and fearful the future looks. On an individual level, *all of us* have *reason* to fear, and if I did not believe in a *good God* that loves me with a more *excellent* love than any other love I can ever experience, I would be fretting, hoarding food, plotting to keep ahead of others, and would be losing sleep over how to protect myself and my future. And if I were a *national leader* or represented a *political ideology* that denied a loving and all-powerful God, I suppose I would act similar to communist China or some of our own politicians that share communist views about God and religions: that is, I would act more like a child by denying the truth, pointing *my* inadequate and guilty finger at someone else, attempt to shift blame to *anyone* but myself, and taking the spotlight off what I could or should have done, perhaps even suggesting that because of *me* things could actually be better. It's child's talk versus *a man or woman of God's talk*.

I cannot see the future, but I believe that this virus will eventually infect most Americans, French, Bolivians, Mexican, Jamaicans, South Africans, Colombians and all the other people on this earth. Even now the virus is *recurring* in the very places it was first seen. But God has not called on His people to live in fear, but rather to "call upon Him." (Psalm 145:18, NIV). This virus might prove to be the *one thing* that brings America and the other nations *back* to a holy reverence for God and away from our smug arrogance. We live in a very, very dangerous world right now, but God is more than able to turn this nightmare into a worldwide revival. May the revival begin tonight…

What I Need vs. What I Want

I prayed to God for *encouragement* this past weekend, and Sunday I was asked to accept a foster-care child in need of encouragement into my home. Although I was happy to help, it's not what I was expecting God to send to me.

That same Sunday, early in the morning, I prayed for a *sign* that He was pleased with me; when I returned to my home after church and opened up my computer, the *first* email I read was from a family that told me, rather uncharitably, that they did not want to receive any more emails or communication from us about our camp.

He seems to be intent on giving me what He thinks I need and using me for His purposes, instead of giving me all that ask for. Although I often wish otherwise, God is not a "permissive Father." His "encouragement" to me is revealed in His *approval* of me to care for a foster child this past weekend. His "sign" that He is pleased with me appears to be that He considers me "worthy" of being insulted for operating a non-profit ministry for youth and children that is non-apologetically Christian.

His idea of "blessing" and my idea "ain't the same." He knows me better than I know me—and He sees what's ahead as well as the present moment in which I live. I know that He hears me because of the things that *do happen*, but the days that I think I cannot handle one more "assignment" or "teaching moment," He gives me more than I think I could possible carry.

It seems likely that He has the secret agenda to make me "holy and set apart" for Him, regardless of my whining or my intentions to delay the transformation. He's pushing me further and further away from where I *think I should be* and closer (I hope!) to a new spiritual plateau.

The truth is, if I had been facing the challenges I have *today,* but *forty* years ago, I do not think for I would still be a pastor or camp director. And if I were not surrounded by family and friends who encouraged me and offered words of kindness, I would have given up any attempt to progress in my Christian walk—at least, that's what I think based upon the young man I was then, versus how I have come to understand Him *now*. The irony is that thirty years ago I was fairly sure that I had *arrived* to just about the highest level a man could attain on this earth in terms of knowing and loving God. God must have been smiling the whole time—if not laughing.

Nan

Recently I went to a family gathering in Florida—the wedding of a nephew. On my way to the wedding I stopped by to see my mom, who has been suffering for the past several years with Alzheimer's. All of you reading this that know a person you love who suffers from dementia or Alzheimer's know how horrible it is to see a life fade away like this.

My mother is now non-ambulatory, non-verbal and rarely responds at all. I sat with her for fifteen minutes, hoping she would open her eyes, smile, wink her eye… anything. I prayed for her; I thanked God for her; I asked God to let her pass in peace as soon as possible and release her in heaven to become the happy, vibrant, talkative, entertaining mother and friend she used to be. My mom at this time was 91 years old but she *never* wanted to leave the world in this manner. It is the *one thing* she dreaded more than anything else: being unable to care for herself.

Many campers and staff knew my mom—they called her "Nan". She made thousands of cookies for our nightly Bible studies. She loved selflessly. She gave beyond what was prudent to give. Nan was always the one that brought laughter and joy into a room. She loved to tell funny stories and attempted to tell jokes, but she never could remember the "punch line" at the end of the joke—yet that somehow made the laughter at the end of her joke all the more uproarious!

My mother also had a testy side to her. She was *fiercely* protective of her children. *Pity* the person that spoke disparagingly of any of the kids. She was *never* sick, *never* slept late, and absolutely would not tolerate coarse, profane or inappropriate conversation. She would not put up with bragging, unkindness or rudeness. She expected *too much* from us and we sometimes complained about it *and we are all better children because of her lofty expectations.*

Nan won't be with us too much longer and the world is already a bit poorer because of her gradual demise. So why did I and my other siblings go and visit this little old lady who can neither talk, hold our hand or feel our caresses? *Because that's how she raised us.* We weren't brought up to do what was convenient, or self-serving, or always pleasant. We were taught to believe that, "what comes around goes around," and that we should honor and respect our parents—even old, feeble, demented parents.

Being with my mom reminded me of *who she was, what she expected of me, the sacrifices she made for me so that I could succeed, and the joy that comes from seeing those you love overcome setbacks.* If there are good things in my character, most can be traced back to what she said, did and demanded from me.

I am not a trained expert in family counseling, but I do believe that many parents don't demand great things from their children and thus later complain that "society," a bad coach, an unfair teacher, or a rude police officer has caused their child to fail. But my mom would quote, "Raise up a child in the way he should go and when he is old he will not depart from it." (Proverbs 22:6, KJV). My mother knew her Bible and knew right from wrong. I am a blessed son.

(Nan passed away five months after this was written. March 2, 2020.)

To Disagree Is to Be Alive

Some time later Paul said to Barnabas, "Let us go back and visit the believers in all the towns where we preached the word of the Lord and see how they are doing." Barnabas wanted to take John, also called Mark, with them, but Paul did not think it wise to take him, because he had deserted them in Pamphylia and had not continued with them in the work. They had such a sharp disagreement that they parted company. Barnabas took Mark and sailed for Cyprus, but Paul chose Silas and left…"(Acts 15:36-40, NIV)

Disagreements are inevitable, even among spiritual giants like Paul and Barnabas! And sometimes it's not a matter of right or wrong, but simply a difference of opinion. These Christian missionaries did not agree about the character of John Mark, and rather than demand that the other see his point as the more valid, they simply "parted ways"—that is, they literally took different paths. And it appears that they departed as friends.

Anyone that has really studied the Word of God would quickly come to the conclusion that there *are valid* points of disagreement in the Bible regarding issues that are *not* essential for salvation but have nonetheless led to a lot of angry debates and name calling—even to torture and murder!

I was raised in a large, conservative Protestant church. But at my university I was a youth pastor at a small church that was borderline "fundamental." Yet in seminary the much larger church I served was far more liberal. In each church I found this to be true: The most tolerant, open-minded, even-handed, gracious and "ready to learn" were the mature Christians that were quite secure in what they believed, and therefore not easily angered by someone with whom they disagreed.

There is plenty of room at His table for various opinions about the Holy Eucharist (the "Lord's supper"), the inerrancy of scripture, what we should eat, wear or drink, etc. But I don't believe that our host (God Almighty) appreciates bickering and arguing at the table. I say this because I find it amazing that some very educated people seem far more dedicated to a denomination, or a creed, or a particular version of the Bible than for whom all this is about.

I have served in Baptist, Methodist, Presbyterian and non-denominational churches; my best friends are both Catholic and Protestant; the men that influenced me the most came from Assisi, Nashville, Glasgow, London and Berlin. The common thread with each of them is a modesty and humility that I found compelling and irresistible. If I am certain of whom I believe and know where I came from, I am able to listen and learn from the least and best.

"A Fool Finds Pleasure in Wicked Schemes…" (Proverbs 10:23, NIV)

This is a verse from the book of Proverbs. Frankly, Proverbs was not a book I read a lot as a young man. The adages seemed a bit archaic and inappropriate for my time and generation when I was younger. The words did not *resonate* with me. I thought some of the warnings were a bit exaggerated and not fit for modern mankind.

But I have come to see the *truth* contained in the proverbs of Solomon in the past few years. Why? Because I can *identify* with the ridiculous things I did and the foolish things I see other young people doing now. I wish I could have taken to heart the wisdom of Proverbs when I was younger and I wonder if there is *any* way to articulate these truths to teenagers today?

I don't want to sound pessimistic about the future, but it brings tears to my eyes to consider how the things that are beautiful and proper and godly *disgust* some children and teenagers today, and how perverse and improper things make some smile and laugh. Perhaps I was the same way when I was a teenager, but for the life of me, I don't ever recall taking pleasure in some of the things I see youth take pleasure in today.

The greatest challenge is the constant negative and questionable information that any child can find on the Internet, television, popular movies, DVDs, video games, social media, and, of course, their cellphones. What scares me is the *celebration* of bad things and the constant *ridicule* of good and proper things. Worse is the suggestion that there *are no absolutes* when it comes to good and evil, or right and wrong.

We will always have "fools" in our families and societies as long as we have free will. I understand that. Many of them are running our government and speaking from pulpits. But the gravest danger for our youth is the attempt to *justify their foolish actions by claiming that it's not their fault and that they cannot be held accountable*. That is what has changed over the past 4000 years. That is what causes me alarm and heartache for the next generation. Until we teach *responsibility* for our choices and actions we should expect more of what we are seeing in our schools, social media, and in juvenile courts.

Please pray that we might be able to teach youth to *desire* what is holy and beautiful and give up on the things that are offensive to God. Please pray that those of us that lead here might *prove* by our lives that we *love* what God loves and *hate* what God hates. It's that simple.

Happy Thanksgiving!

Thanksgiving in the USA is the day we thank God for His blessings and reflect upon all that He has done for us. Every year several families and friends come to the camp for our Thanksgiving dinner and it is truly a joyful day of food, fellowship, and laughter. It has been something we all look forward to each year.

We're told to "give thanks in all things" (I Thessalonians 5:18, NIV), yet it's hard sometimes to thank God when I am in the middle of a catastrophe, or a struggle, or an embarrassing encounter. There are times when I truly to do not *feel* like thanking God. I would rather sit down and cry some days, or give up and walk away from the "call" He has placed upon me, or just hide from everyone; including God. But *that* is the "feeling" I have, and I have learned to *not* trust *or obey* my feelings. My natural response, my instinct and my "gut feelings" are simply inappropriate for a follower of Jesus, and need to be ignored.

Experience has shown me time and time again that God *can* be trusted, that He *is* my friend and guide, and that He *does* love me far more than I love Him. My days often begin with apprehension, disappointing news, impossible challenges, and deadlines…I am tempted to react "naturally" and panic. But if I take control of my emotions and *decide* to thank Him for the challenge, the trouble, the set-back, I give Him the opportunity to bring about a miracle that will not only increase my faith but permit me to a witness to what a man, committed to and totally believing in God, can be and accomplish.

No sane man or woman would look for trouble or sadness, but *no one* "sold out to God" can allow self-pity to dominate his/her life when troubles do come. I am thankful for all the blessings, pleasant moments, kindness, mercy, love, and surprises that I have experienced this year. They brighten my soul. But I also thank God for every difficult and hard thing that He has permitted, because those things—far more than His blessings—have caused me to grow closer to Him and farther away from the "common man" I used to be.

No, I am not where I want to be yet in my walk with Him. *Many* are far ahead of me in their determination to allow Him to have total control of their lives. But I am learning to let go of fear and worry by recalling that He has *never* let me down, He has *never* permitted anything to fall upon me that did not eventually bring about a blessing, and that I do *not* need to understand why He allows me to be on the brink of disaster at times and carefree the next. *He knows what He is doing; He knows what lies around the corner; He knows that I am frail, weak, and a babe in the woods.* And *I know* that He loves me like a father loves a small child. I can rest.

Black Friday

On the Friday after Thanksgiving, I went to the airport to catch a plane to France for an extended trip of presenting the camp to French families. My itinerary had been planned for months. My hotel rooms were reserved and paid for, I made dinner arrangements, I purchased my tickets, and made all the arrangements months in advance to get the very best rates.

But when I attempted to check in at the airport, I was informed that my passport was invalid for travel to France because it expires in February. I knew that I only had three months left on my passport, but why did that matter? Then I discovered that a new law had been passed *in France* requiring more time on a U.S. Passport! No one from the travel agency or airline informed me, and the French law was passed after I purchased the airline ticket!

My reaction at the American Airlines kiosk was not immediately joyful or reflective. I was frustrated, annoyed, and felt sick about the waste of time and money (the airline ticket was not refundable) and a general sense of futility. I thought about all the meetings that would be cancelled, of how disappointed the youth and their parents would be, and wondered how in the world I was going to get this fixed expeditiously.

To make matters worse, the airline accepted no responsibility (no big surprise), but the gentleman at "customer relations" at the travel agency blamed me and told me that I should pay attention to the new laws that were being passed in France!

All day Friday I worked to get a new, emergency meeting with the US Passport services in Atlanta. Finally, three days later I received a new passport, purchased a new ticket to Atlanta, additional tickets from there to France, and then home again at a later date. I had to cancel hotel reservations, attempt to reschedule meetings, and returned to my home with a feeling of utter defeat. But during this entire episode, I was praying, thanking God for being in control, and asking for His peace. I admitted to Him that I had no idea why He caused or allowed this to happen, and I also acknowledged that I might never know why He put this roadblock into my plans (granted He has no obligation to explain His ways to me).

Later that afternoon, I began to experience His presence and peace. That lost flight gave me three days with absolutely no agenda—and there was nothing I could do except rest, slow down, and enjoy the good life He has given me. Frequently, I am far too "fired up" and in too much of a hurry. Now, I realize this. Friday night, alone, I watched *Les Miserables*. I was touched by the priest, in particular, in a way I could not have been if I were focusing on other things. I needed to miss that plane.

He is under no mandate to explain why things go bad for me some days, or to educate me as to why I have struggled for the past two years with our finances because of the fire that took away my home. But, I know that He knows what He is doing and that it is a blessing to be still, from time to time, and recall that He is *God*.

Try to Remember

"He has shown you, O man, what is good. And what does the Lord require of you? To *act* justly and to *love* mercy and to *walk* humbly with your God." (Micah 6:8, NIV)

If these words are true, it means that we are without excuse for much of bad we do—i.e. our lack of compassion, our arrogance. If Micah was truly the "mouthpiece" of God (i.e. a prophet), his words matter to *all men and women, boys and girls.* And perhaps some of the things he said should cause us to pause and reflect.

-*He has shown* us means that we *know* in our hearts these truths. Some things don't have to be introduced to us, but rather *reminded to us.* We innately *know* what is good but have to be reminded, as we get older, because we either forget, get accustomed to following the lead of others, or have found a way to talk ourselves into believing that we are *justified* for not doing good. It is a fight each morning to hold on to the good and let go of the excuses for what is wrong.

But God has shown us what He requires of each of us His creations:

-*To act justly*—that is, to do what is right. *Not* what suits us, or satisfies our urge for revenge or restitution, *but what is right.*

-*To love mercy.* Not merely to approve of someone getting a second chance, or of a criminal getting pardoned, *but loving it.* That is *having joy* about a person receiving something good when we know that he or she deserves something bad. It's a matter of rejoicing *for the other soul* that gets a break and not whining about it when we don't get a break.

-*To walk humbly before Him.* God is God….and I am a fallen creature, a "cracked pot", an imperfect representation of the man that God wanted and wants me to be. Yes, He loves me nonetheless, *but only because of His Son's redemption of my soul on the cross of Golgotha.*

It's easier to talk about these things with *kids* than grown-up folks—-that's why I am so dedicated to summer camping and a youth ministry at this church. Frederick Douglas said, "It is easier to build strong children than to repair broken men." As we get older we're guilty of choosing ignorance—the word in Greek is ἄγνοια: "agnostic". It does *not* mean "not knowing" in this context, but rather "choosing ignorance" with the inference that it is *inexcusable.* We *know* it's wrong to drink and drive, but we think we're smarter than the statistics; we know it's wrong to exaggerate and embellish on our income tax reports, but we hide and tell ourselves that the government is corrupt and we should pay them as little as possible. Then, when we grow up and don't receive justice and mercy we feel we deserve, or when we see the arrogance and pride of others applauded, we can lose sight of our goal and our created purpose and adopt the same "fallen" tendencies.

But teenagers, and even more so children, know right from wrong and are able to apologize for blunders, admit it, confess that it was unfair or not nice. They don't hide behind some conflated explanation for "why" they have chosen to hate Joe Biden or Donald Trump—they *still remember* that to hate someone is wrong (even if they do blurt out that word from time to time.) We hide the words but nurse the same feeling deceptively in our hearts.

May God cleanse our adult hearts from all unrighteousness and give us the heart of a child again. *We know how we should live. We just need to remember.*

Welcome Home

Recently I came home from two weeks abroad. Those of you that travel understand that it's always good to come home; but as a "home-body," I, more than most, really appreciate my home and my country. Travel is fine, and in many regards it helps me appreciate the home and home-folks more and more. But my return this past trip also reminded me about some spiritual truths of the ultimate homecoming we all yearn for.

The first "truth" is that the eldest boy in our home was at airport *on time* to pick me up. That might not be a big matter to you, but after traveling for thirty-five years, I can attest that it is both disheartening and *annoying* to come home and *no one is there to pick you up* at baggage claim. In the past, the camp staff have pretty consistently picked me up *late*. Sometimes it was only a few minutes, sometimes it was an hour or more. Coming home with no one waiting to take you home *is painful*—I don't know how else to describe it. Excuses, traffic jams, having to stop for gas en route, etc. don't allay that sense of disappointment.

On this return I arrived at the airport early, I was at the luggage claim area early, and I knew that the young man would not be there yet because, as I said, I was early. I could already imagine him not being there for me when I got my luggage and how I would begin to get my feelings hurt. But the moment I got my luggage off the conveyor belt and turned around he was walking in the door. He was, in fact, *precisely on time*.

How much energy and how many hours do I waste worrying that God's going to be late? How often does the enemy play with my mind at night when I wonder about the consequences of God *not showing up at all* when I need Him the most? In my life God has never come to my rescue *early*, and there are times I thought He was not coming at all, but then I found out He was with me at the precise time I needed Him—not when I *demanded that I would need Him, but when I really needed Him*. He's never late, but He operates on a different clock than I do.

When I got home the pets were waiting to see me. Their "hero" had returned home! They ran around excitedly while I unpacked, played and seemed to be smiling about the return of their sovereign. That night when I went to my room, exhausted from fourteen hours of travel and six hours of jetlag—I was greeted by both dachshunds and the wolf, already in the bed waiting for me—something they do not normally do. It's as if they were saying, "You're not leaving us behind again!" The dogs showed happiness that they were no longer "abandoned."

How blessed a day is coming when we will be "home" forever. Never alone, never to be abandoned again, never again to be dismayed or given a reason to be anxious again. God sent His only Son here 2000+ years ago so that we could come to know freedom from the overwhelming control and guilt of sin, and experience the certainty of God's love, the peace of knowing that He is in control and is never, ever going to forget us, and that He is waiting for us. And now my greatest hope is to hear Him say gently one day, "Well done, welcome home."

What Am I Saying?!

Who is listening to my *unguarded* words? Those remarks and comments that naturally slip off my tongue when I am annoyed or tired. I know of at least three little boys in my home who seem to pay *more* attention to my cutting discords when I wish no one was paying attention. It's a bit scary to hear the same pungent words I used last week echoing in the little voices in our house the next day. They often repeat and intone the very same things I should not have said, often with the same inflection!

> "Good grief!"…..
> "Do you know how much that cost me?"……
> "Don't make me come up there!"…….
> "Are you out of your mind or something?"…….
> "What is wrong with you?"……

But *am I listening* to His words so often and carefully that I am also *repeating* the very things He says to me? One of the reasons I need to spend intimate, private and focused time with Him daily is so I might *unlearn* the common tongue of the devil and *remember* the very voice and language of God Almighty. *He* never yells or screams at me, He does not bring up my past indiscretions, He does not seek to push me down nor does He seek my destruction or threaten to "skin me alive"—*He is for me.*

What words does He repeat to me when I am alone with Him that I ought to be repeating or living when I am with others? The words, "I love you," "You can be *the* man," "I am for you," "I forgive you," "I have chosen you," "I will never forsake you."

And aren't these the same things we hope and yearn to hear from those we love? Aren't these words the *essential* things that a lover says to his/her beloved?

"Lord, teach me to speak to others like you speak to me."

What Could Possibly Compare

"Just then a man came up to Jesus and asked, 'Teacher, what good thing must I do to get eternal life?' 'Why do you ask me about what is good?' Jesus replied. 'There is only One who is good. If you want to enter life, keep the commandments.'

'Which ones?' he inquired. Jesus replied, 'You shall not murder, you shall not commit adultery, you shall not steal, you shall not give false testimony, honor your father and mother,' and 'love your neighbor as yourself.' 'All these I have kept,' the young man said. 'What do I still lack?' Jesus answered, 'If you want to be perfect, go, sell your possessions and give to the poor, and you will have treasure in heaven. Then come, follow me.' When the young man heard this, he went away sad, because he had great wealth. Then Jesus said to his disciples, 'Truly I tell you, it is hard for someone who is rich to enter the kingdom of heaven. Again I tell you, it is easier for a camel to go through the eye of a needle than for someone who is rich to enter the kingdom of God.'

When the disciples heard this, they were greatly astonished and asked, 'Who then can be saved?' Jesus looked at them and said, 'With man this is impossible, but with God all things are possible.'" - (Matthew 19:26-36, NIV)

This story has *nothing* to do about being rich or poor, but rather it is a question: "What is holding *me* back from entering into God's Kingdom today?" For this young man, it was his dependence, admiration, love and need for money. *This* was his "god" and it would always be competing for his allegiance to God. What is holding us back? Is it our independence? Is it our desire to live without rules or standards? Is it our conceit? Is it our apathy to anything pure and good? Is it family, friend, spouse or child? More often than not, it is the *good* things that keep us apart from God; truly the "good" is the greater enemy of the "best" than something bad or disgusting.

What is holding you back from giving up and giving in to Him? What is it in your life that is more important than the *eternity He offers* with Him? What can possibly compare with what He has to give?

Trust and Let Go!

One week at our camp we talked about the "Prayer of Jabez" (See I Chronicles 4:10, NIV) and how God answered Jabez and gave him all he asked for. It's an encouraging and inspiring story: A good man prays to God for something very specific and God gives him what he asks for. Nice!

But what about the times we ask for *good* things, perhaps even very virtuous and proper things, and God does *not* approve the prayer, or seems to ignore the petition altogether? This has bothered me all day. I know of a good person that was praying for a very, very noble and proper thing to happen, but he has been denied an answer—or the answer is "no."

I personally have been praying for many years for something quite appropriate, noble, and proper; but either God is ignoring my prayer, telling me "no", or telling me to wait. Honestly, I don't know what to do or think at times when I struggle with unanswered prayers or a negative answer. I wonder why He does not answer me, seems to not care or appears to not be listening. My faith is challenged when I pray and pray and pray about something and *nothing* happens.

But perhaps He *is* listening. Perhaps, just maybe, He *believes in me* and is *allowing* me to suffer, lose some sleep, become a bit more humble, and experience some uncertainty about something I want—*for a purpose that I cannot immediately imagine or see.* Maybe God *does* hear every prayer I make and is deliberately remaining quiet to allow me the time to realize that my prayer was inappropriate or that it is best that He does not intervene for the time being.

The question is simply this: Do I trust Him? If I do, at the end of the day I can tell Him that, "I have done all I can do, I have prayed faithfully…it's now in Your Hands, *your will be done. I surrender.*"

I would not be writing this blog, or serving at this camp, or be the man I am today if God had answered the prayer of a *very* righteous man many years ago. When a certain man, my personal hero, *pleaded* with God to protect him from an *illegal* attack, an undeserved punishment and a humiliating execution, *God was silent.* And when the same man was on a cross bleeding, suffocating and dying an incredibly unjust death, God did not even answer Him when He cried out, "My God, my God, why have you forsaken me?" (Matthew 27:46, NIV)

Are we not blessed and overcome with joy that God does *not* always answer our prayers? The Christian faith would not exist if God did everything we begged for. When God is silent or appears to say no, *there is a reason.* Trust in Him and let go…

Suffering and Loss

I have observed in dismay many young people that I thought had great potential *lose* their lives to drug overdose, auto accidents and suicide. My words of comfort and reassurance are woefully inadequate when a teenage life has been snuffed out so early. I simply don't know what to say. On the one hand, I know that disease, decay and death were not a part of God's original plan for mankind; I also know that as omnipotent God He could intervene and stop suffering, pain, accidents and death. And yet He all too often does not seem to lift a finger to intervene. At least that's how it looks to me.

Paul, the greatest evangelist of all time and author of half the New Testament, wasted *years* in dark prisons, and nights and day in the open sea very near to death, and hours and hours hiding from mobs or being lowered over walls in baskets. My favorite 20th century heroes—D. Bonhoeffer, CS Lewis and Oswald Chambers—all died "early." One was murdered by the Nazis before he was 40, the other died in his early fifties, and the last died in his early 40s of appendicitis. All of these men should have lived *longer lives* and accomplished even greater things…or so my reasoning goes.

But the truth that God is ever revealing to me is that He is not in a "business" to grow a bigger and bigger enterprise with great salesmen and superb marketers. No, God's in the habit of taking mortal men and turning them into sons and daughters. And part of that process is to bring them to a place where their mortal life is not their individual focus but rather the goal of perfectly reflecting His Son, Jesus. And if that reflection requires that their life ends at 30, 40, 50 or 100 years of age, God knows what He is doing. God is not obligated to explain to me *why* He lets a 20-year-old young man die in a car crash or why He takes away a Christian apologist at the height of his career. God's purpose is to make me holy in the unusual ways and circumstances that suit His purposes.

I suppose the question is, "Do I believe that God knows what He is doing, and by watching what He does, do I *trust* in the end result?" When a young life is lost I find peace in reminding myself that *God loved and loves that young person infinitely more than I or any other mortal can imagine.*

It's natural to mourn the passing of someone we love or would have like to have known and loved. But God does know what He is doing. Have your way, Lord, and open my eyes to see how you are using tragedy and heartache to further young kingdom.

Walk in the Light

Jesus proclaimed that, "Whoever follows me will never walk in darkness, but will have the light of life." (John 8:12, NIV). This is a great encouragement to me and helps me understand things in the Christian community that just do not make sense at times.

Jesus did *not* say that if we believed in Him we would "walk in the light," nor did He say that if we went to Mass or church services every week we would be "true disciples." He did not even say that if we confessed our sins, received communion and were baptized that we would be living an "ideal life." If we really want to *walk in the light,* i.e. to be free from duplicity, deceit, hidden sins and hypocrisy, we have to *follow Him*—and that's a different matter.

It is the key to the life of light, pure peace, purpose, joy and abundance—*following Him.* Many believe in Him (even the demons) and many more admire Him and quote Him from time to time. But how many of us *follow* Him? To follow means to take the path He has chosen for us, to accept the burdens He places upon us, and even (as He did) carry our cross. Living the self-denying life that Jesus led is the *only* way I can enjoy the *light of life.* My attempts to protect myself, gather for myself, build up for myself, and stand up for myself might not keep me out of heaven, but they keep me out of the pure light of love that He offers to those who trust Him.

Strange as it may seem, when my house burnt down in 2016 and I lost *everything* I have ever owned, along with all those things that identified who I was, I had more peace, clarity and "light" in my soul than I have ever experienced. It's said that either you own things or things own you. And to tell the difference, determine if you can give away something that is special to you. If you cannot, it owns *you;* if you can, you own *it.*

The peace that comes from following Him means having nothing that would "own you" and keep you from keeping up the pace of the walk. I now find myself giving things up, each day, that begin to "own" me. I don't want to be hindered from the race set before me.

Blue Skies!

After several days of gray clouds, rain, hazardous winds and a general "miserable" climate, I woke up today and saw blue skies, green grass and felt a gentle warm breeze. And what an immediate change in my own attitude!

We sing about "Blue Skies", and the "Green, Green Grass of Home" for good reasons. Something the Creator placed within our souls likes the greens and blues better than they gray and darkness. Light, brilliant colors, clear skies—we crave these things because our Creator also appears to love same. Yes, there's a certain benefit to dark days, the drizzle, perhaps even sickness and pain, I suppose; we come to appreciate wellness, the absence of pain and beautiful clear days all the more because we know what it is like to do without.....

A soft wind is blowing the limbs of the tallest trees, the skies are cloud free, the grass seems greener than ever before and all seems well as I write this little devotion. It's as if God is reminding me that this is how life is supposed to be lived; there is a passion within my heart to live my life away from grayness, the cold, bland colors, and (dare I say it) unimaginative and uninspiring people (most of them are now in our national Capitol).

But we are "stimulated" not so much from the Federal Government's handouts as we are by God's unparalleled creative order—and particularly His creation color, clarity and brightness. Thank you, God, for beauty.

A common comment by folks who have had "near death" experiences, or have died, been to heaven and returned, is that they have all seen colors there that are not here. One said, "What I experienced was so incredibly beautiful, words fail to describe it. I saw colors that are not existent on Earth, colors that had so many different shades and hues that I had never seen before. I have tried describing the colors to my friends and family, and the closest I can come to it is by saying that a particular color looked like a mix between blue, green, pink and purple, but it was nothing I had ever seen before in my waking state."

God has great things in store for us—in heaven one day and one day soon after this pandemic has passed. But God's goodness, clarity, light and color will soon be shining brightly.

> Blue skies smilin' at me
> Nothin' but blue skies do I see
> Bluebirds singin' a song
> Nothin' but blue skies from now on
> I never saw the sun shinin' so bright
> Never saw things goin' so right........
> Irving Berlin

All in All?

One thing that seems obvious as we are now being required to live together with our families, is that we're discovering how absolutely intolerable the other members of our clans can be at times. Only the most mature of us can step away and focus upon how intolerable *we* are, but we can have 20/20 vision on how deplorable the others can be!

And in dealing with those that aggravate me, I have a tendency to want to walk away from challenges or stop short of "wresting the problem to the ground" in terms of conflict. This virus seems to cause folks to reconsider their vows and promises! Some of us are having second thoughts about orphanages, divorces and pet cemeteries!

A summer camp tends to exposes who you really are—like being in the army or a foxhole. At camp you live with the same folks 24/7, and people get to *really* know and like you, or really get sick and tired of your bad habits and hypocrisy. You live in a glass house! *But*, I have seen many folk fall in love at camp, get married and establish a Christ-centered family because of that transparency at camp. The truth about who we really are can actually be attractive to some.

But what about the problems we encounter at camp or in our homes? We can get rid of our "problems" (i.e. spouses, kids, annoying people, aggravating pets) by simply *severing* those relationships (as many parents, spouses and friends do every day), or by putting them to "sleep", or by learning to tolerate them, or by finding a way to fall in love with them in such a way that we carry them within our hearts and don't care about their shortcomings. I understand that sometimes it's best to put a pet a down, or send a child to a special clinic, or even get divorced. But these things are not what God originally intended—and I need to be more focused on God's intentions.

There is something about the challenge of not giving up on that marriage, or not putting that child in a special home, or not giving up on that pet, that speaks about our understanding of how we have become connected to His love, compassion, patience and determination to see us through our bad times.

Thanks be to God that He has not talked to me like I've talked to my sons lately! *Praise God* that Christ does not divorce His bride, the church (of which I am a part!)—*God knows* that Jesus has every reason to divorce us! I am encouraged with the *good news* that God is not going to send me to a "special hospital" for Christians that aren't living the way a true son should be living! And *hallelujah*, God is not going to put me to sleep because I am no longer the active, attractive, energetic "pet" I once was! I am *so glad* that God *is not like me,* and that He does not listen to the therapists, psychologists or psychiatrists who would counsel us to give up on children or relationships. (In writing this I am about to lose some donations, I suppose). There are good professionals out there who want to help, not hurt, the family and the Kingdom of God—I know that. But I fear that too often we focus on looking for professionals who will help us be comfortable and at ease as we eliminate the very things that God has purposed in our lives to push us closer to Him. The Christian was regenerated to serve, not be served.

Is He our "All in All", or is it a song we sing but don't believe?

L. DEAN BARLEY

The Idolatry of Work

Sometimes I watch the leisure with which some people lead their lives and wonder if they have somehow found a way to secure *a second life* that they are holding in reserve. I get a bit annoyed when I see people casually take what seems an eternity to complete a simple task, as if they have nothing else to do for the rest of the day.

My closer friends know that I am bit OCD and a workaholic—something in which I don't take pride. But to help me focus, I have created a daily agenda with items on it that I feel must be performed or prayed over each day. My agenda is broken into three-minute blocks so that I can keep on task. Again, this is not a matter of braggadocio for me, but rather a matter of necessity. If I don't do many of these things each day, they won't get done and others will suffer. I have many that depend upon me and I think it is wrong to squander time.

That being the case, why was Jesus *never* in a hurry and *never* stressed about all He had on His shoulders? Good grief, He had the salvation of *all humanity* on His checklist, as well as the demands of those who pressed Him daily for His teachings, healings, interventions, debates. The man was *never* at a loss for time to pray to His Father, minister to His inner circle, take long walks from city to city and so forth. His life almost appears "leisurely" if you read the gospels. And yet, in three years He turned the world upside down.

Yes, He was the Son of God, a part of the Triune God, and so He had a better perspective on life than anyone who's ever lived, but still—*just three years to complete and establish all He did?* It seems that it's not a matter of how many tasks we complete, but instead it's the smaller tasks that God is able to *amplify* because of our devotion to Him. It's not the length and wordiness of my prayers, but the sincerity and simplicity of my talks with Him. It's not my "busy-ness" that causes Him to smile upon my enterprises and plans, but my decision to be about His "business" to the neglect, if needed, of my own agenda.

I cannot waste time, squander my resources, make no plans for the day/week/year, and expect God to do for me what I should have done with my own arms and hands; I understand that. After all, Noah *built* the ark, he didn't pray for God to build it. Paul travelled all over Asia Minor to share the gospel, he did not just write epistles. But it's also possible to plan for a full day of tasks and... not lose my cool when God intervenes with surprise visits, cancelled school days, and opportunities to bear spiritual fruit.

My challenge is to not take my work ethic, planning, and personal goals *so seriously* that they become idols. All work, especially *Christian* work, can become the "good" that usurps the "best". God forbid I ever worship the false gods of "accomplishments" and "success"! My call is to be faithful and alert to the one and only true God... not to a "planner".

Whose Camp Am I In?

As a believer in Jesus Christ I would think that I should have a greater grasp of God's character and habits as I progress in my life and my own sanctification. But I admit that the more I know Him, the more I realize how utterly unlike Him I am, and how totally "other" He is. He is all the more different from me the closer I draw to Him.

I don't mean to speak improperly or in a discouraging manner, but I simply don't understand so many things that He does, and I cannot understand *why* He has the slightest interest in me or my silly little enterprises. Yes, I am frequently guilty of anthropomorphizing God, but how else am I to understand His ways, His laws, His hand in history?

Sometimes when I think about God, I am unspeakably awed about how *different* His ways are from all the ways of mankind. When I think of who He is and what He has created *prior* to the creation of this world, I wonder, Who *are we* that He should give any concern at all to us? What is it that makes us so special and the apple of His eye?

I don't have an answer to this… it's rhetorical but it does cause me to question: If God thinks that I am so special and loves me as He does, what *ever* would permit me to consciously *not* show the same love and special affection to the others, whom He has also loved and called special? What I mean to say simply is this: If God, in all His *incredible majestic splendor, unimaginable perfection, and infinite power,* has looked upon me and every other man, woman, and child and called us the objects of *His love,* who can possibly look at someone else and despise them or look down upon them?

This is why John said that it was *impossible* to know God and *not* love one another! God has called *that* child (or man, woman, youth) *special and worth the price of His Son's blood!* So how can any "creation" of this Holy God dare to suggest that the same child is not worth loving? To *not* love the other and yet claim to love God means simply that I am a liar. John says it clearly in 1 John 4:8 (NIV); "Whoever does not love does not know God, because God is love."

Here is a great test for all of us that claim Jesus as our Redeemer: Do we love others? If we have hate in our hearts towards others, Jesus is simply *not* within or hearts, and we are in the camp of the enemy… not the camp of God.

The Strength of His Joy

"Unless the Lord builds the house, the builders labor in vain. Unless the Lord watches over the city, the guards stand watch in vain. In vain you rise early, and stay up late, toiling for food to eat—for he grants sleep to those he loves." (Psalm 127:1-3, NIV)

Should this encourage you? I hope so. I am learning that the cycle of *all* things, outside of the eternal God, is decay and death….slow, or in some cases, rapid and unexpected. The things *we* build will not last. And the time we devote to our work and ventures will eventually be distant, foggy memories, with no permanence, if God is not inspiring and sustaining the work we do.

But *if* God is our source of strength, vision and inspiration, then we can say with Nehemiah, "The joy of the Lord is my strength…"(Nehemiah 8:10, NIV)

"Nehemiah said, 'Go and enjoy choice food and sweet drinks, and send some to those who have nothing prepared. This day is holy to our Lord. Do not grieve, for the joy of the Lord is your strength." (Nehemiah 8:10, NIV)

So I must ask myself a very simple set of questions: First, do I feel spiritual strength? That is, can I hold on, endure, put up with adversity, persevere, never give up the fight and serve as a spiritual warrior when those around me might be falling? *Do I have inner strength and fortitude?* If not, the reason is that my source of strength is insufficient.

You can work out in the weight room hours every day, or swim hundreds or laps in the pool or run dozens of miles—but if you are not properly feeding your body the proper proteins, amino acids, carb, nutrients, vitamins, and so forth, you will *never* make any progress in your workouts.

The same holds true spiritually. The *source* of our strength is the joy of the Lord. *That* is what not only allows us to enjoy an abundant life, but also to overcome the things that would cause a normal man or woman to turn tail and run!

Paul understood this *superlative* joy. He said, "I can do all this through him who gives me strength." (Philippians 4:13, NIV) Isaiah learned that, "He gives strength to the weary and increases the power of the weak." (Isaiah 40:29, NIV). David wrote that, "The Lord gives his people strength. He is a safe fortress for his anointed king" (Psalm 28:8 NIV), and again, "The Lord is my light and my salvation- so why should I be afraid?" (Psalm 27:1 NIV).

The second question is, 'Do I have His joy?' If I do, I have strength—the ability to overcome…if I don't, I am a spiritual invalid. To have His joy is to have a confidence and certainty of His deliverance, hand and covering that prohibits darkness from invading. There is light and a sense that, "It's going to work out!" that produces this well of expectation and confidence *that the world cannot understand.*

The joy comes from knowing Him, remaining in Him, seeking Him early in the morning and throughout the day! This joy is a fruit, or naturally occurring phenomena, that can only happen if we are connected to the source of joy—the Holy Spirit.

Are you connected? Do you know Him? Have you experienced the Joy of the Lord? Is the strength of the Lord, through His Holy Spirit yours today? *It can be.* You only have to ask for it.

Your Room is Ready

Jesus once comforted His disciples, right before the agony of Gethsemane and the crucifixion, by telling them that He would be going to His Father and that He would "prepare a room for them." (John 14:2, NIV) I have come to understand the significance of those reassuring words as I have grown closer to Him.

Several years ago, I went to see my brother in Hawaii with some other members of my family. It was a long flight and I had just lost my father. I was tired, still mourning my dad's death, and under some pressure in other matters. We arrived at the airport late and we were all suffering from jet lag and the general fatigue of air travel.

My brother and his family met us at the airport with smiles, gentle words of welcome, and Hawaiian leis. It was very nice, but again, we were dead tired. Then he drove us to the hotel, led us to our rooms and explained that all had been taken care of. We were registered, the rooms were paid for, there was mineral water, fruit and refreshments in each room, we had nothing to worry about and he would come by *late* the next morning.

He had prepared a room for us. I "got" the meaning of what Jesus had told His disciples! My brother knew what we needed and craved—rest, some privacy, a hot shower, sleep—he had it all ready for us. How much *more* does Jesus know my cravings, needs and the desires of my heart, and how much *more* is He able to prepare a place for me. *That* gives me peace and a sense of hope when I am down and ready to give up. *He has prepared for me. He "has my back"… He is looking after me.*

I believe that God is *delighted* to take care of me even more than my brother was prepared to take care of me. I merely have to let go and allow Him to lead me to the hotel. If I am submitted to rest in His care, I can be at peace—both here and in my permanent place in heaven.

Jesus said in the same passage, "Let not your heart be troubled. You believe in God, believe also in me"(John 14:1 CSB). I am "troubled" only when I doubt that He is really prepared and able to take care of me.

I believe I have good reason to believe.

Turning to Another Face

When you are under pressure and uncertainty all day long, it can leave you with a sick feeling in the morning. Yes, God is sovereign, and He is good and He is a God of love. But many folks *do* wake up sick, or in pain, or with a broken heart and with an uneasy stomach about all that's got to be done. God permits pain and suffering—just look at the cross, or the suffering of the saints and prophets throughout history. His "goodness" does not prevent us from suffering at times.

But I have learned that *financial* pressure (suffering) is a pain unlike any other. There's no medication you can take for it and the anxiety of financial stress even invades your dreams at night. It's a cancer that is relentless and unforgiving and it breeds fear about the next morning, the next phone call, the morning texts or a visitor.

But the truth is we are *all* afraid of different things at times. When we don't see any way out of the maze of a hurt, or daunting challenge or setback, it can become a bottomless pit. As you sink deeper into the mire, you are reminded that there are any number of things might occur to alter your life *forever*—and for the worse. When all is done and said, you can never be fully bullet proof, well enough insured or totally prepared for disaster or ruin or pain—it just happens.

All things that are important to me are at the same time *fragile*, and all things in nature seem to want to undo or harm me. We are *all* small, finite, limited and, in the scope of vast universe, quite insignificant ("What is man that you are mindful him, oh God?" Psalm 8:4, KJV). What are we to do?

I have found that only *one thing* staves off depression, anxiety and alarm: *Keeping my eyes fixed upon Him.* If my eyes are upon Him, not only for what I *need* but also on what my soul pines for and what my spirit hopes to see, hear and feel, *I will be* satisfied and at peace; at the same time I will not be bitter at family or friends for letting me down, or being unable to give me what clearly only the God who designed me can. Most of humanity goes through life expecting things and fellow humans to satisfy *what only God Himself can provide.*

> "O soul, are you weary and troubled? No light in the darkness you see?
> There's light for a look at the Savior, and life more abundant and free.
> *Turn your eyes upon Jesus, look full in His wonderful face,*
> and the things of earth will grow strangely dim,
> In the light of His glory and grace."
> Helen Lemmell

The Credit of Abraham

I was reading in Genesis about a very important man—Abraham. This man represents the father of the entire nation of Israel and the founder of the lineage of God's own Son Jesus. This man was not only a hero and giant in Hebrew history, but also an incredible Christian witness.

Consider this:

1. God spoke to Abraham and told him to move with all his family and servants to a new land—and Abraham immediately obeyed God. God blessed him with honor, a son, wealth. Do *I* obey Him instantly when He speaks to me and asks me to do something less difficult than changing my entire life's plan and heading out in a totally new direction?

2. Later, in old age, God made a promise to Abraham, and Abraham *believed* God and it was "accounted as righteousness." (Romans 9:3, ESV) *Do I believe Him and trust Him?*

3. But after all of this, God tested him to see where his first love lay. Do I expect anything less from God if He is going to use me in great or small ways? He will test me if I am an obedient son. He will test me if I believe and trust Him. It might sound counter-intuitive, but God does not test those that don't love Him or trust Him or obey Him, but those that *do*.

Why does He do this?

- To make it clear and obvious that *nothing* is more important. Am I willing to lose friends, status, security and even family in order for me to be that obedient son? Abraham *passed* this test. He was prepared to sacrifice his beloved son Isaac as an act of obedience to God. That's what God meant to Him! But the rest of us struggle with giving up video games, porn, a foul mouth or a lying tongue—and then wonder why God does not use us for great things.

- God *already knew Abraham loved Him and would obey Him.* Abraham had proven it, but God was testing Abraham to prove to *Abraham* that he really was the man God hoped He would be. It was not for God's benefit that Abraham was tested, but for Abraham's benefit and for all of Abraham's descendants. *This* is how a man of God is supposed to live, trust, and obey God!

For the rest of his life, Abraham would remember that God had tested him and that he had passed the test. Oh, the joy of Abraham…oh, the honor, affirmation and confirmation to know that we are worthy of being tested.

Praise be to God that He still tests some of us and that some come through that test unwavering and undeterred in serving the Host of Hosts, Lord of Lords.

As He calls us to move or change our direction, let us immediately obey. As He gives us a vision or whispers to us a promise, let us instantly trust Him. And as He tests us, let us not flinch or whine or whimper, but like Abraham, bravely accept the test.

What Am I Reflecting, Really?

Did you ever wonder what God would do, literally, to individuals He would walk past, or what He would say if people were speaking harshly to Him or asking really dimwitted questions? Do you question how God might respond to a woman caught in adultery? How would He react to the biggest "sinners" in town who came to Him repenting and crying? And how would God speak to religious folks that were arrogant and self-righteous?

Jesus was the *perfect* reflection of God. Did you ever think about? All we have to do is read the gospels to see *exactly* what God, the Father would do if He were here, today, walking on the earth. Jesus lived, spoke, responded and reacted JUST like God would if He were living in any town in the world today. Jesus was, in fact, the human embodiment of God Almighty—God in the flesh. He is not only my redeemer, Lord, Savior and friend, He is God *incarnate.*

But am I not supposed to somehow *mirror* Jesus in *my life*? The lives of the apostles *reflected* the life of Jesus right up till the moment they were torn in two, burned alive, crucified, flayed or beheaded. They embodied the character, focus, drive and love of Jesus Christ, and thereby reflected God Himself. Is something missing in our religious services today? To bring the point home, think about your own pastor—whoever that might be. When you see him (or her) in the pulpit, does he represent Jesus in the manner in which the message is given? Does he *focus* upon God, and is he *delighted* in having children come forward? Does he exhibit an unflinching willingness to point out the arrogance of the religious prigs and reserve his greatest condemnation for those that would hinder the work of the Kingdom? Is there *passion* and Spirit-filled power in the messages and leadership that we "catch" from the pulpit of our pastors?

Now I say all of this because **I** am a pastor, and I must humbly admit that quite frequently I am *not* the proper ambassador I should be. But I would also take aim at the contemporary preachers who teach and preach as if they were late night talk-show hosts or motivational speakers—rather than following the example of Jesus. To my knowledge, Jesus never spoke about His childhood, His previous life experiences, or told a joke. He was never the hero of His own stories and never attacked the government or condemned the social sins of His time. He spoke about God, the Kingdom of God and the manner in which citizens of the Kingdom ought to be living. He also talked about the need to forgive, show mercy, have compassion and love others from the heart.

I cannot speak about any specific pastor or his message, but I can attest that it is a *great* temptation to preach to the applause, laughter, "amens" and adulation of the congregation. But that's not really "preaching", it's entertainment or, at best, "Christianity lite." When Jesus spoke, just as when God speaks, the listeners tended to leave the conversation determined to be better, or angry at how His words pierced their hearts, or sad that they were not ready or unable to follow Him and call Him Lord. But *no one* went to hear Jesus speak so that they could "feel good" about themselves, be amused or leave unchallenged. Jesus spoke truth and it penetrated into the heart and soul of those listening and watching—so should our speaking and actions.

Where Do Bad People Go?

Recently a friend of my sons visited us. This was his second visit and he seems to enjoy our home—dysfunctional as it is. He watches how we have our meals together, wrestle, debate, make plans for the following day, and even as we have one of our daily "meltdowns." Yet he seems to want to be a part. Strange as it sounds, he seems to want to visit more and more.

I have been to a few places like that in my life—places I really did not want to *ever* leave. It was not only the climate, the ambiance, the people, the food or the entertainment, but also something going on in my life that was *yearning* for change, for newness, freshness, and something "else."

The Psalmist talks about a place like this, God's "temple"; we refer to it as heaven. Surely, it must be a place like this young man yearns for in his heart of hearts and it is the ultimate place that my soul pines after also. A place where *everything makes sense,* is fair, is transparent, and free from any corruption. Where all the people are kind, generous and gentle. This place, the one *we all hope for*, is a dwelling where all our fears will be removed and all our confusion explained. The older I get the more ready I am to enter into that place.

But, who will be in this "dream place"—His house—one day? And if possible, who can *begin to experience the bliss of living in His house right now?* Only those that *really want it*, it appears. It's for those that look, seek, knock, and ask for it *diligently*. It's not something we are born desiring… it's not a passion we inherit from our parents… we don't catch the yearning just by going to church each Sunday.

In Luke 13 we are told that someone asked Jesus: "Lord, are only a few people going to be saved?" He said to them, "Make every effort to enter through the narrow door, because many, I tell you, will try to enter and *will not be able to*. Once the owner of the house gets up and closes the door, you will stand outside knocking and pleading, 'Sir, open the door for us.' 'But he will answer, "I don't know you or where you come from.' 'Then you will say, 'We ate and drank with you, and you taught in our streets.' 'But he will reply, 'I don't know you or where you come from. Away from me, all you evildoers!'"(Luke 13:23-24, NIV)

Now why would Jesus say something like this? Why did He not say that there was plenty of room in heaven and most folks will eventually make it? What He said makes the Kingdom of God sound "exclusive," suggesting that it takes a lot of effort and *work* to get citizenship there. But I think He is not talking about us being good enough, but rather more about the damage the fall has brought to the hearts of men. *Many* might *want* to go to heaven but most are unwilling to call Him Lord. *A lot* of the folks that fill the churches all over the world have *heard* about Him and *believe* about Him, but are unwilling to *kneel down* and enter through that narrow door. The Kingdom of God is not for good people; they have no need for God and don't look for Him. God has made homes in heaven for *bad* people like me; we realize just how hopeless our life and our destiny is *without Him*. I want to dwell in His house *more than anything else.* And so I shall, not because of how good I am, but because I admit my utter depravity outside of Him and the deepest desire of my heart to live with Him forever.

Who Needs to Be Forgiven in My Life?

If I were keeping a good record of "sins" committed against me, my ledger would be *full* of people that I had good reason to hold a grudge against. It would include some of my former close friends, family members, businessmen, teachers, pastors, people I thought I could trust—and even myself.

I began to think about these "offenders" that went back to my *early childhood* and realized that I *still* resented what they did! It's embarrassing and incredible to think that I would still have some resentment in my life for folks that are probably long dead and gone. But I realized that even though I might have forgotten about what they had done, I *still* have not forgiven them. In fact, I have been nurturing the anger for years and was not even aware of it. I felt wounded, years later, by the slights, insults and attacks I received, but I simply thought that walking away, or growing older, would heal the hurt they caused me.

But I was reminded of *my* need to forgive and get on with living as a true follower of Christ. (My disgust with someone else's actions does not hurt or hinder *them* in the least!) I found out that I needed His healing hand upon my heart for the many injuries I had received from the words, actions and ignorance of others. But the healing that God provides happens only *when I choose to let go and forgive them and can learn to truly pray for their wellbeing and blessing.*

Do I feel His forgiveness, or is there something (or someone) within me suggesting that He has *not* forgiven me? It's either the enemy attempting to whisper to me that my sins are far too great to match up to Christ's perfect sacrifice for me at Calvary (a truly ludicrous suggestion), or something within my soul that has decided that whereas I do want His forgiveness, I *simultaneously* want to hold onto someone's "trespass" against me.

He has given me ample opportunity to prove that I have *repented* of my sins committed against Him and that I am *serious* about letting go of the infinitely smaller sins committed against me. I think that He must be permitting me to recall all the folks I *should have already forgiven,* but have secretly held a grudge against, not for my salvation (because I am already sealed) but for the divine purpose of sanctification—i.e. being made whole and holy.

It's one thing to morbidly torture myself trying to imagine who I have forgotten to forgive, or to let the enemy convince me that God is not forgiving me or providing me the blessed life He wants to because I have failed to spend enough time remembering those long, lost hurts that I have never formally buried. But Paul boldly explained in Colossians 2 that, "God made you alive with Christ. He forgave us *all* our sins, having canceled the charge of our legal indebtedness, which stood against us and condemned us; he has taken it away, nailing it to the cross." (Colossians 2:14, NIV) I am *free* from the penalty and guilt of sin. Thus from the *new birth,* when I first became a Christian, to the *new life,* which is the process of being made holy, I am free from any need for revenge or relishing a chance to get even. I have now come to prefer the peace and joy that comes from surrendering what once could have been called my "right" (for justice or a fair outcome) to trusting Him to give me all that I need or could ever hope for…but I must continue to let go of the insults and hurts that will plague me as long as I live on this earth.

When the Spirit Moves

After Jesus' resurrection, the total number of ardent followers was probably somewhere between 11 and 30 people. These "sheep" scattered after the shepherd was struck, just as Jesus foretold. But then something incredible happened. The Holy Spirit descended upon the eleven disciples right after Christ ascended (just as Jesus promised) and the throng watching these eleven young men were astonished! These simple, unlearned men, received the Holy Spirit and began to speak in foreign languages ("polyglossia") and the Jews observing this were simply overcome by what they witnessed.

Peter then explained to them about the power of the Holy Spirit and the good news of Jesus Christ, and *3000 were added to the eleven.* (Acts 2:41, NIV). That's what happens, it appears, when the Holy Spirit takes hold of a group of people that are filled with the Holy Spirit. It's worth noting that although the early church was *heavily* persecuted, it continued to grow, and by the third century there were over *34,000,000* followers of Jesus. But it *began* when eleven simple men received the power of the Holy Spirit and unabashedly proclaimed the good news of Jesus Christ.

I wonder sometimes if we have become so soft, so lazy, and so accustomed to gimmicks, marketing events, social media, sound systems, and planned visitations, that we've forgotten the very basics of what is required for a spiritual revolution; *The Holy Spirit descending upon men and women that love Jesus,* and those same people finding the resolve to say and do what He says—i.e. being *radically and completely obedient and sold out to sharing the good news of Jesus Christ.*

In my ministerial experience, it has *never* been the planned events, or the thermostatically controlled sanctuary, that have served as the setting for something totally Spirit led to occur (not that these things could stop the Holy Spirit); but rather it's at a waterfall, at the camp pool, behind a home with some youth on an Easter morning, in the living room of my former home, and after a calamity or a catastrophe, that He moves, stirs, inspires, takes control, and changes lives.

There's nothing wrong with planning and preparing and there is *much* wrong in neglecting these things! But He moves when and where He wants at the time that it is most appropriate. My task is to be ready—not to demand the setting or prompt the speakers.

Please pray that His Spirit moves mightily at our camp, that I might not hinder the work of the Holy Spirit, and that ears might hear and eyes are opened.

Whom Do I Serve?

"No one can serve two masters. Either you will hate the one and love the other, or you will be devoted to the one and despise the other. You cannot serve both God and money." (Matthew 6:24, NIV)

Another haunting thought. Whom do I *really* serve? In my mind I want to think that I serve God—first and very enthusiastically. But to determine whom I really serve I must, from time to time, consider whom I am *really* rallying around.

The one I "serve" is the one that consumes most of my time and the one that receives most of my conscious imagination. I might claim to put God first, but the "one" or the "thing" that I ponder upon the most during the day is my *real* master/god.

In my forty plus years of ministry I have seen more than a few parents place their own children in place of God. They claim to be devout and committed in their faith, but their misplaced focus on their children reveals where their real treasure lies. I am not, of course, suggesting that parents should not love and protect their sons and daughters, but many parents transfer their own egos onto the success and recognition of their children *above and beyond other children,* and even beyond what God requires of them as parents.

Christ used money as an example of the thing that often usurps God in our worship. Things have not changed one bit in terms of our focus upon money as the thing that can protect us, give us a warm feeling of security and cause others to respect, admire, and want to befriend us. Money is naturally appealing. But He was quick to point out that if you love money, you will eventually despise God, primarily because God will ask you to give up *whatever it is that is in the way of total devotion to Him.*

Loving God with all my heart, mind, soul, and strength allows my mind, daydreams, and hopes to be focused upon Him. Anything—*anything*—that competes with that will soon enough lead me away from Him. It's not the bad things that will lead me away from Him, but the *good* things. *He* alone is the *best* thing; beware of good things masquerading as best.

What About My Mercy

Every day one of my sons tell me that "it's not fair." They *never* say this when *they* get what the got more than they deserve or when they *do not get* the negative consequence they deserve. But even children are aware of what is "fair" and what isn't.

Much could be said, of course, about how this idea of fairness is *innate* to human beings and how is has nothing to do with animal-like behavior. It is something that points toward our divine creation and our Creator.

But what stuck in my mind today is how *just like the boys* I am. To my shame, I am sometimes a bit satisfied when I see a State Trooper pull over the driver of a new sports car, yet I cringe each time a deputy or trooper starts following me! The *last* thing I want is for that traffic officer to judge me "fairly" (I have a heavy foot quite often).

But as I imagine today how different—and unpleasant—my life would be if I really got what I deserved…I am humbled. How miserable life would be for *all of us* if we received *exactly* what we deserved, and yet how often I want "justice served" to the other person.

Notwithstanding the penalty of sin (something that hangs over all our heads), it's the little lies and little laws that I break that cause me personal grief and shame. What if I really received each day *precisely* what I deserved from my fellow man?

Finally, what if I were treated just like I treated the *least* person I came across today? What if I *truly and literally* did to others (the least one) what was done to me? There are times when I have been accused of being *too* full of grace and mercy, but I think that I am far from that. I am compassionate and merciful to some, but not to everyone, and that's where I fail. It's far better than I am treated unfairly, cheated, disenfranchised and wronged than to deny them the same grace and mercy I that I *desperately* need from a compassionate Father.

Do I want I want to be treated fairly by my fellow man? No, I want to be treated a bit better! Do I want to be treated fairly by God? *Absolutely not!* I beg for His mercy. But am I not required to give in the same manner I hope to receive?

Who Are We to Judge?

One of the things I have to keep clear in my head is what *God* expects of me and what others expect of me. Sometimes those two expectations collide and I have to choose *whom* I will please.

Now it's intellectually an easy decision: Do I obey the Creator of the all that exists and the Lover of my soul, or do I follow the capricious directions of the creatures (humans) that can't seem to make up their minds about right and wrong. As I read the Bible, it seems pretty consistent that what God "hates" is pride, deceit, dishonesty and lying. But in the early church, the things that were additionally considered essential for the believers' "code of conduct" was to "not drink blood, eat meat that was strangled, food that was sacrificed to idols and to not be sexually immoral". (Acts 5:20, NIV) I am not sure about all the reasons for the rules regarding animals strangled or food sacrificed to idols, but the warnings about sexual immorality seems pretty clear-cut. So why do we struggle with those commands (regarding sexual conduct) so much?

Our present generation finds it objectionable and bordering on "ignorant" to even *suggest* that there are certain things, sexually speaking, that we should not do. But I am quite certain that *any* sexual interaction with a person that is not your spouse (call it adultery, fornication, etc.) is immoral, based upon the obvious examples and passages found throughout the Bible.

Which leads me to two questions. Why do so many people who profess to follow Christ fall into this sin and why does the church (i.e. houses of Christian worship across our nation) fail to condemn it? I would *bet my life* that John the Baptist, Saint Paul, *any Old Testament prophet* and all the apostles, would stand amazed at how unmotivated we are to talk about this, let alone *confront* this in our churches. And yet, many of us in Europe and the USA wonder why our attendance at church services is shrinking and why we (Catholics and Protestants alike) are ignored more and more in the media or *maligned* in the movies and television. It seems that we have lost our spiritual backbone and we lack the courage to call things what they are. The Bible is clear (See I Corinthians 5:12b, NIV) that we *are* obliged to judge those within the church when it comes to immoral behavior. Yes, we need to be careful about how we judge the heart, and yes, we should be circumspect about our own behavior(!), but how heartless and cowardly to *not* tell a brother or sister in Christ that what they are doing *wounds the body of Christ and compromises the work of God's Kingdom.*

There are times when I write these little thoughts and I think it might be wise to avoid the topic, but I am not writing from my opinion, or because I am "sin-free", but from frank and direct teachings from scripture. God holds us accountable for *not* saying things that could be helpful, even if those words are initially offensive and/or misunderstood.

I don't claim to have achieved the prize yet, but *I am pressing on* to reach the goal of Christ Himself. And as I press closer to Him, the things that offend Him and God our Father *need* to offend me as well.

Three Years Can Make a Difference!

Why don't I say "no" more often? A *lot* of my troubles come about because I say "yes" too frequently and "no" not nearly enough.

To my sons I hesitate to say "no" so that I will not disappoint them (even though I know that "no" is often in their best interests); I don't say "no" to things I am tempted to do, think or say (that I am certain are wrong) because I am simply weak or lazy; I don't say "no" when cravings or appetites come upon me because I reason that I "deserve" to indulge a little—though I later regret it.

But my heroes had no problem with saying no. These are the men and women I have known or come across in history that really *did not care* what others thought of them! They had enemies precisely because they stood up for something and spoke frankly and courageously that offensive little two-letter word: "*No*".

Paul had *no issue* with saying no—even to the "super apostles" (II Corinthians 11:5, NIV) of his time. But something happened to him in those three years that followed his conversion: the man loved Jesus Christ and had an unwavering loyalty. He prized Jesus' approval over all else. Period. Sadly, I have personally not come across many saints like this, nor have I arrived at that level of devotion/loyalty.

So I've been wondering *what* happened to Paul during those three years? He had that dramatic confrontation with Jesus on the road to Damascus; he was blinded and then healed a few days later; but then he spent three years alone—somewhere sequestered from everyone else—and came back a lion of Jesus. W*hat occurred during those three years that brought about this incredible conversion in his life—something not at all common to other Christians?*

So much of our preaching and teaching appears to focus upon what God could/should do for me, but the early followers spoke about *what He had already* done on the cross and the overwhelming peace, joy and love that followed as the entered from being condemned to redeemed. How have we lost that? *Paul and other giants within Christendom never lost sight of this.*

That's the big difference, I think. *Paul maintained this incredible focus not only on the Christ that saved him, but he also saw in Jesus the only Being that truly was the lover of His soul.* For Paul, and others after him, it was a mystical "Jesus, the very thought of thee…" that caused them to endure or withstand separation, humiliation and suffering most of us will never witness.

May such a thought invade my mind today and never leave me…..

Like Cold Water to a Thirsty Soul (Proverbs 25:25, NIV)

When Christmas time is upon us, we hear about "the joy of Christmas" and "tiding of good news." It makes your heart merry when you are around people full of joy that are speaking about the good news of God's love.

But since I was a child I noticed that some folks seemed to take "pleasure" in being the ones that told the "bad news." It almost seems that some people find "joy" in sharing bad news. I had an aunt who was *always* the first to call my mom when a relative died, or someone was having trouble or in reference to some family scandal. She was *quickly* the first to give bad tidings, but for the life of me I can't think of a single time she called my mom to give her *good news*.

There seems to some hidden delight, at least with some of us, to say things like, "Well …not to burst your bubble, but the truth is…", or "I hate to rain on your parade, but…" In fact, busting bubbles and raining on parades, a la "Mr. Grinch," satisfies some folks' need to contribute to the conversation.

I recall in my first year at college that I "set a friend straight" about some "bad" things. The friend's was being talked about negatively as soon he left a room or a class. He was oblivious to how people mocked him and laughed at him, and, in truth, he *did* think a bit more highly of himself than I thought he should have. So, being a close friend, I told him the truth—and it *was* the truth—but it was not well received and from that day forward I became his enemy. What I told him did him *no* good and actually made matters worse. I should have kept my big mouth shut, but something within me *wanted* to knock him down a notch or two. My foolish and immature ego threw a wrench into our relationship and friendship. I have not seen him for decades, but I would not be surprised if he *still* had very little use for me.

When tempted to "bring tidings of bad news" I am trying think more about three questions:

1. Is the news *really* needed and helpful?
2. Do *I* need to be the bearer of the bad news?
3. Where is my *heart* toward the recipient? I.e. is *love* the motivating factor for me saying bad or sad things?

As it is, there are some folks I rather hide from because I know that they always come bringing bad news. But perhaps I should determine to *thank them* and then offer them some encouraging, kind and good news. The good news far outshines the bad news—that's the gospel. Jesus came here because God wanted Him to be the bearer of the incredible *good news* that God loves us, desires to have us join Him in His home, and has established a place for us where He will call us His own…He will wipe every tear from our eyes…(Revelation 21:4, NIV) He will shield our ears from *ever* hearing any bad news again. Maranatha.

"Like cold water to a weary soul, so is good news from a distant land."

(Proverbs 25:25 NIV). Let's share good news.

He Does Not Spoil Those He Loves

We look forward to the celebration of Christmas, but of course, were it not for the resurrection of Jesus, there would be no celebration of His birth. And were it not for the execution of Jesus, there would never have been a resurrection. But again, what about the suffering that He endured for us? Do we look at the cross and the suffering Man on that cross closely and often enough? Do we see in the baby in the manger for fullness of God's purpose and redemptive love?

I have written about how I considered the suffering of Jesus as He was scourged *prior* to the crucifixion. The image of the incredible *torture* He endured is something we tend to speak of only as a footnote to His execution. The torture He endured for our sins is something that makes us quite uncomfortable—or at least it should.

But in most places of worship it seems to me that congregants are too narcissistically set on creating a sense of worship that feeds their need to feel good about themselves as well as figure out who they can receive His "blessings"; we don't invest too much time on "morbidly" *meditating upon the cross of and suffering of Jesus.*

But it is rather sobering to look at the little baby in the manger and realize that it was *always* God's intention to allow that baby to grow into a young man who would one day suffer and die an excruciating death. Jesus was born to suffer. The irrefutable fact is that God not only *permitted* Jesus to suffer, He *ordained* it. In light of that, the suggestion that abortion makes sense because no baby should be born to suffer is ludicrous. Some babies are conceived out of wedlock, or by poor judgment or unexpectedly, and many do end up being unloved, despised and rejected, but if that is grounds for abortion, Jesus should have likewise been aborted. Praise God it was considered murder, even by an emperor as heartless as Caesar Augustus.

Is there any doubt that God the Father's love for Jesus the Son is profoundly grander than any other love in the universe? Jesus is the only Son and His love for Jesus is the first love that ever existed. They have always existed together in this orbit of love. For all ages, Jesus has loved and honored the Father; for all eternity the Father has honored and blessed the Son—this is the first, primary, most intense and oldest of all loves!

But the fact remains that when it comes to pain and suffering, we seem to be at odds with what suffering means to God and what it means to man. God permitted His beloved to suffer! For mankind, it's something we avoid, fear and want to stop, if possible. And that's the rub: God does not always immediately stop suffering; sometimes He *directs it* for a great purpose, as with Jesus Christ.

Pain, humiliation, suffering…these are things God *Himself* endured in the form of His only Son. So when a man suffers, let's be careful about suggesting that it's a sign of God's displeasure—it might be a sign that he is a true saint—one for whom this world is not worthy.

I just returned from one of my favorite places on earth—France—a country where 5% of Catholics/Protestants attend church regularly. And yet this highly educated country is covered with cathedrals, monasteries, churches and symbols of Christianity. The French government is decidedly "Christian," whether they mean to perform that way or not. They *embrace and show charity* to those without homes along with the immigrants; they provide a free and equal education up through the university along with free national healthcare for all their citizens and in general look after the needs of their population. Everyone can retire—with full benefits—at 62 years of age, and some retire at 52 years (subway, rail and bus drivers). The government takes care of you in France!

But in Nigeria—a true third world home—89% Catholics/Protestants attend church regularly. And yet the people do not enjoy *anything like* the stability, protection and quality of life offered in the secular state of France. So why does it appear that the prosperous, protected, well cared for, *do not* seek God, while those living "on the edge" seek Him so earnestly?

Suffering draws us to Him…material wealth, good health, external protection tend to push us further into personal indulgences, a sense of self-reliance, independence from God, and sometimes, inexplicably, to depression. For as long as men have lived, trouble, pain, suffering and uncertainty have served a *good* purpose for eternal designs: They draw us into the heart of God. The lover of our souls and the One who designed and created us for dependence upon Him for our livelihood, knows that the more He spoils us, the farther we go from Him. Praise God we have a heavenly Father who knows what we need and not a heavenly "Grandfather" bent on spoiling us!

It Has to Mean Something

On Christmas Eve two of my boys got into a fight, and as always, the elder son prevailed and the younger one came running to me as if he had been mortally wounded with only minutes to live. Lately I've been telling them to "stand tall, be a man, don't let them see you cry." But this time I felt the need to cradle my vanquished son and remind him that I loved him and that no one loved him more than me.

And once again my son taught me something: We need to *remind* those we love them that we love them and that they are very special. My youngest son actually said to me that evening, "Please tell me that you love me every time I cry—*like you used to,* and every time I cry, tell me that you love me more than anyone else." I was justifiably embarrassed for being told I did not affirm my love to him more often. What a lesson.

"I love you". Such easy words to say and such a powerful blanket of comfort and security for a child. "No one loves you more than me." Words that can drive away dread, fear, a sense of not being not very important—and a great sleep aid to a child that worries if anyone really cares about him. How many children go to bed every night *not* knowing that they matter to someone else? How many children grow into men and women having *never* known such love?

"Would you please tell me when I am crying that you love me more than anybody else…" The very words of Jesus Christ to the one who comes to Him seeking forgiveness, purpose and divine love! What caused me to seek Christ was a very real dread of eternal death and getting what I deserved. But what draws me *close to Christ* is the certainty that He loves me *more than anyone else ever could.* Even though He knows the most grotesque things about me.

But does that love from Him not also compel me to express and hold that same love for the others that He loves—i.e. my sons, neighbors, friends, associates? How can I experience the love of God and hate others? According to Saint John, it's *not possible* to know God's love and hate another man.

I just don't say it enough. When I say it, I *really do* mean it, but something holds me back from saying it more. The last time I told my dad that I loved him was after all the other family members left his bedside and I held his hand for the last few minutes of his life—"I love you," I told him several times as his hand went from warm to cold. But he could not hear me by then. I should have said it more.

Perhaps some of us hold back on saying I love you because of the weight it *should* carry. It ought to *mean* something, and perhaps we recognize our limited ability to do what love requires if we were to spread that love to all the folks we know. Our emotions, time, energy and creative means of showing and expressing are limited—*but only in proportion to how distant and disconnected we are from the ultimate, unfathomable, and inexhaustible love of the creator and originator of love.*

If you're a bible scholar, you are aware that Jesus is never recorded as *ever* having said to *anyone,* "I love you." No, He did not need to say those words because His life was the perfect epitome of love. But frankly I am not Jesus—and neither are any of you reading this little devotion. Until we're in His Kingdom, quite literally, or until we are perfectly walking as He walked, we need to remind others, particularly our children and our parents, that we love them with our deeds *and* our words.

The Day After

For many years it was the day after Christmas that I felt the "lowest." I am probably not alone in this sentiment; after all the gifts have been given away, the "big day" is over, the parties have ceased and now the credit card invoices are being emailed to me. All the build-up since Thanksgiving has now come to an end. It's a bit hard to get excited about December 26.

But something has been changing in my heart over the past four years. I have found a deep well of both hope and joy as challenges have drawn me closer to Him. I wake up *knowing* two things that make *all* the difference in the world to me: I have *hope* because I *know* that He will not let me go—I can recite the times over the past forty-eight months He has proven to me that He won't let go. And yes, I've gripped His hand until my knuckles were white a few times, but I am secure and safe in His hand. I *know it, I have experienced, He has proven Himself to me.*

And I have joy, each day, knowing that He really *does* want to give me the very desires of my heart. He has *not* forgotten His promises to me, He has *heard* my prayers, He will *not* forsake me, and He will *give me* those things that I have desired for so long. *That is the well that I draw from each day.* And this knowledge allows me to face my lions and my Goliaths.

Am I *ready* for all those "desires"? In my opinion, *Yes!* But time and time again, *after* He has finally given me those *good* things that I have so desired in my heart, I have found that I received them at the proper time and *praise God that I did not get them earlier!*

So the question comes to me quite simply: Do I trust His *timing*? And again, I know from my past experiences with God that His timing is *perfect.*

And so when I wake on the day after the most celebrated day in the year, I can have *real joy and sincere hope* for an incredible day, feeling sure that my tomorrow is secure and know that His timing in life is perfect.

What Is Truth?

Recently I read again how Pilate attempted to free Jesus from death. He appealed to a mob that had been motivated by the Jewish leaders to seek Jesus' death; Pilate wanted to allow Jesus to live. But the crowd had already made up their mind; they wanted Jesus *dead*. Pilate appealed to their logic and reason; "For the third time he spoke to them: "Why? What crime has this man committed? I have found in him no grounds for the death penalty. Therefore I will have him punished and then release him." (Luke 23:22, NIV)

"But they kept shouting, "Crucify him! Crucify him!" (Luke 23:21, NIV) And so he did. Pilate succumbed to the demands of the crowd and caved in. "The majority" ruled in this situation, and Jesus was executed.

Around 500 BC the Greeks came up with the idea of democracy. It's strange how many of us look at democracy as a Christian concept, when in fact it is pagan in origin. I understand that many churches, Christian communities, and even this nation, prefer that the "majority rules," and whereas it certainly beats a dictatorship or communism...the majority is sometimes *wrong*.

Throughout the stories of the Old Testament, the crowds, the mobs, the masses got it pretty consistently wrong, and the small minority, sometimes only the "one", got it right. So whereas I cherish "democracy" as being an improvement over all other forms of governing, it certainly is *not* God's plan.

The spiritual point is that I should not listen and be influenced by what everyone else is saying or doing, but rather by what I know in my heart is the *right* thing to do. And that's not easy! With so much pressure to conform and accept what the majority has *determined* is proper, I am destined to be referred to as a crank, ignoramus, backwards, ignorant, and so forth if I follow Him and not the democratic culture of my time. But again, let me say, I was not called to follow the crowd, the polls, the majority, or the consensus… but Jesus Christ.

Following Him will *never* be the common thing for the majority to do; it will only appeal to those who are prepared to be "set apart", those who will one day be referred to as those "for whom the world was not worthy." (Hebrews 11:38, KJV). Popularity and discipleship simply cannot go hand-in-hand, and Pilate was unable to choose to follow Jesus or even his own conscience. It appears he preferred the admiration of others and his own political ambitions far more than truth.

Who Touches God's Heart?

Consider for a moment the people that we celebrate in sports, politics, entertainment, business and even in the pulpit. Are they not people that are accomplished, polished, witty, the best at what they do, the most beautiful, eloquent, and articulate of all mankind?

But then, I think of the ones that touched God's heart, the ones that *He* celebrated, like Isaiah, a *godly man* of integrity and passion for the Lord, who *cried out* when He saw a vision of God, "Woe to me!… I am ruined! For I am a man of unclean lips, and I live among a people of unclean lips, and my eyes have seen the King, the Lord Almighty." (Isaiah 6:5, NIV) Why this humility? Why did fear grip his heart?

In the gospels Jesus spoke about the lowest of the low… a tax collector… and the most respected, a Pharisee. The tax collector and the very religious fellow (a Pharisee) went to the temple to pray. "But the tax collector stood at a distance. He would not even look up to heaven, but beat his breast and said, 'God, have mercy on me, a sinner.' (Luke 18:13, NIV). Jesus said that the *tax collector,* a man despised for his vocation, left the temple *justified* because of his repentance, remorse, and humility.

In my work at our camp I realize that there are primarily two types of people: those who blame others and those who blame themselves. There are those who constantly hide behind excuses and those who offer up *no* excuses. There are those who point the finger at the faults of others and those who *never* stoop to self-pity. As you can imagine, one of these types is difficult to work and live with, while the other is an inspiration and breath of fresh air!

But what am I? Do I blame others for *my* lazy behavior and ill-advised decisions? Do I admit my own shortcomings (before others are tempted to point them out), or do I carefully orchestrate the situation to make me appear the hapless victim? It's so easy to make myself an innocent prey for all my hardships, but all so humbling to acknowledge *that I am what is wrong* in my business, ministry, or relationship.

Isaiah knew that He stood before God with no excuse for his sin or association with others that sinned. Likewise the tax collector knew that arguing about how it was *not* his fault for being a corrupt tax collector would go *nowhere* with an omniscient heavenly Father. So they both did a very wise thing: They admitted their mistakes and errors were *their own fault* and not the fault of someone else. God takes delight in this, and I can see why. Nobody, particularly God, likes a whiner or coward. It takes courage to accept the blame and admit that you deserve to be held accountable.

Aren't we blessed to worship a God that rewards such a heart with forgiveness and restoration?

"Blessed Are Those Who Mourn" (Matthew 5:4, KJV)

Here is the promise for those of us who mourn—those that are heartbroken and sad about the way things are in this world—we *will* be comforted.

The focus here is on the people of God who mourn, because they are going to be comforted. Everyone experiences sad and tragic losses at some time or another in this life. If it has not happened to you yet, it will one day…and it hurts. But Jesus said "Blessed are you" (Matthew 5:3-12, KJV) when we can rest knowing that *He knows* about our sorrows and that *He will* wipe away our tears and give us His joy! (Revelation 21:4, NIV)

The Messiah came to comfort those of us who mourn, but the comfort comes because the Messiah saves us from our sin, which is the *cause* of the mourning. That's the point here: "*Good for me* when I am truly sad and brought to tears by the wrong things *I have done!" God is going to comfort me and forgive and wipe away the very things that make me sad.*

So the mourning will be mourning not just for the suffering and sadness of life in this dark world, but for the sinfulness that causes it. If I am blessed, it's because I understand that my grieving is ultimately for a world that is lost and ruined, in which God and His will do not prevail. But in my mourning, Jesus opens my heavy heart to the Lord, and I know that my grieving is not without hope. I can know, for sure, that my weeping and grieving is but for a time only. I know that death does not have the final victory. I know that the Messiah will turn all that away someday. And that hope brings me comfort.

As you face the sadness of life, you can do so with hope. If you have mourned over your mistakes bad decisions—"sins"—it is a clear sign that you are placing faith in the Savior—the Lover of your soul.

Who Is My Audience?

"Be careful not to practice your righteousness in front of others to be seen by them. If you do, you will have no reward from your Father in heaven." (Matthew 6:1, NIV)

What is my motivation for being kind, generous, gentle, selfless? Am I really prepared to be "forgotten" in the work that I do for youth and children, or do I have a hidden desire to be celebrated and applauded? These are the things Jesus challenges me to think about. What are my motives? Whose attention do I want to command? Are my selfless actions calculated or a natural reflex because of my intimacy with Jesus?

The happiest and most appealing people I know never seem to talk about themselves—unless they are laughing about something silly they did. These people are always interested in *listening* to what *I* have to say and never seem anxious to interrupt me to tell me *their* story. They play down the good things that *they* do and constantly build *me* or some other soul up. They appear to genuinely *forget* about themselves and consider *others* as far more interesting and worthy for attention. It's been said that you can gain more friends in one year by being sincerely interested in others than you can in a lifetime trying to get others interested *in you.*

If my motivation is God's approval and smile, I will, in every situation, be at peace and a pleasure to be around. But if I try to impress others—even by my charitable actions—there will always be a suspicious eye cast upon my kindness and generosity.

I've noted at camp that the best athletes are *not* the staff or campers that *tell* me how talented they are, but those that quietly *display it.* It's the secret things that we do for Him, when no one else can see, that cause His face to shine upon us. And that approval brings release and purpose to our lives like no parade or celebration of attempted piety ever could!

Do I believe that He sees every "hidden" thing I am doing for Him and His children? Do I trust that He, and He alone, will be pleased with the intention of my heart as I do acts of selfless love to those who never respond or even acknowledge my love? Am I certain that He, the lover of my soul, is ready to bless me *beyond what I can imagine* simply because I love Him and want to behave in manner that brings honor and glory to Him—and comfort and encouragement to those He places in my path?

If I believe these things—*truly hold these things to be true*—I will not look for the approval of others in doing what is right.

What Am I Seeing?

"The eye is the lamp of the body. So, if your eye is healthy, your whole body will be full of light; but if your eye is unhealthy, your whole body will be full of darkness. If, then, the light in you is darkness, how great is the darkness!" (Matthew 6:22-23, NIV)

What I see, physically, allows me to understand how things are in the world. I can avoid stepping into holes or walking into traffic. My eyes permit me to walk carefully across a bridge or adjust myself as I walk up or downstairs. Without my eyes, I would fall, get injured or perhaps even be killed.

Of course, Jesus was not referring to my physical eyes, but the things I ponder about; the things I hope for; the imagination and desires of my heart. If these things are good, pleasing to God, helpful to my fellow man, inspiring and encouraging, there is light.

How is the darkness reflected and evident in my life?

- pleasure in seeing others fail or humiliated
- unwillingness to celebrate and recognize the goodness of others
- a constant negative and sarcastic spirit
- the inability to appreciate and offer compassion to the hurt or suffering of others
- a spirit that manipulates, deceives, and takes advantage of others at every opportunity

How can my eye be made whole and be healed? Only by *the* Physician—Jesus Christ. He comes to offer me light instead of darkness; compassion instead of indifference; spiritual sight instead of total blindness. But... do I *want* to be healed and receive the very eyes and sight of Jesus, or, like Saint Augustine, do I ask God for "chastity"—but not just yet?

Open the eyes of our hearts, Lord—and right now—please.

"I follow this man's creative genius as he describes God's outrageous mercy in ways that way compel us to listen to lessons drawn from the everyday events of life.

Reading Dean Barley's meditations is time well spent."

Dr. Bill Greenwood, Jr, ret.
Adjunct Professor Biblical Studies
Gardner-Webb University

"Dean Barley has distilled and encapsulated, in this remarkable devotional, the God-given wisdom that can only come from running a Christian camp for over 30 years. I can attest to this because I have seen Dean in action with campers from all over the world. The Vineyard Book of Devotionals not only gives us a glimpse into Dean's wisdom but also it provides us with a wonderful recipe on how one should live, pray, humble ourselves and yes, suffer, as true Christ followers."

Wayne C. Guida, Ph. D.
Professor of Chemistry
University of South Florida

"Dean has dedicated his life to teaching and sharing his faith and wisdom. His daily experiences and thoughts captured in these pages will enlighten and assist you through the toughest of times while growing your spiritual foundation. Faith has kept the Vineyard going strong for over 35 years and the passion and drive Dean has put towards that mission is encapsulated in this book. I encourage you to drink from the "vine" daily."

Tommy Walker - camper, counselor, friend, board member and trustee

"Dean has written an easy to read and very helpful devotional. I think this year more than any other, we can use some daily encouragement and this book delivers just that."

Greg Surratt
Founding Pastor Seacoast Church
President ARC